Notebooks in Cultural Analysis

Notebooks in Cultural Analysis

An Annual Review   Volume 2

Norman F. Cantor, Editor
Nathalia King, Managing Editor
Advisory Editors: Harold Bloom, Bruce Mazlish, Robert Wohl

Duke University Press   *Durham 1985*

Notebooks in Cultural Analysis is published by Duke
University Press. It is available for sale in both hard cover
(ISBN 0–8223–0661–1) and paperback (ISBN 0–8223–0694–8).
All orders and business correspondence should be addressed to
Duke University Press, 6697 College Station, Durham, North
Carolina 27708.

Notebooks is edited at the Institute for Cultural Analysis,
New York University. All manuscripts should be addressed to
Nathalia King, Institute for Cultural Analysis, 113 University Place,
New York, New York 10003.

Contents

The Zipper and the Child / *Hillel Schwartz*

The first slide fastener was patented by Whitcomb L. Judson in 1893. Twenty years later Gideon Sundback devised a truly workable "hookless fastener." It would be yet another twenty years before what became known as the "zipper" attached itself permanently to all echelons of the American clothing trade. The resistance of apparel manufacturers to the new fastener had been formidable in the early years of the century; the success of the zipper in the 1930s was such that by 1937 the daring Mme. Schiaparelli of Paris had designed eminently fashionable women's outfits without the usual buttons or hooks and eyes.

This essay will be concerned with the widespread introduction of zippers into all types of children's clothing in the years 1930–35. I argue that the technological improvement and popular acceptance of the zipper ran parallel to changes in ideas about physical movement. I argue further that the increasing zipper sales during the Depression—especially for children's clothing— were a sign of the persuasiveness of a certain kinaesthetic. Finally I suggest that technological innovations, however insignificant economically or ecologically, may have subtle but powerful influence upon human behavior.

I begin by tracing quite briefly the evolution of theories of dance and of handwriting analysis during the nineteenth and early twentieth centuries. Dancers and graphologists were not only quick to recognize changes in a prevailing kinaesthetic; they were often the ones to propose clearly and explicitly a new kinaesthetic—a new ideal of physical movement. Because their theories were adopted by many educators, or because they were themselves evangelical educators, they saw their theories put into practice. Adult ideals of physical movement deeply affected the actual motor training of the young. A new kinaesthetic, developed in the writings of dancers and graphologists over a period of ninety years, implemented by 1930 in the rearing and education of American children, would be a major factor in the reception of the zipper.

The Dance

Between 1840 and 1930 the dance world in Europe and the United States had, by seduction and then concussion, suffered a shift in attitudes toward physical movement. The date 1840 is not haphazard, for by that year François

Delsarte had begun his lectures in Paris, a "Cours d'Esthétique Appliqué." Delsarte taught a system of relating gestures to expression, expression to the soul. There were Orders and Laws of Movement, and a Law of Correspondence: "To each spiritual function responds a function of the body; to each grand function of the body corresponds a spiritual act."[1] Delsarte's system was religiously colored and highly trinitarian, and later exponents made heroic efforts either to explain the intrinsic connection between his theology and his original science of gesture, or to divorce the two entirely.

Delsarte's lectures, designed to help actors, singers, and musicians understand the relationship between gestures, sentiments, and the senses, attracted Steele MacKaye, a young American interested in theatre. Studying with Delsarte in 1869–70, the years before the master's death, MacKaye developed the first of the American offshoots of Delsartean method, Harmonic Gymnastics, "in order to so train and discipline the body that it would become a responsible and expressive instrument through which fluid movement could pass without the obstacles of stiff and unyielding joints and muscles."[2]

The quote is from Ted Shawn, who, with Isadora Duncan and Ruth St. Denis, pioneered modern dance in the United States. Shawn had studied with Mrs. Richard Hovey, a pupil of Delsarte's son, Gustave. The mothers of Isadora Duncan and Ruth St. Denis had also studied with disciples of the Frenchman. In a *New York Herald* interview in 1898, Isadora herself lauded Delsarte, "the master of all principles of flexibility, and lightness of body," who "should receive universal thanks for the bonds he removed from our constrained members."

Ignoring his rigid equations of specific gestures with specific meanings, American dancers took from Delsarte his concern for the absolute integrity of gesture, his attention to the expressive power of the torso, and his desire for movements liberated from artificial codes of motion. What Duncan did was to call for the initiation of movement from the torso, from some physical–spiritual center akin to the solar plexus, and for the free elaboration of movement out of that center, uninhibited by corsets, heavy skirts, and narrow shoes. One used the whole foot, the whole torso, the whole body to move. As Gertrude Colby, one of the first modern dance instructors, later wrote in *Natural Rhythms and Dances*, "The arm positions grow out of the body movements and follow the lift and sway of the body. They do not move independently but grow out of and continue the trunk movements." Katharane Edson, national director of the Denishawn schools, would write, "The art of gesture must come first to a dancer because his gesture represents himself as a whole." She too had studied with Mrs. Richard Hovey, the Delsartian.[3] As Duncan and a long line of modest Epigoni returned to Greek models, as Ruth St. Denis and Ted Shawn looked further east to the Orient, they began to create a new kinaesthetic. The kinaesthetic demanded sincerity, the acceptance of the force of gravity, fluid movement coming out of the body center, freedom of invention, and naturalness of transition from one fully expressive position to another.

About the time that Duncan, Shawn, and St. Denis were exploiting the human torso that had been so rigorously confined by traditional ballet, another master arose in Europe, a Swiss Professor of Harmony at Geneva named Emile Jaques-Dalcroze. In 1910 in Dresden he established his own college to train young musicians and dancers in the principles of Eurythmy, a system of rhythmic gymnastics. For Jaques-Dalcroze, rhythm was all-important, and sensitivity to one's personal physical rhythms was necessarily prior to any mastery of musical rhythms. "The special merit of gymnastics based on rhythm," he claimed, "is that it unites the body and soul in education. . . . What is rhythm? Is it spiritual or corporeal? Assuredly it is both." [4]

Americans first read about Jaques-Dalcroze in an article in *Good Housekeeping* by an English disciple in 1911, but much more influential on the dance world were two German students of and rebels from the master, Mary Wigman and Rudolf Laban. Wigman spent years with Jaques-Dalcroze, but eventually felt oppressed by his emphasis upon the melodic line in physical responses to music. She met Laban through the wife of the painter Emile Nolde, whose vision of the human body was one of force and nervous compression and whose images of motion would later be recreated by Wigman in her choreography. Laban, working as Jaques-Dalcroze's assistant between 1914 and 1917, developed a "Eukinetik," looser and more spacious than the Dalcroze Eurythmics. Both Wigman and Laban made use of rhythm by its fundaments of tension and relaxation, strain and impulse. Their work reached the United States in two forms: as a dance discipline demanding high energy and focus—adapted by Hanya Holm and the Denishawn graduate Martha Graham; as a system of dance notation (Labanotation) whose categories of movement continue today to determine ideas about choreography and dance instruction.

The Dalcroze emphasis upon personal and dynamic rhythms was compatible with the other aspects of the developing kinaesthetic. One bent one's whole body to the whole music; like Isadora Duncan or Ruth St. Denis, one did not dance to beats but to the phrase or the center line out of which flowed the rest of the music. Like music, movement unfolded, and an understanding of rhythm was the key to natural movement. [5]

From Delsarte to the Bennington School, inaugurated in 1934, dancers of "the modern dance" had come to insist upon a human body moving fluidly, rhythmically, naturally, and, in the sense that any part of the body could be called upon, freely. For Isadora Duncan, for the "Greek" dancers, barefoot dancers, and natural dancers who followed in her wake, for Ruth St. Denis and Ted Shawn (who abandoned the ministry for dance), as for Delsarte and Jaques-Dalcroze, physical movement was a crucial means of human expression, a form of worship. If we can find that God-Within, wrote Shawn, we can return to the primitive sources of dance which were "the flowering of man's full self-consciousness." Wrote St. Denis: "To dance is to live life in its finer and higher vibrations, to live life harmonized, purified, controlled." A successful dance found the means to be a good prayer.[6]

Prayer transforms. Dance was not only an expression, it was an experience. What happened between Delsarte and the modern dance of the 1930s was the growth of a kinaesthetic that assumed that movement transforms. As early as 1856, in his *Handbook of the Movement Cure*, Mathias Roth had defined "kinesiatrics" as the treatment of diseases by means of gymnastics or muscular activity. Known also as "kinesipathy" or "kinesitherapy," the treatment was ancestor to our physical and occupational therapies. Even earlier, in eighteenth-century France, C. J. Tissot and Nicolas Dally had written treatises on medical gymnastics and movement cures. But the kinesitherapist sought to treat physical diseases; the modern dancer worked upon character.

The implications of Delsarte's philosophy had been that if one moved wisely, gesture would be a true reflection of the self (or of the role portrayed, or of the music sung). Conversely, moving wisely helped one spiritually: to be attuned to the nuances of a raised arm or a tilted head, one had to be personally in tune. As speech teachers absorbed Delsarte theory, they too began to emphasize the interplay of character in movement and character as movement — to such an extent that by 1920 Charles H. Woolbert's popular textbook, *Fundamentals of Speech*, insisted upon muscular memory, kinaesthetic sets, the good effect of free and fluent movement upon halting speech, and the beauty of curved expressive gestures. Jaques-Dalcroze had gone further: learning the complexities of rhythm would lead to a comprehension of the rhythms of the self. And for the modern dancers, the release of the torso from the prison of classical ballet was a spiritual release as well. In their dances they expressed this release as a flight from plot to painting — from telling a story to the music to telling the story of the music, what Ruth St. Denis called music visualization. Since emotions and movement were to be intrinsically related (rather than customary and formal as in classical ballet), and since there was to be high drama in movement itself, the dance must be a process of character transformation. Movement was at the same time expressive and operative.

Graphology

Delsarte's system had involved an elaborate attempt to specify the absolute meanings of various gestures. An arm extended forward, palm up, meant "It is"; an arm extended downward at a forty-five-degree angle from the torso, palm up, meant "It is improbable," and so forth. This was analogous to the fixed-signs system of abbé Jean Hippolyte Michon, author of the seminal *La méthode pratique de graphologie* (1878). Michon found that physical motions, whose residue were written words, had meanings and some syntax of their own related to the personality. In the same way that Delsarte matched gesture with sense, Michon matched particular letter forms directly and absolutely to character traits, emotional dispositions and psychological states.

The French successor to Michon, Jules Crépieux-Jamin, took a more holistic approach to handwriting. Like Jaques-Dalcroze, he stressed the importance of rhythm—spacing in and between words, variation in sizes of letters, angle of slant. Graphological signs were relative, not absolute, and could usually be deciphered only in the full context of a person's writing. Complex qualities like jealousy showed up only as resultants of several simple qualities, and trained intuition was necessary to construct the equations. With the famed Alfred Binet, Crépieux-Jamin sought to determine scientifically the predictive possibilities of graphology. At the turn of the century they found that handwriting did not disclose the age or sex of an individual, but it did reveal the intelligence of the writer. Somehow—and it was not clear how—motor behavior as reflected in script was an expression of the personality, consistent and reliable.[7]

William Preyer, Georg Meyer, and then Ludwig Klages studied the relationship between handwriting and psychomotor functioning. Klages, the most influential and most respected of the German school of graphologists in the early twentieth century, looked at the entire outlooming motion of handwriting, determined its *Formniveau* (or general form quality), its harmonies and rhythm. Like Wigman and Laban, he identified impulse with expression and constructed a theory based on dynamic oppositions. Handwriting, Klages believed, was the clearest record we have of the personal human context between a restraining mind and a liberating soul. The written line is expressive of psychological state and of spiritual conflict.[8]

Martha Graham would have appreciated this, just as Isadora Duncan would have appreciated the fact that most if not all graphologists interpreted divergence from standardized letter forms (school forms) as a sign of vitality and individuality. (Certain divergences, however, were judged to be unhealthy by criminologists who, for example, identified pasty handwriting with suppressed sensuality or depraved sexuality; this moralizing scientism lingers in much work on handwriting analysis.) After the American publication in 1919 of June Downey's book on the psychology of handwriting, people may have been receptive to the idea that handwriting, like dance, was evidence of a link between physical activity and inner states. But the major impact of graphology was not felt in the United States until 1933, when a book appeared entitled *Studies in Expressive Movement*. Deeply influenced by German gestaltist psychology, the authors Gordon Allport and Philip E. Vernon included a chapter on "matching sketches of personality with script" by Edwin Powers. The book concluded that character was revealed by motions of all kinds, including script, and that physical behavior was not distant from inner state. In script there were no isomorphic or constant relationships between particular letter forms and personality traits, but rhythm, direction, density, and scale of writing were important indices to character.

Graphological theories between 1870 and 1930 had undergone the same series of changes as theories about dance. With less forthrightness than the modern dancers, graphologists had also fashioned a very similar kinaesthetic. Robert Saudek, for example, in a major work, *Experiments with Handwriting* (1929), listed the signs of unnatural handwriting: slow speed of execution, subsequent "touching-up" of letters, frequent change of hold, wavering or uncertain or interrupted pen strokes, marked changes in angle of writing, complexity of initial stroke adjustment, use of the "ornamental fashion of a bygone age." And to write naturally (genuinely) for an adult was to write under an "elementary sentence-impulse," that is, to write from the heart, with an idea in mind, not a word, not a letter-form. In other words, the positive values of Saudek's kinaesthetic were sincerity, fluidity, rhythm, freedom of expression, naturalness of transitions between forms, emphasis upon the phrase, spontaneity.

Saudek's kinaesthetic was as common to other graphologists as it was to the modern dancers. Less common but nonetheless present by 1930 was the graphological assumption that handwriting was not only expressive but operative, that if one changed one's handwriting, one might through the change in motor habits change one's character. Dr. Edgar Bérillon had discussed *la psychothérapie graphique* in 1908, and by 1932 Charles Julliot was reporting on a series of achievements in the field. Milton N. Bunker, who founded the International Graphoanalysis Society in Chicago in 1929, would assure his American readers that "*you can change your character* by changing your writing." If one were failing in business or on the brink of romantic defeat, a new script could effect a new person, a more successful person.[9]

Muscles, Play, and Penmanship

By the 1930s, dancers and graphologists had proposed a kinaesthetic which valued motion as much for its reflexive (operative) as for its reflective (expressive) properties. Integrated, rhythmic movement meant an integrated personality. The free, sincere individual was one who moved fluidly.

On the surface of things, this kinaesthetic was hardly new. The Romantic educator Pestalozzi, like the Greeks, believed that physical exercise shaped character. Edmund Burke in the eighteenth century had described how the assumption of a physical posture and set of gestures normally associated with an emotional state would produce that state in a skilled speaker. The Rev. Gilbert Austin, in his *Chironomia* of 1806, advocated natural, sincere, fluid gestures to accompany oratory.

What gave force and distinction to the kinaesthetic of the dancers and graphologists was the late nineteenth-century work in anthropology and neurophysiology. Through this work, the new kinaesthetic became the center of a powerful theory about education and the origins of culture.

For many anthropologists, "primitive" societies were physical cultures; "savages" were likely to respond emotionally and physically rather than intellectually. Indeed, "savages" were barely speaking animals, and anthropologists looked at them for clues to the original meanings of physical gestures. Since "savages" were somehow the ancestors of modern civilized people, anthropologists also looked at them for clues to the origin of culture. In the 1890s the Germans Karl Groos and Karl Bücher put the clues together: culture developed upon the basis of rhythmic activity, particularly expansive physical play and dance. Rhythm was the energy behind primitive religion and economy, and it was the element common to all "savage" tribes.[10]

While Groos and Bücher enjoyed considerable continental fame for their synthetic works, American physiologists and psychologists were discovering the overwhelming importance of rhythm within the person. Following the lead of German laboratories, they studied reflex arcs, cardiovascular and circulatory mechanisms, the relationship of brain to muscle motions and nerve impulses. They found that the human body was "a device for producing rhythm."[11] Moreover, motion seemed crucial to sensation, growth, and—possibly—intelligence. As the physician Luther Gulick wrote for *Popular Science Monthly* in 1898, "Muscular contraction appears to be closely related to the genesis of all forms of psychic activity. Not only do the vaso-motor and muscular systems express the thinking, feeling, and willing of the individual, but the muscular apparatus itself appears to be a fundamental part of the apparatus of these psychical states." This was but one expression of the motor theory of consciousness, a theory expressed in different forms by William James, by John Broadus Watson and other behaviorists, by Pavlov and other animal objectivists. By 1913, psychologist G. V. N. Dearborn could write that "Kinesthesia is about . . . to come into its own as the primary and essential sense. . . . The very meaning of protoplasm, physically speaking, is motion."[12]

Married quickly to genetic psychology and culture epoch theory, the ideology of rhythm and the motor theory of consciousness became a pedagogical strategy. As Lilian E. Appleton explained in her *Comparative Study of Play Activities of Adult Savages and Civilized Children* (1910), the subject of instruction during any period of individual personal growth should consist of the cultural products of the race in its comparable epoch; since rhythmic movement was natural and primitive, mastery of rhythm must precede mastery of more "civilized" forms of expression. Like "savages," children were primarily physical beings whose intellectual faculties had not fully developed.

ing rhythmic activity and the vigorous exercise of the large muscles.

This was more than a stealthy means of introducing songs and dances. It was good neurophysiology. As the graphologist Preyer explained in his highly admired book on *The Mind of the Child,* repetitive (rhythmic) motions made passable the nervepaths between muscles and brain; others would go so far as to claim that physical activity was responsible for the laying of those paths. G. Stanley Hall, whose work in genetic psychology served as the underpinning for much subsequent child study, praised Preyer for his double emphasis upon will and kinaesthesia. Hall himself had been early excited by the study of motor functions in relation to mental function. Education, in the sense of the cortical development of the brain, might very well be a physical process. The child begins by responding with the entire body; slowly motor specificity is established, slowly the child coordinates muscles, slowly the child gains the ability to execute complex serial physical maneuvers.[13]

Play therefore must be the child's work, the means by which the neural network was fixed. Rhythmic play would facilitate learning, which must begin with the large (or fundamental) muscles and pass carefully to the small, finer, accessory muscles.[14] John Dewey was pleased: "The manual-training movement has been greatly facilitated by its happy coincidence with the growing importance attached in psychological theory to the motor element." Dewey himself actively promoted Alexander technique, a system for postural and personal alignment founded upon a theory of mind-body unity. F. Matthias Alexander, like Delsarte, had set out for a career on the stage; also like Delsarte, he had encountered voice problems which led him to the study of the body and motor habits. His *Use of the Self* (1932) attracted physiologists, genetic psychologists, the comparative anatomist Raymond A. Dart, and an ailing Aldous Huxley. As with Alexander's fiercely manipulative orthopedics, Dewey's "learning by doing" philosophy was justified because, in fact, doing *was* learning.[15]

The kinaesthetic of the small population of graphologists and modern dancers was carried into larger society through widespread reforms in the motor training of young children based upon rhythmic play and large-muscle activity. The graphologist's positive evaluation of natural, full-bodied rhythms and flow in handwriting was reflected in penmanship instruction which involved the writing of whole letters, whole words rather than artificially designated constituent movements. The modern dancer's insistence upon the free torso and fluid, rhythmic motions in long phrases was reflected in the nursery school teacher's insistence upon wholesome play and individual expression, and in the collegiate insistence upon natural gymnastics rather than rigidly uniform calisthenics.

The evolution of penmanship instruction followed closely the evolution of graphological theories between 1870 and 1930. Instruction at first concentrated upon drill in the various constituent movements requisite to the shaping of a letter, later upon the general movements requisite to the shaping of any letter, then upon the letters and the letters in context. Instruction gradually moved away from the copybook to the chalkboard and the large pencil and soft paper. By 1930, students no longer practiced the standard forty-eight-degree slant of 1870 Spencerian script; the slant would come naturally, would vary with the individual, and, according to the major pedagogues, was part of the rhythm of the handwriting. Rhythm and ease were uppermost considerations, especially in the first grades, during which time students were still struggling to coordinate finger movements. Penmanship supervisors constantly redesigned desks and chairs to afford younger children free arm motions and good posture; they studied the advantages of pencils, pens, and paper surfaces for the awkward fingers of young children. In the classroom teaching of writing, "a very complex muscular movement involving the use of some five hundred or more muscles altogether," they stressed legibility rather than strict imitation of forms, writing as an act of expression rather than as a mechanical exercise. They used singsong chants, metronomes, and the new Waterman split-feed fountain pen to help the children toward a fluid, simple, rhythmic script.[16]

The changing pedagogy in penmanship entailed a changed script. Austin N. Palmer, who died a millionaire in 1927 after promoting his penmanship system for thirty years, wrote in 1896, "the masses have no use for ornate penmanship; the people do not ask for it, and do not want it. . . . I would define practical writing for the people as a style devoid of all superfluous lines; made up of letters that can, to the greatest possible extent, be formed without lifting the pen, or checking the motion; an unshaded style, executed with medium pointed or coarse pen." [17] But even he did not anticipate the introduction, in the mid-twenties, of the form most devoid of all superfluous lines: manuscript writing or, as we now call it, printing. Printing was easier; the children themselves liked it in the early grades because without much training they could produce legible words. They printed more rapidly and fluently than they could write in cursive, and they appeared to have no difficulty switching to the cursive in later grades. Printing required mostly downstrokes, strokes bringing the hand in toward the body, and physiologists agreed that arm motions toward the body could be executed with less strain than the outflung motions demanded in most cursive forms. Rhythm was not lost (even in cursive, *pace* Palmer, the good writer lifted the pen from the paper in rhythmic sequences), and the child gained a sense of personal accomplishment which had often eluded youngsters well into their practice with cursive.[18]

The reforms in penmanship instruction were not limited to progressive schools. They spread widely and resulted in a significantly different set of motor experiences for many young children. Consider the amount of time children spent writing: in 1926, American students in grades one through six received direct penmanship instruction for seventy to eighty minutes each week, on the average, according to grade level. If spelling practice, arithmetic, art and drawing be taken into account, weekly writing or equivalent manual practice occupied an average of more than four hours in first grade, more than seven hours at its peak in fourth grade.[19] These figures must be immediately supplemented, of course, by the incidental writing practice in subjects such as grammar, geography, history, and the social sciences. Penmanship supervisors encouraged teachers to introduce writing as an integral part of tasks in all areas of the curriculum.

Like penmanship, drawing had also been undergoing a pedagogical change during the same period and in the same manner. The reform in drawing instruction was particularly remarkable in Kimon Nicolaides' *The Natural Way to Draw* (1941). Nicolaides, who finished the initial draft of his book in 1936 after decades of experience as an instructor at the Art Students League, advocated a drawing pedagogy perfectly parallel to the notions of movement in modern dance: start with the core, the imagined center of the form; start with the impulse and not the position; remember with your own muscles the movement of the model; think of gesture as dynamic and outward bound. Drawing reforms, however, proceeded more slowly and narrowly than reforms in penmanship instruction, since fewer schools could afford specially trained art instructors.

Behind the momentum of the reforms lay not only a desire for practical penmanship in an age of typewriters, or a desire to train the muscles in proper order, or an appreciation for the value of rhythm. There was also that other element in the kinaesthetic, the operative quality of motion. Colonel Francis W. Parker's *Talks on Pedagogics* of 1891 were reprinted in 1937, and the implicit argument he had made against the old penmanship teaching stood behind much of the urgency of the reforms: "The imperative rule for an adequate act of expression is that the whole body, every muscle and fiber, is concentrated upon the act: a person should sing, write, speak, by means of the freest action of the entire physical organism. When agents are isolated by premature attempts at precision before poise and ease of body become habitual, the inevitable knotting and tension of muscles react, cripple the body, and constrain the mind." If graphologists could read one's character in one's script, then penmanship instructors were partly responsible for the true expression—and the healthy formation—of character.

Penmanship training normally ceased with the coming of puberty and/or high school. The kinaesthetic promoted by modern dancers reached beyond: to physical education in high school and college; to children outside of school, in playgrounds, in nurseries, at home manipulating a toy.

"I do not know what research has been made as to the exact correspondence of body structure to mental and psychic condition, but from general observation I hazard a guess that there must be a close relation between motion and emotion; that failure or inhibition of movement, especially of movements which (so to speak) answer the call of the muscle for action, bespeaks decadence. On the other hand, can we not premise that with the discovery of new and more subtle rhythms and movements, new and fuller experience of life is attainable?" So speculated Ruth St. Denis in 1932 in an article for the *Journal of Health and Physical Education.* Seventeen years earlier, in his very influential book, *Play in Education,* Joseph Lee wrote, "Play is the child. In it he wreaks himself. It is the letting loose of what is in him, the active projection of the force he is, the becoming of what he is to be. . . . And rhythm is the method of the soul's progression, the natural manner—not indeed the ruling motive, but the gait and habit—of the human spirit." To physical education instructors who had been fighting since 1880 for creative play rather than gymnastic drill, these were key statements. As with changes in the teaching of penmanship, changes in physical education depended upon a growing recognition of the congruence between psychological health and fluent, rhythmic, spontaneous movements. First came the informative change in names: from physical "training" to physical "education." In 1886 Chautauqua University sponsored the first classes to prepare physical "education" teachers. By 1891 there were 130 graduates of the program, and many of them had studied with Emily Bishop, whose Americanized Delsarte system of dance sought to "make the body a temple for the indwelling soul." Next came Melvin Ballou Gilbert's "esthetic calisthenics," taught at Harvard beginning in 1894, with the explicit approval of the physical education director, Dudley Allen Sargent. This too derived from Delsarte. Then there was educational gymnastics, defended by Lura Sanborn in the *Child-Study Monthly*; she quoted from John Dewey: "I believe that consciousness is essentially motor or impulsive; that conscious states tend to project themselves in action." By 1930, in *Athletics and Education,* Jesse F. Williams and William Leonard Hughes could ask, "Is physical education an education of the physical [or] . . . an education through the physical?" By 1930, too, gymnastics had been defined as work, consciously directed and thoroughly systematic; its opposite was physical play, free and spontaneous, pleasurable and unspecialized, operative on the whole body and the whole person.[20]

The new kinaesthetic was even more prevalent among nursery school and kindergarten teachers. Wrote Edna Dean Baker, president of the National Kindergarten and Elementary College, in 1922: "In this very wonderful provision of movement in response to stimulus, a continuous reaction of the organism to environing conditions, lies the possibility of education." [21] The active, playing child was a learning child. Alice Corbin Sies, a professor of childhood education, was more outspoken in that same year: "Movement is 'the cry of the being to be,' the I AM of the human organism." She called for a progressive use of the nearly perpetual motion of children, for more playgrounds and for more tolerance of spontaneous play.[22]

She would get them. Through Arnold Gesell's campaign for nursery schools and kindergartens, teachers began to be aware of the applications of genetic psychology and physiology. Although the kindergarten owed its inspiration to the European educator Froebel, whose work early in the nineteenth century favored play as a means of education, kindergartens made little headway in major American school systems until teachers linked play with character on a physiological and genetic psychological model. Part of the kindergarten reforms begun in the 1890s included the redesigning of Froebelian activities to compensate for the small-muscle imprecision of younger children.[23] Physical tasks, like handwriting, were more carefully graded; correlations between nutritive needs and common growth curves were studied by school hygienists; children's toys were occasionally age-graded. Through the Playground and Recreation Association of America (founded 1906), the number of public playgrounds was multiplied five-fold by 1929, and new pieces of equipment —slides, jungle gyms—were anchored to the ground.[24]

Above all, the early years of the child of the Twenties were to be rhythmic, playing years. Educators adopted enthusiastically Joseph Lee's encomium to rhythm and play. As they did so, they turned more and more often to the principles of Dalcroze eurythmics. They found Dalcroze rhythms in the motions of a four-month-old baby, they sought to adjust the Dalcroze method to very young children, and in moments of exuberance they envisioned a new creature as the final outcome of a eurythmic world. Wrote music critic Walter Damrosch, "If [Jaques-Dalcroze's] teachings were accepted and taught to the children of the entire world, it would effect a revolution, and a finer, a nobler race would be the result."[25] (Meanwhile, Rudolf Bode, an early student of Jaques-Dalcroze and an avid reader of the works of Ludwig Klages, was developing a spiritual nationalistic theory of gymnastics, based upon rhythm, that lay behind much of the Nazi preoccupation with physical culture.)[26]

At play children were to be independent, mobile, natural, spontaneous, fluent, supple, and, of course, rhythmic. In the kindergarten one could promote independence and refine the rhythmic sense by employing the theories of child psychology and eurythmy. At the very least, one could give children opportunities to develop large-muscle coordination and to express themselves fully.

This very least was fingerpainting. Uniting the kinaesthetic of penmanship reforms and the play movement, it was meant to be the ideal form of recorded expression for a playing child. Ruth Faison Shaw invented children's fingerpaints in 1931; she had been seeking a medium for expression that would eliminate the small-muscle strain of holding brushes, chalk, pens, or pencils. Actually, according to Shaw, "fingerpainting" was a misnomer: "When a child begins to finger paint, his whole body contributes to the rhythmic movements which register characteristic arcs and sworls of extraordinary grace in color. As one small boy put it, 'I paint with the spot in the middle of my back.' " Had she questioned the boy more closely, I suspect that the spot in the back would have been the modern dancer's center of movement—the solar plexus of Isadora Duncan, the Graham center of tension and release in the torso. For Ruth Shaw, the child was dancing and painting at the same time, and the result was startling: the fingerpainting was more than an honest expression of "inmost fancies"; it was also therapeutic. "Once [problem children] were given direct means of free expression for the impulses smothering inside them, the 'problems' solved themselves." Fingerpainting might also be good medicine for "the affliction sometimes described as 'oral constipation' " or stammering, for "few locked doors can resist that master key of rhythm." [27]

On Getting Dressed

I have been following the process by which the new kinaesthetic of modern dancers and graphologists came to affect the motor training of children in the early twentieth century. I have shown that the ways children wrote, played, and painted were being changed in accordance with the new kinaesthetic. There were similar changes in other less formalized areas of motor training: the manipulation of table utensils, the brushing of teeth, dressing. Emily Post in 1940 was newly concerned with the awkwardness of children confronted by heavy or thick silverware. Dentists, insisting that dental hygiene should begin with three-year-olds, found that young children could not easily be taught the ideal method of brushing teeth (rotary and vibratory). They did, however, discourage children from the old-fashioned crosswise horizontal (stiff) brushing and proposed a circular continuous motion compatible with the new kinaesthetic.[28]

Applied to the act of dressing, the new kinaesthetic entailed a demand for new kinds of clothing for children. It may be evident at last what all this has had to do with zippers.

If children were to be active, independent, and rhythmic, they needed clothing which would not hamper their motions, which would not distract them from their play, and which they could put on and take off by themselves. Maria Montessori, "discovering the child" in Italy, had designed fastening frames by which children would learn the intricacies of buttons, snaps, and hooks-and-eyes; this was part of their "education in movement." Restrictive, awkward, hard-to-manage clothing would inhibit personal mastery of the environment; the child would lose her/his mobility and rhythm, and would suffer psychologically. Clothes were a type of training ground; as one related clothes to the body, so one would relate self to world. Watson, in his 1928 behaviorist guide to childrearing, took the nineteenth-century feminist argument against tight, heavy clothing one drastic step forward: "The present mode of dressing children," he wrote, "seems eminently adapted to encourage rage behaviour." [29]

Whether or not one accepted the behaviorist model, Watson's dictum, "*Let the child learn as quickly as possible to do everything for itself*," was extremely popular in the twenties and thirties. The dictum was part of the new kinaesthetic cherishing independence in the young child—a child who could print legibly before he could write legibly, a child who could fingerpaint without much preparation or instruction. Maud Fetherston wrote in 1928 in the *Journal of Home Economics*: "The child gains for good habit formation as well as proper mind-sets by learning to do things for himself—not in having them done for him. The process of dressing himself will give him assurance which will carry over in his work and play in other matters than dress." The motor habits of dressing would contribute to the shaping of character, and the United States Bureau of Home Economics was designing children's clothing "that will permit the greatest possible physical and mental development."

The object of rearing was in part to increase self-reliance. It followed that the child should be as independent of (in control of) clothing as possible. According to Ruth O'Brien in 1929, the Bureau's designs for little girls' dresses had them "open down the front so that the wearer can manipulate the buttons without assistance. There is an abundance of fullness across the chest, the sleeves are non-restricting, the panties are comfortable, and the drop-seat has four buttons so grouped that they are easy to fasten and unfasten." O'Brien's comments on the Bureau's boys' clothing illustrated the new kinaesthetic's concern for mobility and rhythm. It is not merely the freedom of the external body which is of concern; the freedom of the internal systems is also affected by clothing, for clothes which immobilize the wearer may make him constipated or irregular: "The present vogue for collars, many buttons, and complicated belts on such garments, results in suits that are uncomfortable and, in many cases, discourage good toilet habits. Many a mother has complained that the effort required to loosen complicated trouser fastenings causes her small son to delay visits to the toilet." So the Bureau devised "plackets and fastenings easy to manipulate." [30]

Fasteners, then, were the prime determining factor in the mobility, spontaneity, and rhythm of the clothed child. Spurred by genetic psychology and the physiology of small-muscle growth, educators began to determine the ages at which a child should be expected to conquer various dressing operations, and parents began to learn when they should expect their children to buckle belts, button coats, tie ribbons, lace and tie shoes. Certainly, the easier the fastening, the earlier the mobility and free expression of the child, but even at three children could do little with buttons, though some months later they could deal with buttons in loose buttonholes. Bow-tying did not come until age seven. The perfect garment would have "the fewest possible and the simplest fastenings." [31]

What if there should be a new fastener, manipulable by two-year-old children, lightweight, placed accessibly, and priced reasonably? What if it should require minimal small-muscle coordination and encourage self-help by fascinating children with its mechanism? What if it should be hygienic, reliable, long-lived, launderable, and stylish? And what if it should give children confidence, security, mobility, and versatility? What if it should contribute to the shaping of character?

The Zipper

Between 1880 and 1920, a set of mechanical inventions and applications had made possible a different appreciation of physical movement. By repeating operations along a continuous track, the escalator, the motion picture camera and projector, and the central conveyor belt in the Ford assembly line integrated series of elements into products which had, it seemed, a rhythm of their own. The escalator actually yielded the rhythm of motion along a stairway. The motion picture camera, preceded by Etienne Jules Marey's photographic gun, and Eadweard Muybridge's multiple cameras, recorded natural human expression and movement so well that people could begin the scientific study of physiological and anatomical changes in a man jumping or running. The assembly line produced automobiles so cheaply that the middle class consumer might do more than dream of increased mobility, and the wealthier customer could move in streamlined, expensively fluid cars. The purpose of the roller coaster (1885) was almost solely kinaesthetic, and the spiral track of the phonograph brought the musical rhythms of great symphonies into the home. Alive to the new quality of motion, Mary Moss wrote in 1904, "Carried along by mechanical contrivances and the elaborate organization of commerce, a man is now compelled to move quickly, but in grooves." [32]

The dynamic of mid-nineteenth-century invention had been the dynamic of Delsarte, of laws of conversion and expression, of motion invested with a spiritual presence: the electric telegraph, the dynamo, the steam locomotive all had this aura about them. Camera, escalator, and conveyor-belted assembly line were within the realm of Dalcroze Eurythmy: bodies could be made (or made to appear) whole and mobile if one understood the principles of rhythm. To improve the camera and projector, one had to take into account the optical rhythm of after-images; to improve the escalator, one had to smoothe out the rhythm of the moving stairs; to improve the assembly line, one studied the rhythms of the worker.[33] In 1880, Carroll D. Wright defined the factory system so as to stress "continuous, harmonious processes," just as Jaques-Dalcroze would stress continuity of harmonious motions. Time-and-motion studies reflected the new kinaesthetic in their transition from the stopwatch technique of Taylor to the emphasis of the Gilbreths upon fluid movement and use of the movie camera. In each case, one sought a natural, fluid transition from frame to frame, or step to step, or task to task. If the naturalness was a fraud, as it was in the case of the contrivance of the projector, it was a fraud in the interests of the new kinaesthetic.

Whitcomb L. Judson had been experimenting with a street trolley network in which the trolleys would be propelled by compressed air. They would move smoothly along a track. But when Judson patented his "clasp locker or unlocker for automatically engaging and disengaging an entire series of clasps by a single continuous movement," he slid into another kinaesthetic world.[34] The pull of the movable guide brought into being and—this was the trick— then dissolved the track. In other words, motion did not simply follow a track, nor was motion (as it was with camera, escalator, assembly line) the result of the track; instead, motion gave meaning to the series of clasps. Motion brought all elements together. The motion of the zipper came amazingly close to one formulation of the ideal in (Americanized) Delsarte gesture theory: "Love, fear, anger, hate, surprise, are all indicated by a movement of the shoulder, which translates itself along the arm from joint to joint until it reaches the tips of the fingers. . . . Now these movements, from joint to joint should, as it were, overlap each other, slide into each other, and make a graceful gesture."[35]

The new fastener, I suggest, was an ectype of the motor theory of consciousness. This was analogous to the *Bahnung* of the neurophysiologists, who believed that physical motion led to the laying down of fresh neural tracks.[36] As one manipulated the fastener, one experienced first the fluidity and simplicity of the motion, then the operative, creative aspects of motion by which the clasps were made to unite—in a manner which may today still intrigue the technologically innocent.

Unfortunately, Judson's fasteners did not work very well. Marketed by 1905 as "C-Curity" fasteners, they were difficult to manufacture and repair, likely to snag or come apart. Despite the zealous entrepreneurship of Colonel Lewis Walker, they were not a financial success during Judson's lifetime. Neither boots, mail pouches, nor the plackets of women's skirts proved at first to be commercially viable locations for the fastener.[37]

Judson devised a way to make the fastening elements more machinable and the fastener itself more integral to clothing: he clamped the clasps along the edge of a fabric which could then be sewn on to dress material. But he died in 1909, vaunted in his Muskegon, Michigan, obituary for his patents on a pneumatic car.

It was Gideon Sundback, a Swedish engineer formerly employed by Westinghouse on their turbo-generator project for Niagara Falls, who took the crucial step of redesigning the fastener so that its parts were consistent with the basic conception. Working for seven years in Colonel Walker's Automatic Hook and Eye Company, Sundback finally acted as if he had realized that the name of the company was the clue to the failure of the device. What he needed was not an automatic hook and eye system but one that took advantage of the sliding motion which was the central feature of the device. At the end of 1913 Sundback produced the "Hookless No. 2," a fastener whose design remained fundamental to the industry until the 1960s. It was composed of "nested, cup-shaped members" that interlocked without complication and which resembled neither snaps nor buttons nor hooks and eyes.[38]

Sundback had changed the character of the parts to suit the motion of the whole. Like the penmanship reformers, he based his reform of the fastener upon the nature of the motion desired. Only by keeping the fundamental motion in mind could he escape the tyranny of the previous forms, the hook and eye. In this he was also like the dancers whose invention of the modern dance was the result of a desire for a new kinaesthetic experience.

For forty years more Sundback would continue to fiddle with fasteners, sue over patent infringements, and extend the range of slide fastener applications. Four improvements upon the slide fastener were not completed until the late 1920s or early 1930s: the engineering of a cam lock to ensure secure fastening; the perfection of a separable fastener—that is, a fastener in which both ends of the fastener tape can be freed from one another—for jackets and girdles; the gradual reduction in the weight and size of the slide fastener so that it could be attached to less sturdy materials or be manipulable by less powerful hands; the development of a non-metal (pyroxylin) slide fastener which could be thoroughly and permanently dyed to match colors in fashion and to blend in and move with folds of cloth.[39]

And the zipper had yet to be named. The word "zip" apparently did not enter the English or American languages until the 1830s. Why then it occurred to someone to use that onomatopoetic syllable may bear some relation to the use of higher-powered rifles in warfare. But the word was early applied to the sound of mosquitoes and of needles passing through cloth as well as to the "zip" of bullets, and it would be unwise to make too much of samples in historical dictionaries.[40] In 1923, B. G. Work of the B. F. Goodrich Company, examining the Mystik Boot (rubber galoshes) with its new hookless fastener, searched for an action word to describe the boot and came up with "zipper." He had wanted a word which would draw attention, as he said, to the way the fastener seemed to zip. He did not mean, of course, that the fastener had a particular mechanical action associated with zipping, for that association arose from the popularity of the boot, whose sales reached half a million units that year.[41] But what *did* he mean? Was he referring to the ease of the slider, its speed, the sound of the interlocking, the quality of pull, or the entire visual-aural-motor set? And was the appeal of the zipper (boot) the security of the zipper—as in the postwar moneybelts and Locktite tobacco pouches from which the Hookless Fastener Company drew its first large profits? Or the durability of the zipper—as in work garments, overalls, sleeping bags, and life preservers produced in the twenties? Or the speed—as in the Whizzer Flannel Shirt? By 1933 "zipping" had reference to speed, to security, to fluency and spontaneity.

The kinaesthetic associations of the words "zip" and "zipper" corresponded well to elements of the new kinaesthetic. However, advertising the slide fastener's "snugness in fit, smoothness in contour, flexibility and convenience" did not sway the major children's apparel manufacturers or retailers toward the use of zippers. Nor was the appeal to the time-saving virtues of the zipper markedly effective; the popularity of the zipper, when it arrived, was due to more than the increased pace of American life. The major zipper producers by 1930 had volume sales only for children's leggings and some snowsuits. Not until the Hookless Fastener Company undertook a concerted campaign which brought together both halves of the new kinaesthetic, not until the company associated the zipper with freedom of movement *and* the shaping of character, did zippers begin substantially to replace buttons.

"Bye-Bye Buttons"

George Earnshaw read Watson's behaviorist manual in 1928. The Earnshaw Knitting Company started using the "Self-Help" motto for its children's clothing on July 13th of that year. Imitated shortly after by the Dalby "Me-Do" garments, Earnshaw's "Vanta" line of infant apparel reduced the number of buttons, made them larger, and put them where the child could reach them. Already the inventor of the innovative sunsuit, Earnshaw gradually replaced the buttons entirely with tapes and simple belts. Others used elastics as substitutes for buttons. Whatever the means, the goal was clear and the logic formidable: children ought to dress themselves and buttons got in the way, so eliminate the buttons (each of which required from seven to eighteen distinct motor operations to be done up or undone).[42]

Babies ate buttons. For this reason manufacturers had removed buttons from baby shoes. And buttons came off in the wash. For this reason a woman in Forest Hills suggested that mothers sew the buttons on upside down, and for this reason the manufacturers of washing machines had to wage an uphill battle for electric washdays. Sewing buttons on again and again was time-consuming, dull, annoying: "Buttons!" you sigh, "Heavens above . . . how do youngsters do away with so many buttons!"[43]

So began a 1930 advertisement for the slide fastener, which did not rust, laundered beautifully, would "actually *improve* with age!" The zipper was promoted as a technological marvel saving mothers time and giving children "complete freedom of motion." "Zip-on" suits were "So comfortable and snuggly fitted children like to 'live' in them. . . . Active bodies have plenty of room to climb, run and stretch." As yet, however, there was no focus on the psychological values of self-help, and the boom in zipper sales had just begun.[44]

In April, 1930, Ruth O'Brien of the Bureau of Home Economics appealed to the five thousand firms involved in the $66,425,000 annual children's clothing business. Since October, 1929, some 45,581 people had requested copies of the Bureau's booklet on suits for the small boy. Like the Bureau's other publications, this too emphasized that every garment should assist in the small child's physical and mental development by aiding self-help. Self-help, she claimed, "has therefore become a part of the vocabulary of many a mother of young children, and, as a result, she is in the market for everything from self-help toys to self-help trousers. . . . But, for some reason, the clothing and pattern manufacturers have not caught the lead and women are complaining that they can find neither patterns nor garments in which these ideas are incorporated."[45]

One year later, in the fall of 1931, the Hookless Fastener Company began to run full-page ads for their trademark "Talon" slide fasteners, which emphasized self-help (see figures 1 and 2). The first ad in this new mode read in part: "No longer is mother's day filled with the plaintive plea 'button me, please!' Nowadays Talon fastened youngsters take pride in being able to dress themselves without help—*three full years before the average buttoned baby is able to put on or take off a thing!*" "Only two an' a half," read the banner of a December ad, "*but he can dress himself.*" In an April, 1932 ad, the psychological and characterological values of the zipper were the main pitch. We find a physician advising a well-dressed mother, and the banner, "DRESSING WITHOUT HELP DEVELOPS SELF RELIANCE," CHILD PSYCHOLOGISTS SAY. And we read below, "Eager baby hands . . . fumbling with buttons and snaps. So anxious to help as you dress them. So anxious to fulfill the urge to be independent, to strike out for themselves!" In October, 1932, we find Robert, six years old, still fumbling with buttons. "Needs aid in simplest dress problems. Helpless complex growing. James, age 3, dresses alone quickly with Talon fasteners. He's independent, self-reliant, as psychologists advise." Do we wonder why some children lack confidence, seem shy, almost afraid? "Much of the tendency toward an inferiority complex, modern child psychologists say, can be averted in a way that's simple for the child, and convenient for mothers. It's this: begin moulding the character of the smallest youngster . . . give him courage and ingenuity . . . by teaching him to dress himself! A simple idea. A sound idea."[46]

The two halves of the kinaesthetic had been united. The zipper enabled freedom of movement, flexibility, and spontaneity at the same time that zipping actively affected character. Wrote Anna E. Bayha in *Practical Home Economics* (1932), "If the speed, skill, effectiveness, neatness in dressing essential to character building is to be acquired, the problem of fastenings may

Figures 1 and 2. Talon advertisement, *Parents' Magazine* (Sept., 1934), pp. 50–51. Reprinted by courtesy of Talon Inc. and the Free Library of Philadelphia. Photo: Arthur Soll.

"They'll be Self-Reliant Children"

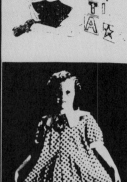

Attractive Flannel Pajamas. Belt-controlled drop-seat and Talon fastener front closing make it easy for tiny tots to dress themselves for bed.

Full weight Underwear. Made on the self-help principle with elastic drop-seat and the Talon fastener which closes it snugly, opens it easily.

Dainty "dress-up" Frock . . . new checked design. Invisible Talon fastener closing in front makes it easy to slip in and off in a jiffy.

In those important growing-up years, it's the everyday routine that forms character. In the matter of dressing, for instance. Children who learn to clothe themselves are building self-reliance, sturdy independence!

In the new completely Buttonless Garments, the Talon Fastener replaces clumsy button closings with the easy-operating, snug-closing slider!

In a jiffy, even smallest tots can easily dress or undress without a bit of help from mother.

There's another happy side to this picture, too. Talon-fastened garments eliminate button upkeep, the repairing of buttonholes and lead the way to new leisure time!

Entirely Buttonless Garments for night and day, for dress and play, are available in leading stores.

be the nucleus around which the design should be built. . . . Zippers are the easiest and take the least time to manipulate." Now that the Hookless Fastener Company (and other zipper producers) had followed up on the self-help campaign of child study groups, nursery schools, and the Bureau of Home Economics, it remained for apparel manufacturers and large retailers to be convinced that self-help was a marketable idea, and that zippers were ideal for self-help clothing. The first breakthrough came in the fall of 1932, in Newark. Bamberger's department store announced the creation of a self-help clothing section. This was the crucial paragraph of the announcement: "We aren't sure we'll ever make another announcement of greater social significance. You're catching us in the very act of pioneering. For, though the United States Government itself has organized an elaborate program to introduce self-help clothes into as many homes as possible, the movement has made slow progress. Amazing as it may seem, self-help clothes for children have never before been available to the public at large at any store in the country or in the world." An article in the *Infants' and Children's Review* on the new buying habits of mothers reproduced in full the Bamberger manifesto and, citing Watson, advised salespeople to remind parents that the emotional dispositions of children were fixed by age three.

By late spring of 1933, that same trade journal carried advertisements for what amounted to a new fashion wardrobe: Sweeney-Block Self-Dress Clothes, Craig-Musgrove "Do Self" sleepers and "Me-Fix-It" union suits, Acme Underwear "All-by-myself" pajamas, a recently patented Dalby "Me-Do" union suit, and zippered self-help jackets, leggings, shirts, shorts, and frocks in Wiz-O, Zip-On, Play Boy, Klad-Ezee, and "Quik-Drest" versions. Gimbel's in New York rounded up a jury of children to select the spring fashions; this was lauded as "a forward step in fending off many infant inhibitions which are often directly traced to the choice of inappropriate clothes for youngsters." [47]

Soon, disregarding the children's clothing fastened with tapes, simple belts, large buttons or elastics, the Hookless Fastener Company began to assure the industry and the consumers that the slide fastener made "self-help" possible. Hookless Fastener also told the industry that zippered self-help was marketable: "What a merchandising idea it is . . . what a story you have to tell! For these Talon-fastened "Self-Dress" clothes teach children sturdy independence. They appeal in a superlative degree to the maternal instinct of mothers whose eagerness for information which will instruct, protect and care for their children dominates all other thinking. Seldom has a selling idea had such a basic, powerful appeal. No mother can resist it!" Hookless Fastener told the consumers that zippers solved the self-help problem: "A company manufacturing slide fasteners has become much interested in the self-help idea for children's clothes and believe that in this type of fastening lies a very satisfactory solution to this problem. The promotional head of the children's division of the company, a man with young children of his own, is convinced of the importance of self-help clothing and is interested to sponsor authentic self-help designs." [48]

That man with young children was John Keilly, sales manager of the infants' wear division of the Hookless Fastener Company. He promoted the zipper as a revolution in child care, but the true revolution may have been technological. Keilly's engineers had had to redesign much of children's clothing to sell the idea of a zipper. They placed all openings in front, made the drop-seat more easily manipulable, had the garments cut more fully to avoid binding. They designed a smaller, lightweight zipper for cotton clothing, since one of the handicaps in sales had been the kinds of material to which a zipper could be attached. Finally, they had to design new machinery for clothing manufacturers; zippered flies especially entailed a revision of assembly-line procedures. [49]

I suspect that Keilly's sales tactics—prime examples of the mobility and fluidity of the new kinaesthetic—were also somewhat revolutionary. Besides creative window displays in major department stores and radio broadcasts on self-help, Keilly encouraged retailers to sponsor talks by child study professionals, demonstrations by amateur four-year-old models such as his own daughter Joan, and perhaps even parent education conferences. Keilly and daughter Joan toured the country until Keilly realized that children must also play; then Joan became a movie star.

That film promotion for clothing should have been pioneered by a zipper manufacturer is additional evidence for the strong connection between the zipper and the new kinaesthetic. The same year that Judson patented his clasp locker or unlocker, the Delsartian Steele MacKaye was fighting to finance and construct a giant Spectatorium, an 1800 theatrical display across vast moving stages, "a picture-of-motion done in the round to the life—an actual 'movie,' not a photograph." Psychologist G. Stanley Hall, fascinated by the power of gesture in silent films, hoped for the revival of Delsartian studies. Motion pictures as technology were a metaphor for the new kinaesthetic's concern with fluid motion along a "natural" path, while motion pictures as theater were instrumental in re-educating young and old alike in posture, gesture, and gracious movement. Silent movie stars such as Lillian and Dorothy Gish, Ina Claire and Myrna Loy had studied at Denishawn studios. Even though modern dance training might immediately affect only a small minority of men and women, the indirect impact through film was far more considerable. So now, too, a child pulling zippers, like Lillian Gish pulling heartstrings, would appear on celluloid. [50]

In 1934, while Bloomingdale's was hosting a marionette show, "Lucy Late-to-School," in which Lucy had nightmares about buttons and alarm clocks, other department stores across the country were showing the film "Bye-Bye Buttons." A booklet, with stills from the film, was sold in the stores as *A Picture Book in Rhymed Prose That Tells the Story of Children's Clothes.* One stanza read: "Little Miss Nancy / Took a great fancy / To dressing the self-help way; / There came a young actor / And tried to distract her. / But she was too busy to play." Zipping was training, it was the child's work, the child's labor of love toward independence. The trade journal reported that self-help promotions were sweeping the country, and the "significant thing about all these promotions is not the discovery of Self-Help Clothing but the promotion of Self-Help and Self-Dress Garments as a complete wardrobe." [51]

The zipper was part of each element in the wardrobe, and when self-help was discussed, the illustration almost always showed the act of zipping. With the confidence of the self-enlightened, the Hookless Fastener Company re-wrote history. Looking back, they told the consumer in November 1934 that the self-help idea was given birth by the zipper: "The Talon Slide Fastener brought to outdoor garments an easy-operating, fumble-proof closure that fastened up snug and fast against all kinds of weather! By doing away with all those tiresome buttons children were able to dress alone. Thus the self-help idea was born." [52]

This was a deft reversal, particularly for these years of despair. Even the adult might zip himself or herself into a new mood, and one could sell self-help clothing—a most pleasing advantage to retailers—"on the basis of ideas rather than price." Buttons did not disappear, but Meadville, Pennsylvania, home of the Hookless Fastener Company (Talon Inc.) would make headlines during the thirties as the town without a depression. Zipper sales climbed throughout the bad years. The total value of zipper products rose from less than five million dollars in 1929 to nearly nineteen million dollars in 1939; the figures for buttons were twenty-nine million in 1929, twenty-nine million in 1939. [53] The ten million children under the age of seven who were in the province of John Keilly were learning to sleep, dress, and play in zippers. Students at Princeton in 1940 favored the zipper over buttons by a four-to-one margin. (Princeton alumni of classes before 1929 generally preferred buttons on their flies.) In August 1941, *Good Housekeeping* was casually reminding readers that "Slide fasteners in your children's clothes encourage them to become self-reliant and help save your valuable time."

Although zipper advertisements had stressed and would continue to describe the mobility, freedom, spontaneity, and rhythm (regularity) afforded children by the zipper, this expressive aspect of the new kinaesthetic had had to be complemented by the operative aspect before the sales boom. Further, the boom depended upon a campaign to put zippers in all clothes for all occasions, to associate the zipper with the whole body. As was the case in the progress of penmanship reform and the play movement, the virtues of a certain sort of physical motion were put into increasingly larger contexts; as the

zipper moved from boots and leggings to cover the entire body, so the significance of the zipping action acquired a psychological component.

Kinestruct and Kinecept

I have shown how the campaign for zippers in children's clothing was tailored
to a new kinaesthetic ideal (or kinestruct). Is it possible to go beyond this
history of ideas in the explanation of the success of zippers? Is it possible to
identify a change in the ruling kinaesthetic experience (kinecept) which would
have been compatible with acceptance of the zipper? [54]

The primary kinecept of the button, for children, had been the push. The
primary kinecept of the zipper, according to instructions and advertisements,
was the pull and slide along a smooth track. "One slight pull of the Talon,"
read an ad in 1932, "and the drop seat glides open. Another and it's closed.
One pull on another small light Talon fastener and the front of his suit is
sealed. No fumbling with buttons. No jamming or sticking. Just one smooth,
easy operation for even the smallest child." [55] I wish tentatively to suggest
that the new kinaesthetic ideal evolved to the accompaniment of a kineceptual
change from push to pull-and-slide.

Elizabeth Selden, writing in 1930 on *Elements of the Free Dance*, distinguished classical (pre-1900) ballet from modern dance in these ways: the main
action for speed in ballet was the kick, in the modern dance it was the swing;
ballet was a technique of thrust, modern dance a technique of winding and
unwinding; ballet dancers worked to the beat, modern dancers to the phrase,
legato; ballet was composed of a disjointed series of highly articulated motions, modern dance was composed of pull and relaxation; ballet artists made
quick changes in direction, modern dancers worked along the path of the
motion.

The playing children whose teachers were influenced by dance likely learned
the pull and swing rather than the push. I find this in books on games and
rhythmic movement for children in the 1920s. I find this also in the most
popular new playground equipment, the junglegym (1923), the backyard
swingset, the metal slide.

The same children, learning to write, were taught to pull their strokes
toward themselves and then to slide the arm and hand to the right (along an
imaginary horizontal track, or on lined paper). This was the vertical writing
of 1896, this was printing, but the principles were also applied to the cursives
of the 1920s. The handwriting process was structurally analogous to the contemporary physiological theory of the nerves: the "direction of growth of
medullation was not from the highest cerebral centers toward the periphery
[push], but rather, through the mediation of the medulla, in the opposite
direction [pull or slide]." [56] A signal shift in graphological theory between
1870 and 1930 was congruent: "freedom" as a trait had been identified with

movement away from the body; by 1930, "freedom" related to motions toward the body, for muscles, literally, could but pull.

Of course, people had been pulling on door knobs before 1870, and they would push on bicycle pedals after 1870. But the issue is vital. Can one identify ruling kinecepts as well as kinestructs? Should I have suggested instead a shift from punch to press, or from beat to phrase? Have I chosen poor examples? Have zippers, graphology, and dance somehow misled me? Perhaps the crank on the phonograph, on the Model T, on the clothes wringer, was a more important determinant of the kinecept.[57]

Dudley Sargent, Harvard director of physical education, wrote in the *Educational Bi-monthly* in 1908, "This demand for rhythmic exercises is felt all the more keenly at the present day, because the introduction of steampower, electricity, and labor-saving machinery has taken this factor out of our lives. . . . What wonder that ragtime music (which is all rhythm) has been taken up by the best society." Sargent's assumption was that a kinestruct had been set against the ruling kinecept. Social dance forms were not consistent with but protests against the kinecept of working life. Perhaps, then, the childrearing and educational kinestruct which I have described as the new kinaesthetic was actually designed to run counter to the kinecept controlling most working adults. If so, it might well be profitable to consider "adolescence" during the last forty years as a stage during which the young must accommodate a disjunct kinecept.[58]

H. C. Dent, defending the use of a fast print-script in 1929, wrote, "We have swept from our drawing-rooms the *bric-à-brac* of the Victorian age; we furnish our houses to-day in spare and severe fashion. Our dress has become similarly simplified. The elaborate courtesies of social life in the nineteenth century are disappearing rapidly. We may ascribe, if we like, these changes in fashion to a change in taste, but behind them all is the desire to economise time. . . . So we replace our coal fires by gas and electric stoves, we cut short our courtesies and our hair, we scribble short and illegible notes where our grandparents wrote long and careful epistles." Dent's assumption was that kinecept, kinestruct, and technology run in generally the same direction. In good measure I have shared his assumption. His position—and mine—is plagued by the question, what then causes a change in kinecept or kinestruct? The answer, too often and too easily, has been that technological innovation provokes such changes. I have shown that the refinement of the zipper—and perhaps its very invention—was not independent of the evolving new kinaesthetic. Still, I have shown how, not why, the kinestruct changed during the late nineteenth century.[59]

In 1932, with some prescience for fashion, Aldous Huxley filled the *Brave New World* with zippers. I do not know whether he realized the extent to which zipper promotions were beginning to exploit the behaviorism which Huxley was attacking, but the zipper comes to be paradigmatic of that entire post-Ford society. During his confrontation with the Controller Mustapha Mond, the Savage asks, "But isn't it *natural* to feel there's a God?" The Controller replies, "You might as well ask if it's natural to do up one's trousers with zippers." [60]

For Mond, "natural" is a meaningless word. For the Hookless Fastener Company, which presented the zipper to society in the 1930s as something which preserved spontaneous fluidity of motion and promoted a sense of independence, the zipper *was* natural, far more natural than buttons. Had then our human nature changed, or would it be changed by the experience of zipping at an early age? This was the essential tension between the expressive and operative aspects of the new kinaesthetic. It was a tension upon which the zipper's success was based. It was a tension ignored by the reporter in 1935 who was so bold as to claim that "the zipper is more than any other novelty or innovation the expression of contemporary American culture, Yankee ingenuity and 20th century salesmanship." [61]

Notes

For the sake of editorial economy and consistency, the scholarly apparatus of this essay has been severely curtailed. I use these abbreviations throughout: *DM, Denishawn Magazine*; *ESJ, Elementary School Journal*; *ICR, Infants' and Children's Review*; *JHPER, Journal of Health, Physical Education and Recreation* (before 1949, *Journal of Health and Physical Education*); *LHJ, Ladies Home Journal*; *NCAB, National Cyclopaedia of American Biography*; *PM, Parents' Magazine*. First edition dates for books and monographs are indicated in brackets where important to the chronological argument.

1   "Delsarte's Address Before the Philotechnic Society of Paris," in Genevieve Stebbins, *Delsarte System of Expression* (New York, 1902 [1885]), p. 67.

2   Ted Shawn, *Every Little Movement: A Book about François Delsarte* (New York, 1963 [1910]), p. 49; Claude L. Shaver, "Steele MacKaye and the Delsartian Tradition," in Karl R. Wallace, ed., *History of Speech Education in America* (New York, 1954), pp. 202–18.

3   Isadora Duncan, *The Art of the Dance*, ed. Sheldon Cheney (New York, 1969 [1928]), pp. 48, 54–55, 100, 129, 136–37; Gertrude K. Colby, *Natural Rhythms and Dances* (New York, 1933 [1922]), p. 13; Katharane Edson, "The Art of Gesture," *DM* 1/1 (1924), pp. 9–11.

4   Emile Jaques-Dalcroze, "Eurythmics and Its Implications," *Musical Quarterly* 16 (1930), p. 360, and his *Rhythm, Music and Education*, ed. Harold F. Rubinstein (New York, 1972 [1921]).

5   Margaret Naumberg, "The Dalcroze Idea: What Eurythmics Is and What It Means," *Outlook* 106 (1914), pp. 127–31; Ruth St. Denis, "Music Visualization," *DM* 1/3 (1925), pp. 5, 15.

6   Ruth St. Denis, "The Dance as Life Experience," *DM* 1/1 (1924), pp. 1–3; Ted Shawn, "The History of the Art of Dancing: Part I," *DM* 1/1 (1924), pp. 4–6.

7   See Gabriel Tarde, "La graphologie," *Revue philosophique de la France et de l'Etranger* 44 (1897), pp. 337–63, reviewing Crépieux-Jamin's *L'écriture et le caractère* (Paris, 1896 [1889]), which was freely translated by John A. Schooling as *Handwriting and Expression* (London, 1892) and more literally as *The Psychology of the Movements of Handwriting* by L. K. Given-Wilson (London, 1926); Alfred Binet, *Les révélations de l'écriture d'après un contrôle scientifique* (Paris, 1906).

8 Ludwig Klages, *Handschrift und Charakter* (Leipzig, 1917), and his *Ausdrucksbewegung und Gestaltungskraft* (Leipzig, 1913), the latter translated as *The Science of Character* by W. H. Johnston (Cambridge, Mass., 1932); William Preyer, *Zur Psychologie des Schreibens* (Leipzig, 1895).

9 Ch.-L. Julliot, "La graphologie et la médecine," *Presse Médicale* 40 (1932), pp. 188–90, 803–5; Milton N. Bunker, *Handwriting Analysis: The Science of Determining Personality by Graphoanalysis* (Chicago, 1974 [1959]), pp. 9–13. Bunker's first publication was *Physical Training for Boys* (Boston, 1916).

10 Karl Groos, *The Play of Man*, trans. Elizabeth L. Baldwin (New York, 1908 [1898]), pp. 20–25; Karl Bücher, *Arbeit und Rhythmus* (Leipzig, 1896).

11 One later outcome of this study of physiological rhythms was the development of a more reliable rhythm method of contraception: Leo J. Latz, *The Rhythm of Sterility and Fertility in Women* (Chicago, 1932).

12 G. V. N. Dearborn, "Kinesthesia and the Intelligent Will," *American Journal of Psychology* 24 (1913), pp. 204, 225.

13 William Preyer, *The Mind of the Child*, trans. E. W. Brown, 2 vols. (New York, 1890–93) 1, p. 339; G. Stanley Hall and Joseph Jastrow, "Studies of Rhythm, I," *Mind* 11 (1886), pp. 55–62, and see Dorothy Ross, *G. Stanley Hall* (Chicago, 1972), pp. 279–308.

14 Frederic Burk, "From Fundamental to Accessory in the Development of the Nervous System and of Movements," *Pedagogical Seminary* 6 (1898), pp. 5–64; George E. Johnson, *Education by Plays and Games* (Boston, 1907), p. 24; Edward L. Thorndike and Arthur I. Gates, *Elementary Principles of Education* (New York, 1931), esp. pp. 273–74.

15 John Dewey, "The Place of Manual Training in the Elementary Course of Study (1911)," in his *Middle Works, 1899–1924*, ed. Jo Ann Boydston, 2 vols. (Carbondale, 1976) 1, pp. 231–32, and Dewey's *Art as Experience* (New York, 1934), pp. 162–71; F. Matthias Alexander, *The Resurrection of the Body*, ed. Edward Maisel (New York, 1969), reprints Dewey's introductions to Alexander's books, pp. 169–84.

16 See esp. Platt R. Spencer, *Spencerian Key to Practical Penmanship* (New York, 1872); Annie E. Hills, "Vertical Writing," *N. E. A. Proceedings* 35 (1896), pp. 541–53; A. N. Palmer, "Penmanship," *ibid.* 53 (1915), pp. 888–93; Mary E. Thompson, *Psychology and Pedagogy of Writing* (Baltimore, 1911), p. 49 (quote); H. W. Nutt, "Rhythm in Handwriting," *ESJ* 17 (1917), pp. 432–45; Frank N. Freeman, *The Handwriting Movement* (Chicago, 1918); Frank N. Freeman and Mary L. Dougherty, *How to Teach Handwriting* (Boston, 1923); Harry Houston, "A Turning Point in Penmanship Instruction," *Normal Instructor and Primary Plans*, 33/1–33/3 (1923); Oscar E. Hertzberg, *A Comparative Study of Different Methods Used in Teaching Beginners to Write* (New York, 1926); Joseph S. Taylor, *Supervision and Teaching of Handwriting* (Richmond, 1926); Paul V. West, *Changing Practice in Handwriting Instruction* (Bloomington, 1927).

17 Austin N. Palmer, "Practical Writing—A Course for Colleges and Public Schools to Answer the Needs of the People," *N. E. A. Proceedings* 35 (1896), pp. 825–26.

18 See esp. Marjorie Wise, "Manuscript Writing," *Teachers College Record* 26 (Jan. 1924), pp. 26–38; Arthur I. Gates and Helen Brown, "Experimental Comparisons of Print-Script and Cursive Writing," *Journal of Educational Research* 20 (June 1929), pp. 1–14; William H. Gray, "An Experimental Comparison of the Movements in Manuscript Writing and Cursive Writing," *Journal of Educational Psychology* 21 (1930), pp. 259–72; Harry Houston, "Large or Small Writing for Beginners?" *ESJ* 30 (1930), pp. 693–99; Jean Corser, *Manuscript Writing* (Cleveland, 1931); S. Lucia Keim, "Present Status and Significance of Manuscript Writing," *Journal of Educational Research* 24 (1931), pp. 115–26; Edith U. Conard, *Trends in Manuscript Writing* (New York, 1936).

19 Carleton H. Mann, *How Schools Use Their Time* (New York, 1928), pp. 20, 25, 86–87, tables 42–47.

20 See esp. George W. Beiswanger, "Physical Education and the Emergence of the Modern Dance," *JHPER* 7 (1936), pp. 413–16, 463.

21 Edna Dean Baker, *Parenthood and Child Nurture* (New York, 1922), p. 23.

22 Alice Corbin Sies, *Spontaneous and Supervised Play in Childhood* (New York, 1922), pp. 209 (quote), 211, 214, and see 273–77, which relies on the work of Jaques-Dalcroze.

23 Friedrich Froebel, *The Education of Man*, trans. W. N. Hailmann (New York, 1887 [1826]), esp. Hailmann's comments, pp. 18–19, 36–39, 55–60, 103, 107; Kate D. Wiggin and Nora A. Smith, *Froebel's Occupations* (Boston, 1899), pp. 34–39, 57, 94–96; Elizabeth D. Ross, *The Kindergarten Crusade* (Athens, Ohio, 1976).

24 "Puzzled Parents Offered a 5-Year Toy Plan," *Business Week* 60 (Nov. 18, 1931), p. 8. On play and playgrounds, see esp. Dom Cavallo, *Muscles and Morals: Organized Playgrounds and Urban Reform* (Philadelphia, 1980).

25 Jo Pennington, *Importance of Being Rhythmic* (New York, 1925), p. iv.

26 Rudolf Bode, *Expression-Gymnastics*, trans. S. Forthal and E. Waterman (New York, 1931 [1922]), pp. 11–48; Hans E. Schroder, *Der Rhythmus als Erzieher. Festscrift zum 60. Geburtstag von Rudolf Bode* (Berlin-Lichterfelde, 1941); Hayden V. White, "Klages, Ludwig," *Encyclopedia of Philosophy*, 8 vols. (New York, 1967) 4, pp. 343–44.

27 Ruth F. Shaw, *Finger Painting* (Boston, 1934), pp. 14, 22, 30–32, 38; "Finger Painting," *Fortune* 11 (May 1935), p. 52.

28 See Emily Price Post, *Etiquette* (New York, 1940), pp. 742–47, with Lillian Eichler, *New Book of Etiquette*, rev. ed. (Garden City, 1934), pp. 402–8. On brushing, see William J. Charters, "Ideal Tooth Brushing," *Journal of Dental Research* 4 (1922), pp. xi–xviii; Russel F. Rypins, "Incidence of Dental Caries in the Pre-school Age," *ibid.*, pp. 369–73; Isador Hirschfeld, *The Toothbrush: Its Use and Abuse* (Brooklyn, 1939), pp. 27, 366–84, 412.

29 John B. Watson with Rosalie Watson, *Psychological Care of Infant and Child* (London, 1928), pp. 26–27, 81 (parts first published in *McCalls*).

30 Ruth O'Brien, "New Developments in Designing Children's Clothing," *Journal of Home Economics* 21 (1929), pp. 748–49.

31 Lovisa C. Wagoner and Edna M. Armstrong, "Motor Control of Children as Involved in the Dressing Process," *Pedagogical Seminary* 35 (1928), pp. 84–97, quote p. 85; Watson and Watson, *Psychological Care*, pp. 94–95.

32 Mary Moss, "Machine Made Human Beings," *Atlantic Monthly* 94 (Aug. 1904), p. 266.

33 Edward C. Kirkland, *Industry Comes of Age: Business, Labor, and Public Policy, 1860–1897* (New York, 1961), pp. 171–74; Henry Ford, "Mass Production," *Encyclopaedia Britannica* (Chicago, 1929) 15, p. 38; Frederick W. Taylor, *Principles of Scientific Management* (New York, 1911); Clarence B. Thompson, ed., *Scientific Management* (Cambridge, Mass., 1914); Frank B. Gilbreth, *Motion Study* (New York, 1911); Samuel Haber, *Efficiency and Uplift: Scientific Management in the Progressive Era, 1890–1920* (Chicago, 1964).

34 James Gray, *Talon, Inc.*, ed. Stanley H. Brown (Chicago, 1963); F. J. Federico, "The Invention and Introduction of the Zipper," *Journal of the Patent Office Society* 28 (1946), pp. 855–76.

35 Cora Linn Daniels, "Delsarte Philosophy at Lunch," *The Voice* 6 (Dec. 1884), p. 207.

36 See Maurice H. Krout, "A Preliminary Note on Some Obscure Symbolic Muscular Responses of Diagnostic Value in the Study of Normal Subjects," *American Journal of Psychiatry* 88 (1931), pp. 30–33.

37 Gray, *Talon*, pp. 10–28; Lewis Walker, *"The Lengthened Shadow of a Man," Colonel Lewis Walker, 1855–1938* (New York, 1955); "Lewis Walker," *NCAB*, 28, pp. 6–7; "History of Talon, Inc.," *Meadville Tribune-Republican* SesquiCentennial Edition (May 12, 1938), pp. C1–C9; "100,000,000 Units," *Fortune* 6 (Sept. 1932), pp. 58–61.

38 Gray, *Talon*, pp. 28–40; Federico, "Invention," pp. 864–71; "Sundback, Gideon," *NCAB*, 47, p. 18.

39 Gray, *Talon*, pp. 66–68; Federico, "Invention," pp. 871–75; "Zipp Goes Another Custom!" *Modern Plastics* 12 (May 1935), pp. 44–45.

40 See "Zip," *Oxford English Dictionary*, 12, p. 95, and "Zip" and "Zipper" in supplement (1933), p. 325; "Zip," *Dictionary of American English on Historical Principles*, 4 vols. (Chicago, 1944) 4, p. 2528; "Zip," *Dictionary of American Slang*, eds. Harold Wentworth and Stuart B. Flexner, 2d ed. (New York, 1975), p. 594. The word occurs first in the phrase "Zip Coon," for which see "Zip," *Dictionary of Americanisms on Historical Principles*, ed. Mitford M. Mathews (Chicago, 1951), pp. 1910–11; Constance Rourke, *American Humor* (Garden City, 1931), pp. 84–86. I am not certain whether "zip" in this earliest context had reference to motion (the laziness and itinerary of the character Zip Coon) or to status (his being a "zero," as in student slang circa 1900).

41 Gray, *Talon*, pp. 57–61; "100,000,000 Units," pp. 59–60; S. V. Jones, "50 Years of Zip," *New York Times Magazine* (April 28, 1963), pp. 108–9. See comments by Goodrich executive L. H. L'Hollier on the impact of the 1923 Zipper Boot in E. Grosvenor Plowman, *Fashion, Style, and Art Spread to Other Lines of Business* (New York, 1929), p. 26.

42 "The Merchant and the Child," *Fortune* 4 (Nov. 1931), p. 100; "Earnshaw, George Frederick," *NCAB*, 30, 408–9; Talon ad, *PM* 8 (March 1933), p. 47; Allan D. Craig, "A New Opportunity for Children's Departments Helps Children to Dress Themselves," *ICR* 16 (March 1934), p. 51; Eugene Du Bois, "Who Said Depression?" *Brooklyn Daily Eagle* (May 7, 1935), p. 19; Wagoner and Armstrong, "Motor Control," p. 89, on the time required by nursery school children to work various buttons.

43 Talon ads, *PM* 5 (Nov. 1930), p. 48; *LHJ* (Nov. 1930), p. 193. On washing machines, see "Save the Buttons," *PM* 7 (June 1932), p. 51; General Electric ad, *PM* 9 (Oct. 1934), p. 53.

44 Zip-On ads, *PM* 5 (Oct. 1930), p. 51 and (Nov. 1930), p. 49. Zipper sales industry-wide were 13,100,000 units in 1928. The volume nearly tripled to 35,500,000 units in 1933; in the next two years, sales tripled again, to 109,350,000 units in 1935. See "Early History of the Slide Fastener," pamphlet from Coates & Clarke (n.d.), p. 1; "Zippered Imports," *Business Week* 70 (July 18, 1936), pp. 30–32.

45 Ruth O'Brien, "Thousands of Mothers Want Clothes That Teach Self-Help," *ICR* 8 (April 1930), p. 59; "Merchant to the Child," pp. 72, 77.

46 Talon ads in *PM* 6 (Oct. 1931), p. 47; *PM* 6 (Dec. 1931), p. 45; *PM* 7 (April 1932), p. 39; *PM* 7 (Sept. 1932), pp. 40–41; *PM* 7 (Oct. 1932), pp. 44–45; *LHJ* (Nov. 1931), p. 122; *LHJ* (Dec. 1931), p. 137; *LHJ* (May 1932), p. 83; *LHJ* (June 1932), p. 67. Although *PM* catered to a wealthier, more elite audience, self-help and zippers were promoted to a far larger (and less "progressive") audience through *LHJ* and *Woman's Home Companion*. The additional cost of zippers in clothing was normally a hidden cost to the consumer, since zippered clothing was not strictly comparable in design to unzippered clothing. The wholesale cost of a slide fastener declined from 15 cents in 1931 to 8.5 cents in 1936. Considering ad placements and zipper prices, I would argue that the increase in zipper sales was due to middle-class buying. The first large sector of the adult world to wear zippers was probably among the working class whose heavy worksuits and overalls had been zippered since the mid-twenties.

47 Ads in *ICR* 14 (April 1933), pp. 11, 30, 39, 45; (June 1933), pp. 4–5, 24; (July 1933), pp. 3, 11, 12, 14, 17, 35, 41.

48 Talon ad, *ICR* 15 (Sept. 1933), p. 11; Winifred Davenport, "Self-Help Clothes," *PM* 8 (Nov. 1933), p. 29.

49 "Designing to Sell," *Sales Management* 29 (Feb. 20, 1932), pp. 254, 274–75; "Hookless

Fastener Gets Store Buyers Active Support with Industrial Film," *ibid.* 35 (Oct. 10, 1934), pp. 364–66; "Slide Fasteners Battle to Hold Up Tots' Togs," *ibid.* 36 (March 1, 1935), p. 274; "Tough Market Capitulates," *Printers' Ink* 170 (March 14, 1935), p. 34.

50 Percy MacKaye, *Epoch: The Life of Steele MacKaye*, 2 vols. (New York, 1927) 2, p. 331; G. Stanley Hall, "Gesture, Mimesis, Types of Temperament, and Movie Pedagogy," *Pedagogical Seminary* 28 (1921), pp. 171–201; Gregorio Maranon, "The Psychology of Gesture," *Journal of Nervous and Mental Disease* 112 (1950), pp. 469–97 and written before 1939; Robert S. Lynd and Helen M. Lynd, *Middletown in Transition* (New York, 1937), pp. 260–63.

51 Crete M. Dahl, "Self-help Promotions Sweep the Country," *ICR* 16 (May 1934), pp. 17–18; "How Bloomingdale's Successfully Promoted Self-help Clothes," *ICR* 17 (June 1934), pp. 25, 51; "Hookless Fastener Gets Store Buyers Active Support with Industrial Film," *Sales Management* 35 (Oct. 10, 1934), pp. 364–66.

52 Talon ad, *PM* 9 (Nov. 1934), pp. 58–59.

53 See U. S. Bureau of the Census, *Sixteenth Census, Manufactures, 1939* (1942) 2, part 2, pp. 605, 606, 648; William H. Dooley, *Economics of Clothing and Textiles* (Boston, 1934), pp. 115, 123, 128–35.

54 I borrow these terms from Eleanor Metheny, *Connotations of Movement in Sport and Dance* (Dubuque, 1965), pp. 58–60.

55 Talon ad, *PM* 7 (Sept. 1932), p. 41.

56 Thompson, *Psychology and Pedagogy of Writing*, p. 40.

57 There have been fewer studies of kinecepts than of kinestructs, and fewer still of relationships between kinecepts, kinestructs, and technology. On kinestructs, see esp. Martha Davis, *Towards Understanding the Intrinsic in Body Movement* (New York, 1975); Jonathan Benthall and Ted Polhemus, eds., *The Body as a Medium of Expression* (New York, 1975); Gregory Bateson, *Steps to an Ecology of Mind* (New York, 1972), pp. 107–27; Joann Kealiinohomoku, "Hopi and Polynesian Dance," *Ethnomusicology* 11 (1967), pp. 343–57. Studies of kinecepts have generally remained within fully psychological frameworks, beginning notably with Wilhelm Reich, *Character-Analysis* (New York, 1949 [1933]). In a study singularly relevant to this essay, Morton Schatzman correlated the physical experiences of children in the Schreber pedagogical and gymnastic contraptions of the late nineteenth century with their psychological development; see *Soul Murder: Persecution in the Family* (New York, 1973). Three valuable methodological discussions are Marcel Mauss, "Techniques of the Body," *Economy and Society* 2 (Feb. 1973), pp. 70–88 (first presented in 1934); Franziska Boas, ed., *The Function of Dance in Human Society* (New York, 1944), pp. 17–18, 46–52; Luc Boltanski, "Les usages sociaux du corps," *Annales: economies, sociétés, civilisations* 26 (1971), pp. 205–33. On the relationship of kinecept, kinestruct, and technology, see above all Alan Lomax et al., *Folk Song Style and Culture* (Washington, D.C., 1968); Edward T. Hall, *The Hidden Dimension* (Garden City, 1969); Andre Leroi-Gourhan, *Le geste et la parole* 2 vols. (Paris, 1964–65).

58 The complex relationships between fashions in social dancing and the development of the new kinaesthetic must be left unexamined here, but see a fine study by Adrienne L. Kaeppler, "Preservation and Evolution of Form and Function in Two Types of Tongan Dance," in Genevieve A. Highland et al., *Polynesian Culture History* (Honolulu, 1967), pp. 503–36, and a provocative work by Julie M. Taylor, "Tango: Theme of Class and Nation," *Ethnomusicology* 20 (1976), pp. 273–91.

59 H. C. Dent, "The Schools and the Nation's Handwriting," *The Nineteenth Century and After* 105 (1929), p. 389. The compatibility of kinestruct and kinecept is also assumed by Robert F. Thompson, *African Art in Motion* (Los Angeles, 1974).

60 Aldous Huxley, *Brave New World* (New York, 1946 [1932]), p. 159.

61 Du Bois, "Who Said Depression?" p. 21.

L'Enfant Terrible Comes of Age
William Moebius

In the criticism of children's literature, we tend not to want to say too much, lest the spell be broken. In an arresting prologue to his *Childhood Regained*, the contemporary Spanish philosopher Fernando Savater goes further: "Now I need only clarify what I want to do in this book, since I seem to have rejected the sacred viewpoints of the criticism and laying-bare of texts. Very simply, the only thing I want to do here is provoke an evocation, a sort of literary spell." [1] Writing on *Treasure Island* and other favorites from his childhood, Savater draws us into his memory, while the books he has read remain as ethereal, as otherly real, as the childhood that appropriated them. The path of memory is not a well-traveled one in the current criticism of children's literature; the watchful shepherds who tend an ever increasing flock of texts stick to the high roads, preferring the survey of the field to an invocation of the mother of the muses.

Why not, I wonder, read the children's book for its spell? Are those of us who flourish in the reading of children's books crippled when we begin to figure forth the experience? May we not adopt the spectator role, accommodating ourselves entirely to a given text without modifying it in some "transactional" way? [2] Especially when we slip between the covers of a children's story, may we not also escape? This, indeed, is the route Savater invites us to take:

> And yet, when we are older, almost mature, we sometimes return to the forbidden sphere of stories, where jungles full of gleaming eyes and the ghostships of our childhood still lie in wait. We descend to our souls' misty homeland, anesthetized by grownupness, swaddled in that sensation of controlled escape that comes over us on Saturday afternoons. We raise like a banner a word that for some is censure, for others an incentive, and for everyone a proper defense against the fatal poison of nostalgia: escape. [3]

We know full well that escapes are often plotted in advance. That escape is theme and hermeneutic device. Perhaps a genre unto itself, if we listen to Paul Oppenheimer: "For Eulenspiegel's is a book that belongs to what might be called the literature of middle-class escape, in which the hero, or anti-hero, succeeds in triumphing over the dull repetitiousness of much middle-class life, while implicitly acknowledging the futility of having been born a man in a universe that insists on cruelty, injustice and death." [4] For Oppenheimer, "the distinguishing feature of such books, though, is that they seem to depict an escapist version of lower-class and middle-class economic life, regardless of the nature of their audience. Their delight for any audience thus lies in their brash treatment of serious circumstances." [5] We see reflected in these comments the dilemma of the mapmaker: do we trace the hero's or the reader's escape? Are hero, treatment, and audience all traveling the same route?

The stories of *Curious George* and *Pippi Longstocking*,[6] those *enfants terribles* of the forties, provoke questions like these. I took time out for Pippi and George only after I myself had become a father. Whatever vague memories they evoked, they were not, like Savater's, those of my childhood reading experiences. But indeed, these books cast a spell, enabled a certain escape. Yet in the middle of my escape, and among their many, I stumbled. It was not that the narrative device was unfamiliar or that the psychology of the runaway was difficult to grasp. The convention of the breaking away from conventions was not new. But a core of meaning eluded me; I was not just escaping, but escaped from. Here were stories that had undergone the "realistic displacement" [7]: their time was plausibly ours, their places somewhere on this or the other side of the Atlantic. In the man with the yellow hat I glimpsed the serene detachment of some fellow parents; in Tommy and Annika, Pippi's friends, I recognized some of my younger acquaintances. But none of these witnesses, whether the man with the yellow hat or Tommy and Annika, articulated what the mischief meant, what the escapes were all about. Even the narrator's voice, so often in children's books the editorial shield-bearer or over-the-shoulder Athena, was not always persuasive. Whether they conveyed amazement or disapproval, the voices in the text offered little sense of discovery. It seemed that the chronic misbehavior inscribed on the page was not completed there, not quite rounded off or buckled in, but was gleefully and impatiently demanding interpretation. It was up to the reader to steer the mischief off the page, to chart the course; as a reader, I was already collaborating in George's next escape and Pippi's further mischief, and in effect imagining a flight manual of my own. In this essay, I distill instructions from that flight manual.

The story lines of George and Pippi are not hard to recall. George, a monkey, is lured into captivity by a suave European-American, the man with the pale yellow hat. George tries to fly like a seagull, takes a plunge in the sea, is rescued, inadvertently dials a fire alarm in his captor's office, is apprehended by the gendarmerie and jailed, but escapes his prison, grabs the dangling strings tied to a balloonman's wares, is lifted high, drifts down to a traffic light, and is delivered for resettlement to an island of his own in the zoo. The first installment ends here. One later installment depicts George washing skyscraper windows, painting an apartment wall to look like a jungle, and becoming a screen idol.[8] George's story is told in words and pictures, one at variance with the other. Pippi's story, in the twelve chapters of *Pippi Longstocking*, unfolds primarily in the text, with complementary sketches in pen and ink that accent rather than recreate the story. Like George, Pippi's penchant is for getting into things; unlike George, Pippi has the gift of gab, and easily invents whopping but usually harmless lies. In or near Villa Villekulla, Pippi goes "thing-finding," turns away the officers who come to make her a ward of the state, spends an hour at school as a somewhat recalcitrant pupil, joins, without being invited, a circus act, dances two thieves out the door of her home, makes herself an unwelcome guest at the home of Tommy and Annika, rescues two children from their blazing home, and plays hostess and pirate for Tommy and Annika. Her rescue earns her public esteem, but her "primitive mentality" seems unsuited for the Swedish way of life. Always she fancies returning to the man of her dreams, her father, the supposed Cannibal King, down in the South Seas. The sequels to *Pippi Longstocking* build on Pippi's longing for her father's world; her climactic reunions with him on her territory and then on his provide a fulfillment for Pippi that one wishes the reader could share.[9]

Precocious at their play, both George and Pippi share social and cultural disadvantages. They cannot abide by laws, cannot grasp the lessons imparted in schools, and cannot read books. As their tales unfold, we bear witness to their constant overdoing, a hyperactivity that not only exasperates local authorities, but leaves both Pippi and George worn out, ready for sleep; when their tales are ended, we find them in places apart, smiling at their exclusion. Both curious and elusive, Pippi and George are creatures of other realms, Africa and South Seas, strangers to the northland, members of an endangered species that perhaps only fiction can save.

Not that children's literature has neglected to preserve other monsters. Unruly or mischievous children have played important roles in children's literature, but not usually as escape artists. Their difference from Pippi and George is reflected in many ways, but especially in their beginning and their end. If they prove incorrigible, as Max and Moritz do, they are "eliminated". If, on the other hand, they exhibit the potential for growth and adjustment, they escape death but face a series of lessons. Wilhelm Busch's Max and Moritz, the progeny of "Scherz und Phantasie," (Jest and Fancy) are introduced as examples of not just bad behavior, but of bad or wicked children: "Ach, was muss man oft von bösen / Kindern hören oder lesen! / Wie zum Beispiel hier von diesen, / Welche Max und Moritz hiessen."[10] ("Oh, about bad children so often we must hear or read, like these, for instance, Max and Moritz.") Their exploits suggest somewhat sadistic motives; not only do they bring about the death of a poor widow's chickens, but they contrive the near drowning of the tailor, the mutilation by burning of the schoolmaster, and the infestation with lice of their Uncle Fritz's bed. But these motives are not limited to Max and Moritz. The baker thrusts them into the oven in suits of dough; soon they are crisp and ready, gingerbread boys, yet not quite done for. In their one and only escape from the custody of an elder, they step out of their ovenwear. An attempt to hide in piles of grain after a break-in at the miller's is foiled; captured in a sack, they are ground up in the mill.

The narrator's judgment of Max and Moritz as "bad children" is reaffirmed by that of their victims in the end. These survivors, pictured as lanky, somewhat pinched oldsters with slightly bulbous red noses, spell out the lessons of two abbreviated lives: "Bösheit ist kein Lebenszweck!"; "Dies ist wieder ein Exempel!"; "Das kommt von dumme Witze!" [11] ("Wickedness is not to be aimed for in life"; "Yet again another example!"; "What comes of hare-brained jokes!").

Much as the boys' behavior is seen to merit these moralizing declarations at the end, still their truth as characters is just a bit more complicated. Their redeeming qualities are recognized by two healthy geese, shown in the final illustrations snapping up ground-up pieces of Max and Moritz. As figures of the reader, these geese, their backs turned to us, remind us that we owe Max and Moritz our thanks for satisfying a certain curiosity. What happens when you tie pieces of bread to both ends of a string and place the matter before a jury of chickens? What happens when you saw a footbridge almost through? What happens when you pour gunpowder instead of tobacco into a pipe? The answers are clear: someone gets hurt, the perpetrators are labeled criminals, and a certain poetry is born:

> Rums, da geht die Pfeife los
> Mit Getöse, schrecklich gross!
> Kaffeetopf und Wasserglas,
> Tabaksdose, Tintenfass,
> Ofen, Tisch und Sorgensitz —
> Alles fliegt in Pulverblitz. [12]

> (Pow, it goes off with a blast,
> that pipe, horrendously loud!
> Coffeepot and water glass,
> Tobacco-tin, inkstand,
> Oven, table, and easy chair —
> All fly up in a powderflash.)

Unfortunately, Sophie, another nineteenth century perpetrator of mischief and misfortune, hardly seems to merit poetic utterance. Judged from the beginning by both the narrator and her mother, she practices lachrymose contrition long before she learns obedience to mother's rule or honesty before charges of misbehavior. Yet the cumulative weight of her sorrows does seem to effect a change in Sophie: she will grow up, she will be well-adjusted. For example, her callousness towards animals, beginning with the mutilation of her mother's tropical fish and of a bee (Sophie reproaches it for all the stinging it has done), softens as she mourns chicken, squirrel, cat, donkey, and turtle, each her victim. The cat, the most domesticated brute to suffer under Sophie's care, bears the stigma of "défauts;" his death is an expiation of his own wickedness, but it is also a consequence and an instructive emblem of Sophie's "faute." [13] Sophie can never escape consequences (none fatal, even a wild ride in a donkey cart, perhaps her closest call) whether she steals her mother's special candied fruits or covets what she believes to be her mother's sewing box. Every sin she commits is known to her mother almost at the hour of commission, and every sin is punished, once by whipping. Her feminine wiles, lexified as this or that "idée," cannot transcend those of a mother who apparently knows the practices of little girls: " 'mais toi, Sophie,' " her mother intones, " 'tu as toujours des idées si singulières, que j'ai peur d'un accident causé par *une idée.*' " [14] (" 'But Sophie, your ideas are always so singular I'm afraid of an accident on account of *an idea.*' ") This risky and ill-fated wantonness that can never gain official clearance as imaginative play is in sharp contrast to the earnest and almost stark righteousness of her cousin Paul. Paul's model conduct, in which sympathy and compassion for the sinner outweigh the impulse towards correction and punishment, illuminates the good name of the apostle; Sophie's conduct obscures the gift her name implies, or rather perhaps reveals the difficulty one faces in earning it. Although the narrator endorses the relentless child-rearing techniques of Sophie's mother, there is nevertheless a trace of Paul's sympathetic understanding: "Sophie était étourdie; elle faisait souvent sans y penser de mauvaises choses." [15] ("Sophie was heedless; she would often do bad things without thinking.")

Both *Max und Moritz* and *Les Malheurs de Sophie* present the child as malefactor, experimenter on the verge of crime; the child becomes the vehicle of an indoctrination in proper conduct. Social pressures dictate conformity or extinction, submission to human laws, or summary liquidation. The tendency of these children's books to freeze the figure of the "free-thinker" in moral platitudes has the effect of blocking the reader's escape. We can think the way the experimenting, wondering minds of the main characters do for only a moment before finding ourselves curbed, even crushed, by adult edicts and controls. Precedents for the kind of *enfant terrible* we encounter in Pippi and George are not to be found, I believe, among the denizens of children's literature, but rather among the creatures of folktale and myth.

The denomination of the type "mischief-maker" is problematic. Among the figures of childish misbehavior I have encountered in the tradition, I have found many to choose from, each with its own epithet, for example, the merry prankster, the trickster, the *enfant terrible* and the *enfant malin*. These epithets evoke different monsters, Till Eulenspiegel, Peer Gynt, Hermes, Loki, Ananse, Br'er Rabbit, even Kronos. And I am not sure that we can ignore a Hungarian *táltos* such as Csucskari, a gypsy boy who needs neither food nor drink, can pass in and out of natural forms such as a cat or a flame, write with his finger, make fools of old women and the blacksmith, and for no personal reward, give the world back the sun, moon, and stars. There is more than the hint of the shaman in the *táltos* figure,[16] as there may be in the figure I have chosen as analogue to Pippi and George. Tom Thumb, in the Grimm versions, is prankster and trickster,[17] and as he contributes to the destruction of fortunes and livestock, *enfant terrible*, yet not quite the murderer we meet in the tales of the Dogon and Bambara tribes from North Africa.[18] And like Pippi and George, Tom is both terribly underdeveloped and at the same time uncapturable, beyond ownership.

Tom is literally conceived for enjoyment. One version begins with a sort of invocation by his parents. His father offers his first: " 'Wie ist's so traurig, dass wir keine Kinder haben! Es ist so still bei uns, und in den andern Häusern ist's so laut und lustig.' " [19] (" 'How sad it is that we have no children! It's so quiet where we live; in other houses, it's so noisy and jolly!' ") His mother follows with, " 'Ja, wenn's nur ein einziges wäre, und wenn's auch ganz klein wäre, nur Daumens gross, so wollt' ich schon zufrieden sein; wir hätten doch von Herzen lieb.' " (" 'Yes, even if it were only one of its kind, and even if it were perfectly small, only as big as a thumb, I would still be satisfied; then we would have our hearts' desire.' ") His parents want a noise-producer like themselves; the effect of their talk is to produce a boy-noise who will continue their meaning. Born prematurely, Tom is all his parents need; despite his shortcomings, he has a way, a very nimble and verbal way, one that gives him access to a horse's ear and to a snail's shell. But his small size offers his admirers in the world the possibility of total possession, like the girl whom the boy in "Die Nelke" turned into a pink, and pocketed. His diminutive size coupled with his mature voice mark him as an attractive commodity. Entrepreneurs of the "world-at-large" can make something of Tom. Bought from his father, Tom escapes his buyers, like the pupil who learned the trick of turning into a horse and then back into a boy. It is only the mask they purchased, not the actor himself. Tom merely lends himself to roles, from playing horseman to playing stage material. By owning the conventions, Tom Thumb disowns the masters.

Throughout his adventures, Tom, *táltos* or prankster, shifts from one "occupation" or "habitation" to another. Teasing or cajoling his superiors, he makes a game out of cooking or stealing. But the games are over when Tom suddenly finds himself in the windowless stomach of a cow, and later in the belly of the wolf, or encased in sausage. Tom appears to be in trouble. He may perish, we might think, or be altered by such confinements. But he is merely soiled by them. The temporary metamorphosis of Tom into talking cow (or so think the sexton and his milkmaid) is an illusion. Tom can be assimilated to another's being, but like the sperm in Barth's "Night-Sea Journey," he cannot lose his voice.[20] He is always the parasite that betrays the host, always the illegitimately possessed, never the unwittingly transformed, as in tales in which person becomes animal, or as in Steig's *Sylvester and the Magic Pebble*, where Sylvester, a donkey, becomes a rock.[21] Cow and wolf are killed for their ownership of Tom Thumb, their incorporation of his value. Tom's survival is usually at the expense of his numerous hosts.

We have been looking at Tom Thumb's story as a set of variations on the theme of emergence from captivity. That this captivity is to conventions of space and object as well as to persons will not need further proof. But it may be worth another moment to reflect on Tom's continual disengagements from the material world. Insofar as Tom is an escape artist, he upholds a principle of reversibility, from the not-seen to the seen to the not-seen, or from the unowned to the owned to the unowned. But one thing about Tom is irreversible: his size. Several cues lead us to connect his small size with inherent fragility. His parents doubt his ability to be of use on the farm. That he can lie unnoticed in the ear of a horse (a fly might be rejected with a twitch) suggests his weightlessness, as does his standing on the brim of the entrepreneur's hat. When he ducks into a mouse hole, and finds that unsafe, we have to adopt new standards for "safe place," modeled for us by the contrast with the safe snailshell. What Barthes calls the reference code is at work here, as we formulate an estimate of Tom's viability in our world. That estimate has to take into account Tom's given likeness to a grasshopper, in one version, and to a straw, in another. The figure of Tom Thumb is clearly marked by its vulnerability, especially to normal human weight and force.

But his vulnerability is not only a matter of small size. Unlike folk tale heroes who seem to earn tangible credits with each test they pass, whether it is simply the right to continue taking the test or to possess a magic instrument whenever another one comes along, Tom earns no such tangible credits. Dirtied and soiled, he is demeaned, expelled from animal entrails or sausage. Upward mobility, progress toward wealth or happy marriage: these are not available to Tom. The world will never catch Tom, but then he will never be able to cope in it. So both versions have Tom back at home, in the care of his parents. He is an infant who cannot make permanent the step out of the nest. His underdevelopment has its rewards, but only by virtue of the anecdotes it generates. His nimble responses to life-threatening situations earn him passing respect, but he will never be ready for the world except as a curiosity.

Tom's incompatibility with the world does not prevent him from playing mediator between the animal and the human. Human in form, he is vulnerable to consumption by both domestic and wild animals. The gap that we assume between what we are for animals, especially domesticated ones, and what we are for people, cannot be taken for granted in Tom's case. Although his disadvantageous position toward grown-ups is clear from the start, we may not see him as bite-size until near the end. Then we may question what difference there is between the human and animal forces that prey on Tom, between the civilized entrepreneurs or sausage-makers and the hungry wolf or fox. It is against such a world of exploitation, of economic savagery, that Tom Thumb's pluck and ingenuity are measured. He knows only what he needs to "not be" himself momentarily; but to be more than a jumping jack across the gap of the animal and human is beyond him, unless it is to live to tell the tale.

Whereas Tom Thumb's experience leads him deeper and deeper into the "old world" of brute consumption, ultimately into the belly itself, what occurs to Curious George is no more than a series of groundings in the new world, of startling contacts with shipdecks and ocean, cabin and office, jail and stoplight, sportscar and zoo. In between these seemingly ritual returns, Curious George enjoys the "life above," an existence he shares with the birds, one of whom, during his sea journey, he fancies himself to be. His life story begins in Africa, declares the text, and high up in a tree, declares the illustration. Once transported to "the zoo!" he is once again found perched in a tree, albeit one without bark, clutching a single balloon as he once clutched a liane. Shown smiling when he is up high, frowning more often than not each time he is grounded, George belongs not so much to a particular stretch of land in the southern hemisphere as to the air, where boundaries disappear. And the world looks very different from on high: the narrator tells us that "the houses looked like toy houses, and the people like dolls" to George as he hangs on tight to the balloons. As an aerial explorer, George knows no political or legal boundaries, only hard physical facts such as the sack in which he is first captured, or the ocean, or the jail cell walls. Nor can it be said that he develops a more sophisticated awareness of the difference between public and private property, or between situations that require respect for law and those that admit a degree of playfulness. George's anomie, the basis of his poetic license, is incorrigible. His power resides strictly in the looking into or down on things, but stops short of grasping their rules.

The verbal narrative reminds us again and again that the root of George's problem with human society, the basis of his impish behavior, lies in his push to perceive, the impulse to feel, handle, and discover, without arriving at judgment. When George thinks "it would be nice" to try on the hat, or to fly like the seagulls, or to dial the telephone, the editorial narrator knows otherwise. Nearly every graphic image of George moving in characteristic abandon is accompanied by a written affidavit of illegitimacy. From the very beginning, the scriptural aspects of the narrative constitute an attempt at the reader's moral enlightenment:

> This is George.
> He lived in Africa.

> He was very happy.
> But he had one fault.
> He was too curious.

Original happiness and original sin are syntactically on a par, but curiosity, the original sin, occupies, as it were, the bottom line. The man in the yellow hat, for whom George is precious as a commodity, enjoins George to "run along and play," then adds, "but don't get into trouble." The moral "objectivity" of the narrator is thus translated into the economically motivated injunctions of the suave master. George does not answer these injunctions because he cannot speak, and of course, cannot read. Yet as he descends the gangplank, entering the land of opportunity, he holds open some sort of printed matter, no doubt the papers of legitimacy that attach him to his master. George's silent phonecall that inadvertantly rings the alarm at the fire station calls forth a string of graphic images that suggest keystone cop hilarity; here are uniformed men dancing over office furniture after a wild ride down the page on their hook and ladder. But these images are thwarted, so to speak, by the text which first underscores the urgency of men doing their duty ("HURRY! HURRY! HURRY!") and then reports their finding: "No fire. Only a naughty little monkey." Next to this sober determination of George's culpability we come face to face with the gaiety of the firemen as they tumble after George. Finally, beside a full page spread, one of the most extraordinary images of the book, that of George hovering with glee over a cityscape that bears so much the stamp of H. A. Rey's European origins, goes the forbidding text: "George was frightened. He held on very tight." The contradiction between spoken and graphic representation is at its most acute on these two pages (figure 1).

Like Tom Thumb, George makes only aesthetic gains; economic gains are for the grown-ups, who borrow, so to speak, from George's power as image. The man with the yellow hat, armed with shotgun, spyglass and a smile, obtains George by simple deceit. From this point on, George lends himself to the business of others. His actions require not individual but group response, the cooperation of sailors and firefighters, and the opportune presence of many balloons on sale to many children, and the happy occasion of a stoplight designed to regulate the flow of traffic including buses, trucks, horses, and cars. Finally his donation of himself on the tree at the zoo benefits many visitors. Much as it may seem that the man in the yellow hat is the merciful lord bestowing his blessings on a child of nature, it is George who becomes an object of public worship, who receives the awe, if not the tender of the world. It is because of loose phenomena like George that the servants of law and order get paid. He is the key to the hubbub no laws can ever get straight, or ever get rid of, the veritable master of the revels. It is no surprise that in one of the sequels George becomes a movie star.

Figure 1. From *Curious George* by H. A. Rey. Copyright 1941 and copyright renewed 1969 by H. A. Rey. Reprinted by permission of Houghton Mifflin Company. Photo: Jamie McEwen.

Before we let George's monkeyshines fade from our view, let me ponder briefly a Lithuanian children's story about a monkey like George, who shares George's fate. This story, which was brought to my attention by a Lithuanian-American, and has not been translated, is called *The Curious Monkey* and it is both written and illustrated by Martynas Vainilaitis. It appeared in Vilnius in 1964, 21 years after the publication of *Curious George* in the United States.[22] Written in rhymed verses of irregular length, it records the short-lived freedom of a runaway pet, imported from "the south," who is unable to adapt to the rules of the particularly urban and automotive culture of the north. There are two lines of action: one follows the monkey as tricycle rider from first pedaling to a minor accident; the second displays him as "tourist" on and above city streets, until his capture and incarceration in the zoo. The first episode underlines the monkey's likeness to active boys: like "you" the reader, he is athletic and is shown playing soccer with boys. However, he is endowed with a tail and demonic coordination: he wins the tricycle race he organizes. The second episode identifies this boy-monkey as an outlaw, whose disregard for traffic and pedestrian law constitutes criminal behavior. The monkey answers for his misbehavior as follows: "The rules I don't know, and I don't care to know them." As a final proof of his incorrigibility, he states clearly that he is a monkey, not a human; where he was born, in the Brazilian jungle, there are no cars. Concluding his misadventure, he confesses to the law-abiding children who visit him in the zoo, "I was a rascal, and I just fooled around too much."

The narrator, who purports to have brought the monkey up "like a boy" adopts and sustains a critical attitude towards his pet's behavior, pronouncing sentence as of the very first frame: "He was very happy and bright, but not very careful." By the end of the second frame, however, the narrator has dispatched the monkey into the world with words of caution, and is not heard from in any self-reflexive way again. Instead, the children, who ask where he is going, the blackbirds, who tell him to fix his tricycle, and finally the people on the streets, who call attention to his jaywalking, all set the pattern of legality and conformity. Vainilaitis illustrates this critical attitude throughout by playing on the equivalence in perspective of the background, which is situated "high" on the page, with the superior vantage point of the community, whose members regularly figure in that background. While the monkey enjoys proximity to the reader by always appearing in the foreground, neither his larger image nor his obviously dynamic mobility can compensate for the inferiority of his position on the page, made all the more transparent in the final scene at the zoo, in which the monkey appears in a cramped cell, on the lower left hand side of the left hand page. It seems evident that in the graphic code of this text, judgment is represented by vertical up or down perspectives, while pleasure and excitement operate on the horizontal plane. Whereas in *Curious George*, the monkey alights on a traffic signal overlooking a massive traffic jam below, the curious monkey without a name crosses the street in front of and under, so to speak, the gaze of pedestrians and busdrivers. In only two frames, those which follow this one, does the monkey occupy a superior position while retaining his privileged spot in the foreground. In the first, a cop blows a whistle, pedestrians lift their arms in outrage or hysteria, and two ambulance personnel bring a stretcher to catch the monkey, who hangs by his tail from the bus's powerline. It is on this page that the monkey states his indifference to rules. In the second frame, the rules of chronology themselves are broken as the monkey is shown in a flashback to the Brazilian jungle. The text continues the monkey's defense of his alien behavior.

If there are gaps or blanks in this text, the major one must be that break in chronology, not very common in picturebooks. On nearly every other page, text captions picture, and picture provides a mirror of text. Where the discrepancy between text and picture in *Curious George* is itself a constant source of uncertainty of meaning, as we do not know whether to join in the pursuit of aesthetic or of moral goals, that in *The Curious Monkey* is carefully reserved for a key moment, in which the hero's unfortunate fate is clearly decided. This fate sheds no light on particular economic laws, as it does in "Tom Thumb" and *Curious George*. It does not exemplify except in that flashback a particularly imaginative view of reality. The content of text and illustration of the monkey back in the jungle suggests an anthropological *explanation* of his reality, rather than a *poetic vision* of it. George, on the other hand, though defined by his African origins, extends his ecstatic vision of reality to everything from seagulls to telephones to wires to balloons. At the same time, George is incapable of explaining or of apologizing for anything. His vision is corporal, not yet invested in the language of the new world. The "curious monkey," though never given a proper name, has, like Sophie, learned the language of the north, developed an alibi, and lost, as his abject confession on the final page shows, the vision.

In each of the stories we have examined so far, origins tell us something about the *enfant terrible*'s incompatibility with the normal westernized world. The grownup world is in the northern hemisphere; the curious incorrigibles are imported from south of the equator. Tom Thumb, I should point out, is spoken of as an object of desire while the speaker, his father, pokes the fire. Both monkeys and Tom are elemental creatures of heat; it is hardly surprising that Tom plays near the stove (even goes up the chimney in one version) and that George calls in a false fire alarm.[23]

Pippi Longstocking too, though Swedish, is far from the pure stock represented by her friends Tommy and Annika. In one sense, she has no parents, except in imagination. If we trust her account, her mother died at Pippi's birth, and is now watching her through a peephole in the sky. This is not the

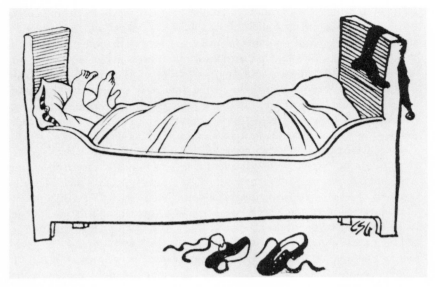

Figure 2. From *Pippi Longstocking* by Astrid Lindren, illustrated by Louis S. Glanzman. Reproduced by permission of Viking Penguin, Inc. Photo: Jamie McEwen.

fond mother of Aschenputtel[24] who promises to look down from heaven, but a voyeuse. Her father has disappeared overboard in a sailing adventure. His daughter reckons that he has become a king of the cannibals. Although the text does not tell us what cannibals do, Pippi's proud evocation of her father as a prince of the primitive recalls an "other" world not as civilized as the one we meet her in.

Pippi's looks tell us more about her esoteric origins. She wears outlandish shoes "from South America"; her feet are planted, so to speak, in another realm. Her hair is the color of a carrot, her nose, "the shape of a very small potato"; her affinity with two root crops gives her, one might say, a somewhat raw, unfinished look, that of a Würzelmannchen.[25] And then there is her monkey, Mr. Nilsson. I note that in one Swedish edition, illustrated by Ingrid Nyman, Mr. Nilsson's image occurs more than fifteen times, more often in fact than that of Pippi herself.[26] In the American edition illustrated by Louis Glanzman, the monkey figures but twice. To the reader of that Swedish edition, monkeyhood and Pippi may be synonymous.

Pippi's underdevelopment, apparent in her root crop face and monkeyhood, may also be signified by her sleeping habits, feet on pillow, head under the blanket (figure 2). While this inversion mocks a norm in our world, it seems to confirm one in Pippi's private world, that of her head being in the "low" position, beneath her feet; her viewpoint is from below, starting with the Cannibal Island. Seen in this light, all of the elements of her name itself point below the belt.

Pippi's mouth, so full of attractive lies, is "it must be admitted," a wide one. The tales that stream out of this little Amazon offer wild glimpses of life in pre-industrial countries such as the Congo and Borneo, and in "underdeveloped" ones such as Arabia, Argentina, Egypt, and China. Her account of the Congo is quite revealing:

> Let me tell you that in the Congo there is not a single person who tells the truth. They lie all day long. Begin at seven in the morning and keep on until sundown. So if I should happen to lie now and then, you must try to excuse me and to remember that it is only because I stayed in the Congo a little too long.

Later, Pippi announces, "I'm lying so my tongue is turning black." These spurious explanations of the causes and effects of lying render still more palpable a moral geography, in which anything south of the border is both suspect and tantalizing.

Further evidence of Pippi's alliance with the "lower" world appears when, at the coffee party, she gabs on and on about a houseservant, appropriately named Malin, whose service is atrocious, and whose worst sin is that "SHE NEVER SWEPT UNDER THE BED." Like Pippi herself, this Malin finally goes to sea. Despite these associations with underworldliness, Pippi maintains that she will always come out "on top."

To Tommy and Annika, Pippi's superiority stems from her bountiful nature. She gives freely from her secret storehouse, a hollow tree-trunk, and from her father's endowment. To those who would extract something from her, such as the schoolteacher or the burglars, she offers gifts, a gold watch, gold coins. To her guests, she offers food, pancakes and her own version of birthday cakes. She also offers her strength where it is needed, and where it is not. She outdoes the circus-lady on horseback, the trapeze artist, and the strongman. Finally, at her most demonic, she emerges from a burning house, from which she delivers two children; she celebrates the occasion with singing and dancing, worshipping the blaze.[27]

Pippi's functions as 'donor' and 'sender' require that she not be held back within conventional boundaries. As one who provides access to the underworld, whether it be the world of ghosts or of teeming jungles, she is a sort of pre-teen Hermes. But if the mode of the arch-thief were dominant, Pippi's story might lose much of its appeal. For Pippi is not an infallible little goddess, stunt-woman that she would sometimes appear to be. Like Curious George and Tom Thumb, she is subject to failure and to great fatigue. There are gaps in Pippi's awareness of the world and these must be filled in by a sympathetic reader.

It is through the eyes of Tommy and Annika that we read Pippi's great weaknesses. It is they who call her bluff. Strangely, Pippi does not deny their accusation: "Pippi thought a moment. 'You're right,' she said sadly, 'I am lying.'" Not only does she confess, but even draws sympathy to herself by rendering her fault the shortcoming of an orphan,[28] whose memory is somehow defective.

> "Yes, it's very wicked to lie," said Pippi even more sadly. "But I forget it now and then. And how can you expect a little child whose mother is an angel and whose father is king of a cannibal island and who herself has sailed on the ocean all her life—how can you expect her to tell the truth always?"

That Pippi's memory is beyond discipline is suggested in other ways. Ordered to attend school, she asks why. "'To learn things, of course.'" But if learning is equated with memorization of the multiplication tables, then Pippi cannot learn. Asked to name the capital of Portugal, Pippi expresses regret that she does not know this sort of fact and will "'lie awake nights and wonder and wonder.'" Then standing on her hands, she remarks, "'For that matter, I've been to Lisbon with my papa . . .'" Pippi has *lived* the answer, but it is one she cannot automatically name. Like George's, hers is a corporal knowledge, not easily articulated in our categories and language.

It is easy to read Pippi's behavior at school as a piece of buffoonery in the manner of *Le Petit Nicholas*.[29] Pippi's response to a quiz question is a classic: "'Well, if you don't know that yourself, you needn't think I'm going to tell you.'" This remark scandalizes her teacher, even as it amuses us. Yet the scandal it provokes is unintentional; Pippi is sorry for it, yet continues to be offensive: "'See that!' said Pippi. 'You knew it yourself. Why are you asking then?'" Pippi, like George, cannot grasp the rules of this discourse. And this renders her somewhat pathetic:

> "Have I behaved badly?" asked Pippi, much astonished. "Goodness, I didn't know that," she added and looked very sad. And nobody could look as sad as Pippi when she was sad. She stood silent for a while, and then she said in a trembling voice, "You understand, Teacher, don't you, that when you have a mother who is an angel and a father who is a cannibal king . . ."

Although much of Pippi's misbehavior is antidote to a world that takes itself too seriously, it can also act as poison to the automatic desire on the reader's part to enjoy it at society's expense. Pippi is at her best overthrowing those especially masculine characters who would exploit or correct her. Her wisecracks undercut the authority of policemen, ringmaster, and strongman. But at school, and especially at the coffeeparty, Pippi's outrageous routines, while perhaps originally laden with satiric purpose, play themselves out in a manner that is, upon reflection, of a wearying whimsicality. As she runs on in her description of Malin's disservices, interrupting the other guests, gobbling the cakes and pie meant for the general company, she tries even the most sympathetic reader's patience. The hostess pronounces a sentence it is hard not to agree with: " 'You must never come here again . . . if you can't behave any better than this.' " This sentence is tougher than those exclusionary pronouncements (stay away from school, from the circus) we have heard before because it comes from the mother of Tommy and Annika. For these two Pippi feels great affection, and for the reader, these two are representative of inoffensive norms. The reader is presented with an awkward choice: to take Pippi's increasingly obnoxious behavior as a radical critique of adult conventions, preferring her ill-timed and relentless make-believe to the predictable seriousness of others, or to accept the norms and somewhat dull routines of life represented by these others as an increasingly resilient response to the mad pretentions of this pirate princess. The reader may well want to avoid the choice, but we are not allowed to forget that Pippi will not reform, as Pippi confesses to Mrs. Settergren: "Pippi looked at her in astonishment and her eyes slowly filled with tears. 'That's just what I was afraid of,' she said. 'That I couldn't behave properly. It's no use to try; I'll never learn. I should have stayed on the ocean.' "

Banished from the Settergren home, Pippi is on her own. Having committed the sin of gluttony, Pippi does not suffer indigestion or increase in weight; she does not, like Augustus Gloop,[30] get reprocessed and reformed. Instead, she goes out and spectacularly saves two lives and earns resounding praise. As in "Tom Thumb" and *Curious George*, an unwritten law or principle not unlike that of eroticism, that pleasure is to be sought in authenticity and intensity of feeling and sensation (or, to put it figuratively, in "taking the heat"), governs Pippi's activity and is only partially curbed by the forbidding language of the legal norms borrowed from beyond the text.

Pippi's confabulations, at first a sin, ("it's wicked to lie," says Annika) then a treat, then an embarrassment, finally a dreadful calling, signal the ways, through discourse, by which the imagination demands to be recognized. Pippi, like George and Tom, challenges the reader to know her, not just as a little wonderwoman, but as a dangerous, yet vulnerable insight.

As we ponder an afternoon of escape among these *enfants terribles*, do we still have scruples? Is our conscience still not quite at ease because, after all, the children's book is child's play? Let us listen, finally, to the British critic and teacher Fred Inglis:

> . . . the idea of escape is often too happily used in the condemnation of what are obviously poor works of literature. We may "escape" from our immediate world into a much darker and more horrifying one; "escape" may be narcotic or reassuring. When we escape with the most

intense relief into a novel, it may be that the novel is a relief because it is much more intelligent and rewarding than the tedious staff meeting from which we have "escaped." We regularly need respite when repairs (or repression and evasion) can go on. "Repair time" is a valuable concept in any developmental graph worth having. We cannot say any work is necessarily a form of "escape," but we can say a good deal about its quality. We can speak censoriously of escape as regression only when the activity is self-deceiving, a deliberate manipulation of our humanity in order to alter feelings without altering conditions, a pursuit of a fraudulent solace in which we purposely retreat from our usual level of cultural interest and stamina.[31]

Inglis reminds us that escape need not be self-deceiving. We need not run away from ourselves, or from our "usual level of cultural interest and stamina" in order to be spellbound, to enter realms where only the most adventurous dare take flight.

Notes

1   Fernando Savater, *Childhood Regained*, trans. Frances M. Lopez-Morillas (New York: Columbia University Press, 1982), p. xiii.
2   See essays by James Britton and D. W. Harding in Margaret Meek, Aidan Warlow, and Griselda Barton, eds., *The Cool Web: The Pattern of Children's Reading* (London: Bodley Head, 1977); and Arthur Applebee, *The Child's Concept of Story* (Chicago: University of Chicago Press, 1978).
3   Savater, *Childhood Regained*, p. 22.
4   Paul Oppenheimer, trans. and ed., *A Pleasant Vintage of Till Eulenspiegel* (Middletown, Ct.: Wesleyan University Press, 1972), p. xxiii.
5   *Ibid.*, p. 289.
6   All further references will be to the standard American editions: H. A. Rey, *Curious George* (Boston: Houghton Mifflin, 1941); and Astrid Lindgren, *Pippi Longstocking*, trans. Florence Lamborn (New York: Viking Penguin, 1978).
7   See Northrop Frye, *The Secular Scripture* (Cambridge: Harvard University Press, 1976).
8   See H. A. Rey, *Curious George Takes a Job* (Boston: Houghton Mifflin, 1947). There are six books in the series.
9   I find these sequels disappointing. In *Pippi Goes Aboard*, trans. Marianne Turner (Harmondsworth, Middlesex, England: Penguin, 1977), the mystery of her father is dispelled; in *Pippi in the South Seas*, trans. Marianne Turner (Harmondsworth, Middlesex, England: Penguin, 1979), the magic of the Cannibal Island is laid to rest.
10 Wilhelm Busch, *Max und Moritz* (Munich: Sudwest Verlag, 1979), "Vorwort." There are no page numbers.
11 *Ibid.*, "Letzter Streich."
12 *Ibid.*, "Vierter Streich." The translation is my own.
13 Comtesse de Ségur, *Les Malheurs de Sophie* (Bruges: Désclee de Brouwer, 1965), p. 96. Translations are my own.
14 *Ibid.*, p. 121.
15 *Ibid.*, p. 20.

16 See Linda Dégh, ed., *Folktales of Hungary*, trans. Judit Halász (Chicago: University of Chicago Press, 1965), esp. pp. 15–28 and note on pp. 306f.

17 The Nordic trickster, as recently described by Siegfried Mandel, bears some of the features we encounter in Pippi and George: "In all the mythologies and folklores (discussed so far), the trickster is distinguished by his fearlessness and absence of shame or an inhibiting sense of honor; he thrives on comic exposure. Whatever great benefits he brings to society are achieved through trickery; society cannot condone the one nor refuse to accept the other. Precisely because he breaks taboos, he is condemned by the convention-minded but is at times also rewarded and secretly admired for doing what others dare not do. He is the visible embodiment of private fantasies and plays them out to comic proportions. . . . With laughter and defiance he oversteps boundaries and flirts with the pathological, but he incurs no permanent scars and most often comes out of his farcical adventures unscathed though bruised. The trickster accepts whatever fate doles out, with commonplace laughter, but in general the tragic hero and his audience brood over heaven's arbitrariness." See Siegfried Mandel, "The Laughter of Nordic and Celtic-Irish Tricksters," *Fabula: Journal of Folktale Studies* 23, no. 1/2 (1982), p. 41. See also Carl Jung's discussion of a "trickster cycle" in "The Psychology of the Trickster," in *The Collected Works of C. G. Jung*, 2d ed. (Princeton: Princeton University Press, 1968), vol. 9, pt. 1, pp. 255–72, and the application of his model of a trickster's "development" to the monkey in *Journey to the West* in Jing Wang, "A Generative Grammar of Stone: A Study of the Transformation of Stone-Images from Folklore Texts to Three Classical Chinese Novels" (Ph.D. diss., University of Massachusetts, 1985). Evidence of such "development" is missing in the cases discussed here.

18 See Veronica Görög, Suzanne Platiel, Diana Rey-Hulman, and Christiane Seydou, *Histoires d'enfants terribles* (Paris: Maisonneuve et Larose, 1980). In Görög's view, the *enfant terrible* "vise par son action non l'acquisition d'avantages ou de biens mais précisément des 'valeurs immatérielles' " (p. 41). I believe this also describes the bent of Tom Thumb, Curious George, and Pippi Longstocking.

19 The Brothers Grimm, "Daumesdick," in *Kinder-und Hausmärchen*. See also "Daumerlings Wanderschaft."

20 John Barth, "Night-Sea Journey," in *Lost in the Funhouse* (Garden City, New York: Doubleday, 1968), pp. 3–13.

21 William Steig, *Sylvester and the Magic Pebble* (New York: Simon and Schuster, 1969).

22 My sincere thanks to Daiva Matulaitis for this reference and for her rough translation. See Martynas Vainilaitis, *Pramustgalvis Bezdzioniukas* (Vilnius, Lithuania, 1964).

23 Pippi herself will chant praises to the fire from which she rescues two children. The *enfant terrible* described by Görög derives power from his association with fire. "Le rôle du feu, omniprésent soit comme force destructice soit (dans la scène finale) comme élément bénéfique, permet de penser que le héros possède des attaches particulières (. . .) avec les maîtres du feu. Ce manipulateur du feu terrestre et céleste deviendra, au terme de sa quête, tonnerre, maître des eaux célestes et dispensateur de pluie. La pluie est bien un don des plus précieux du ciel, principe de fertilité." See Görög et al., *Histoires d'enfants terribles*, p. 49. Max and Moritz show themselves to be "children of the fire": standing on top of the chimney, they suspend chickens on strings to let them roast in the fire below; they put gunpowder in the teacher's pipe; and they survive their own baking as doughboys. Yet unlike George, Tom, and Pippi, their mischief costs them their lives.

24 I.e., Cinderella in the Grimm Brothers' version.

25 My thanks to Albert Cook for this reference, and for the opportunity to present a draft of this paper to a conference on Aspects of Narrative held at Brown University in November, 1983.

26 Astrid Lindgren, *Pippi Långstrump*, illus. Ingrid Vang Nyman (Stockholm: Raben & Sjogren, 1969). See, for example, pp. 21, 27, and 29.

27 See note 23 above.

28 Pippi's claim to sympathy may also have roots in our most profound dreaming. As an orphan with godlike power, she participates in the archetype of the divine child, as described by Karl Kerényi (with Carl G. Jung) in *Essays in a Science of Mythology*, trans. R. F. C. Hull (New York: Bollingen Foundation, 1949, 1963), and by Gaston Bachelard in *The Poetics of Reverie*, trans. Daniel Russell (Boston: Beacon Press, 1971). Bachelard writes: "In every dreamer there lives a child, a child whom reverie magnifies and stabilizes. Reverie tears it away from history, sets it outside time, makes it foreign to time. One more reverie and this permanent, magnified child is a god" (p. 133). In a review of Astrid Lindgren's life and work, Jonathan Cott draws on the work of Bachelard. See "Profile," *The New Yorker* 59 (February 28, 1983), pp. 46–48, continued on later pages.

29 Sempé-Goscinny, *Le Petit Nicholas* (Paris: Denoel, 1960).

30 Roald Dahl, *Charlie and the Chocolate Factory* (New York: Bantam, 1973).

31 Fred Inglis, "Reading Children's Novels: Notes on the Politics of Literature," in Geoff Fox, Graham Hammond, Terry Jones, Frederick Smith, Kenneth Sterck, eds., *Writers, Critics, and Children* (London: Heinemann, 1976), pp. 165f.

"Le Plus bel amour de Don Juan" or
a Child's Phantom Pregnancy / *Julia Przyboś*

As divergent as they may at first appear, all reception theories agree on a fundamental point: literary works act upon the reader. With this in mind, some critics have suggested that the act of reading changes the reader. Among those who analyze such changes, some describe reading as an activity that brings the reader to question social or moral orthodoxies. And because of the changes that such questions provoke in the reader's mind, reception theorists believe that reading is a means of gaining privileged access to an understanding of self and world.

This would appear to be the fundamental (and founding) principle of Wolfgang Iser's theoretical construct—the implied reader—whom he endows with the attributes of an active, perceptive individual.[1] Iser's favored field of research, that of so called "realist literature," yields an optimistic, if not idealistic, view of the reading process. But what of texts that one hesitates to class with the novels of Smollett and Thackeray?[2] What of works that do not present uniform or easily graspable value systems and which, though raising important questions, frustrate the efforts of even the best-intentioned readers to answer them? By indirectly postulating the aesthetic inferiority of such works, Iser casts a blind eye on their (to his mind justifiably) "imperfect" or "failed" reception. Yet every literary theory should take into account works both accepted and rejected by the prevailing aesthetics of their time. It is as important to discover why certain texts fail to act on the reading public as it is to know why certain texts succeed in doing so.[3] In this context, it might be worth asking if literary extremes do not provide the best test of a theory's validity: in the case of so obviously optimistic a theory as Iser's, works which are built on a more pessimistic view of world and reader make for disarming case studies. The "proto-decadent" writings of Barbey d'Aurevilly are a case in point. The analysis of one of his *Diaboliques* will enable me to evaluate Iser's theories of reading and, at the same time, to conceive of the reading process from a different vantage point.

This essay will focus on a work that has always provoked a variety of responses. Ever since their appearance in 1874, *Les Diaboliques* have been the object of lively controversy.[4] Already apparent in the reactions of Barbey's contemporaries, these range from condescending derision to outraged moral condemnation. "Risible" sneers Flaubert; "filthy" and "unnatural" vociferates the young Zola; "monstrosities" conceived by "a self-proclaimed champion of throne and altar" *Charivari* exclaims.[5] But only a few years later, Théodore de Banville will claim "epic grandeur" for *Les Diaboliques.*[6] The book will also eventually arouse the enthusiasm of Léon Bloy, Remy de Gourmont, and Huysmans, who casts one of his protagonists, Des Esseintes, to find it "particularly enthralling."[7] And the author? In the prefaces and the judicial questionnaires in which he responds to the accusations leveled at him, Barbey d'Aurevilly insists on the uplifting qualities of his tales.[8]

Are they then moral tales, these *Diaboliques*: stories in which the author visibly delights in displaying such aberrations as a profaned eucharist, a heart devoured by dogs, an infant buried in the flowerstand of an elegant drawing room! At first glance it would seem highly improbable that these stories either mask or reveal a moral code of any description. These are not edifying allegories written to foster specific rules or precepts of conduct. The moral or immoral aspects of *Les Diaboliques* are, however, only incidental to this essay. If Aurevilly spent time over the writings of Saint Thomas Aquinas, Saint John Chrysostom, and the mystics, his own works typically reveal epistemological rather than religious preoccupations.[9] In one of the more unusual *Diaboliques,*"Le Plus bel amour de Don Juan," Barbey seems to broach a specifically epistemological issue, namely that of the restrictive effect of moral and ethical systems on perception and, more specifically, on the interpretation of narrative.

In this story, I shall first attempt to trace the tangled network of mythic and legendary elements. I shall then broach the narrative techniques themselves, analyzing the interplay between narrators and narratees in more detail.[10] Such an examination will illustrate the essence of Aurevilly's ideas on perception. It should also shed some light on the usual reactions the story elicits from its readers: admiration or disquiet, laughter or indignation. And it may then offer an explanation of the reading mechanisms set in motion by a text dedicated to ambiguity.

Let me first summarize the tale. An anonymous first narrator sets the story's framework: he tells the aged and devout Marquise Guy de Ruy of the supper that twelve women held for the Count Ravila de Ravilès, a man of the same lineage as Don Juan. He knows the tale from Ravila himself and before long concedes the narrative voice to Ravila/Don Juan, who, during the course of that meal, at the promptings of his former mistresses, tells the story of his greatest love. He speaks of a marquise he once loved and of her daughter's hostility to him. But the tale that Ravila now undertakes to tell has come to him second hand—he repeats it as it was told him by the marquise. She herself is describing a meeting that she had with her daughter's confessor. The latter, incredulous and embarrassed, declares that he has come on behalf of the girl, who has beseeched him to inform her mother of her crime. She had confessed to the priest that she was pregnant. Astounded, the marquise questions her daughter, who explains that one evening she unfortunately sat in an armchair which Ravila had just occupied and had left still warm. In the end (and at the story's end as well), we discover that the child's pregnancy is merely a phantom.

"Le Plus bel amour de Don Juan," containing neither violent death nor profaned eucharist, is in sharp contrast with the other *Diaboliques*. It harbors none of the scandalous secrets that lie at the heart of Aurevilly's other tales.[11] Some have pointed to the frustration of certain readers who, having reached the center of this Chinese box of a text, are disappointed to find only a young girl's uncanny naiveté.[12] Many critics seem to share the same impressions: they are almost all in agreement in judging the story peculiarly insubstantial.[13]

Current criticism focuses primarily on the mechanism of the story's narration.[14] Critics, having posited at least five levels of narration, are generally astounded that so many narrators should be so involved in unveiling so little. "The gullible reader swallows the bait of a promised revelation indefinitely postponed and finally altogether avoided."[15] This kind of surprise is at the heart of an analysis of "the tale's neutralization by the process of its own narration."[16] In the throes of deconstruction, critics went so far as to label the tale "une machine à faire du vide" (a vacuum-making machine). Like Penelope, Barbey was supposed to have amused himself in the unravelling of his own creation. "Le Plus bel amour de Don Juan" would play at giving narrative shape to this "unravelling" itself.[17] But if there is any undoing (or doing-in) here, it is definitely being done by (and to) those critics who view the tale from either an exclusively moral or formal angle.

I

A couple: a Don Juan and a young girl. Don Juan, alias the Count Jules-Amédée-Hector de Ravila de Ravilès. "A providential name" (p. 99) suggests the anonymous narrator, who hastens to add that Ravila de Ravilès "always lived up to the expectations of his lordly title." It has been said, perhaps hastily, that "Barbey assumed a demiurgic role in name giving: in baptizing his characters, he damns them."[18] "Expectations" then, but which ones? Though Spanish-sounding, the name Ravila de Ravilès is forged of French elements. It is not difficult to find a "ravisher" in it.[19] But if we listen to the blasphemies that fleck the conversation of the first narrator and the devout old lady, we begin to hear in Ravila's name less of the ravisher and more of the object of ravishment, an echo of vilification (*ravilir*). A veritable "ontological gauge," the count's name is open to various interpretations:[20] on the one hand, it condemns Ravila de Ravilès to seduce, degrading those seduced; on the other hand, it hints at idolatry of which he is himself the object.[21]

If Don Juan clearly emerges as the Other, the Evil-doer,[22] in the tell-tale motto of the story ("Le meilleur régal du diable, c'est une innocence"/The

Devil's favorite delicacy is innocence), some of his characteristics do not gibe with a demonic nature. Ravila is a Don Juan "in his final act" (p. 106), a lover already past his prime. This does not hinder his twelve former mistresses from forming "a chain, like mesmerists round their tub, round that magnetic man" (p. 99). This "aged sultan" (p. 106) meant "more to them than all of Asia did to Sardanapalus." What matters here is not the count's seductive prowess as much as the collective adoration of his former mistresses. This difference is crucial and serves to underscore Marquise Guy de Ruy's devout fascination. Like an Orgon on the subject of a Tartuffe, she incessantly leads the conversation back to Ravila.

As well as allusions to Molière's "froid Commandeur" (p. 100), Barbey exploits elements evoking Lord Byron's Don Juan. Ravila's mistresses are not like "those soft green youth, those little maids that Byron loathed" (p. 102); they are full-blossomed beauties. Like Byron's *Don Juan*, Ravila is not a vile seducer who roams the earth collecting women with evil intent. Both authors depict their character as one who seduces those placed in his path by social and cultural circumstance.[23] Furthermore, Ravila's love, the young girl's mother, is a "blonde with black hair," echoing Byron's theme of the blonde with black eyes.[24] She is "awkward in love"; an unusual, a surprising choice for a Don Juan.[25] But she literally worships Ravila: for her he becomes the Mass that she recites "with all ceremoniousness and sumptuousness, like a cardinal" (p. 108).

The details characterizing Ravila de Ravilès reveal a tension between the concepts of power and fascination. Don Juan's demonic and supernatural power and the collective adoration of his person come into play by turns. Both as a bold seducer and as a figure visibly lacking the attributes of a classic Don Juan, Ravila is always the object of a profound devotion. Barbey postpones the resolution of this apparent flux between active and passive roles, accentuating now one, now the other side of the character.

But in the end he will have to settle the issue. When the women ask Ravila for the story of his greatest love, he recounts instead the greatest love that he has inspired—a distinction marking yet again his slippage from activity to passivity. The evening in honor of Ravila turns into a truly edifying exercise in humility. During the supper that has brought the twelve women around their Lord and Master, Ravila/Don Juan sacrifices his vanity by unveiling an adventure which casts doubt on his reputation as a seducer. An unusual reversal is here at work. Perversely patterned on the mystery of transubstantiation,[26] Ravila's narrative is one in which a man cast as the Don Juan of his era, confesses himself to be the object of a childish fantasy, the victim of a strange seduction.

Who is the Devil's cohort? "She was . . . a puny child . . . ugly even by her mother's admission . . . a small, burnt topaz . . . a half-finished study in bronze with black eyes . . . Sorcery!" She has "sickly-looking hair, black with tinder highlights" (pp. 111–12). Such is her physical appearance. Her psychological portrait is more difficult to sketch. Four complementary concepts emerge in the narrative progression: hostility and piety, aggression and submission. These categories incorporate all the details of the girl's character. Extremely shy, she is sullen, taciturn, somber, and icy. But she is furtive as well: at Don Juan she casts the glances "of a spy, dark and menacing." She feels "an almost convulsive horror" toward her mother's lover (p. 111). We learn, moreover, that she is very devout. "An angel of purity and piety," says the aged priest (p. 116). If the child knows the canons and precepts of her religion, hers is a peculiar kind of piety: a "somber, Spanish, medieval, superstitious sort of devotion" (p. 113). This array of adjectives evokes a Spanish mysticism associated by Barbey himself with the ecstasy of Saint Theresa of Avila. "Ravished and ravishing" he writes of her: "she died for the love of her God, consumed by desire just like one consumed by desire for a fellow being."[27] And we might further specify with Bataille that there is a disquieting resemblance between religious ecstasy and erotic sensation, that "the saint turns away in horror from the sensualist, unaware of the unity of his shameful passions and her own."[28] The girl's phantom pregnancy is thus explained: it betrays her desires, hidden for so long under the mask of piety. In the end, they become violently manifest. For it is in fact she who "ravishes," by means of the imagination, Ravila de Ravilès.

The theme of seduction around which the narrative is structured, thus centers not on Don Juan, but on his seductress. In her case, Barbey initially appears to relinquish his predilection for giving "ontological" names. He contents himself with calling her "little mask." But are we not intended to recognize in this cold, menacing, and "black-eyed" child a youthful incarnation of Lilith, the veiled seductress with "eyes . . . like dark stars?"[29] Lilith, the immodest one. In Christian tradition, she appears above all as the female demon of seduction. Over the centuries, folk imagination and scholarly "investigation" have caused her to undergo countless transformations.[30] Romanticism, Symbolism, and Decadence abound with images of the vampire, specter, siren, water-sprite, snake-woman, and phantom-woman. Beautiful or ugly, inevitably striking, they pour forth from the pens of poets and prose writers alike: Hoffmann, Poe, Pushkin, Mickiewicz, Rosetti. Among the French, Vigny, Nodier, Gautier, Hugo, Baudelaire, Mérimée, Dumas, Villiers de l'Isle-Adam, and Huysmans all describe their charms and the erotic fascination they hold for the great-grandsons of Adam. As a protean, mythic figure, the eternal seductress haunts the canvases of Rosetti, Böcklin, Gustave Moreau, and Edward Burne-Jones.[31]

Barbey's title points to the seducer, but the prefaces of *Diaboliques*, which assert women to be their sole concern, point to the seductress. The tension underlying the story's framework is between a youthful incarnation of Lilith and that of an aging Don Juan, linked in any case by their common demonical ancestry. By putting into play the notion of oppositional complements in the age and sex of the protagonists, Barbey hints at what Lévi-Strauss would later document—that, "d'une certaine manière, les mythes se pensent entre eux" (to some extent, myths think each other).[32] Don Juan and Lilith are head and tail of a single myth of seduction, allowing Barbey to play a double hand. He puts his chips simultaneously on an "aging" myth (the seducer) and on an emerging, or so to speak "pubescent" myth (the seductress). And he wins on both accounts, since the story successfully yields a prolific mirroring of meanings.[33]

II

Age and sexuality: Barbey uses physicality to tackle more spiritual matters. "Le Plus bel amour," told in an erotic vein, explores that human dimension which is intellectual, psychic, and religious. The focal point, the young girl's story, is simple, some might say simplistic, only at face value.[34] But to a well-attuned ear the girl's story resonates within a sufficiently broad range to allow for the discovery that Barbey, through this supposedly "naive" and "disappointing" tale, touches upon the founding myth of Christianity.

> "—Mère, c'était un soir. Il était dans le grand feuteuil qui est au coin de la cheminée, en face de la causeuse. Il y resta longtemps, puis il se leva, et moi j'eus le malheur d'aller m'asseoir après lui dans ce fauteuil qu'il avait quitté. Oh! maman! . . . c'est comme si j'étais tombée dans du feu. Je voulais me lever, je ne pus pas . . . le coeur me manqua! et je sentis . . . tiens! là, maman . . . que ce que j'avais . . . c'était un enfant! . . ." (p. 118).

> (Mother, it happened one evening. He was in the big armchair by the fireplace, across from the settee. After sitting there for a long time, he got up and I had the misfortune of sitting down in the armchair he had just left. Oh! mama! . . . it was as if I had fallen into a fire. I wanted to get up, but could not . . . I hadn't the strength and I felt that what hurt me . . . right here, mama . . . was a child! . . .)

Would we be accused of reading into the text if we were to discern in it a reference to the dogma of the virgin birth, more specifically to the Annunciation?[35] Let me point out that the tale provides us with the whole cast for the reenactment of this truly seminal scene. Does not the girl wear Virgin Marys and Holy Spirits around her neck (p. 113)? There is no doubt that the text takes the pains to provide us, between the lines, with the key that would open the door to such an interpretation.

One is tempted, in the structuralist mode, to trace inverse parallels between the evangelical and Aurevillian annunciations. The details of Barbey's text mimic and invert the elements drawn from the original scene.[36] It is known that the Annunciation preceded the Conception: God sent the angel Gabriel to announce to Mary the miracle of Incarnation that was about to take place in her womb. The little mask, however, "conceives" first, then announces the "miracle" herself to the priest and to her mother. It can not be a mere coincidence that the little mask is thirteen years old. Such was the age of the Virgin Mary when the angel appeared to her.[37]

The Annunciation took place one beautiful morning in spring: the serene skies, the clear and golden light, depicted in the canvases of the Old Masters attest to this. "It happened one evening" begins the little mask's confession. This much is conceivable. Don't demons perform only under cover of the night? Let us be more specific: an autumn or winter evening, since there is reference in the girl's episode to the fire lit in the fireplace.

For centuries, the church fathers and saints have maintained that the Virgin is a passive figure. In the scene of the Annunciation, she receives the Divine Word in either a kneeling or seated position.[38] By contrast, Aurevilly's girl seems singularly active: it is she who gets up, it is she who goes to sit down in the armchair impregnated with Don Juan's essence. It is an act of usurpation—was not Satan himself damned for having sat on the throne of the Almighty?[39] A revealing act, all the more significant as it marks the transition of power: from this moment on a gradual transformation will take place. The active Don Juan will slip into passivity.

The angel tells the Virgin that "the Divine power of the Heavens will take her under its shadow" (Luke 1:35); for the little mask it is "as if /she/ had fallen into a fire" (p. 118), into the flames of Hell.[40] Divine shadow and hellfire—here the inverse parallel is obvious. Mary received the Word in her ear, by the salutation of the Angel. Western painting usually depicts a band of luminous rays joining the beak of the Dove to the Virgin's ear. For Barbey's young girl, an entirely different orifice comes into imaginary play. Ear and vagina—we have here yet another reversed parallel.[41] This reversal was well understood by Félicien Rops, a friend of Baudelaire's, Barbey's, and Huysmans'.[42] To illustrate "Le Plus bel amour," he portrayed a barely nubile girl, thin and sickly. He shows her seated in an armchair and from the spot where the nude body touches the seat emanates a series of rays leading nowhere. In the background we glimpse a Don Juan who bears a resemblance to Barbey, and whose cape spreads like a black wing.

What purpose does it serve to know that Barbey transposes and reverses a seminal mythical event? What purpose is served by multiplying echoes, references, and allusions? Is the author doing no more than creating a story from a myth that, finally, seems to reverberate only in the imaginings of a thirteen-year-old girl? The answer lies within the text. The little mask is superstitious: she wears Virgin Marys and Holy Spirits, amulets intended to protect her from evil glances and demonic powers. And yet the inconceivable happens: one fine evening she believes that she has been impregnated by Don Juan.

The mystery becomes clear once we examine the function of amulets. They guard against attacks on the person who wears them: but their "impregnable" shield works only in one direction—from the outside in. No amulet, it would appear, can stand in the way of forces interior to the self.

Beneath the young girl's behavior and phantom pregnancy we can thus glimpse another meaning. In the girl's "superstitious devotion" we discern a pubescent asceticism reminiscent of certain religious fanatics.[43] In her attitude towards the count, whom she flees, we recognize an example of avoidance behavior. The hostile and sullen mask distorting her features suggests a reaction formation. And since these measures prove themselves ineffectual, she redoubles her efforts to master her libidinal impulses. A special kind of defense mechanism sets itself in motion here: she ascribes to her mother's lover her own thoughts and desires. In the scene of the conception, the girl clearly projects her instinctual desires onto their object.

It is not necessary to enumerate parallels and analogies in order to perceive the relationships linking "Le Plus bel amour de Don Juan" to theories of psychoanalysis. The nineteenth century played with the very concepts to which the twentieth century subsequently gave a doctrinal formulation. Thomas Mann asserts that Freud is the true son of Schopenhauer's and Ibsen's century, and, we might add, that of Barbey d'Aurevilly.[44] Freud bears this out when he notes that "demons are bad and reprehensible wishes, derivatives of instinctual impulses that have been repudiated and repressed."[45] He adds in another text that "the devil is certainly nothing else than the personification of the repressed and unconscious instinctual life."[46] He was himself the troubled witness of the first documented instance of transferance and countertransferance between Anna O. and Breuer. In Jones' account, Breuer's patient, "who . . . had appeared to be an asexual being and had never made any allusion to such a forbidden topic throughout the treatment, was now in the throes of a hysterical childbirth, the logical termination of a phantom pregnancy that had been invisibly developing in response to [his] ministrations."[47]

This projection of repressed desires is reminiscent of the way in which the Aurevillian girl appropriates for her own narrative a reversal of the original Annunciation. The power of Barbey's disturbing syllogism is such that it forces us to reflect upon the evangelical scene. The veiled reference to Saint Theresa of Avila, the "ravished and ravishing" Saint, already announces or, more precisely, denounces the erotic aspect of the two scenes: the announcement (or, if you will, "annunciation") made *by* the little mask and that made *to* Mary. Suddenly a new ambiguity comes to the fore: announced "to" or "by"? In such a light, the foundations of Christian theology could be seen to rest upon the choice of a preposition . . .

Barbey is playing here with the dogma of the Word's incarnation by drawing attention to the issue of Christ's divine and miraculous birth. But in questioning the fundamental dogma of the Church, he also questions the notion of salvation: a Redemptor of dubious origins would be able neither to purge the stain of original sin, nor to redeem the human race through his death: in short, he would not be able to ensure eternal life. Man would be thus irrevocably condemned as the descendant of his first parents, those who succumbed to the temptation of the snake-woman wrapped around the tree of Good and Evil.[48]

The fruit offered to Eve by the Snake Lilith and the fruit in the womb of Mary, the second Eve—the fruit that condemned humanity and the fruit that saved it—these two have mirrored each other since their inception.[49] But whereas the Church has sought to demonstrate their fundamentally opposite nature in the supposition that such algebra will negate original sin, Barbey insists on the intrinsic similarities between the myth of Seduction and that of Annunciation. Likewise he raises the issue of the world's and humanity's guilt and innocence, emphasizing the universality of sin and the indelible nature of vice. This same pessimism is reflected in his preface to Les Diaboliques, in which he expresses the doubt that he could ever write a corresponding collection of Célestes: "And after les 'Diaboliques,' les 'Célestes'? . . . perhaps, if one could find a blue that was pure enough . . . but does it exist?" (p. 43). If Barbey implicitly questions Christian dogma, he seems to believe "in Satan and in his influence on the world" (p. 41).

Satanism and the blasphemy of pessimism readily lend themselves to a translation into secular terms. In a century that put so much faith in progress, an optimistic century that preached the perfectibility of the human race and its institutions, Barbey's voice is dissonant. It challenges all the moralisers, philosophers, and builders of better futures. Aurevilly's remarks against "the great Hegel" bear this out. He writes of Hegel that he "saw neither the outside nor the inside of man, the political prisoner of God, and that man would have pointed an accusing finger at himself, even if History . . . had remained silent on that issue."[50] Barbey's challenge was not fully comprehended by his contemporaries. Nonetheless, the sacrilegious tone of this literary neo-Catholic (to adopt Anatole France's phrase) was taken up again by a number of writers who, a few years later, looked to Barbey as a master. Les Diaboliques by "the Holy Father of the Decadent Movement"[51] bears witness to "that state of mind, at once devout and impious,"[52] which engendered works like those of Barrès, Bloy, and Bourget.

What lurks behind these inversions that tempt a modern mind to see the defense mechanism in action? Why so complex a skein of themes? What can it hope to gain, this text, positively "à rebours," that fixates on great myths? It can be agreed that the tale is not an easy one to read. And since it lacks an authoritative narrator, the reader's task is made all the more difficult. It may seem that Barbey seeks to orient the reader: he describes, for example, the effect of the girl's story on the listeners. Yet given the diversity of their reactions, such description says both too much and not enough. It provides no single confirmation. The parish priest suggests that the girl "is mistaken . . . by her very innocence, perhaps" (p. 116). The mother's behavior is ambiguous: she distances her daughter by marrying her off.[53] Ravila's twelve listeners "are pensive. . . . Had they understood?" (p. 118). Barbey implies a certain hypocrisy on their part by alluding to Joseph's and Potiphar's wife and by describing the thoughts of one of the listeners as being as murky as the green of her crystal goblet. The story of the little mask is exiled to the daydream-provinces of the twelve listeners, who are reassured by her young death because in life she acted out their own blindness and desires. A prolonged silence, an exclamation, a question, and the final "if it weren't for that . . ." typographically suspend the tale. This finale underscores the author's refusal to retrace the narrative hierarchy so carefully established. The first narrator and his narratee have long since vanished—the punctuated silence with which we are left is in strange contrast to the orchestrated voices that have come before.

III

Today's critics are not much more perceptive than the maligners and sneerers among Barbey's contemporaries. Starting with the typical reactions the story evokes may assist in establishing a general pattern in its reception. The nature of such reactions depends on the informational baggage of the two "ill-matched" parts: that of the story's frame, in which we discover a whole hierarchy of narrators, and that of the "naive" account of the little mask.

The frame of the tale is crowded with characters, events, echoes, and allusions, whether religious, mythological, folkloric, or literary. Christ and the Devil, the Bible and the Koran, Don Juan and Melusine, Sardanapalus and Alcibiades, Machiavelli and Prince de Ligne, Molière and Byron—all are there, to the dismay of a novice reader and to the delight of an experienced one. Frustration and pleasure: such are the opposite reactions that the text may elicit. But even the most enthusiastic reader will find it impossible to track down all the references. He will conclude that he is grappling with a text that takes in the entire Western tradition, a text so complex and rich that it does not lend itself to any one exhaustive and coherent interpretation.

One might object that almost any reader sets off into this labyrinth equipped with Ariadne's threads, namely, the references to the Devil and to innocence. It is not by happenstance that Barbey highlights the provocative sentence "Le meilleur régal du diable, c'est une innocence." However these two referential poles are modified by contradictory details and epithets: Don Juan is an aging seducer, the young girl is pious but hostile. These oxymorons call into question generally accepted values and cultural clichés. Faced with the contradictions, the typical reader chooses the path of least resistance: he retains only those pre-conceived ideas that conform to his expectations—those ideas that correspond to the prevailing doxa of piety and seduction. Of the expression "aging seducer," the reader will retain only the notion of "seducer," and of the "pious and hostile girl," he will remember only the piety. If initially reflective, a reader confronted with too many contradictions is quite happy to retain familiar elements while rejecting those that seem anomalous to him. The plethora of references makes it impossible to focus on particular details and to recognize them individually. To invert Victor Shklovsky's theory but in his own terms, one could say that this text, by "defamiliarizing" too many elements, sets in motion, paradoxically, a process of "automatization."[54] Thus, for many readers, critical thought is more often than not subordinated to habitual reflexes.

Furthermore, as the young girl's story unfolds, one is struck by its informational and referential impoverishment. This sudden moderation in narrative mode is confusing to a reader already accustomed to narrative abundance. Because of so obvious a contrast, the reader could well be tempted to find the young girl's narration "quite unsubstantial." In his perplexity, the reader may cast a blind eye to the tale's erotic aspects, avoid translating it into religious terms, and make no connection between the little mask and the Virgin. Such is, I would contend, the typical reading process set in motion by "Le Plus bel amour de Don Juan," one which differs considerably from that outlined by Wolfgang Iser.

"The implied reader"—the intelligent, independent, imaginative person open to new ideas that Iser places at the heart of his theory has a predisposition to reading texts in an active manner. While letting the text guide him, he never fails to meet its challenge. Yet the most striking works—those which question established norms—put the reader in a position both conflictual and stimulating. I question Iser's assumption that the reader will make the text's new and subversive ideas his own. What of the reader who firmly embraces established orders? What of the more or less self-proclaimed partisan of the dominant ideology? And most importantly, what of the unpredictable role of the unconscious in the reading process?

In the act of reading, two fundamental questions arise: the work's verisimilitude and its conformity to the social and moral norms of the reader. Starting from these basic concepts, one may formulate a schema that accounts for four possible situations. A narrative that conforms to the reader's accepted norms and presents plausible events will no doubt be accepted as authentic. The reader's views, in such a case, are reconfirmed (A). A narrative of implausible events that threatens the values embraced by the reader will, on the other hand, be rejected as inauthentic (B). Things become more complicated, however, when the reader is faced with an implausible narrative that reflects values he accepts (C), or when he is faced with a narrative that does not conform to these values but seems to present "real" events (D).

The latter two cases will allow us to perceive what takes place during an incomplete reading of the little mask's story. Her account, because it suggests an inverted Annunciation, forces a comparison between itself and the story of the Virgin. By marking the stories' conformity to established values on the vertical axis, and their plausibility on the horizontal axis, we can represent the reader's experience in the following schema:

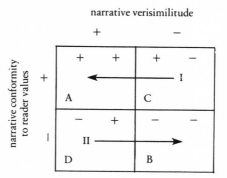

Stipulating the presence of an angel, the story of the Annunciation is quite likely to seem implausible. But since it conforms with Church dogma accepted through the ages, a modification takes place in the reader's mind; he gravitates from C to A, a movement indicated by the arrow (I). It is in this way, if at all, that the reader will accept the story of the Annunciation.

On the other hand, the little mask's story is rejected because it is situated in a "diabolic" context. The troubled reader follows the opposite movement indicated in our schema by arrow (II), concluding that the little mask's account is inauthentic. If he cannot help but discern the blasphemous elements linking Eros with religion, which frame the girl's account, he will, this time on a pre-conscious level, automatically reject those associations which create conflict for his value system.[55]

Paradoxically, Aurevilly's tale seems more dangerous than those satirical writings of the Age of Enlightenment ridiculing Church dogma in which the authors openly developed subversive thoughts. Recognizing their true colors, the reader can keep his distance. It is quite a different matter with Aurevilly: with him the reader risks conceiving blasphemous ideas of his own.

Perhaps we can now evaluate the applicability of Iser's theory of reading. The defense mechanism often at work in the mind of a recalcitrant reader demonstrates that active and open-minded reading is not always possible. Our thoughts on the reception of literary texts also helps to explain why certain types of reading are made possible with the passage of time. If the dominant values of a particular epoch have not been contested, the reader will refuse to recognize the new or subversive aspects of the work he is reading and hence will reject the text as bizarre or merely whimsical. With time and in direct proportion to the decline of the system of entrenched values, new interpretations will begin to emerge, questioning the established norms.

According to Iser, the most striking works are those that transform the reader: a melioristic conception that implies the reader's potential "betterment." Those who rig literature with such power make themselves the advocates of progress. In order to influence the public, however, these works must keep step with transformations that are gradually occurring in the collective psyche: in short, they can only precipitate changes that are already taking shape. It follows that "transformative power," Iser's primary aesthetic criterion, is temporally limited. Hence, in spite of his affirmations to the contrary, his theory is burdened with historicity, in contrast to other critical theories in which aesthetics are based on an appreciation of the timeless and universal.[56]

In lingering over the effects produced by the little mask's story, Barbey presents different versions of its reading. Thus the tale lucidly both predicts and describes the public's most typical reactions. Under the veil of light irony, the text holds out to the reader a distorting mirror in which he may see himself in the act of reading and interpreting. Where Iser favors perceptive and optimistic reading, Aurevilly's concept of his reader shows a deep pessimism, encompassing even the power of art. He compels the reader to compare his own reactions with those of the lovely listeners in the narrative, a potentially disquieting process. The effect sought by Barbey is thus the reader's own embarrassment or exasperation. Judging from the general consensus of critics he has not failed to produce these very reactions. A blind alley of unresolved conflict—such is the essence of Barbey d'Aurevilly's aesthetics.

Translated by Sophie Hawkes

Notes

1   Quoting from Iser: "Reading reflects the structure of experience to the extent that we must suspend the ideas and attitudes that shape our own personality before we can experience the unfamiliar world of the literary text. But during this process something happens to us" ("The Reading Process," in *Reader-Response Criticism: From Formalism to Post-Structuralism*, ed. Jane P. Tompkins [Baltimore and London: Johns Hopkins University Press, 1981], p. 65); "The reader discovers the meaning of the text, taking negation as a starting-point; he discovers a new reality through a fiction which, at least in part, is different from the world he himself is used to; and he discovers the deficiencies inherent in the prevalent norms and in his own restricted behavior" (*The Implied Reader: Patterns of Communication in Prose fiction from Bunyan to Beckett* [Baltimore and London: Johns Hopkins University Press, 1978], p. xiii); "The nineteenth-century novel achieves its artistic effect by sharpening its readers' reactions so that they can discover the conditionality of their world and so be better able to deal with the mounting strain of the increasingly complex situations to which they are exposed" (*The Act of Reading: A Theory of Aesthetic Response* [Baltimore and London: Johns Hopkins University Press, 1980], p. 206.)

2   Iser's analyses of writers such as Beckett and Joyce follow the same pattern.

3   Michael Riffaterre writes: "A theory of literature will not be valid unless it explains bad literature as well as good, for literariness manifests itself in variants both acceptable and

unacceptable to an aesthetic within a society" ("The Unshackling of Theory," *Proceedings* 9 [1980–81], pp. 84–87).

4   *Les Diaboliques*, ed. Jean-Pierre Seguin (Paris: Garnier-Flammarion, 1967). All page references to *Les Diaboliques* are to the Garnier-Flammarion edition and will henceforth be given in parentheses in the text. All translations from the French are my own.

5   These facts are described in Jean-Pierre Seguin's preface to the Garnier-Flammarion edition of *Les Diaboliques*.

6   Théodore de Banville, *Lettres chimériques* (Paris: Charpentier, 1885), p. 242.

7   Joris-Karl Huysmans, *Against Nature*, trans. Robert Baldick (Harmondsworth: Penguin Books, 1959), p. 160.

8   For additional details, see Pierre Boissard's article "Poursuite contre *Les Diaboliques*," *Mercure de France* 1191–92 (November-December 1962), pp. 460–71.

9   Readers are referred to "Memoranda" III, IV, and V, where Barbey jots down impressions from his readings, in *Œuvres romanesques complètes*, vol. 2, ed. Jacques Petit (Paris: Bibliothèque de la Pléiade, 1966). A letter reveals that in 1868 he is busy with his *Diaboliques* and that he is reading Saint John Chrysostom (p. 1288). Barbey is familiar with J. J. von Görres' *La Mystique divine, naturelle et diabolique*, published in French in 1854. See Barbey's *Disjecta Membra* (Paris: La Connaissance, 1925), 2:27–31).

10   For the concept of the narratee, see Gerald Prince's study "Introduction to the study of the Narratee," in *Reader-Response Criticism: From Formalism to Post-Structuralism*, pp. 7–25. Prince defines the narratee as "someone to whom the narrator addresses himself." He distinguishes between the narratee as opposed to the real, virtual, or ideal reader.

11   See Mario Praz's classical study *The Romantic Agony* in which the author talks about the *Diaboliques*' satanism but fails to discuss "Le Plus bel amour de Don Juan" (Oxford: Oxford University Press, 1970), pp. 325–29.

12   Anne Giard mentions her students' reactions in the article "Le Récit lacunaire dans *les Diaboliques*," *Poétique* 41 (1980), pp. 39–50.

13   Jacques Petit writes: "The story is rather insubstantial and it is solely its narrative structure that by means of a sort of trompe-l'œil endows it with some depth" (*Essais de lecture des Diaboliques de Barbey d'Aurevilly* [Paris: Minard, 1974], p. 26).

14   Quoting Pierre Tranouez's phrase from his "La Narration neutralisante: Etude de quatre *Diaboliques*," *Poétique* 17 (1974), p. 47.

15   Jacques Petit, *Essais de lecture des Diaboliques*, p. 20.

16   See Pierre Tranouez, "La Narration neutralisante."

17   Marie-Claire Ropars-Wuilleumier, " 'Le Plus bel amour de Don Juan': Narration et signification," *Littérature* 9 (1973), pp. 118–25.

18   Philippe Berthier, *Barbey d'Aurevilly et l'imagination* (Geneva: Droz, 1978), p. 320.

19   Petit, *Essais de lecture des Diaboliques*, p. 157.

20   Norbert Dodille, "L'Amateur de noms: Essai sur l'onomastique aurevillienne," *Revue des Sciences Humaines* 46, 174 (1979), pp. 131–50.

21   The ambiguity stemming from Ravila's name becomes truly disquieting when the reader recognizes in it an echo of Barbey's expression referring to Saint Theresa of Avila. Barbey describes the saint as "ravie et ravissante" (ravished and ravishing). See "Sainte Thérèse," in *Les Œuvres et les hommes*, vol. 22, *Femmes et Moralistes* (Geneva: Slatkine Reprints, 1968), p. 59.

22   See Gregorio de Marañon's classical study *Don Juan et le donjuanisme* (Paris: Librairie Stock, 1958). For a more recent treatment of the subject, see *Le Mythe de Don Juan* by Jean Rousset (Paris: Arman Colin, 1978).

23   We refer the reader to Byron's letter of February 16, 1821. He writes about his hero to Murray: "I meant to have made him a Cavalier Servente in Italy, and a cause for divorce in England, and a Sentimental 'Werther-faced man' in Germany, so as to show the dif-

ferent ridicules of the society in each of those countries" (*Don Juan*, ed. T. G. Steffan [New Haven and London: Yale University Press, 1982], p. 9.

24 This is a popular theme with Gautier, Musset, Nerval, and Dumas. See Georges Poulet's essay "Nerval, Gautier et la blonde aux yeux noirs," *Trois essais de mythologie romantique* (Paris: J. Corti, 1966).

25 Petit, *Essais de lecture des Diaboliques*, p. 121.

26 Barbey studied in depth the writings of Saint Thomas Aquinas, to whom we owe one of the best formulations of the dogma of transubstantiation, i.e., the conversion of the substance of the bread and wine into the substance of the Body and Blood of Christ, only the appearances of the bread and wine remaining.

27 Barbey, "Le Cachet d'onyx," *Une Histoire sans nom suivi de trois nouvelles* (Paris: Gallimard-Folio, 1972), p. 180.

28 Georges Bataille, *L'Erotisme* (Paris: Les Editions de Minuit, 1957), p. 11. The author states that there exist "glaring similarities or even relations of equivalence and exchange, between the systems of erotic and mystical expressions" (p. 250).

29 Victor Hugo, "Lilith-Isis," *La Fin de Satan*, in *La Légende des Siècles; La Fin de Satan; Dieu*, ed. Jacques Truchet (Paris: Bibliothèque de la Pléiade, 1950), p. 859–60.

30 Readers interested in the legendary figure of Lilith are referred to Maximilian Rudwin's classical study *The Devil in Legend and Literature* (Chicago and London: The Open Court, 1931), and to Mario Praz's *The Romantic Agony*. For a more recent treatment of the subject, see Jacques Bril's *Lilith ou la mère obscure* (Paris: Payot, 1981), and Sidney Braun's "Lilith: Her Literary Portrait, Symbolism, and Significance," *Nineteenth-Century French Studies* 1 and 2 (1983–84), pp. 135–53.

31 E. T. A. Hoffman, "The Devil's Elixirs"; E. A. Poe, "Berenice," "Morella," "Ligeia"; Pushkin, "The Queen of Spades"; Mickiewicz, "Switezianka"; Rossetti, "Lilith," "Eden Bower"; Vigny, "Lilith"; Hugo, *La Fin de Satan*; Gautier, "La Morte amoureuse"; Nodier, "Inez de las Sierras"; Baudelaire, "Le Vampire"; Mérimée, "La Vénus d'Ille," "La Femme est un diable"; Villiers de l'Isle-Adam, "Véra."

32 Claude Lévi-Strauss, "Ouverture," in *Le Cru et le cuit* (Paris: Plon, 1964), p. 20. He writes that "each myth considered individually is only an exemplification of general scheme, through which this myth becomes intelligible when placed among other myths" (p. 21).

33 By the middle of the nineteenth century similar attempts were not uncommon. Some writers tried to reconcile the two dominant and seemingly contradictory myths. Alexandre Soumet found a solution as brilliant as it is bizarre. In his *Divine Epopée*, Don Juan recounts how his seduction of a vampire caused his own death. For more detail, see *L'Epopée humanitaire et les grands mythes romantiques* by Léon Cellier (Paris: Société d'Edition d'Enseignement Supérieur, 1971).

34 Faced with such a "naiveté," critics are hesitant to pursue their analyses. At most, they ask questions, but then they leave them unanswered: "But is the little girl's most disquieting discovery truly insignificant? If she is pregnant only in her imagination should we not account for her desire which manifests itself in this fantasm?" (Jacques Petit, *Essais de lectures des Diaboliques*, p. 28). Jean Pierre Boucher writes that "questions which arise in our mind make the 'little mask' even more mysterious—a disturbing mixture of vice and virtue that we shall never be able to set apart" (*Les Diaboliques de Barbey d'Aurevilly: Une esthétique de la dissimulation et de la provocation* [Quebec: Presse Universitaire du Quebec, 1976], p. 41).

35 We are following the theological tradition which specifically distinguishes the Immaculate Conception of Mary by Saint Ann from the Virgin Birth of Jesus-Christ by Mary.

36 Barbey follows the demonological tradition that commonly transforms Church dogmas. J.-K. Huysmans adopts the same principles in *Là-Bas* in which he describes black masses.

Ernest Jones analyzes the imitations and mirror-imagings at work in folklore and popular beliefs. See his *On the Nightmare* (London: Hogarth Press, 1931). At the time, the theme of virgin birth was often developed and transformed. One finds it in writings of Chateaubriand ("Atala"), von Kleist ("The Marquise of O"), and Alexandre Dumas (*Joseph Balsamo*). It received a theatrical treatment in Victor Ducange's *Il y a seize ans*, and a satirical one in Pushkin's "The Gabriliad," a sacrilegious poem forbidden during the author's life but reprinted by the *Playboy* magazine for the Christmas issue of 1975. Barbey d'Aurevilly takes up the same theme in "Une histoire sans nom."

37   This is Mary's age in the *Protevangelium* of Saint James and in *De Ortu Beatae Mariae et Infantia Salvatoris*, an apocryphal Latin text attributed to Saint Matthew. In the thirteenth century Jacob of Voragine restates this fact in his exceedingly popular *Golden Legend*. We refer the reader to the French translation of the Latin work: Jacques de Voragine, *La Légende dorée* (Paris: Garnier-Flammarion, 1967), pp. 171–83. To obtain information, we shall rely on Saint Luke, the sole Evangelist who provides us with a brief synopsis of the Annunciation. On issues on which the Evangelist remains silent, the talking will have to be done by the *Golden Legend* and the Christian iconographic tradition.

38   Primarily in the Western iconographic tradition (Simone Martini, Fra Filippo Lippi, Sandro Boticelli). See Louis Réau's *L'Iconographie de l'art chrétien* (Paris: Presses Universitaires de France, 1957).

39   Maximilian Rudwin, *The Devil in Legend and Literature* (New York: AMS Press, 1970), p. 6.

40   Petit, *Essais de lecture des Diaboliques*, p. 29.

41   Barbey transforms an old folk tradition that had already been appropriated by Rabelais. Garganelle gives birth to Gargantua through her left ear. Molière takes up the same theme in his *L'Ecole des femmes*, act 1, scene 1, where Arnolphe says:

> "Elle estoit fort en peine, et me vint demander,
> Avec une innocence a nulle autre pareille,
> Si les enfants qu'on fait, se faisoient par l'oreille."

Readers interested in this particular aspect of the Annunciation and virgin birth will profit from Ernest Jones' "Madonna's Conception through the Ear," in *Psycho-Myth, Psycho-History: Essays in Applied Psychoanalysis* (New York: Hillstone, 1974).

42   Baudelaire writes for Félicien Rops his "Sonnet pour s'excuser de ne pas accompagner un ami à Namur." See "Poèmes divers" (XVII), in *Les Fleurs du mal* (Paris: Classiques Garnier, 1961), p. 232. Huysmans wrote an illuminating essay "Félicien Rops: Étude de son imagination satanique." See *L'Art moderne/Certains* (Paris: Union Générale d'Editions, 1975), pp. 331–63.

43   Anna Freud, *The Ego and the Mechanisms of Defence* (New York: International Universities Press, Inc. 1946), p. 167. We refer the reader to the twelfth chapter of the book which is devoted to the instinctual anxiety during puberty. Possibilities of a psychoanalytical interpretation of "Le Plus bel amour" had been noted by Philippe Berthier in his *Barbey d'Aurevilly et l'imagination*, p. 290.

44   Thomas Mann, "Freud and the Future," *Life and Letters To-Day* 15 (Autumn–Winter 1936), pp. 80–94.

45   Sigmund Freud, "A Seventeenth-Century Demonological Neurosis" (1923), in *The Standard Edition of the Complete Psychological Works of Sigmund Freud* (London: Hogarth Press, 1961), 19:72.

46   Sigmund Freud, "Character and Anal Erotism" (1908), in *The Standard Edition of the Complete Psychological Works of Sigmund Freud* (London: The Hogarth Press, 1959), 9:174.

47   Ernest Jones, *The Life and Work of Sigmund Freud* (New York: Basic Books, 1961), pp. 147–48.

48 See *The Pedigree of the Devil* by Frederic T. Hall, first published in London in 1883 (reprint, New York: Benjamin Bloom, 1971). Lilith's presence in Christian imagination is attested by Van Eyck's *The Adoration of the Lamb*. One sees there a talisman bearing the inscription: "Adam Havah shutz Lilith." See F. de Mély's study "Nos premiers parents dans l'art: Adam, Eve, Lilith," *Mélanges Hulin de Loo* (1931), pp. 116–22.

49 The Eve/Mary reversed parallel has been acknowledged by early church theologians. "Justin Martyr . . . was the first on record with the argument that Mary should be regarded as a Second Eve," writes J. A. Phillips in his *Eve: The History of an Idea* (New York: Harper and Row, 1984), p. 133. See also Marina Warner's *Alone of All Her Sex: The Myth and the Cult of the Virgin Mary* (New York: Vintage Books, Random House, 1983).

50 Barbey d'Aurevilly, *Les Philosophes et les écrivains religieux* (Paris: Amyot, 1860), p. 80.

51 Mario Praz, *The Romantic Agony*, p. 325.

52 Huysman, *Against Nature*, p. 164.

53 We recognize here the last episode echoing the life of Mary. After the virginal conception she was obliged to leave Nazareth. In contrast with the little mask, however, she dies in old age surrounded by the Apostles.

54 Founding his theory on the general laws of perception, Victor Shklovsky develops the concepts of automatization and defamiliarization. See his "Art as Technique," in *Russian Formalist Criticism: Four Essays*, trans. and ed. Lee T. Lemon and Marion J. Reis (Lincoln and London: University of Nebraska Press, 1965), p. 3–24.

55 The relationship between the pre-conscious and conscious phenomena entering into the reading process suggest that the Iserian phenomenological model may profit from some psychoanalytic refinements. My mechanistic description of the reading process assumes that in addition to the conscious cognitive processes postulated by Iser, one has to take into account emotional factors that he chose to overlook. Psychoanalytic critics have argued that the reading process may be compared to a successful psychoanalytic session, a "good analysis" in which "a movement from symptom to insight" takes place. See Meredith Skura, *The Literary Use of the Psychoanalytic Process* (New Haven: Yale University Press, 1981), p. 229. Psychoanalytic criticism, however, should be more aware of the defense mechanisms operating in the reader the way they operate in the analysand. Unfortunately Skura concentrates on successful readings only and thus her approach suffers from the same shortcomings as Iser's. Case histories abound in descriptions of analysands resisting the interpretations of their actions and dreams put forward by the analyst. Their resistance occurs when the interpretations are threatening to them. I would like to argue that these resistive reactions would provide a model for the actions of a reader who blocks those interpretations that are threatening to his/her ego.

56 On this issue let us quote Henri Peyre, who writes: "Beauty in literature and the arts is often found to reside most lastingly in works which offer different generations ever-renewed secrets and multiplicity of parallel interpretations, among which each age will choose its own" (*The Failure of Criticism* [Ithaca: Cornell University Press, 1967], p. 225).

Huysmans: Conversion, Hysteria, and the "French Unconscious" / *Jeffrey Mehlman*

In the hundred years since its publication in 1884, few books have contributed as broadly to the Anglo-American idea of French culture as Huysmans' *A rebours.*[1] For the middle-brow, it is as though the aesthetic and sensual experiments of the reclusive des Esseintes—world-weary and perverse, anti-American and effetely aristocratic—were in themselves sufficient to underwrite the French usage *fin-de-siècle* to designate the closing years of the century. That the refinements of Huysmans' protagonist all seem linked to prodigies of high-class consumption—*liqueurs*, rare flowers, perfumes—further contributes to what one might vulgarly thematize as their "Frenchness." Add to this matrix the cultural commonplace that Proust would later draw on Huysmans' model, Robert de Montesquiou, for the creation of one of his most memorable characters, M. de Charlus, and the going intuition that *A rebours* provides privileged access to the wellsprings of French culture seems confirmed.

A convenient perception of the high-brow debt to Huysmans' novel is afforded by Frank Kermode's influential study, *Romantic Image.*[2] The author expertly sketches the image of grace, or intelligence, incarnate in the body of the female dancer and its role as emblem of the poetic image per se in the European tradition that culminates in Yeats. To this extent the poetic myth par excellence for symbolist modernism is Salome dancing before Herod. In Kermode's words: "It is hardly too much to say that whenever Yeats refers back to the historical concept of unity of being, or to the esthetic one of beauty as a perfectly proportioned body, the image of Salome is likely to occur to him."[3] But if integrity of poetic form is somehow commensurate with the formal perfection of Salome's dance, *A rebours* would appear to constitute a key juncture on the path to that aesthetic consensus. For the myth of Herodias' daughter is twice present in Huysmans' novelistic essay at canon-formation—in the *tableaux* of Moreau and in the poem of Mallarmé. Indeed, an aesthetic paroxysm cherished by des Esseintes consists in murmuring lines of *Hérodiade* while gazing at the Byzantine Salome of Moreau. *A rebours*, if we may extrapolate from Kermode, comes as close as any text in French to providing, in Salome, the expressive emblem of the poetic *symbol* per se.

Whether it be through middle-brow interest in the decadent aristocrat or high-brow fascination with the mythic dancer, *A rebours* would appear to

epitomize a *consciousness* of French culture. Which is why the unspoken un-
derpinnings of that consciousness may be of particular interest for cultural
analysis. Consider, for instance, that *A rebours* recycles as an aristocrat the
lamentable *petit-bourgeois* functionary of an earlier Huysmans novel, *A Vau-
l'eau*. As though the exemplary aristocrat were always already a *petit-bourgeois*—more specifically, the nausea-stricken *petit-bourgeois* Folantin, who,
from the moment he first ponders a platter of Roquefort, appears to await
service as prime "source" of Sartre's Roquentin.[4] But then the notion of the
dubious aristocrat as political revery of the *petit-bourgeois* is perhaps already
present in my use of the term middle-brow to allude to the general fascination
elicited by des Esseintes.

More interesting is the role of *A rebours* in the high-brow emblematization
of the "organic" poetic symbol. And what it masks. Consider in this light
the famous preface Huysmans wrote twenty years after completing the novel
from the vantage point of his subsequent conversion to Catholicism. He
speaks of *A rebours* as "a supremely unconscious work (*un ouvrage parfaite-
ment inconscient*)," by which he means that his apparent abandonment of
naturalism in 1884 was not accompanied by any awareness of the religious
vocation which would erupt years later.[5] Yet the novel's "unconscious" status
seems to take on a certain positivity. It would consign the aesthetica of des
Esseintes to the status of allegories cut off from their sense. Huysmans' initial
example is the book's discourse on gems:

> The chapter on precious stones I have recapitulated in *La Cathédrale*, in
> the second case treating the matter from the point of view of the sym-
> bolism (*symbolique*) of gems. I have there given life to the dead stones
> of *A rebours*. Of course I do not deny that a fine emerald may be
> admired for the flashes that gleam in the fire of its green depth, but, if
> we are ignorant of the idiom of symbols, is it not an unknown being, a
> stranger, a foreigner with whom no talk can be had and who has no
> word to say himself, because we do not understand his language? (p. 63)

The excursus on flowers is endowed with a similar muteness in the preface
of 1903: "*A rebours* considers them solely from the point of view of shapes
or colors, in no wise from that of the significations they disclose" (p. 66).
Meaning would have to await conversion and *La Cathédrale*.

Having begun, then, with Kermode and the path to a more "organic"
or "unified" consciousness, we have come to the retroactive scheme through
which the novel emerges as fundamentally *unconscious*. And whereas consciousness was to be consolidated through the poetic symbol, "unconsciousness" finds its mode of insistence in the flaws of allegory. Huysmans, moreover,
seems curiously willing to maintain the specificity of *A rebours*' "unconscious"
even beyond its ultimate redemption—into meaning—by *La Cathédrale*. An

important passage of the preface sketches the "subterranean labors" of the soul prior to conversion:

> There was no doubt at the date when I was writing *A rebours* a shifting of the soil, a delving of the earth, to lay the foundations, of which I was all unconscious. God was digging to lay his wires, and he worked only in the shadows of the soul, by night. Nothing was visible on the surface; it was only years after that the spark began to run along the wires. (p. 75)

Thus runs the two-phased instauration of grace. But what somehow exceeds the illumination of religion, remains opaque in the face of grace, is the unconscious "period of incubation," the phase during which the foundations of faith were laid despite the unawareness of its subject. In Huysmans' terms: "I understand, in brief, up to a certain point what befell between the year 1891 and the year 1895, between *Là-bas* and *En Route* (i.e., the period of the conversion), nothing at all between the year 1884 and the year 1891, between *A rebours* and *Là-bas*" (p. 76). The "unconsciousness" exceeding grace is linked to the span separating *A rebours* and *Là-bas*. Its mode, we have seen, is the essential unfulfillment of allegory. It is that "unconscious"—of *A rebours*, with its complement of implications for our perception of French culture in general—that this essay would sketch.

Allegoresis and the "unconscious." That link brings us back to (Moreau's) Salome. In one formulation, Huysmans speaks of the painter's "hieratic and sinister allegories, made yet more poignant by the restless apperceptions of a nervous system altogether modern in morbid sensitiveness" (p. 154). The modernity of his *nervosisme* entails, in the case of Salome, the evocation of a specific condition: "She became in a sense the symbolic deity of indestructible Lust (*Luxure*), the goddess of immortal Hysteria" (p. 149). On the one hand, then, Lust, and the tradition originating in Prudentius; on the other, hysteria, and the discourse that would soon be deciphered by Freud.[6] What both share is a splitting off from the totality of "organic" meaning, a propensity to manifest apparently arbitrary signs. The gems of *A rebours* were said to be an allegory oblivious of its meaning. Just so do the stones of Salome's gown perversely activate each other: "Over her robe of triumph, bestrewn with pearls, broidered with silver, studded with gold, a corselet of chased goldsmith's work, each mesh of which is a precious stone, enters into combustion, criss-crossing coils of fire, swarming over the pink flesh" (p. 147). The dead —allegorical—surface has taken on a baroque autonomy fundamentally unsettling to any affirmation of substance. Allegory as—the aesthetic mode of —decadence.

But what of the "unconscious"? Earlier we spoke of the interest of constructing the "unconscious" of *A rebours*. But at this juncture, we find ourselves in some proximity to the origins, in Freud, of the motif or concept of the unconscious in contemporary discourse. As though, with Huysmans, we were midway between an application and a genealogical elaboration of the concept itself. In the crucial period between *A rebours* (1884) and *Là-bas* (1891), Freud, after all, was to come to Paris and frequent assiduously the lectures of Charcot on hysteria at La Salpêtrière. He would later evoke the "theatrical" presentations in which the French master, *un visuel*, would put his patients through the erotic paces of a hysterical fit, while *staring* the truth of each case into clinical awareness.[7] The scenario is not far from that of Herod demanding that Salome (or Hysteria) dance and remaining enraptured by the result. We are, then, in *A rebours*, close by the historical context in which the discourse of the unconscious first emerged.

Huysmans' "unconscious," we recall, was specifically invested in the period between the decadent *A rebours* and the proto-Christian *Là-bas*. His principal novel of that period was *En rade* (1887), third in the series initiated by *A Vau-l'eau*. This time the hero, Jacques Marles, undergoes his martyrdom of disgust in the country. A *petit-bourgeois* down on his fortunes, he escapes Paris with his ailing wife to the abandoned *château* of Lourps, where his wife's uncle and aunt maintain the decrepit property as peasant guardians. The experience is one of utter abjection, more deserving perhaps of the title *Against Nature* than *A rebours* itself. At novel's end, Jacques, like des Esseintes before him, returns to Paris. Now the stylistic novelty of *En rade*, a vicious satire of peasant life, is its interpolation of three almost surreal dream sequences. The first sounds for us an oddly familiar note. An ornate palace of mineral splendor rises in Byzantine glory: "On every side there shot up vines etched out of unmatched stones; on every side blazed a clear flame of incombustible shoots, a fire nourished by the mineral brands of leaves cut in differing shades of green" (p. 51).[8] Soon the two principal characters in some primal drama appear. First, an aged and world-weary king, seemingly beyond all sentiment; then, the young girl on whom he fixes his gaze as she sheds her gown of hyacinth. "The King's eye bored (*vrilla*) into the child's nudity and slowly he extended to her the diamantine tulip of his sceptre, whose extremity she approached, faltering, to kiss" (p. 55). Shortly thereafter Jacques awakens.

The dream at first seems an enigma for him, but it is one which the reader of Huysmans' previous fiction is tempted to provide with an odd solution. For the otherworldly monarch staring lasciviously at a fragile virgin against a backdrop of Byzantine splendor appears to be a repetition of Moreau's Salome. It is as though in recycling the experience *against nature* of des Esseintes in the ironically conceived harbor (*rade*) downstream from *A rebours*, Huysmans somehow felt impelled to include the crucial Salome motif even if the rural setting allowed no inclusion of a discussion of nineteenth-century painting.

Or so it seems. For a chapter later, the "interpretation" of the dream scene gradually dawns on the protagonist: "Little by little, however, a flickering light began to gleam and the recollections of sacred volumes adrift in his memory regrouped and converged on the book in which Ahasuerus, attentive to the demands of a waning virility, rises before the niece of Mordechai, the august procuror and blessed spokesman (*truchement*) of the God of the Jews" (p. 74). The king and the virgin, that is, were not Herod and Salome but Ahasuerus and Esther. And yet no sooner have we corrected our initial suggestion than the limitations of that correction become apparent. For the appeal to the Salome motif is based on something more far-reaching than *trompe-l'œil*. Consider that whereas Salome, in the New Testament, uses her charms to extort from the king the head of John the Baptist, Esther, in the Old, seduces a king to demand from him the head of Haman. It is, oddly enough, precisely what is *missing* in the visual *tableau*, the victim's head, which confirms (while displacing) the initial surmise. The Esther scene, even in its intentional structure, repeats the Moreau Salome, and the difference of the repetition is insistent in precisely what the scene fails to manifest. Which is to suggest that the subterranean continuity between the Salome and Esther scenes approximates something of what might be provisionally construed as the "unconscious" of Huysmans' fiction.

We were first drawn to *En rade* by the suggestion in the 1903 preface to *A rebours* that the period between that work and *Là-bas*—the period of *En rade*—constituted the region of maximal opacity in Huysmans' *œuvre*: "I understand nothing at all between the year 1884 and the year 1891." So that the Esther/Salome conjunction seems to function in mythic counterpoint to the programmatic statement of the preface. That impression is confirmed upon examination of Jacques Marles' thoughts in the wake of his dream analysis. He speculates on the source of his Old Testament dream: "He had thus to believe that this Biblical passage had been smoldering for years in a province of his memory so that once the *period of incubation* was over Esther could explode like some obscure flower in a dreamscape" (p. 75). That term is precisely the one used in the preface to *A rebours* to designate the residual opacity of the period 1884–91: "If surprise there were, it could continue only over the *period of incubation*, the period when one sees nothing and notices nothing, the period of the clearing of the ground and laying of the foundations of which one never had even a suspicion" (p. 76). Similarly, the hero of *En rade*, in the wake of his dream, proposes an almost electrical metaphor of the unconscious: "Was there as well a necessary association of ideas so tenuous that its thread or wire (*fil*) escaped analysis, an underground wire functioning in the darkness of the soul, carrying the spark (*l'étincelle*), illuminating in a flash its forgotten caverns, linking cells unoccupied since childhood?" (p. 76). Now that passage anticipates the conclusion of the Preface of

1903: "It was only years after that the spark (*l'étincelle*) began to run along the wires (*fils*)." As the mobile spark of *En rade* (1887) travels forward—or backward—to the preface of *A rebours*, the perversely retroactive temporality of Huysmans' "unconscious" brings us again to Esther and her vicissitudes.

With Salome become Esther, we have moved beyond what with Mario Praz's *The Romantic Agony* had become a *locus classicus* of thematic criticism: the motif of Salome in decadent literature.[9] Indeed we have gone as well beyond a purely *visual* confusion between, say, Salome and Judith, the two Biblical figures whose iconographic merger in the Renaissance has been charted by Panofsky.[10] For the Salome-Esther connection is ultimately authorized by an invisible difference: that which posits a homology between John the Baptist, saintly precursor of the faith, and Haman, would-be exterminator of the Jews. Now our initial consideration of Salome in *A rebours* insisted on the analogy between Herod inviting Huysmans' personification of Hysteria to dance and Charcot putting his hysterics through their paces at La Salpêtrière. Psychoanalysis originated as a going beyond that scenario. We shall see eventually that the sequence of texts we are considering—from *A rebours* to *Là-bas* by way of *En rade*—ends explicitly as a project to go beyond Charcot's relation to hysteria. But that sequence has interested us as the locus of what Huysmans himself, in 1903, thematized as the region of his fiction most resistant to his own comprehension, most fundamentally "unconscious." In Huysmans as in Freud, then, the elaboration of the "unconscious" lay in transcending the model of La Salpêtrière. But the superimposition of Salome and Esther and, more subliminally, of John the Baptist and the unmentioned Haman, has already brought us a measure beyond the "theme" of Salome. To that extent, we may already posit, or intuit, a transformation of our structure that takes us beyond the *tableau* of Moreau—beyond the gaze of Herod and/as Charcot—into the emergence of psychoanalysis itself.

On his trip to Paris in 1885, Freud took with him the case history of Breuer's patient Anna O., a woman whose decision and ability to talk her way out of her hysterical symptoms has been generally recognized as the invention of psychoanalysis. Now that mythical discovery—of the unconscious—was marked by two devastating challenges to the mastery of the therapist. The first lay in the substitution of the hysteric's discourse for the doctor's gaze as the medium of comprehension and cure. The second is tied to the trauma of Anna O.'s "hysterical pregnancy" in the course of her therapy and the abrupt flight of Breuer once she attributed the imaginary paternity to him.[11] It is that second threat which invites the homology this essay would elaborate: Salome or Hysteria dances at Herod's command only to shock him with the demand for the Precursor's head; Esther submits to Ahasuerus in order to shock him with the demand for Haman's life; Anna O. submits to the therapeutic wisdom of Breuer only to traumatize him with the revelation of her fantasied child and his responsibility for it. The interruption of a relation of male-female mastery by the hallucinatory insistence of an intensely cathected "partial object"—an anatomical part whose availability for fantasy is inseparable from its apparent capacity to become detached and circulate in a chain of substitutions—is constant: John's head; Haman's; and Anna's unborn child (whose price might be Breuer's head). As we approach *Là-bas*, then, and its will to go beyond Charcot's Salpêtrière, we observe what Huysmans calls his "unconscious" figure, on the one hand, what psychoanalytic discourse, through the superimposition of Salome and Esther, would call as much, and, on the other, a historical phase of the elaboration of that discourse itself in the wake of Freud's Parisian sojourn of 1885.

Before turning to *Là-bas*, however, we shall pursue our reading of the interim, or "incubatory," text, *En rade*. Shortly after the Esther dream, the protagonist takes off on a tour of the lower chambers of the abandoned castle. Upon penetrating into one sealed room, he is deeply moved by the fragrance emanating from it: "A strange odor escaped the room, an odor of warm dust at whose core filtered through an extremely faded fragrance of ether" (p. 83). From *Esther* to *éther* . . . Now by novel's end, Jacques Marles indulges in a particularly grisly fantasy on the subject of science's capacity to recycle human flesh as fragrance, and the use to which it might be put in order to perpetuate familial memory: "And then think of the endless remembrance, the perpetual freshness of memory one might obtain with such sublimated essences of the dead!" (p. 196). For the twentieth-century reader, no doubt, the cruelest anticipation in *En rade* is that of the manufacture from human remains of perfumed soap: "Ah! I know many women of the people who would be happy to purchase for a few *sous* whole cups of pommades or bars of soap laced with essence of proletariat!" (p. 196). From *Esther* to *éther*, it is as though the spectre of Jewish genocide were kept alive in Huysmans' text by the ghastly fragrance of a pun. Shortly before the final dream of *En rade*, reference is again made to the intoxicating odor of ether, which by then has totally evaporated. The dream that ensues seems as closely linked to *Là-bas* (which would follow *En rade*) as the first dream (of Esther) is to *A rebours*. In that final dream, Jacques finds himself installed in an Escher-like construct, which turns out to be the bell tower of Saint-Sulpice: "Atop the monstrous scaffolding, criss-crossed beams enclosed in an inextricable cage a huge bell. Ladders zigzagged midst the network of planks, hugged girders, descended abruptly, broke off, lost their rungs, rested on wooden platforms only to climb again, suspended without bearings in the void" (p. 203). The protagonist accepts the position of bell ringer in the church. His dream turns to nightmare when he finds a horrendous slut rising to the top of the tower, where she is perched provocatively. At that point Jacques intuits her identity along with the strange inversion characterizing the tower:

What was it? Jacques wondered in his dismay. Then he recovered, tried to be reasonable, managed to convince himself that the tower was a well, a well erected in the air instead of sunk into the ground, but, in any event, a well. A wooden bucket rimmed in iron and resting on the well's lip attested as much; everything could then be explained; the abominable trollop (*gaupe*) was none other than Truth. (p. 211)

He awakens shortly thereafter. E. M. Forster wrote quaintly of the novelist's ability to let a bucket down into his unconscious. If the final dream of *En rade* is participatory in what Huysmans calls his unconscious, it is in a sense that crucially exceeds Forster's image. For the bucket here must be sent undecidably up *and* down into a tower that is an inverted well. To suggest as much, however, is to move toward a consideration of transcendance in *Là-bas*, and it is to that novel that we now shall turn.

The image of the bell tower as an ascending well in fact occurs at an important juncture in *Là-bas*. Des Hermies escorts the protagonist, Durtal, up a winding staircase toward the lodging of Carhaix, bell ringer of Saint-Sulpice: "The climb seemed endless. Finally they came to the barred door, opened it, and found themselves above the abyss on a frame balcony, the wooden lip of a double well—one, dug beneath their feet, the other rising above them" (p. 55).[12] It will be from Carhaix's perch, *là-haut*, overlooking Paris that Durtal will gain his principal insights into the depravity of the nether-regions, both medieval and modern, designated by the book's title. But the novel's enigmatic quality lies largely in its openness to a fundamental relation *between là-haut* and *là-bas*, extremes of valor and corruption, the rising and descending wells. It is in terms of such a relation, in fact, that *Là-bas* is best evoked.

In his effort to work his way beyond the aesthetic of mediocrity with which he has come to identify "naturalism," Durtal, a surrogate of the author, happens on the monstrous subject of Gilles de Rais: "the Satanist who was, in the fifteenth century, the most artistic, exquisite, cruel and villainous of men" (p. 49). Gilles had been a companion in arms of Joan of Arc and one of the great feudal lords of France. After Joan's death, however, he withdrew to his castle of Tiffauges and devoted himself to the arts of astrology and occultism. Gradually, he pressed his cult of the Satanic to the point of engaging in the kidnapping, rape, and murder of numerous young boys. Through an understandable confusion, he has been regularly conflated in popular memory with Bluebeard (*Barbebleue*). Now it is this monster, with his dandified dreams of "holocaust," whose reinvention releases in Durtal sources of energy, or "health," otherwise repressed (p. 46). His task, as he sees it, is to create the myth of Gilles: "to forge for himself, with adroitly selected details, a fallacious coherence" (p. 47). Of the many speculations on Gilles' career, let us retain one that praises his audacity in wanting "to accumulate in crimes what a saint accumulates in virtues" (p. 74). It reminds us, to be sure, of the mirror-like relation of the descending and ascending wells, but also of the homology between Saint John the Baptist and the monstrous Haman in our superimposition of the Salome and Esther *tableaux* in the earlier novels. Haman and/as the Precursor . . . of Gilles.

Now Durtal's fascination with Gilles is doubled by an ambivalent suspicion that the transgressive tradition of Satanism may indeed survive in modern times. He is taunted in this interest by Hyacinthe Chantelouve, who will ultimately bring him to a black mass celebrated in Paris by a Satanic priest named Docre: "the Gilles de Rais of modern times!" (p. 150). The discussion of contemporary Satanism, moreover, is inseparable from a consideration of the ambiguities of exorcism:

> The celebrants of Deicidal masses dissemble and declare themselves devoted to Christ. They even affirm that they defend him by using exorcisms to counter the possessed. That, in fact, is their biggest gimmick. The "possessed" are made so or kept so by the priests themselves, who are thus assured of subjects and accomplices, especially in the convents. All kinds of murderous and sadistic follies can be covered with the venerable and pious mantle of exorcism. (p. 85)

Once again a certain undecidability between saint and criminal becomes manifest. And it is in this context that Charcot and hysteria are invoked:

> No, upon reflection, the effrontery of the positivists is appalling. They decree that Satanism does not exist. They lay everything at the account of *la grande hystérie* and don't even know what this frightful malady is and what are its causes! No doubt, Charcot determines very well the phases of the attack, notes the illogical and passional attitudes, the contortionistic gestures; he discovers the hysterogenic zones and can, by skillfully manipulating the ovaries, arrest or accelerate the crises. But as for foreseeing them, learning their sources and curing them, that's a different story! (p. 153)

Charcot would appear to be an unwitting Satanist, staging and exacerbating fits of hysteria (i.e., possession) he is unable to cure. Huysmans' Durtal, disappointed by Charcot's results, would choose a more medieval understanding of the scenes at La Salpêtrière: " '*Peuh*' said Durtal, who was now in front of his door. 'Since anything can be maintained and nothing is certain, let's stick with Succubacy [as opposed to Hysteria]. At bottom, it's more literary—and cleaner!'" Two years later, Freud would offer thoughts on the limitations of Charcot that sound a similar note:

> Let no one object that the theory of dissociation of consciousness as a solution to the enigma of hysteria is too far-fetched to suggest itself to

the untrained and unprejudiced observer. In fact the middle ages had chosen this very solution, in declaring possession by a demon to be the cause of hysterical manifestations; all that would have been required was to replace the religious terminology of those dark and superstitious times by the scientific one of today. Charcot did not choose this path.[13]

Like Freud in his essay of 1893, Huysmans in his novel of 1891 looked toward the middle ages in an effort to go beyond Charcot and the rituals of hysterical performance. And *Là-bas* does, in fact, manage to salvage from the ambiguities of "exorcism" one figure who seems to work cures that Charcot can only envy. He is called Dr. Johannès, and here is an evocation of his therapeutic style:

He claims that when such or such a stone is placed in the hand or on the affected part of the bewitched a fluid escapes from the stone into his fingers and informs him. In this connection, he told me that a woman whom he did not know came to him one day to consult him about a malady, pronounced incurable, from which she had suffered since childhood. He could not get any precise answers to his questions. He saw no signs of venefice. After trying out almost his whole array of stones, he placed in her hand lapis lazuli, which, he says, corresponds to the sin of incest. He examined the stone. "Your malady," he said, "is the result of an act of incest." "Well," she replied, "I did not come to you to be confessed"—but she ended up admitting, nevertheless, that her father had violated her before she attained the age of puberty. (p. 273)

Before commenting on Johannès' feat, let us observe the scene, in Lyon, of his "impossible cures":

Lyon is celebrated for her *charcuteries*, chestnuts, silk, and also her churches. The peaks of all of her ascending streets are strewn with chapels and convents, and Notre Dame de Fourvière dominates them all. From a distance, it looks like an eighteenth-century *commode* turned upside down, its legs in the air, but the interior, which is in process of completion, is stunning. You ought to go and take a look at it some day. You will see the most extraordinary jumble of Assyrian, Roman, Gothic and God knows what, jacked together by Bossan, the only architect capable of creating a cathedral interior in a century. The nave glitters with inlays and marble, with bronze and gold. Statues of angels diversify the rows of columns and break up, with solemn grace, the known harmonies of line. It's Asiatic and barbarous; it reminds one of the constructs raised by Gustave Moreau to surround his Herodiades. (p. 266)

We are given, in brief, a further repetition of the *tableau* of Salome in *A rebours*, which recurred as Esther in *En rade* only to resurface in *Là-bas* as the

stone-bedecked hysteric relieving her symptoms by confessing the scene of incest that lay at the root of her condition. We earlier evoked the primal scene of
psychoanalysis: Anna O. revealing her "pregnancy" and asking in the process
for "Breuer's head." That hysterical fantasy was seen as homologous with
the demand for John the Baptist's head. This time the therapist's name is
Johannès, or John the Baptist. And Salome's ultimate revelation is a "scene"
of paternal incest. As the elements in our structure return to circulate from
position to position in the recurrent fantasy, the Biblical myth gives way to
the scene of the origin of psychoanalysis, or, rather, finds itself inscribed as an
instance in a fantasmatic transformation of the sort that psychoanalysis itself
would eventually come to elaborate.[14]

Johannès' hysteric, it is true, evoked a *scene* of paternal incest, therein par-
ticipating in the seduction theory Freud would eventually relinquish. *Là-bas*,
however, offers an inflection of the paternal incest motif that moves it beyond
that theory as well. Hyacinthe Chantelouve isolates within the province of
Lust a sin of particular gravity: "what I shall call Pygmalionism, which embraces simultaneously cerebral onanism and incest" (p. 179). Pygmalionism is
worse than "normal incest," in which one loves a child who is also another's,
for in this case "a father violates the daughter of his soul." The object of his
rape is not a palpable being, but "an unreal entity" (p. 179). There is thus a
move from incest as content of a scene (or fantasy) to incest as relation to
fantasy, the mode whereby any element of consciousness may be split off and
promoted to fantasmatic status. Huysmans speaks elsewhere of the process in
terms of a will to inhibit instinctual gratification in the interest of "isolated
erotic ideas, without either material basis or biological sequel to appease
them."[15] Such a process of generalized perversion is already present in the
displacement of the Salome myth toward Pygmalion, the "propping" of a
relation to fantasy on the content of an alleged recollection or scene. Add to
that complex the disqualification of instinctual satisfaction ("without biological sequel to appease them") and we have the wherewithal to reconstruct
a crucial phase of the Freudian model of sexuality: the auto-erotic propping
(*Anlehnung*) of drive on instinct construed as the genesis of fantasy per se.[16]
"Pygmalion" is to "Salome" (or "Herod"), in brief, as drive is to instinct in
Freud's *Three Essays on the Theory of Sexuality*.

The repetition and displacement of one myth as another brings us to the
motif of sexualized repetition as displacement in general in *Là-bas*. The name
given that demonic instance in the novel is *incubus*: "The Incubus steals the
seed a man loses while dreaming and puts it to use" (p. 146). The work of
the incubus consists in sexually reinscribing the real as fantasy, assuring its
dissemination as other than itself. But that dissemination—of incubi—has
emerged in Huysmans' fiction at the end of the sequence he calls the "period
of incubation." It is as though the capacity for displacement—"matter removed and instilled in an other"—were inseparable from a fundamental

mode of deferment (p. 200).[17] The incubus would appear to be always already incubating its return as difference.

Dr. Johannès, the therapist-exorcist of *Là-bas*, was, in fact, one of the names assumed by Huysmans' sometime mentor, a heretical theologian named abbé Joseph-Antoine Boullan.[18] Boullan's obsession was vicarious suffering, the capacity of one soul to suffer the ills, and eventually commit the sins, of another. He called this aptitude for performing displacements "le pouvoir transpositeur" or "transference (*le transfert*)."[19] The Freudian tenor of that latter term may give us pause in the present context. For Freud's "transference," the medium of therapy, entailed a virtual contagion whereby the therapist would become the object of the neurotic's suffering. Even so would Boullan transfer to himself the ills of his sufferer. In Freud, before designating the reactivation of neurotic conflict within analysis, the term "transference" referred to "displacement" itself: affect transferred from ideational representation to ideational representation in symptom or dream.[20] Which is why the potentiality of Boullan's *transfert* to designate as well something of the order of the uncontrolled displacements of Freud's primary process is worth noting. Why, for instance, suppose that the *pouvoir transpositeur* respects the integrity of persons? Thus the question of Boullan's radical disciple, A. Poulain: "Is it easier to transfer the malady from one person to another than to displace it onto a different organ in the same subject? That appears to me to still be substitution or transposition."[21] Here then is (the) transference reverting to its primal Freudian sense of displacement. And what if those displacements were to proliferate beyond the will of any subject? Poulain asks: "Can the person exercising *le pouvoir transpositeur* limit at will the process to bounds he deems it imprudent to exceed? Or better yet: does *le pouvoir transpositeur* include the capacity to impose restrictions on the transference, to endow it, as one would a river, with a bed which channels without impeding it?"[22] It is this horizon of uncontrolled displacement which sounds the Freudian note. Organ-to-organ, after all, is the formula for hysteria, or symptom formation in general. But was it not, we may wonder, always already the formula for synesthesia in the experiments of *A rebours*: from the triumphant "symphonies" for the mouth to the desperate menus—or "lavements nourrissants"— for the rear? In Freud as in Huysmans, the death instinct plays itself out within the medium of grotesque displacement.

From Salome to Esther to the hysteric of *Là-bas*, our effort has been to delineate the return of a mobile fantasy as it crucially exceeds the scenario of La Salpêtrière. Like Freud, Huysmans in the late 1880s was to write his way beyond what one is inclined to call *les Folies-Charcot*. And like him, he was to elaborate by implication a theory and praxis of fantasy within which this essay may be situated. On the path to Catholicism, however, Huysmans was not alone in undergoing a fascination with La Salpêtrière. Léon Bloy, in *Le Désespéré*, comes close to summarizing a portion of our argument in his visionary refrain: "*L'Eglise est écrouée dans un hôpital de folles* (the Church is bolted in to a hospital for madwomen)." [23] I have elsewhere attempted to chart the stylistic and polemical debt of Lacan to Bloy, who was one of the central figures of the Catholic renascence of the late nineteenth century. [24] His importance to the present analysis—of the intersection of French letters and what would later emerge as psychoanalysis in La Salpêtrière—may be gauged from his early essay in praise of *A rebours*. [25] For the myth around which it organizes Huysmans' anti-humanism is none other than Oedipus: "Oedipus was convinced he had vanquished it, the undying monster, defeated it for good! and for his victory the imbeciles of Thebes made him king and quasi-god." [26] The news Huysmans is said to bear is that of the return of the Sphinx in a form traditional humanism can no longer assuage: "The Sphinx has come back, a thousand times more formidable. Its riddle no longer concerns man, but God, and there is not a single Oedipus at hand to solve it." [27] The casualty of Huysmans' Oedipus, like Freud's, is the autonomy of the ego: "His book . . . denounces on every page the nullity, the irreparable nullity of all the supports (*étais*) with which the old psychical entity pretends to continue to sustain itself." [28] In Bloy's essay, then, we have, as it were, an Oedipalization of the proto-Catholic complex we have been reading as consonant with psychoanalysis. It is a convergence pregnant with the future of the discourse of the unconscious in France. Let a single example suffice: "His mode of expression, perpetually armed and eager to defy, allows of no constraint, not even that of Mother Image (*sa mère l'Image*), whom it outrages at the first hint of tyranny and drags endlessly by the hair or by the feet down the worm-eaten stairway of terrified Syntax (*dans l'escalier vermoulu de la Syntaxe épouvantée*)." [29] We have, here, the Oedipal motif of the sacrifice of maternal proximity, but interpreted specifically as the disruption of Image (or the Imaginary) by Syntax (or Structure). It is as though Bloy were approaching a strict Lacanian exposition of what we broached in our allegorical critique of Kermode on the image of Salome. Lest the link to Lacan be in doubt, I return to the *tone* of Bloy's essay, specifically the paragraph that in its will to offend sounds as though it had been scripted by Lacan: "If I could forget the wretched stupidity (*l'horrible sottise*) of the majority of those who read me, and if I had been vouchsafed a talent for sacrilege, I would be less afraid of touching on this redoubtable subject. It is perhaps the most troubling matter I have yet encountered (*ce que j'ai rencontré de plus troublant*). . . . But rest assured, dear heart, nobody will understand a thing." [30]

An incipient theory of the unconscious, but a symptom as well . . . In the fantasy structuring Huysmans' "unconscious," the most recessed sequence is that of *En rade*: Esther, Ahasuerus, and, in the wings, Haman. In our discussion of that novel, we followed a trace of *ether* from the dream of Esther (and the thwarting of a plan for Jewish genocide) through speculations on the manufacture of soap from human remains to the concluding fantasy of bell tower as ascending well. The reproduction of that image in the novel on Gilles de Rais, *Là-bas*, leads us to hypothesize a link between the extreme cruelty of Haman and the "holocaust" of Gilles.

Gilles de Rais, introduced to French literature by Huysmans, has continued to haunt a number of central figures in contemporary French letters. Pierre Klossowski translated the complete proceedings of his trial from the medieval Latin, and Georges Bataille supplied a lengthy preface for its publication.[31] For Bataille, in his somewhat rambling text, Gilles is the tragic hero of a nobility no longer permitted that totality of expenditure and "sovereignty" of risk without which it has no raison d'être. In the present context, what is most curious in his evocation is his willingness to link Gilles with a primitive Teutonic cult: "Rais is noble in the sense in which primitive Germanic warriors were."[32] His reference to Germanic war, however, is marked by the contemporary context: "see Dumézil, *Les Dieux des Germains*, Paris, 1939."[33] And indeed Bataille finds it hard to avoid an undeveloped reference to Hitler when confronted with the case of Gilles: "Before Gilles and his grandfather, it is possible to think of the brutality of the Nazis."[34]

Here, then, quite carelessly, in the margins of a marginal text that knows not what to do with it, is, nevertheless, an explicit connection between Gilles de Rais and the Nazis. It is a link, I would suggest, already scripted by Huysmans' Haman as the Precursor . . . of Gilles. "La Tragédie de Gilles de Rais" is, however, a minor text. More interesting in this context is what is arguably the major novel of the most important novelist to have emerged in the last twenty years in France, Michel Tournier's *Le Roi des Aulnes*.[35] The novel's title—*Erlkönig* in French—plainly refers to the German myth of the child-murdering ogre and may be read as such. Abel Tiffauges, a mediocre French *garagiste* is captured by the Nazis in 1940 and marched off to East Prussia. In Tournier's summary: "But whereas his companions are overcome with grief by the endless and desolate plain, Tiffauges sees in it the magical land he had awaited and knows a strange liberation in captivity."[36] He finds an occasion for service with the Germans, and becomes "the Ogre of Kaltenborn, an ancient Teutonic fortress in which young boys destined to be the finest flower of the Third Reich are selected and trained."[37] In the final section of the novel, the German camp is destroyed by the liberating armies, and Tiffauges in flight is stunned to learn of the plight of the Jews in Germany from an abandoned Jewish child, whom he now carries on his back in what one suspects to be an eroticized version of penance. He has become the Horse of Israel and perseveres at novel's end midst the muck into which his new found charge sinks him ever deeper. Tournier's summary, moreover, contains two programmatic statements. The first concerns the deeper ambition of his novel: "to deduce the 'phoney war,' Hitlerism, the concentration camps, and the unleashing of the Red Army according to a purely symbolic mode and without recourse to the traditional categories of history and psychology." [38] The second would situate *Le Roi des Aulnes* as "an effort (*un essai*) to delineate a new model of non-genital sexuality." [39]

What Tournier, in his own terms, has given us, then, is a bizarre myth of sexual liberation centered on the experience of a French collaborator with the Nazis. For there can be no doubt that the new sexuality of male child-rearing (or bearing) is evoked at its most intense at the youth training center of Kaltenborn. True, Tiffauges will live to learn and regret that the "inverse" counterpart of his idyll is the destruction of European Jewry. But if the new sexuality has received any room for experimentation in the novel it is in the arena of Tiffauges' collaboration with the Germans. The conclusion of *Le Roi des Aulnes* complicates that situation, but does not efface it. Now my reason for introducing this discussion of *Le Roi des Aulnes* is that the myth of Gilles de Rais was manifestly a subtext of Tournier's novel.[40] Tiffauges, it will be recalled, was the name of Gilles' castle in Brittany. And Gilles' horse was a barbary steed or *barbe* he called *barbe-bleu*. He was, we read, "another version of (Gilles) himself." [41] Let us educe a final fragment of the novel in our elaboration of this bizarre legacy of Huysmans. The young Jewish boy, Ephraïm, tells Tiffauges of the horrors of Auschwitz. All began for him, however, midst a certain air of celebration. No sooner were the Jews stripped and disinfected upon arrival than they were invited to improvise costumes for themselves from a pile of shabby clothing put at their disposal. Ephraïm: "We played at putting on women's dresses; some limped as they ran because they had only two left—or right—shoes. You would have thought it was Purim!" [42] The drama of Jewish genocide was first experienced as a travesty of the book of *Esther*. But consider, then, that with the scenario of *Esther* as the netherside of the myth of Gilles de Rais, we have reconstructed one of the most idiosyncratic nodes of our reading of Huysmans. And the historical experience most susceptible of allowing that nexus to be forged is the one that *En rade*, with its human soap, seemed almost to anticipate: the Nazi extermination of the Jews. Surely "Bluebeard's Castle," Steiner's metaphor for Western culture itself, has few corridors as surprising in the rigor of its construction as the one we have traversed from Huysmans to Tournier.[43]

As will be seen from a retraversal of the same span in opposite direction. In "Le Roi des Aulnes," a chapter of Tournier's quasi-memoir *Le Vent Paraclet*, the author speaks of the pleasures he experienced as an adolescent during the Nazi occupation of France.[44] He lived June 1940 as "a gigantic party," the schoolboy's version of the famous "divine surprise" of Charles Maurras.[45]

Nowhere is the will to provocation more offensive than in Tournier's comments on the execution of Robert Brasillach for collaborating with the Nazis. He writes:

> *Ergo* the indictment which resulted in the death sentence for and execution of Robert Brasillach — a mediocre writer and superior traitor, moreover — was no more than a sinister cacology thrown up by a pack of barely washed aliens (*un ramassis de métèques mal débarbouillés*). As a French writer, I possess the privilege accorded by my superior degree of Frenchness (*ma francité supérieure*) of subjecting France to the worst criticisms, the filthiest insults. As for you who read me, if you are not yourself a French writer, I grant you no more than the right to remove your hat, stand at attention, and listen to me as if you were hearing "La Marseillaise." [46]

The humor of Tournier's tone is undeniable, but seems intended to authorize a decidedly risky proposition. Were one to encapsulate the self-indulgent arrogance of Tournier's mock profession of superior Frenchness, the phrase "cruelle niaiserie," mean-spirited fatuousness, might well be deemed adequate. I adopt it from Bataille, who writes of "the personal tragedy of Rais, that of a world best figured by a bloody face, and which, from the *Berserkir* to M. de Charlus, betrays in any event *une cruelle niaiserie*." [47] From Gilles de Rais to Proust's Charlus. But Charlus was modeled, like des Esseintes, on Robert de Montesquiou. And for Huysmans, Gilles was no less than the "des Esseintes of the fifteenth century." Once again, this time through the mediation of Proust, the Huysmans-Tournier link is confirmed.

I have insisted on Tournier partly because of the apparent centrality of his writing to French fiction, partly because of the enthusiastic blandness with which formalists have been tempted to read *Le Roi des Aulnes*. It should be stated that Tournier's *œuvre* offers some resistance to the network of relations we are drawing. On the one hand, the philosemitic conclusion of *Le Roi des Aulnes* has Tiffauges serving as Horse of Israel. On the other, in *Le Vent Paraclet*, after regretting that, were it not for Hitler, the world today would be German (and better), Tournier offers "the German Jew" as the pinnacle of human perfection: Marx, Freud, and Einstein.[48] But the praise for Marx and Freud are short-lived. A chapter later, we read: "For fully a century, moreover, two pseudo-sciences have ventured with equally reductive pretentions into domains where authentic sciences cannot pretend to tread. Marxism and Freudianism "reduce" the most delicate and multifaceted creations to a few lamentably indigent *schema*." [49] My point here is not to defend Marx or Freud, but to underscore that they were celebrated — as German Jews — just long enough for the wish for a German world order to be acknowledged. If we read the conclusion of *Le Roi des Aulnes* in this light, we are brought up short by the realization that the philosemitic image of a Frenchman straining under the weight of his Jewish burden—"the charge which grew heavier at each step was crushing him"—is ultimately no different from the anti-Semitic image current in French prose until World War II.[50] One may wonder how many aggravated steps further before the "malign inversion" (Tournier) might again enter into effect.

With the diversity and depth of his affiliations, Huysmans, ardent "naturalist" who became, in *A rebours*, a prime forger of the "symbolist" canon, has long appeared to straddle in strategic manner the two great aesthetic currents of the nineteenth century. We are somehow not surprised to read in *En rade* that the family that formerly owned the château of Lourps also owned a second property at Saint-Loup. It is as though the elements of the monumental synthesis Proust would later make of the two traditions are already in suspension in Huysmans. Our reading, however, has insisted on two rather different legacies of Huysmans. The first began with the implicit critique of Charcot on hysteria and charted the transformations of a recurrent fantasy which—upon undergoing "Oedipalization" in Bloy's article—seems to anticipate the future of psychoanalysis in France. The second seems less theory than manifestation of the "unconscious." In observing the re-emergence of the link between the myths of Esther and Gilles de Rais in *Le Roi des Aulnes*, we appeared to be broaching the tradition of anti-Semitism in France. In a realm in which the claims of metalanguage are notoriously unstable, it would no doubt be naive to insist on a rigid distinction between model and manifestation of the "unconscious." In recent years, moreover, it has been possible to write a history of psychoanalysis in France which is essentially coextensive with that of French anti-Semitism.[51] As though the early history of French psychoanalysis consisted of solutions to the dilemma: to what extent might the ideas of a Viennese Jew, whatever his technical ingenuity, permit access to the deepest traits of French character? Our Huysmans, in brief, is less the author who managed to short-circuit the divergence between the "naturalist" and "symbolist" series a generation before Proust than the writer whose heretical Christian matrix contained the seeds of the discourse of the unconscious —in both senses of the phrase—in France.

A final element of our original complex remains to be developed. For *A rebours*, it will be recalled, characterizes (Moreau's) Salome as a personification not only of Hysteria, but of *Luxure*: the allegorical figure of Lust. It was, in fact, Huysmans' subsequent characterization of his novel as allegory cut off from its meaning which initially allowed us to disrupt the aesthetic consensus echoed in Kermode's *Romantic Image*: Salome as modernity's image par excellence of organic unity. Now our gesture, in following Huysmans' text,

prolongs the principal move of the final chapter of one of the great and elusive works of the critical canon, Benjamin's thesis on *The Origin of German
Trauerspiel*: "Where man is drawn toward the symbol, allegory emerges from
the depths of being to intercept the intention, and to triumph over it." [52] Our
own allegorical "interception," I believe, is dictated by a profound relation
between the object of this essay (the fiction of Huysmans) and the genre
(*Trauerspiel*) Benjamin sought to examine. [53] As though the unspecified "future" that *Trauerspiel* was said to have might well be read as the novels we
have been interrogating. [54] It is that legacy which this concluding section will
attempt to sketch. That the future of *The Origin of German Trauerspiel* lay
in its author's death in France at the very moment in 1940 that Tournier's
Tiffauges was to know his greatest triumph is the ironic horizon against which
this parallel is sketched.

Our reading of Huysmans has insisted on a series of silent interpolations
into the text: the *tableaux* of Moreau in *A rebours*, the dreams of Jacques in
En rade. Both the silence and the heterogeneity are thematized by Benjamin
as quintessential traits of *Trauerspiel*. Silence: "With all the power at its disposal the will to allegory makes use of the 'dumb show' to bring back the
fading word." [55] Heterogeneity: "The use of the drop-scene permitted the al-
ternation between actions on the forestage and scenes which extended to the
full depth of the stage." [56]

The primal scene of our recurrent fantasy was Herod staring at Salome.
For Benjamin, if *Trauerspiel* was the drama of a tyrant, "above all it was the
figure of Herod . . . which was characteristic of the idea of the tyrant." [57]
Now the strangeness of our sequence is best metonymized as the crossing
over of John the Baptist from the martyr's position in *A rebours* to Herod's
—as Johannès or John the Baptist—in *Là-bas*. That mobility of terms informed our use of the Freudian model of fantasy: a battery of mobile terms
circulating through the recurrence of a constant structure. But the specificity
of *Trauerspiel* lay in the odd interchangeability of martyr and tyrant: "The
sublime status of the Emperor, on the one hand, and the infamous futility of
his conduct on the other, create a fundamental uncertainty as to whether this
is a drama of tyranny or a history of martyrdom." [58] And further on: "Deeper
examination is therefore not necessary in order to ascertain that an element
of martyr-drama lies hidden in every drama of tyranny. It is much less easy
to trace the element of the drama of tyranny in the martyr-drama." [59] And if
the Huysmans sequence is silently pursued against a Byzantine backdrop, in
Benjamin's *Trauerspiel* also, "it is the theocratic Empire of Byzantium which
figures most prominently." [60]

It would, in fact, be possible to assemble quotations from Benjamin's
"mosaic" and constitute them as a running commentary on *A rebours*. The
materiality of *Trauerspiel*, "the precision with which the passions themselves
take on the nature of stage properties," recalls the variety of ingenious devices

through which des Esseintes cultivates while displacing the aesthetic capacities of the bodily orifices.[61] The general project of "striking Christian sparks from the baroque rigidity of the melancholic" nicely recaptures the author's retrospective view of the novel.[62] Allegory's investment in the merely "decorative," *Trauerspiel*'s "stylistic law of bombast," the "nightmare burden of realia" impinging on its action, all are evocative of the overcrowded, even ostentatious texture of *A rebours*.[63] But we shall conclude rather with what Benjamin calls the "third type alongside the despot and the martyr": the intriguer, "the evil genius of the despots." [64] For it completes our recurrent fantasy by restoring the recessed middle sequence: Haman as deceptive counselor in murder. By the end of Benjamin's "baroque dialectic," the intriguer's "mood permits the paradoxical demand for saintliness to be made of the courtier or even, as Grácian does, actually to declare that he is a saint." [65] With murderous court intriguer in the position of saint, we have reproduced the homology between the Precursor and Haman in our reading of Huysmans. Benjamin comments that the "German dramatists did not dare to plumb the vertiginous depths of this antithesis in one character." [66] It is a division whose measure in our reading is the difference through which the fantasy returns.

Luxure/hystérie. Beyond the proto-Freudian critique of Charcot, then, we conclude with "Huysmans" as baroque allegory, a French afterbirth of *Trauerspiel*. On the one hand, Benjamin's thesis as exemplary guide to the novels culminating in *Là-bas*. On the other, the legacy of those novels in Tournier's reinvention of Gilles de Rais triumphant at the outset of World War II. On the one hand, a thesis on mourning. On the other, the celebration of the very circumstance of the critic's death. This concluding section, then, to evoke the Benjamin-Huysmans encounter as the virtuality—in time—of a mortal embrace.

Notes

Unless otherwise indicated, all translations from the French are my own.

1   In Edmund Wilson's *Axel's Castle* (New York: Scribners, 1931), p. 264, for instance, the novel's protagonist seems to rival Villiers' Axel as the "type" of the hero of French symbolism: "Above all, Huysmans' des Esseintes . . . set the fashion for so many other personalities, fictitious and real, of the end of the century." More recently, Richard Gilman, in *Decadence: The Strange Life of an Epithet* (New York: Farrar Straus Giroux, 1975), p. 103, sees Huysmans as offering the "paradigm" of "decadence."

2   Frank Kermode, *Romantic Image* (New York: Knopf, 1964).

3   *Ibid.*, p. 76.

4   In his remarkable preface to *A rebours* (Paris: Gallimard, 1977), p. 9, Marc Fumaroli underscores Sartre's debt to Huysmans. See also Jean-Pierre Richard, *Microlectures* (Paris: Seuil, 1979), p. 147: "We may imagine . . . that through some return of the repressed, *Roquefort* resurfaces in *Folantin*—which will give us the name of another celebrated bachelor hero, just as nauseous, but perhaps harder and more thoughtful than Huysmans': *Roquentin.*"

5   Joris-Karl Huysmans, *A rebours* (Paris: Gallimard, 1977), p. 59. Subsequent references to *A rebours* in the text are to this edition.

6   Huysmans grants Prudentius' *Psychomachia* an important role in his virtuoso "para-phrase" of "L'Ouverture de *Tannhäuser*" (1885): "It appears that the Wagnerian Venus attracts and ensnares much as did the most dangerous of Prudentius' deities, she (*celle*) whose name the writer invokes only in trembling: Sodomita Libido." See *Croquis parisiens* (Paris: 10/18, 1976), p. 436.

7   Sigmund Freud, "Charcot (1893)," in *Early Psychoanalytic Writings* (New York: Colliers, 1963), p. 14. For an important evocation of Charcot's legacy to French psychoanalysis, see Elisabeth Roudinesco, *La Bataille de cent ans: Histoire de la psychanalyse en France* (Paris: Ramsay, 1982), 1: 34–70.

8   Page references in the text refer to *En rade* (Paris: 10/18, 1976).

9   Mario Praz, *The Romantic Agony* (New York: Oxford University Press, 1933), pp. 301–19. The principal authors mobilized by Praz in his discussion are Flaubert, Wilde, Laforgue, Heine, Mallarmé, and Huysmans.

10 Erwin Panofsky, "Iconography and Iconology," in *Meaning in the Visual Arts* (Chicago: University of Chicago Press, 1939).

11 For a discussion of Anna O. and the myth of the birth of psychoanalysis, see the presentation of H. Ellenberger's critique of Jones' version in Roudinesco, *La Bataille de cent ans*, p. 31.

12 Page references in the text refer to *Là-bas* (Paris: Flammarion, 1978). I have occasionally quoted from Keene Wallis' translation, *Down There* (New York: Boni, 1924).

13 Freud, "Charcot," p. 22.

14 For the psychoanalytic notion of fantasy, see Jean Laplanche and Jean-Baptiste Pontalis, "Fantasme originaire, fantasme des origines, origines du fantasme," *Les Temps modernes* 215 (1964), pp. 1833–68.

15 Huysmans, "Félicien Rops," in *Certains* (Paris: 10/18, 1975), p. 333.

16 For a discussion of "propping (*Anlehnung, étayage*)" and/or "anaclisis" in Freud, see Jean Laplanche, *Vie et mort en psychanalyse* (Paris: Flammarion, 1970), chapter 1.

17 For a discussion of "deferment (*Nachträglichkeit, après-coup*)" in Freud's elaboration of the unconscious and its relation to *Anlehnung*, see Laplanche, *Vie et mort en psychanalyse*, chapter 2, as well as my "*Poe pourri*: Lacan's Purloined Letter," *Semiotext(e)* 3 (1975).

18 For Boullan's proclamation of himself as "John the Baptist," see Robert Baldrick, *The Life of J.-K. Huysmans* (Oxford: Oxford University Press, 1955), p. 156. For a general discussion of his work, see Richard Griffiths, *The Reactionary Revolution: The Catholic Revival in French Literature (1870/1914)* (New York: Ungar, 1965), pp. 130–38.

19 Boullan, *La Divine Réparation par J. J. M., missionnaire de Marie*, quoted in Griffiths, *The Reactionary Revolution*, p. 169.

20 Jean Laplanche and Jean-Baptiste Pontalis, *Vocabulaire de la psychanalyse* (Paris: P.U.F., 1967), p. 494: "Transference for Freud was originally but a particular case of displacement of affect from one representation to another."

21 A. Poulain, Letter of 18 March 1873, quoted in Griffiths, *The Reactionary Revolution*, p. 173.

22 A. Poulain, Letter of 8 April 1873, quoted in Griffiths, *The Reactionary Revolution*, p. 173.

23 Léon Bloy, *Le Désespéré* (Paris: Mercure de France, 1964), p. 223.

24 See my *Legacies: Of Anti-Semitism in France* (Minneapolis: University of Minnesota Press, 1983), chapter 2, "The Suture of an Allusion: Lacan with Léon Bloy."

25 Reproduced as chapter 1, "Les représailles du Sphynx," of *Sur la tombe de Huysmans* (Paris: 10/18, 1983). Bloy's violent break with Huysmans is charted in Baldrick, *The Life of J.-K. Huysmans*, pp. 167–69. Huysmans appears as a (despised) character, Folantin, in Bloy's *La Femme Pauvre*.

26 Bloy, "Les représailles du Sphynx," p. 235.

27 *Ibid.*, p. 237.

28 *Ibid.*, p. 236.

29 *Ibid.*, p. 241.

30 *Ibid.*, p. 236.

31 Georges Bataille, *Le procès de Gilles de Rais*, trans. Pierre Klossowski (Paris: Pauvert, 1972).

32 *Ibid.*, p. 47.

33 *Ibid.*, p. 37.

34 *Ibid.*, p. 28.

35 Michel Tournier, *Le Roi des Aulnes* (Paris: Gallimard, 1970). B. Vercier and J. Lecarme, in their effort to hammer out a canon of *La Littérature en France depuis 1968* (Paris: Bordas, 1982), p. 69, proclaim Tournier "the most important of the new writers of the period," a "new classic."

36 Tournier, *Le Roi des Aulnes*, p. 8.

37 *Ibid.*, p. 8.

38 *Ibid.*, p. 8.

39 *Ibid.*, p. 9.

40 Since the publication of *Le Roi des Aulnes*, Tournier has written explicitly on Gilles de Rais in *Gilles et Jeanne* (Paris: Gallimard, 1983).

41 Tournier, *Le Roi des Aulnes*, p. 403.

42 *Ibid.*, p. 555.

43 See George Steiner, *In Bluebeard's Castle: Some Notes towards the Redefinition of Culture* (New Haven: Yale University Press, 1971), p. 136: "We open the successive doors in Bluebeard's Castle because 'they are there,' because each leads to the next by a logic of intensification which is the mind's own awareness of being."

44 Michel Tournier, *Le Vent Paraclet* (Paris: Gallimard, 1977). For a discussion of heretical beliefs in the coming of the Paraclete or Third Reign in Huysmans' *milieu*, see Griffiths, *The Reactionary Revolution*, p. 127.

45 Tournier, *Le Vent Paraclet*, p. 74.

46 *Ibid.*, p. 86.

47 Bataille, *Le procès de Gilles de Rais*, p. 53.

48 Tournier, *Le Vent Paraclet*, p. 143.

49 *Ibid.*, pp. 202–3.

50 Tournier, *Le Roi des Aulnes*, p. 580.

51 See Roudinesco, *La Bataille de Cents Ans*, "L'inconscient 'à la française' (de Gustave Le Bon à l'affaire Dreyfus," pp. 181–222, and "Judéité, israélisme, antisémitisme," pp. 395–411. The most interesting chapter in this regard concerns the efforts of Edouard Pichon, psychoanalyst, linguist, and militant of *Action française*, to reorganize the Société Psychanalytique de Paris on the model of a 1930s militant *ligue*, and his recognition of the young Jacques Lacan as perhaps best suited to lead it (pp. 309–10). It was from Pichon's writings on linguistics that Lacan adopted the term *foreclusion*. See Roudinesco, *La Bataille de cent ans*, pp. 314–17. For Huysmans' own anti-Semitism, see his letter of 28 February 1898 to Arij Prins on the Dreyfus affair (*Lettres inédites à Arij Prins* [Geneva: Droz, 1977], p. 313): "It is true, on the other hand, that it has augmented the ranks of anti-Semitism, all of which is not without giving me a certain pleasure."

52 Walter Benjamin, *The Origin of German Tragic Drama*, trans. J. Osborne (London: NLB, 1977), p. 183.

53 Fumaroli, in his preface to *A rebours*, p. 35, develops at some length the "strange similarity between the Golden Age of Loyola's *Spiritual Exercises* (the end of the sixteenth century and its prolongation in the seventeenth) and the Decadent *fin-de-siècle* of Huys-

mans." The Jesuit theater was crucial to *Trauerspiel*, and the late sixteenth and seventeenth centuries its golden age.

54   Benjamin, *The Origin of German Tragic Drama*, p. 113.
55   *Ibid.*, p. 192.
56   *Ibid.*, p. 194.
57   *Ibid.*, p. 70.
58   *Ibid.*, p. 73.
59   *Ibid.*, p. 73.
60   *Ibid.*, p. 68.
61   *Ibid.*, p. 133.
62   *Ibid.*, p. 158.
63   *Ibid.*, pp. 188, 210.
64   *Ibid.*, pp. 98, 95.
65   *Ibid.*, p. 98.
66   *Ibid.*, p. 98.

Terror and Historicity in Giovanni Battista Piranesi as Forms of Romantic Subjectivity / *Jürgen Klein*

Giovanni Battista Piranesi (1720–78), who celebrated his greatest artistic triumphs in Rome, used Roman antiquity as a metaphor for mortality, a theme which was to become one of the most important in the Romantic movement. His etchings of Roman ruins depicting their intrinsically massive proportions, reveal his intense preoccupation with the contrast between human mortality and human aspirations to immortality. His engravings of ruins transcend the treatment of the same theme by his predecessors, who saw their sovereigns as omnipotent, representing them both in the image of God and as the recipients of God's mandate.[1] Piranesi's images are deployed in an unlimited architectural hierarchy which no longer seeks to conceal the smallness of rulers by means of complicated allegorical representations, but rather emphasizes the absolute insignificance of human kind.[2] Pascal's deeply felt anxiety about the emptiness of an infinite universe is graphically formulated in Piranesi's schemas, which contrast gigantic architectural spaces and structures with men who appear as flyspecks on the paper. As Pascal wrote in his *Pensées*:

> Quand je considère la petite durée de ma vie, absorbée dans l'éternité précédente et suivante, le petit espace que je remplis, et meme que je vois, abîmé dans l'infinie immensité des espaces que j'ignore et qui m'ignorent, je m'effraie et m'étonne de me voir ici plutôt que là, car il n'y a point de raison pourquoi ici plutôt que là, pourquoi à présent plutôt que lors. Qui m'y a mis? Par l'ordre et la conduite de qui ce lieu et ce temps a-t-il ete destiné à moi?

> [When I consider the short span of my life, absorbed by eternity past and to come, and contemplate the small space that I occupy, or even that I see, swallowed by the infinite immensity of space about which I know nothing and which has no knowledge of me, then I shudder and marvel that I am here and not there; for there is no reason why I should be here and not there. Who put me here? By whose order and act have this time and space been destined for me?][3]

While Pascal conquered his anxiety with Christian faith, which provided him with the unique revelation of a hidden God, Piranesi turned to historicity, acknowledging at most that anonymous and undefinable if suprahuman powers are responsible for man's place on earth. Piranesi's edifices could hardly have been erected by the men who wander through them. But it is in the architectural fervor of the "heros" of Roman antiquity that Piranesi could best exemplify the aspiration to immortality while simultaneously expressing the mortality to which both man and edifice are subject. Norbert Miller spoke rightly in this regard, of a "meglomania of impotence" [4] (figure 1).

It is precisely this theme which enabled Piranesi to achieve the success he did in eighteenth century Europe. It was taken for granted that the best houses possessed one or more Piranesi works. Goethe, although critical of Piranesi's "Pyramid of Cestius," owned a series of his etchings. The fascination which Piranesi's plates exerted upon artists, collectors, and antiquaries in the 18th century, was nourished by the fact that his imaginative powers provided him with creative methods of synthesizing material, temporal, and spatial opposites. He rendered visible the contrasts between eternity and finiteness, between human individuality and the omnipotence of the natural laws.

It is the artistic imagination that unifies the immense echeloned spaces and architectural structures in the partially real, partially fictive Piranesi landscapes. His waking dream imagination contains a nightmarish element, and in this respect Piranesi can be compared to writers in the Gothic tradition who were his contemporaries. Sir Horace Walpole, author of the first Gothic novel (*The Castle of Otranto*, 1764) writes to his friend Cole on March 9, 1765:

> (I) had a dream, of which all I could recover was that I had thought myself in an ancient castle (a very natural dream for a head like mine filled with Gothic story), and that on the uppermost bannister of a great staircase I saw a gigantic hand in armour. In the evening I sat down, and began to write, without knowing in the least what I intended to say or to relate.[5]

The proportions of the hand in Walpole's dream correspond to Piranesi's use of dimension in his drawings, depicting an oversized or imagined, rather than realistic, sense of proportion. This is indeed the aspect of Piranesi's "Pyramid of Cestius" which Goethe found cause to criticize:

> Die Pyramide des Cestius ward für diesmal mit den Augen von aussen begrüsst und die Trümmer der Antoninischen oder Caracallischen Bäder, von denen Piranesi so manches Effektreiche vorgefabelt, konnten auch dem malerisch gewöhnten Auge in der Gegenwart kaum Zufriedenheit geben.
>
> [This time the eyes greet the exterior of the Pyramid of Cestius, and the Antonian and Carcallian Baths, from which Piranesi has fancied many an effective illusion, though they are hardly satisfying to the contemporary, artistically schooled eye.][6]

Piranesi's artistic power stems from his ability to transform a model into a chiaroscuro, idealizing it. The gigantic, combined with the somber and the

Figure 1. Giovanni Battista Piranesi, *Carceri*, Plate V. Photograph courtesy of the New York Public Library. Photo: Jamie McEwen.

picturesque, give his etchings an extraordinary intensity. Magnitude, loftiness, and infinite space in contrast with insignificance and transitoriness, lead to their mutual intensification. The function of the imagination as an observer directive is built into Piranesi's work, or, to quote Hans Blumenberg, the "Vulcanicity of his imagination" and the "Neptunicity of his choices" are indissoluably intertwined.[7] The imagination, as a generative source of multiplicity, has in Piranesi's case been aided by the systematic review of manifold historic forms. Hence, in the "temporal resistance" of fragments, ruins, and myths, there is a potential futuricity, albeit an obscured one.

Piranesi's controversy with Jean-Louis Mariette on the originality of Etruscan architecture and its exemplary relevance for Roman building typifies his kind of artistic imagination. Piranesi filled his book "Della Magnificenza ed Architettura de Romani" (1761) with all kinds of decorative and structural reconstructions based on Etruscan architecture. His imagination supplied him with all those details that historical evidence was not able to provide. Mariette contested Piranesi's opinions on this ground. He accused him of having obfuscated true chronology as well as having misinterpreted Roman architectural history.[8] But in Piranesi's "failure" as an antiquarian can be read a sign of his originality.

When Sir Roger Newdigate bought two Piranesi candelabras in 1775 for the embellishment of the Radcliffe Library in Oxford, his acquisition was made according to standards exemplifying Piranesi's artistic principles:

> They are important to the student of antique sculpture. They are indispensable to the student of New-Classicism in Europe, and in particular in England. Their completeness, richness, variety, and assurance provide the aesthetic justification of Piranesi's teachings; his insistence upon the validity of an assimilation of elements of styles into a personal manner of expression, and his claims that the study of antiquity must result in invention rather than in repetition.[9]

Newdigate's observations are typical of his time. In the late eighteenth century ruins were considered works of art in and of themselves, not merely as apt subjects for graphic representation. Castles only seemingly in ruins were designed by architects for residential use. But Gothicists of the late eighteenth century also constructed "mere ruins," which could never be used at all, except, as Carl Justi has postulated, to project the internalized sense of historic relativity as a concrete, spatial experience.[10]

According to Justi, Piranesi offers similar projections in his two-dimensional work:

> Eine andere Wirkung, über die [Piranesi's] Nadel gebot, war der Zauber der Vergangenheit. Denn Piranesi konnte die Unendlichkeit der Zeit wie des Raumes malen. Er versinnlicht die Wirkung der Jahrtausende und des Verfalls durch das unauflösliche Mysterium seines Helldunkels, seinen

dusteren Metallglanz. Bei ihm lernt man erst, was Druckerschwärze vermag. Und so schliessen die poetischen Freiheiten keineswegs die Anerkennung aus, dass sein Stil wie kein anderer aus dem malerischen Charakter jener Ruinen hervorgewachsen sei, und wollte man paradox reden, so konnte man wohl behaupten, seine Prospekte seien teurer als die Aufnahmen derer, deren nüchterne Trockenheit ihnen phantasielose Treue leicht machte.

[Another effect, over which [Piranesi's] needle had control was the magic of the past. Piranesi was able to draw the infinity of time as well as that of space. He materialized the passing of the millennia in the mystery of his chiaroscuro and his somber, metallic glow. One learns from him for the first time what printer's ink is capable of. Poetic license by no means excludes the recognition that his style, more than any other, grew out of the picturesque character of those ruins. And one could well maintain that his renditions have more value than the reproductions of those whose sober tedium makes unimaginative loyalty easy.] [11]

Justi's further description of Piranesi's men as flies caught in the meshes of a spider's web is noteworthy. The enormity and sinister power of his Cyclopean architecture, the rampant growth and impenetrable nature of his undergrowth, transform humanistic anthropocentrism into an entomological discipline. The opposition of limitless forces reduces mankind to a subordinate existence, in which self-idolization finds its end in a motionless gesticulation, in a hollow, chitinous armor. Justi touches upon a pivotal point when he characterizes Piranesi's world as a reversal of Leibnitz's optimism. In the place of a preordained harmony, a weblike pattern of subordination and repression is woven by anonymous, unknown forces. This viewpoint makes Piranesi a radical in his own time. While his contemporary, J. H. Füssli, in a drawing entitled "The Artist, Despairing before the Magnitude of his Antique Dreams," places the despairing, still possessed of his human dignity, next to oversized fragments of a foot or a pointing hand, in Piranesi's work we discern at best grotesque insects in motionless commedia dell'arte postures before the ruins. [12]

Reinhart Koselleck's principle of "absence of synchronism between contemporary elements" applies to the relationship between Piranesi and Füssli. [13] It seems particularly relevant because it ascribes the meaningful gain made in the "exemplary and educational reproducibility of history" to Piranesi rather than to Füssli. Enlargement of the aesthetic distance between object and human subjectivity in Piranesi's work intensifies the aesthetic terror as Edmund Burke defined it. [14] In his *Philosophical Enquiry into the Origin of Our Ideas of the Sublime and Beautiful* (1756), he proposes interrelated definitions for the concepts "terror" and "the sublime": "pleasure" and "pain" are not necessarily mutually exclusive. Burke also divides the concept of taste into "general" and "individual" taste. For him, emotional exhilaration is more important than "pleasure." He stresses the joys of melancholy and sets forth the principle behind the new Gothic novel: the joys of destruction in a paroxysm of horror. Provided that it does not proceed directly from unmitigated pain, the satisfaction of passions through "delightful horror" becomes a postulate for the new art and the concept of the sublime. There are even intimations of a pleasure derived from the sufferings of others. Burke says, "Terror is a passion which always produces delight when it does not press too close, and pity is a passion accompanied with pleasure, because it arises from love and social affection." [15] The "sublime" is thus constituted in the relationship between individual security and a dangerous situation or a dangerous object: "Whatever is fitted in any sort to excite the ideas of pain, and danger that is to say, whatever is in any sort terrible, or is conversant about terrible objects, or operates in a manner analogous to terror, is a source of the strongest emotion which the mind is capable of feeling. . . . When danger or pain press too nearly, they are incapable of giving any delight, and with certain modifications, they may be, and they are delightful, as we every day experience." [16] According to Burke's theory, the indirect aesthetic effect of a portrayal of terror increases the imagined threat to the reader or spectator of a sublime work of art, which, displaying situations of "sublime terror," rouses intellectual and aesthetic processes of association.

In his analysis of eighteenth-century views of Roman ruins, Justi has shown that very different personalities, such as Winckelman (1717–68) and Piranesi, could find inspiration in the same subject. Indeed, Piranesi's relativity perhaps meets nowhere with so marked an opposition as in Winckelman's optimistic idealism.

> Winckelmann recognized only one objective in art—beauty. To this he sacrificed both character and expression. It was the sun around which his thinking, searching, and feeling all revolved. Piranesi indulged himself in the ugly, the distorted. . . . Winckelmann's sensibility was Greek: volume and form, simplicity and nobility of line, quietude of the soul and sensitive perception were the words of his credo, crystal clear water his favorite symbol. Piranesi was a modern, passionate, yes, demonic nature, the infinite, the mystery of the sublime—its space and power were his subjects. The sight of his engravings makes one shudder, we are spellbound by his magic, an irresistible longing pulls us into his spaces, into the depths of a spirit domain.[17]

Carl Justi's appreciation (1866) of Piranesi's work was invaluable. For although the stylistic and artistic syncretism of nineteenth-century art and architecture led pedagogues and philologists, especially in Germany, to an intensive study of Greek language, literature, and culture, these were used for models of intellectual and aesthetic purity along the line of a neo-idealistic philosophy. The Greek classical ideal of the late nineteenth century goes back to Winckelmann's normative classical aesthetics developed in his *Geschichte der Kunst des Altertums* (1764).

It is curious that the nineteenth-century authorities on the arts in Germany concentrated on classical Rome and Greece as well as on the Renaissance, but neglected artists like Piranesi. Jakob Burckhardt, for instance, identifies Piranesi with a follower of the French style "a la greque", fashionable in the 1770s, and as the architect of the Priorato di Malta in Rome.[18]

Piranesi—with the exception of the attention paid him by Carl Justi—was not a prominent figure in nineteenth-century art history and has remained a mysterious personality. Not much is known concerning his youth. His drawing skills became apparent at an early age and he was first trained as an architect by his father's brother-in-law.[19] He studied the work of Andrea Palladio (1508–80)[20] thoroughly and gained familiarity with the architectural theories of the Roman Vitruvius, whose *De Architectura* (25 B.C.) included a detailed compendium on architectural methods, town planning, and construction.[21] Piranesi studied under Carlo Zucchi in Venice and in 1740 he was employed by the Signoria of Venice as a draughtsman, and would accompany the new Venetian ambassador to Rome. In Rome, Piranesi started to draw the antique ruins. Through the models he used for this work he became acquainted with the "study of classical spacial harmony and dimensionality as well as with the classical decorative order."[22] His first artistic work appeared in 1743 under the title of *Prima Parte Architetture e Prospettive*. Piranesi placed a special emphasis on draftmanship—it came to constitute his own particular outlet for his ideas, since his architectural dreams, partially visible in Roman architecture, could no longer, for various reasons, be actualized.

In 1745 Piranesi's *Invenzioni capric . . . di Carceri* appeared, a work that he revised and expanded in 1760–61. These plates, depicting fantastical prisons, are among the most daring and modern illustrations produced in the eighteenth century. This series of graphics exercised an irresistible fascination on the Romantics, sensitive to the darker side of the artistic movement since the mid-century. The *Carceri* can be considered a derivative of Piranesi's "waking dream about Rome's historical greatness as the world's architectural empire."[23] Local references play only a subordinate role: these plates show a nowhere and everywhere, their intransitive eminence is especially apparent in this use of abstraction.

Piranesi's other major works include the *Antichita di Roma* which appeared in four folio-volumes in 1756. The dedication of this work to Lord Charlemont was probably instrumental in Piranesi's nomination as honorary member of the "London Antiquarian Society" the following year. In 1762 Piranesi published both the *Della Magnificenza de Architettura de Romani* and the *Il Campo Marzio dell'antica Roma*. In these works he deliberately intensified the grandeur of antique Rome, as if in opposition to the discovery of the northern "antiquity," then permeating the genesis of early English romanticism and the German "Storm and Stress" movement. It is interesting when one thinks of Herder's (1744–1803) reflections on the cultural differences between North and South,[24] that Piranesi entered into an argument with an unknown Englishman (The Investigator, anon.) in 1755. The controversy began when the Englishman, much to Piranesi's consternation, preferred the Goths to the Romans.

In England as in Germany a model of northern antiquity was conscientiously set against the exemplary image of Rome, so that finally there existed the parallel of cultural patterns: classical antiquity (south) and Germanic culture (north). For the northern cultural "ideology" within eighteenth-century England one might refer to Mallet's Northern Antiquities (1770). Piranesi advocated instead the ancient Roman art of construction which existed before Greek influence: for him the Tuscan-Etruscan was the primary architectural model, a thesis also upheld by Vitruvius.[25]

In spite of such disagreements, close cultural ties existed between England and Rome during the mid-eighteenth century, predominantly involving the study of antiquity, but also facilitating the export of ancient art objects from Italy to England even when political relations between the Kingdom and the Vatican were not especially friendly.[26] The British interest in classical art by no means begins in the eighteenth century. In the Elizabethan age the Earl of Arundel had already brought together one of the most splendid antique collections of northern Europe. The Renaissance had not only favored the inclination for collecting, but in England as elsewhere had related, in what Hans Blumenberg has called a "linguistic secularity," the revival of interest in antiquity with the rebirth of Christ, so that classical and Christian metaphors at times intersected.

> Perhaps such . . . boldness can be exemplified in the traditional anecdote told about Francis Bacon. In the gardens of the Earl of Arundel, who had installed a great quantity of antique statues of naked men and women, Sir Francis suddenly stopped in amazement and exclaimed: "the resurrection."[27]

But a Christian-Platonic orientation, such as prevailed in the seventeenth century and up to the time of Milton, cannot be claimed for the eighteenth. Religious concepts in the eighteenth century clearly stood under the influence of the Enlightenment and under the level of Deism, although occasional visions of terror, death, or hell coexisted with the elevating and predominantly didactic thoughts of redemption.

It can be said generally of the intellectual and historical mainstream of the eighteenth century that its relationship to antiquity was less religious than it had been a century before, when the Platonism of the Renaissance was an active cultural element.[28] While the England of the seventeenth century was especially preoccupied with the Neo-Platonic school in Italy,[29] English interests during the eighteenth century focused less on the mixing of Christianity and Platonism than on classical art and architecture—a trend that might be interpreted as running counter to Christian culture. The popularity of Greek and Roman research continued throughout the entire eighteenth century and did not abate until the early nineteenth. The excavations at Pompei and Herculanum certainly helped to stimulate a general interest in classical history. By the mid-eighteenth century, the British interest in archeology had grown enough to influence the English arts and crafts movement—those of antique design were an enormous success by the end of the century.

As Peter Gay has shown in his book *The Enlightenment, An Interpretation*, Greek and Roman antiquity restrained the Christian influence in Western Europe in favour of an "affirmation of worldliness and cultivation," [30] which implied skepticism and intellectual discrimination, stressed logical and proportionate thought, but also curiosity.[31] Any assessment of Piranesi has to take into account that in his concept and practice of art, subjectivity is seen from a double perspective, namely from the classical point of view in the sense of proportion and from the psychological potentality conveyed by the sublime, the picturesque, the diffuse, the archetypal. The conjunction between these two points of view is provided by the concept of permanent historical change, which connects the constructive energies of man with his demonic aspect.

Within the framework of the reception of classical art and architecture in eighteenth-century England, it is remarkable that Piranesi's work is connected with the specific classical language of architectural forms. His innovations are established by his use of structure, by the relation of architectural elements, perspective, light and shadow, and especially atmosphere.[32] It therefore makes sense to suggest that his view of classical antiquity is tinged with his empirical knowledge of the classical ruin and that it leads back to the analysis of architectural language in order to construct a synthesis providing a new aesthetic quality. Piranesi's influence in Britain was important during the eighteenth century. Not only did he influence architects, artists, and antiquarians, but also poets and novelists like Ann Radcliffe, William Beckford, Horace Walpole, Coleridge, De Quincey. His direct influence on British eighteenth-century classicists is indicated by different personal relationships; his friendships with Sir William Hamilton, Sir Roger Newdigate, and Robert Adam.[33]

It was tremendously important for the history of English culture and art that two such esteemed artists and experts on antiquity as Piranesi and Robert Adam should become friends. Piranesi dedicated his essays on *The Field of Mars* (*Campus Martius*) to his English friend and colleague. Piranesi intensified Adam's taste for "the grand"[34] during Adam's stay in Rome in 1755–57. Before Adam left for Rome he was already "antique mad," but when he came to know Piranesi, the scale of his fascination for Roman antiquity was given quite a new dimension. In a letter to Margaret Adam dated June 18, 1755, Robert wrote: "[Piranesi] is become immensely intimate with me and as he imagined at first that I was like the other Englishers who had love for Antiques without knowledge upon seeing some of my sketches and drawings, was so highly delighted that he almost ran quite distracted and says I have more genius for the true noble Architecture than any Englishman ever was in Italy." [35] A friendship between Piranesi and Robert Adam developed, which lasted until Piranesi's death. Besides dedications of works to one another, there were a number of mutual references in their publications. Most important for Piranesi's influence on Robert Adam and, via Adam, on English taste in the eighteenth century, is the fact that both he and Piranesi based their work on the three aesthetic principles: novelty, variety, and freedom from absolute rule. [36] Robert Adam was a master of architectural design and of neo-Classicist decoration, but he also loved the romantic touches in the Piranesi etchings. About some of Adam's own work it was written that: "A strong romantic bias appears in his beautiful pen and ink drawings of mountain landscapes and fantastic ruins, as well as in his architecture and in his admiration of the work of his friend Piranesi." [37]

As mentioned above, Piranesi had turned away from the standard aesthetics of Andrea Palladios between 1743 and 1765 to acquire his own independent concept of art, one that would combine the Constructive with the Sublime in an urgent and forceful form. Piranesi pledged his individual development to a new aesthetic direction centered on the thesis of breaking with the constraint of standards. This thesis was by no means limited to the fine arts but was very soon expressed in the *Poetic Theory of the Original Genius*. Thomas Gray gave very clear expression to this trend when he wrote: "Rules are but chains, good for little, except when you can break them." [38] Albert Giesecke, whose important monograph on Piranesi appeared in 1911, wrote of him "that he was always happier if he created spontaneously than if he merely contrived something in order to demonstrate his intentions and his capability." [39]

The Piranesian landscape, initially realistic, goes through an obvious change between the 1740s and the 1770s, one corresponding fully with the transition from the Beautiful to the Terrible-Exalted in Burke's terms. Piranesi's first rendition of the *Carceri* contrasted with later renditions support this description of his artistic development. Piranesi combines the austerity characteristic of Roman antiquity with a rare, spatially creative imagination, a combination which is subsequently presented to the viewer in two modes. The first (1745) is light, picturesque, bright, reminiscent of Guardi, Canaletto, and Tiepolo. The later (1760–61) is increasingly heavy, materially oriented, chiaroscuro, "sublime." Piranesi's predeliction for the bizarre became noticeable in the work after 1760 as did the brilliant demonic-melancholic aspect of his character, particularly evident in Polanzani's famous portrait of him (1756). [40]

Piranesi's realistic landscapes evolve from light, picturesque views and sil-
very airspaces to the detailed architectural subjects of which Rome offered
him a great plenty, evoked here by Kenneth Clark:

> Rome in the middle of the eighteenth century must have been the most
> beautiful place in the world—and the most paradoxical. First there were
> the vast buildings of papal Rome. . . . Although the great epoch of
> building was over, a succession of benevolent Popes and Cardinals had
> given the feeling that this colossal stability would go on forever. . . .
> Next to those came certain buildings which had survived from antiquity
> and were still used for human habitation. In these conversions the level
> of prosperity had gone down—there were broken pediments and crum-
> bling walls. There was an uncomfortable feeling of devouring time. Then
> came those ruins of antiquity which, because of their location or insta-
> bility had been allowed to decay, magnificent, complex structures that
> no reasonable architect would have dared to restore. And finally there
> were those great projects of antiquity . . . subjects of dread and melan-
> choly, emotions at the opposite extreme to the pure, limpid water which
> Winckelman was proposing, at the same epoch, as the proper analogy
> for art.[41]

Piranesi's early veduta display the quality of theatrical scenes, which profit
from the light that characterizes Rome for every artist. Examples are the
"Veduta della Basilica e Piazza di S. Pietro in Vaticano" (1748) or the "Veduta
della Basilica di S. Giovanni in Laterano" (ca. 1748). One can compare the
transformation of Piranesi's art to the changes in a day: from an early afternoon sun on a realistic and pastoral landscape to southern evenings such as
those portrayed by Anne Radcliffe in her novel *The Italian* (1797). The black-
green pines and the massive threatening ruins in the early edition (1750) of
Veduta degli Avanzi del Triclino della Casa aurea di Nerone are in striking
contrast to those in the later edition (1774).

The structure and light of Piranesi's etchings make the viewer reflect; they
bewilder him. As Norbert Miller has written: "Maybe the first to do so in
the history of the eighteenth century, Piranesi has not only consciously destroyed the assured and reliable relation between the I and the outer world,
between dream and reality, but he also visually cancelled it."[42] Norbert Miller
has justifiably noted that Piranesi the melancholic falls back on the fiercely
grim *Vanitas*—a concept current in the early Baroque. The individual is cog-
nisant of his own skeptical subjectivity in relation to an overpowering history;
the individual's claim to totality is exposed to doubt and melancholy. A collective human effort is under attack from the natural world just as the ruins
of Rome are being overwhelmed by undergrowth.

Piranesi anticipates the future tendencies of an art which will be called
"Romantic" and which produces a transition towards the "no longer Fine

Figure 2. Giovanni Battista Piranesi, *Carceri*, Plate XIV. Photograph courtesy of the New York Public Library. Photo: Jamie McEwen.

Arts."[43] His concept of art is in clear opposition to Winckelmann's, which left no room for either the grotesque or the melancholic. The *Carceri*, especially, convey a grandiose spectacle of the battle between freedom and necessity: man, though his aspirations may reach to the heavens, has always to experience suppression by Chronos' powers. The interplay between hope and despair in plainly metaphysic proportions contribute to the concept of the sublime in art, or, as Martin Christadler has emphasized, the *Carceri* confront the viewer with a dialectic between escape and negation.[44] There are steps and staircases which seem to lead to a destination, but Piranesi's spaces and their inbuilt structures present gaps, dead ends, abolishments of any spatial "procedure." Every bias is cancelled by its opposite. A rope gives rise to both the associations of hanging and of swinging out through a breach in the battlement (figure 2). There is, however, no definite possibility of breaking out of the prison because of the principle of reflexivity, which simply determines all flight, progress, and captivity as products of the human mind itself.

The *Carceri* are not actual prisons, but fantastic constructions of imprison-
ment and escape in constant opposition. Norbert Miller has articulated their
importance for the Romantics:

> Not until Romanticism did this cycle reach its almost legendary impor-
> tance as one of the earliest and most sinister products of pre-romantic
> ideology. They rediscovered their own nightmares, their own horror of,
> and secret desire for, a distorted reality where the borderline between
> inner and outer world had disappeared, the game with the powerful
> sphere of the subconscious, which through the haschisch or opium in-
> duced intoxication liberates itself from the tight grasp of reason. Pira-
> nesi's *Carceri* became a hieroglyphic text for the changing generations
> of the artistic avantgarde, a text about the secrets of a reality which
> were mastered by the subject only in appearance; they became a coded
> message, the decoding of which promised insight into the individual
> existence.[45]

We cannot then refer to Piranesi as an artist of affirmation. He is much more
the artist who conveys how startling and frightening the uncertainty of language is. He is more closely connected with the Atomism of Democritus than
with the Christian conviction of an eschatological "safety net." Atomism is
the "subject's unprotected fear of an empty cosmos, being caught in an incessantly regenerating chaos."[46] Constancy is found neither in man nor in the
world, but only in atoms, the indivisible unit. Constant growth and decay
then become a premise adding to the uncertainties of the spatial world in
which man exists. Time and space take on importance not only as ideologies
of existence but also of a possible non-existence.[47]

Whereas the brilliance and unfilled architectural space still evident in the
first edition of the *Carceri* stand in obvious juxtaposition to infinity, the plates
of the second edition take on the shape of the worlds in which there is no
difference between a "within" and a "without." The world of the image
converges with that of the prison—there are no more allusions to alternatives.
Lord Clark correctly wrote of the *Carceri* series: "Every square inch is made
horribly factual, so that one cannot avoid climbing up those spiral staircases
and hurrying along those terrible dizzying gangways which end in air."[48]
Piranesi's prisons paint a world in which everything is architecture, in which
enormous arches merge into one another transversing changing shades of light
and dark (figure 3). One penetrates into different dimensions of depth, down
secretive steps that disappear into darkness, or up towards ledges and bridges
also lost in obscurity long before one can even suspect the presence of a ceiling.

Hans Hollander, in his essay "The Image in the Theory of the Fantastic"
("Das Bild in der Theorie des Phantastischen"), lets the *Carceri* speak through
a number of interesting extracts from Lars Gustafson's essay "About the Fan-

Figure 3. Giovanni Battista Piranesi, *Carceri*, Plate VII. Photograph courtesy of the New York Public Library. Photo: Jamie McEwen.

tastic in Literature." The fantastic, he specifies, is able to arouse fear; it is surrounded with coldness. It transposes its focus to a point outside the text, outside that which has been expressed, even outside grammar itself. The fantastic in literature finds a congenial parallel or anticipation in Piranesi's *Carceri*. Fear, dread, eerieness are as recognizable in Piranesi's work as they are in the Gothic or fantastic novel. The phenomenon of the labyrinth is to be found in both disciplines.[49] Gustafson's concluding thought very suggestively proposes that the language of Piranesi's *Carceri* is no longer able to communicate an immediate meaning to the viewer and that it points toward that which cannot be stated, i.e., to a language that does not yet exist, to a statement which has not been made nor cannot be made yet. A language is only a screen which selectively reflects objects. Just as is expressed in the last sentence of Ludwig Wittgenstein's *Tractatus logico-philosophicus* (1918), we cannot conceive of objects that our language cannot cope with: "What we cannot express, we must be silent about." The question remains whether it is possible to transform silence into utterable silence, so that one could unlock a "tacit knowledge" from fantastic art and or pictorial representations.[50]

The symbolism of the *Carceri* contradicts Gustafson's statement precisely because there never is any notion of a ceiling on the prisons: because of the conditions of our existence and the consequences of our own ideas, we are simply prisoners of space and time. Man cannot break through the limits of his ideology, or his cognition, or his language. The "estrangement" of Piranesi's genius is based on having made all these problems accessible to the modern consciousness without being comparative in his description. The truth that Piranesi offers is rather like Lord Byron's, about which Goethe once remarked to Eckermann, "only, one does not feel well at ease with it" (Goethe to Eckermann, November 29, 1826). Ivan Nagel makes Piranesi's principle theme the breaking of limits:

> His graphic work has a singular theme. Structure as transgression, as incomprehensible will and failure. The will and the failure divide both of Piranesi's genres: Construction as Plan, Construction as Ruins. . . . The fate of the plan is the ruins, the demon of the ruins is the plan.[51]

With this in mind Piranesi's landscapes of ruins do not come across as snapshots of a historical situation, but rather as an elucidation of the "longue durée" of the historical process. In the landscapes, as in the *Carceri*, time is made spatial. Piranesi rises to the monumental in the late realistic views of the *Carceri*. Impressive walls tower on top of each other in his prisons, but are always broken. His spaces are designed for an aimless wandering which finds a close parallel in the genre of the Gothic novel — in William Beckford's 1786 novel, *Vathek*, for example. Traveling in the realm of Eblis, Kalif Vathek experiences the unprecedented glamour and luxury of a subterranean, labyrinthine palace, piled high with treasures. But hope is not possible in his directionless roaming: it must be interpreted as a sign of damnation. It is interesting to note that Beckford knew Piranesi's work very well indeed.[52] It might also be noted that Beckford built his Fonthill Abbey as a mixture of monastery, castle, and cathedral in overwhelming proportions—a structure in which he suffered his loneliness and took pleasure in excess, one which makes Horace Walpole's little castle Strawberry Hill look like a gothic toy.[53] The massive structures which are so apparent in the realistic landscapes and in the later *Carceri*, are complemented by Piranesi's predilection for openness and limit-lessness. We can recognize that which Edmund Burke calls the Sublime, de-fined by "infinity" and "power." [54] The artistic imagination bursts through the regularity of classical architecture by the arrangements of rooms and spiral movements. Thus the geometrical harmony of the Proportionists gives way to an alteration which Thomas De Quincey, elucidating the objects of the *Carceri*, characterized as a "progressive power and conquered opposition." [55]

One would, however, underrate Piranesi's mastership as an architect and as a geometrist, if one assumed his distortions of classical harmony and per-spective to be mere products of arbitrariness. Under no circumstances may one forget that Piranesi controlled the central perspective thoroughly. The key for explaining the *Carceri* is that Piranesi transformed a given central perspective thus rendered no longer visible. In other words, Piranesi first con-ceptualized the *Carceri* with a central perspective and subsequently worked out his geometric displacements.[56] Piranesi's alteration of the central perspec-tive could be read as the addition of a fourth dimension, namely that of time.

Thomas De Quincey did not comment on Piranesi's startling of geometry, but he tried to assess the *Carceri* from the point of view of individual psy-chology. His remarks concerning Piranesi constitute an important statement from an English Romantic attempting to read the *Carceri* as the results of hallucinations or feverish delirium. This view of Piranesi says something about reception in the Romantic era, but does not hold its own against the current Piranesi research, which interprets the *Carceri* as the creations of a fully con-scious artistic mind. However, the difference between levels of consciousness is a troublesome one to define and De Quincey's view of Piranesi is not to be overlooked.

Many years ago, when I was looking over Piranesi's *Antiquities of Rome*, Mr Coleridge, who was standing by, described to me a set of plates by that artist, called his *Dreams*, and which recalled the scenery of his own visions during the delirium of a fever. Some of them (I describe only from memory of Mr Coleridge's account) represented vast gothic halls; on the floor of which stood all sorts of engines and machinery, wheels, cables, pulleys, levers, catapults, etc., etc., expressive of enormous power put forth, and resistance overcome. Creeping along the sides of the walls you perceived a staircase; and upon it, groping his way upwards, was

Piranesi himself: follow the stairs a little further, and you perceive it come to a sudden and abrupt termination, without any balustrade and allowing no step onwards to him who had reached the extremity, except into the depth below. Whatever is to become of poor Piranesi, you suppose, at least, that his labours must in some way terminate here. But raise your eyes, and behold a second flight of stairs still higher on which again Piranesi is perceived, but this time standing on the very brink of the abyss. Again elevate your eye, and a still more aerial flight of stairs is beheld: and again is poor Piranesi busy on his aspiring labours: and so on, until the unfinished stairs and Piranesi both are lost in the utter gloom of the hall. With the same power of endless growth and self-reproduction did my architecture proceed in dreams. In the early stages of my malady the splendours of my dreams were indeed chiefly architectural: and I beheld such pomp of cities and palaces as was never yet beheld by the waking eye, unless in the clouds.[57]

Thomas De Quincey's "Opium Eater" reinterprets Piranesi with an oriental vision as he describes the *Carceri* as figments of an imagination that had been sensitized to the overdimensional and superhuman through intoxication. It is very tempting thus to connect Piranesi with Beckford, Coleridge, and possibly with Byron. But neither the influence of "opium" nor the concept of the "gothic" are really applicable to Piranesi. "The gothic" might apply as a metaphor of "height," reminding us that architectural height was seen as non-form[58] by the English Augustans and was not subject to an aesthetic re-evaluation until the early Romantic. The *Carceri* could then be called gothic only in a figurative sense, if compared with the spatial conception in the gothic novel.[59]

De Quincey correctly recognized the ominous in the *Carceri*, called forth by the constant transcendence of spatial limitations. The spaces suggest a state of suspension, repeatedly renewed by the co-existence of greatness and destruction: "These violations of visional logic in no way lessen their expressive power."[60] Already Horace Walpole had written with admiration of Piranesi's *Carceri* in the fourth volume of his *Anecdotes of Painting* (1771):

The sublime dream of Piranesi, who seems to have conceived visions of Rome beyond what is boasted in the meridian of its splendour. Savage as Salvator Rosa, fierce as Michael Angelo, and exuberant as Rubens, *he has imagined scenes that would startle geometry*, and exhaust the Indies to realize. He piles palaces on bridges, and temples on palaces, and scales Heaven with mountains of edifices. Yet what taste in his boldness! What labour and thought both in his rashness and details.[61]

Walpole was an astute and clever observer. His remarks on the law-defying geometry of Piranesi are clearsighted. Walpole also recognized Piranesi's giganto-mania, when he describes him as someone who scales the heavens. With good reason, he points to a situation in Piranesi's work which mythologically speaking could be said to predate the Olympian Gods. It is the Titanic in Piranesi's renditions which distinguishes them, but also gives them a sense of the tragic: fulfillment and endurance stand in an antagonistic relationship to man's "heaven-assaulting" will. And Walpole's comment that the *Carceri* "startle geometry" is fitting, especially when one considers Ulya Vogt-Göknil's comment that Piranesi had depicted non-Euclidean spaces.[62] This point of view was also taken by Hans Hollander and interpretively expanded to show that Piranesi's architectural polysyllogism points towards the principle of relativity.[63] The continuously transcending expansion of spaces thoroughly questions the theoretical and ontological concepts of man. Just as in Bruno's universe there exists a multiplicity of sun-systems without a center and without a periphery, Piranesi's perceivable space expands in the imagination to such a degree that an equivalent sensual capacity for its perception becomes a problem. The transition from Romanticism to Nihilism is already anticipated in Piranesi's work.

Absolute confinement, simultaneously arousing the idea of liberty, is simply transmitted to the observer by means of the prison metaphor. As Andräs Horn has written in his essay "Literature and Freedom":

> Cages, prisons, and scenes of incarceration therefore can become powerful devices for dramatizing notions of liberty, especially when these devices are to have a sharp emotional impact.[64]

Liberty, therefore, should not be understood to represent an alternative world, but rather an alternative practice which realizes itself when the appeal made by art is accepted.[65]

The fact that Piranesi's *Carceri* are built mostly with blockstone, jointed by wooden bridges and beam projectiles fitted with a multiplicity of iron reinforcements, would appear to suggest the open palaces of the Age of Iron, a time in which the incarceration of man stands in closest relationship to his knowledge and ability.[66] Not without reason is it suggested that with the transformation and debasement in the purity of metals—gold/silver/bronze/iron—a parallel can be seen to the intensified harnessing of man to what Kafka identifies as self-manufactured complexities.[67] The *Carceri*, then, anticipate the monstrousness of the Age of Positivism. They represent industrial miracle-works and implements of torture (figure 4), and thereby bear witness to an age of material and mechanical enslavement that was to become reality in the nineteenth and twentieth centuries.

By the same token, the immense and terror-arousing command of the subject matter can be perceived as a form of dread, long before existentialism was able to reflect it. Consequently, the terror the "I" exercises over the hu-

Figure 4. Giovanni Battista Piranesi, *Carceri*, Plate XVI. Photograph courtesy of the New York Public Library. Photo: Jamie McEwen.

man imagination turns into the terror of the masses, who are gripped by the powerful machinery of modern organizations and their modes of production. The extension of the *Carceri* into a Kafkaesque world is not only plausible, but it is to be viewed as an indication of Piranesi's foresight.

Dürrenmatt's comment that writers should be categorized, not by chronology, but by their primal structures, motives, and images, is eminently appropriate to Piranesi's case. Dürrenmatt's self-definition applies to Piranesi as to no other eighteenth-century representative of the fine arts:

> While I depict the world, into which I see myself placed, as a labyrinth, I try to achieve a distance from it, to step back, to fix my eyes upon it as would a tamer of a wild animal. The world, as I experience it, I confront with a counter-world of my own invention.[68]

Piranesi's art, then, grows out of the struggle between the attempt to gain an objective distance and the impossibility of attaining such distance. At its foundation, the concept of dread converges with the recognition of historicity and so marks a significant point in the development of the modern perspective.

Translation by Erika Segall and Vibeke Rützou Keith

Notes

1   In the eighteenth century Louis XIV of France made his idea of absolutism visible in the symmetrical structure of Versailles, the "absolute" architectural, symbolical, and political center of which was the king's bedroom. See Wolf Lepenies, *Melancholie und Gesellschaft* (Frankfurt, 1972), p. 66–75.

2   Norbert Miller, *Archäologie des Traums, Versuch über Piranesi* (Frankfurt/Berlin, 1981), p. 35.

3   Blaise Pascal, *Pensées*, ed. Jacques Chevalier (Paris, 1965), p. 59.

4   Miller, *Archäologie des Traums*, p. 10.

5   I quote from *Three Gothic Novels*, ed. Peter Fairclough (Harmondsworth, 1968), p. 17. The Reverend Cole (1714–82) was a friend of Walpole's (1717–97), whom he had met at Eton College. Cole became a Tory country parson and was an ardent collector of antiquities as well as an antiquarian. Walpole chose Cole as one of his correspondents on antiquarian subjects. See R. W. Ketton-Cremer, *Horace Walpole, A Biography* (London, 1964), pp. 184–86.

6   Johann Wolfgang Goethe, *Italienische Reise* (Berlin, 1966), 3:177.

7   Hans Blumenberg, *Arbeit am Mythos* (Frankfurt, 1979), p. 180.

8   See Pierre Grimal, *Auf der Suche nach dem antiken Italien* (Bergisch Gladbach, 1978), p. 245.

9   Michael McCarthy, "Sir Roger Newdigate and Piranesi," *Burlington Magazine* 114 (1972), p. 470.

10   Carl Justi, *Winckelmann und seine Zeitgenossen* (Cologne, 1956), 3:436.

11   *Ibid.*

12   See Marcia Pointon, "Romanticism in English Art," in *The Romantics*, ed. Stephen Prickett (London, 1981), pp. 77–80.

13   See Reinhart Koselleck, "Geschichte, Geschichten und formale Zeitstrukturen," in *Geschichte—Ereignis und Erzählung* (Munich, 1973), p. 216.

14   Edmund Burke, *A Philosophical Enquiry into the Origin of Our Ideas of the Sublime and Beautiful* (London/New York, 1967), p. 45.

15   *Ibid.*, p. 39.

16   *Ibid.*

17   Justi, *Winckelmann und seine Zeitgenossen*, pp. 436–37.

18   The most widespread handbook in Germany, Wilhelm Lübke's *Grundriss der Kunstgeschichte* (1882), does not even mention Piranesi. See Jakob Burckhardt, *Der Cicerone* (Leipzig, 1924), p. 377.

19   John Harris, "Le Geay, Piranesi, and International Neo-Classicism in Rome, 1740–1750," in *Essays in the History of Architecture Presented to Rudolf Wittkower*, ed. Douglas Fraser, Howard Hibbert, and Milton J. Levine (London, 1967), p. 195.

20   Reinhard Bentmann and Michael Muller, *Die Villa als Herrschaftsarchitektur* (Frankfurt, 1970), pp. 29–38.

21   C. Fensterbusch and R. Heidenreich, "Vitruv," *dtv-Lexikon der Antike. Philosophie, Literatur, Wissenschaft* (Munich, 1978), 4:341; and Ernesto Grassi, *Die Theorien des Schönen in der Antike* (Cologne, 1980), p. 209.

22   Miller, *Archäologie des Traums*, p. 24.

23 *Ibid.*, p. 25.
24 Johann Gottfried Herder, "Shakespeare," in *Sämmtliche Werke*, ed. B. Suphan (Berlin, 1891), 5:218–23.
25 Albert Giesecke, *Giovanni Battista Piranesi*, p. 22. Also see Otto-Wilhelm von Vacano, *Die Etrusker in der Welt der Antike* (Hamburg, 1959).
26 See Brian Fothergill, *Sir William Hamilton, Diplomat, Naturforscher, Kunstsammler* (Munich, 1971), pp. 121 ff. About the tradition of British journeys to Rome, see Thomas Frank, "Elizabethan Travellers in Rome," in *English Miscellany*, ed. Mario Praz (Rome, 1953), 4:95–132; and L. D. Ettlinger, "With All Convenient Speed to Rome," in *ibid.*, 4:133–46.
27 Hans Blumberg, *Säkularisierung und Selbstbehauptung* (Frankfurt, 1974), p. 122.
28 See Edgar Wind, *Pagan Mysteries in the Renaissance* (Oxford, 1980); and Paul O. Kristeller, *Humanismus und Renaissance* (Munich, 1961), pp. 50–68.
29 See Ernst Cassirer, *The Platonic Renaissance in England* (New York, 1970).
30 Peter Gay, *The Enlightenment, An Interpretation* (London, 1973), 1:63.
31 *Ibid.*, pp. 72–126.
32 Miller, *Archäologie des Traums*, p. 381; Mario Praz, *Liebe, Tod und Teufel, Die Schwarze Romantik* (Munich, 1970), 2:375–79; Maurice Levy, *Le Roman "Gothique" Anglais 1764–1824* (Toulouse, 1968), pp. 273, 634.
33 See Fothergill, *Sir William Hamilton*, p. 147; Basil Williams, *The Whig Supremacy, 1714–1760* (Oxford, 1965), p. 404; Grimal, *Auf der Suche nach dem antiken Italien*, pp. 110–63, 197–211.
34 Damie Stillmann, "Robert Adam and Piranesi," in *Essays in the History of Architecture Presented to Rudolf Wittkower*, p. 197.
35 *Ibid.*, p. 198.
36 *Ibid.*, p. 201.
37 Olive Cook, *The English Country House* (London, 1974), p. 185.
38 Thomas Gray, *The Complete Poems of Thomas Gray*, ed. James Reeves (London, 1973), p. 26.
39 Giesecke, *Giovanni Battista Piranesi*, p. 38.
40 *Ibid.*, p. 116.
41 Kenneth Clark, *The Romantic Rebellion* (London, 1975), pp. 50, 52.
42 Miller, *Archäologie des Traums*, p. 9.
43 See Hans Robert Jauss, ed. *Die nicht mehr schönen Künste* (Munich, 1968).
44 See Martin Christadler, "Giovanni Battista Piranesi und die Architekturmetapher der Romantik," in *Miscellanea Anglo-Americana*, Festschrift for Helmut Viebrock (Munich, 1974), pp. 78–108.
45 Miller, *Archäologie des Traums*, pp. 11–12.
46 See *Griechische Atomisten*, ed. Fritz Jürss, Reimar Müller, Ernst Günther Schmidt (Leipzig, 1973), p. 83.
47 Miller, *Archäologie des Traums*, p. 73.
48 I quote from Clark, *The Romantic Rebellion*, p. 50.
49 Hans Hollander, "Das Bild in der Theorie des Phantastischen," in *Phantastik in Literatur und Kunst* (Darmstadt, 1980), p. 71.
50 See Dan Sperber, *Rethinking Symbolism* (Cambridge, 1975), especially the preface and chapter 1; Edmund Leach, "Michelangelo's *Genesis*, Structuralist Comments on the Paintings on the Sistine Chapel Ceiling," *Times Literary Supplement* (March 18, 1977), pp. 312–13.
51 Ivan Nagel, "Der Mythos des Baumeisters, Zu Piranesi's 200. Todestag am 4 November," *Die Zeit* (November 3, 1978), p. 55.

52 See Jorgen Anderson, "Giant Dreams, Piranesi's Influence in England," in *English Miscellany*, pp. 49–60.

53 See Heinfried Wischermann, *Fonthill Abbey, Studien zur profanen Neugotik Englands im 18. Jahrhundert* (Freiburg im Breisgau, 1979).

54 See my *Der Gotische Roman und die Ästhetik des Bösen* (Darmstadt, 1975), pp. 48–55.

55 Thomas De Quincey, *Confessions of an English Opium-Eater* (London, 1886).

56 Miller, *Archäologie des Traums*, p. 418.

57 De Quincey, *Confessions of an English Opium-Eater*, pp. 92–93.

58 See Josef Haslag, *"Gothic" im 17. und 18. Jahrhundert* (Cologne/Graz, 1963).

59 See Klaus Poenicke, "Schönheit im Schosse des Schreckens, Raumgefüge und Menschen im englischen Schauerroman," *Archiv für das Studium der neueren Sprachen und Literaturen* 207 (1970), pp. 1-19.

60 Lorenz Eitner, "Cages, Prisons, and Captives in Eighteenth Century Art," in *Images of Romanticism, Verbal and Visual Affinities*, ed. Karl Kroeber and William Walling (New Haven/London, 1978), p. 21.

61 I quote from *Three Gothic Novels*, ed. Fairclough, p. 16 ff. my italics.

62 Ulya Vogt-Göknil, *Giovanni Battista Piranesi: Carceri* (Zurich, 1958), p. 28.

63 Hollander, "Das Bild in der Theorie des Phantastischen," p. 72 ff.

64 Andräs Horn, "Literatur und Freiheit," *Sprachkunst* 12 (1981), pp. 186–211.

65 Eitner, "Cages, Prisons, and Captives in Eighteenth Century Art," p. 14.

66 *Ibid.*, p. 21.

67 See Franz Kafka, *Erwählte Prosa* (Frankfurt, 1965), especially "In der Strafkolonie," pp. 9–47.

68 Friedrich Dürrenmatt, *Stoffe I–III* (Zurich, 1981), p. 77.

Fraternity and Anxiety, Charles Allston Collins and *The Electric Telegraph* / *Martin Meisel*

Among the manuscripts associated with the Pre-Raphaelite Brotherhood now in the Huntington Library is a document rich in implication on a painting that was never painted. The document, printed here for the first time, furnishes the text for this essay. But the painting that was never painted is also a text in its own right, perhaps all the more so because it remained in the realm of ideas—conceptual art by force of circumstance.

Knowledge of the painting comes from language about an image that tells a story; but language that is also charged with the artist's own disabling anxiety and desire, the substance of another, concurrent story, about himself. Knowledge of the painting comes as well from several drawings that survive from the hundreds that Collins seems to have made. Despite these drawings, and despite evidence that the artist began working on canvas, the idea of the painting (in the language of the nineteenth century) never achieved a completed pictorial realization, although with implications, contexts, and indeed a certain prospective importance in its time and place, it had a shadowy life of its own.

The painting was never realized, not because of any intrinsic flaw or impossibility in the concept, but because of an inhibition in the painter, an uncertainty in the individual that opened through some unbalancing strain in the dynamics of mutual support within the first avant-garde group in the modern experience. The part played in the debacle by fraternal relations is critical to a reading of the documentary text and—if I am correct—exemplary and revealing with respect to the long succession of similar groups in modern art and the fates of their members and aspirants. The written document is a systematic inquest into the matter of originality. The imagined painting, by no great coincidence, is a vivid representation of unresolved anxiety.

The painting is also a text in its own right because it was intended to tell a story. More precisely, it was to have embodied a situation that was the concentration of a story in its crisis. This situation was the greater part of the idea of the painting, its originating thought and its conceptual center. The idea of the painting, then, was not an arrangement in line and color, not an effect of light and shade, not a matter of style or expression, not an investigation of nature or the fixing of an evanescent scene, but a narrative situation.

For the beholder to apprehend the painting, to introject and respond to it, he would have to read it for its story as he would have to read a novel, or, in the nineteenth-century theater, the arrested image encapsulated in a "tableau." If a painting of another kind, without narrative content, had never been realized—one whose "idea" was clouds reflected in water, for example—it would probably have achieved much less presence and specificity than this situational painting. It would offer less to know and judge, and provide less of a text for commentary.

The artist in question was Charles Allston Collins, whose best-known work, *Convent Thoughts* (1851), had earlier shared the sensation and opprobrium of the third Pre-Raphaelite incursion into the annual Royal Academy exhibitions (figure 1).[1] The painting not painted was one whose "dramatic agent," in Collins' phrase, was "the Electric Telegraph"; and it is likely that *The Electric Telegraph* was to have been its title as well.[2] The idea for the painting came to Collins in the latter part of 1854. He intended initially to have it on canvas for the Royal Academy exhibition of May 1855, and he still had that expectation in February when he first mentioned the painting in a letter to Holman Hunt, whose Pre-Raphaelitism had taken him to Jerusalem. But Collins missed the sending-in date for 1855, and as the 1856 exhibition approached, his telegraph painting was still unrealized. It was then (April 22, 1856) that he wrote a careful assessment of the project and its history, and dispatched that to Hunt, now back in England, for review. Hunt wrote a reassuring reply which is probably not extant, but whose burden can be deduced from Collins' acknowledgment. On May 10, the day the important weeklies (many of them shaking their heads over Hunt's *Scapegoat*) carried their first exhibition notices, Collins wrote back:

> My dear Hunt
> Many thanks for your friendship in making your way through the documents, and for your encouraging review of them. I only write this to thank you. I must see you to talk the matter over a little. I see that you recommend a healthful rest. I do not think it would do me much good. Neither rest nor travelling alter facts. I ever find them awaiting me on my return. The rest over—the journey concluded—you find care perched upon the top of your easel when you enter your studio or earlier still he is sitting on the end of your bed and strikes you a blow that turns you sick when you wake in the morning.[3]

Collins—who signs himself "yours ever affectionately"—says he will present himself at Hunt's lodgings for further counsel. What that counsel was we can guess, for it is clear that Hunt located the cause of his friend's anxiety, not in the problematic originality of the painting, but in Collins' mental state. Whatever Hunt's counsel, however, it was without therapeutic effect, for Collins never found, then or later, sufficient respite from his Fuselian nightmare to

Figure 1. Charles Allston Collins, *Convent Thoughts* (1851), oil on canvas, 82.6 × 57.8 cm., Oxford, Ashmolean Museum. By permission of the Visitors.

complete the telegraph painting, or any other. Instead—in crude synopsis—he gave up painting, set up as a writer like his older brother Wilkie, began publishing in Charles Dickens' weeklies, and married the boss's daughter. His success was modest.

Collins saw *The Electric Telegraph*—rightly I believe—as the painting that promised to be the making of him. His confidence was unqualified, and it was founded upon the manifest excellence, in that time and that place, of its narrative and pictorial idea. The two aspects of the idea that assured a great success were the structured intensity and affective interest of the narrative situation, and the bold modernity of the "dramatic agent." These are the focal concerns in the first two parts of the succeeding discussion, which start out from the idea of the painting and are largely contextual and historical. The third part, "Liberty and Fraternity," is in a measure psychosocial, concerned with group character and dynamics, and arguing the primacy of fraternal as opposed to progenitive anxieties. The fourth part, "Being There," attempts to educe another, more personal element in Collins' crisis. Here Collins' unexecuted painting is set in the light of his earlier work, and what seem to be refractions of a latent private anxiety expressed in his pictorial imagery. The anxiety that was to have been the dominant emotion in *The Electric Telegraph* was embedded in a development of that imagery. Consequently the fifth part, "Sticking Fast," brings the discussion back to the abandoned painting with the help of the extant drawings and the document that someone other than Collins, probably Hunt, labeled "Charlie Collins Apology for his Art." The sixth and last part attends to some echoes and refractions of Collins' terminal ordeal as a painter during his subsequent career as a writer.

The principal document on Collins' ordeal remains his "Apology," which follows in the appendix. Unlike the painting and the conjectures to which its nonexistence give rise, the "Apology" and the drawings have an actual rather than a hypothetical reality. Despite their position in this text (a matter of convenience) the "Apology" and the drawings are where one properly should begin.

A Modern-Life Painting

The daring modernity of his pictorial idea was not a source of anxiety for Collins. If anything, he turned to this modernity for relief and reassurance, to distract himself from his uneasiness. So much appears in a letter, written while Hunt was still in the East, wherein Collins first tells Hunt about his current project. The letter is long and contains important news of Millais, Rossetti, and others of the connection. One thing he could have wished for, Collins remarks, is a definite prospect of Hunt's return:

But there is more hint of that in a letter which Egg[4] sent me to read, in which, by the bye, I noted what was cause of comfort to me, I mean indications that I do not stand alone in the extreme suffering and anxiety which painting causes me and which I never have found so wearing and torturing as in what I am at this time engaged in. It is a picture in which the Electric Telegraph plays a prominent part and every day for months past or almost every day has been loaded with anxiety so great that I almost wonder that I have not given up what so distresses me. But the subject is one so pregnant with the greatest interest to me that I go on thankful that I have got it. People are apt to groan over these times. They look back to the old days when half a town was voluntarily engaged in piling up a Cathedral whose strength and beauty we cannot approach and then they divide their time between, the aforesaid lamentations that we produce nothing like these now, and miserable attempts at pseudo Gothic dilettante imitations—forgetting (narrow minded souls that they are) that we have now things around us, natural emanations from the modern mind, just as glorious as these triumphs of masonry, or rather much more so. For surely this little mahogany Instrument not two foot high which tells the wife whether the wreck she has had news of has made her a widow or whether her children are fatherless through the railway accident which has befallen the Train in which she knew her husband was travelling[—]something of this is my present subject—which summons a physician to one in extremity or one to a death bed whose pardon the dying man desires—surely the Instrument which does these and a thousand other marvels—setting time and distance at defiance is a thing to glory in. This, and the lighting of this town by gas, and our railways and machinery are the natural production of the nineteenth century mind just as these buildings so justly admired were of the thirteenth—and it is worse than useless to ignore these colossal achievements of our own day and try to force back the stream to its source again [,] an experiment the pitiable results of which there are abundant opportunities of judging of in every cheap new Gothic structure which is added to the list of London edifices. For the right view of such wonders as the Electric Telegraph &c refer to Exodus 31. 1 to 7. a most wonderful passage.[5]

The biblical passage celebrates artisans and craftsmen in the service of the Lord.[6] Collins applies it conspicuously, not to the artist as such, not even to the ideal artist/artisan of the past who captured the imaginations of Ruskin and Morris, but to the makers of the new technology: inventors, industrial organizers, and engineers. Collins' explicit rejection of both historical nostalgia for the era of great communal art and present-day Gothic archaizing is actually a little surprising. (Ruskin's *On the Nature of the Gothic* from *The*

Stones of Venice had just appeared as a separate publication in 1854, and the archaizing impulse, though with a revolutionary rationale, was strong in the initial phase of Pre-Raphaelitism, as both the name and the paintings testify.) Between its positive and negative assertions, Collins' entire homily deserves notice as an artistic manifesto for the painting of modern life, an enterprise still seen in the England of the 1850s as fraught with difficulties that disqualified it as Art.

Yet a change was in the air. After a decade of longing to paint contemporary life but shrinking from the ugliness of modern dress, W. P. Frith had only just exhibited the first of his modern-life panoramas, *Life at the Sea-Side* (he was still far from the modernity of *The Railway Station*). In the same year, 1854, Holman Hunt had exhibited *The Awakening Conscience*, whose fallen-woman subject, here in a brand new suburban interior, would be a characteristic motif of modern-life art and literature. Ford Madox Brown's *Work* and Rossetti's *Found* had been begun, but remained incomplete. Millais, however, was hard at work on *The Rescue*, dramatizing the possibilities of modern-day heroism in the figure and action of a fireman who is rescuing two children from a blaze and delivering them to their delirious mama.

There had been earlier ventures in modern-life painting in nineteenth-century England, but they had been rare, and a program for such painting comparable even to Hogarth's had yet to emerge when Collins declared himself to Hunt. In fact no school of modern-life realists with a shared stylistic rationale would appear until the 1870s, as the group of artists associated with *The Graphic*. The mid-fifties were nevertheless something of a turning point, and it is noteworthy that all the major Pre-Raphaelites, and Brown who was their mentor and associate, at this moment set their hands to works that had a modern-life character. Collins' manifesto, along with the aggressive modernism of his pictorial idea, bid fair to put him near the forefront of a fruitful and important development in the art of the century.

The situation in Collins' painting was to be read from setting and configuration. According to his explanatory account, having thought of the electric telegraph as a dramatic agent, he decided that "the subject should be a wife enquiring by means of it after her husbands safety."[7] He thought first to make her the wife of a traveler by sea responding to news of a shipwreck. "Then I thought it would be more completely a subject of our own day if it was a Railway accident which had caused her fears." The setting then had to be a railway-station telegraph office with the instrument itself made prominent. The configuration had to involve the instrument, the clerk, and the wife, though for a while Collins intended a third figure, "her child reading one of the advertisements in large letters which the Railway Accident Insurance Company post about stations." The child would be present, one deduces, not simply for pathos, nor only to complete the threatened domestic circle, but to give visual emphasis to an element of the setting that supplied essential specification, of the place and nature of the wife's anxiety. By reminding the viewer of the frequency and fatality of accidents on the modern miracle, the characteristic poster gives a clue whose generality the reader of the picture converts into particularity, a clue that structures the narrative situation. The woman must be there because she is fearful concerning *one* particular railway accident. A narrative painting, Millais' *Huguenot*, for example, that is not simply illustration of a familiar literary text, renders history or general experience as a story of individuals, and invokes history or general experience to make that story readable.

Collins reveals that among his first steps was to investigate the locale and the operation. The desire for authenticity in a modern-life painting had much in common with the archaeological and ethnographic urge that drove Hunt to the Holy Land; but Collins could expect his audience to be equipped with better information on the authentic features of the local scene. High among the pleasures of his painting would be, necessarily, the pleasure of recognition. In the station office, Collins discovered that the telegraph clerk writes down the message word by word as it comes over the machine, and that an anxious individual might watch over the clerk's shoulder (see figure 2). That discovery set the essential configuration, which remained constant through all Collins' fretting over position and detail. Collins further perceived "that it would be a wonderful increase of the dramatic effect of the picture if this writing were shown." From that observation followed the obvious corollary of using a scale that would make the writing easily legible. It should be noted that Collins uses the term "effect," not in the painterly sense having to do with immediate visual impact or the manipulation of light and shade, but with reference to the impact of the narrative image.

At this point in the history of drama, especially popular drama, "effect" and "situation" were the watchwords of the art, and were virtually identified.[8] The intensity of a dramatic effect was much influenced by the implicit temporal pressure on a visually articulated situation moving towards dissolution or resolution. Situation required a moment of poise, where the forces were in equilibrium. But drama—and narrative implication—depended on the conviction that the configuration embodying the situation was inherently unstable, that the moment would pass and the picture dissolve. The moment of arrest or equilibrium had to be plausible, but the "period" of the configuration, its implicit duration, was always in tension with the imminence (or desirability) of change, a tension that is the structural analogue of anxiety. Among the Pre-Raphaelites, Hunt would go furthest to intensify the imminence of change, by internalizing it in one of his figures, and psychologizing it. Millais took another route, creating impasse situations which nevertheless could not last, but whose effect was to mute action and extend pathos.

From the point of view of dramatic effect, the message coming over the machine ideally would resolve the situation at the next word. The reader-

Figure 2. Charles Allston Collins, Design for *The Electric Telegraph* (1), pen and ink, 24.3 × 14.8 cm., London, British Museum. By courtesy of the Trustees.

viewer of Collins' picture and the reader-protagonist within it would share knowledge and suspense. The "effect" would come through the viewer's empathy with the protagonist, whose anxiety and impatience would be at its height. Accordingly, Millais, who sometimes sat for the clerk, urged the model for the wife "to press closer to him to seem more eager," as Collins duly notes in his reckoning of originality. But shortening the period before the resolution, and so intensifying the emotion, did not mean favoring gestures and attitudes that expressed intensity at the expense of plausible duration. Plausible duration in gesture and attitude becomes all the more important, paradoxically, when situation as the vehicle of suspense is about to dissolve. So Collins, who was attracted to the notion of giving the lady a veil and having her lift it to see better, expresses a doubt to Millais "whether this was not too momentary an action for painting." Millais then played the lady "and assumed the action of one *holding up* a veil while following the words the man was writing rather than of one hastily throwing it back once for all." This tableau solution apparently appealed to Collins, for he worried that it continued to influence his drawing of the figure.

Sending and receiving telegraph messages from a telegraph station did serve suspenseful situations and incorporate the fascination of modern technology in later drama, as we shall see. All such uses exploit the temporal aspects of telegraphy, but aside from Collins' painting, none that I have noticed take advantage of the suspense available in syntax and word-by-word linearity. Perhaps only a painting could do so with maximum effect, by bringing the viewer to the very edge of a resolution, by putting before him (and the wife, whose anxiety would accordingly reach an extreme) a message that is one word short on a matter of life and death, and *remains* one word short despite the temporal pressure of the informing device.

In *Oedipus the King*, Sophocles' self-conscious characters create an intensifying pause in which they play the roles of poet and audience: "I am on the brink of dreadful speech," says the Messenger; "And I of dreadful hearing," says Oedipus. It is such a moment of high anxiety, of arrested, condensed, and heightened drama, but drama enhanced by the distinctive *techné* of modern life, that Collins intended to make everlasting.

Telegraph Drama

The efficacy of the electric telegraph as a dramatic agent was better established in life than in art when Collins conceived his painting. It was, in fact, its intervention in the denouement of a real-life criminal melodrama, rather than any immediate benefits to transport, commerce, or military intelligence, that established the electric telegraph in the British popular imagination as a modern wonder and a social benefit.

The first British patent for the device had been entered in 1837, and the first regularly working line was established in 1838 for the Great Western

Railway Company. The wire ran between Paddington and West Drayton, and was extended to Slough in 1842. The alliance with the railways, so important in Collins' conception, became the norm in this early development, thanks to rights-of-way; and the Paddington-Slough connection soon became famous.[9]

On New Year's Day, 1845, an ostensibly respectable Quaker named John Tawell, middle-aged and married, visited and poisoned a former servant named Sarah Hart in Slough, where she lived with her two young children. Tawell in his distinctive dress was seen leaving the premises just before the dying woman was discovered. A clergyman named Champneys then took a hand:

> Hearing of the suspicious death of the deceased, and that a person in the dress of a Quaker was the last man who had been seen to leave the house, I proceeded to the Slough station, thinking it likely he might proceed to town by the railway. I saw him pass through the office, when I communicated my suspicions to Mr. Howell, the superintendent at the station. He left for London in a first-class carriage. Mr. Howell then sent off a full description of his person, by means of the electric telegraph, to cause him to be watched by the police upon his arrival at Paddington.[10]

At Paddington Station, Sergeant Williams of the Railway Police waited on the platform, identified Tawell from the description, and followed him through a complicated course to a lodging house. (At one point the resourceful Williams collected Tawell's fare on an omnibus.) Williams reported by telegraph, and the next day, on orders from Slough, Tawell was arrested.[11] As the *Times* observed (January 4, 1845), "had it not been for the efficient aid of the electric telegraph, both at Slough and Paddington, the greatest difficulty as well as delay would have occurred in the apprehension of the party now in custody." By the time Tawell's story reached its punitive conclusion, the telegraph had been established in moral as well as social terms as a force for good, produced by human ingenuity, but working behind the scenes like Providence itself.

Credit for the invention of the electric telegraph and the right to its exploitation were notorious subjects of dispute, and one result is that England and America have different popular inventor-heroes as the creator of the device. Both Cooke and Wheatstone in England and Morse in America drew on technology and conceptions that had been developed by their predecessors, but as one historian put it, Cooke and Wheatstone's instrument was rather more of an "evolved" achievement than Morse's.[12] The result of Morse's relative originality was a design difference probably of greater importance to a painter or playwright than to an electrical engineer; a transatlantic difference that persisted into the decade of Collins' painting and affected its visual and dramatic conception. Morse's system and the first lines to embody it used an acoustic receiver for its familiar dot-dash code. The Cooke-Wheatstone system used a visual receiver, usually two dials with needles, and a visual code. The operator manipulated levers and read and decoded by eye rather than by ear (see figure 3). At least two different forms of such visual sending and receiving devices, one with its double dials manifest (see figure 4), appear in Collins' four extant drawings. It seems reasonable to suppose that in conceiving the electric telegraph as a visual system, Cooke and Wheatstone were affected by the proximity and importance of the modern semaphore system (also called a telegraph and where the name originated) which had been created in the crisis of the French Revolution, persisted in England for Admiralty matters until 1847, and flourished in France until 1852.[13]

It is significant that in the theater the electric telegraph made its effect in auditory terms even in England where the familiar system was visual. It is surprising, however, that the first playwright (a transatlantic figure) to exploit the drama of the electric telegraph waited until 1866, more than a decade after Collins had had his pictorial idea. By then the imaginative possibilities of the electric telegraph had already made themselves felt in literature; and the most notable of these early entries, ambivalent in its attitude, reflects the notoriety of the murder at Slough. In his flight by railway from the dead Judge Pyncheon in *The House of the Seven Gables* (1851), Clifford speaks of the liberating agency of "this admirable invention of the railroad," and then of the sublimation of matter by electricity, turning the whole world into a vibrating nerve, into thought. But, with his own case in mind, he deplores the debasement of "an almost spiritual medium, like the electric telegraph" into a source of anxiety when the murderer or bank robber fleeing by railway is deprived by its agency of his biblical city of refuge.[14]

The power to transcend distance and difference, abstracted and intensified, struck Dickens a decade later as an idea for the opening of a story. His biographer quotes from a "Book of Memoranda" a passage that Dickens probably entered in 1862:

> Open a story by bringing two strongly contrasted places and strongly contrasted sets of people, into the connexion necessary for the story, by means of an electric message. Describe the message — *be* the message — flashing along through space, over the earth, and under the sea.[15]

Through Dickens' gift of empathy with energy itself and his habit of informing the material and the phenomenal with ego, he projects an escape from the limits of prosaic representation as visionary as Clifford's spiritualism, but rather at odds with Collins' earlier pictorial conception. In Dickens' condensed idea, Collins' modern-life miracle is made strange, released from the ordinary and the familiar. But it was the ordinary and the familiar investing the technical miracle that Collins had conceived as the essence of his modern-life painting.

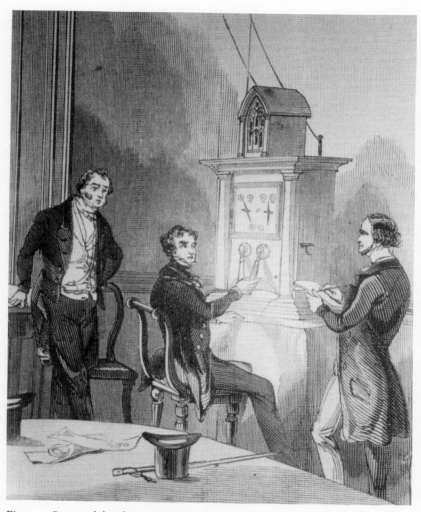

Figure 3. *Room of the Electric Telegraph, Nine Elms Station* (detail), wood engraving, *The Illustrated London News* 6 (April 12, 1845), p. 233.

Figure 4. Charles Allston Collins, Design for *The Electric Telegraph* (2), pen and ink, 18.9 × 14 cm., London, British Museum. By courtesy of the Trustees.

The potential of the electric telegraph for a scene of sustained dramatic effect only found expression in the modern theater with Dion Boucicault's *The Long Strike* (1866), an adaptation of Mrs. Gaskell's *Mary Barton*. The once-famous scene in the telegraph office in the fourth act was Boucicault's own invention, and characteristic of his interest as a playwright in the fruits of modern technology and modern organization. The dramatic situation is founded on the fact that the only witness who can save Jane Learoyd's sweetheart from the gallows has gone to take ship for distant parts. In the account of the *Times* reviewer (September 17, 1866):

> Off go the good-natured lawyer and his distress[ed] client to the telegraph office, and here we have an instance of the great effect which a bit of closely copied reality has upon a modern audience. The stage becomes, for the nonce, an actual telegraph office, with its clerks employed like real clerks, and its dials working with the correct click. Various difficulties seem to render hopeless all chance of communication with Johnny Reilly. Jane and her adviser have come too late, for the telegraphic message sent to Liverpool receives no response, and hence it is clear that the man at the Liverpool station is gone. Presently, however, a click is heard—the man has unexpectedly returned. But the good ship Eliza and Mary has already sailed. More despair. No, she can be overtaken by a pilot-boat, and the expenses of that mode of communication are at once deposited by the lawyer. The rise and fall of all these difficulties, accompanied by all the minutiae of telegraphic correspondence, raise the audience to the highest pitch of excitement, and there is no doubt that this scene will be considered the greatest attraction of the piece.[16]

The dramatic excitement of the scene is sustained by transmitted question and answer, mediated by the operator and intensified by the mechanics of transmission and reception and the necessity of translation. The pathos of the scene, however, had to be sustained by the figure with most to lose, Jane Learoyd, who variously falls on her knees, sobs, prays, swoons, listens breathlessly, and finally kisses her lawyer's hands as the scene closes. For the *Athenaeum* reviewer also this was "*the* scene of the piece," but "chiefly made so by Mrs. Boucicault's acting."[17]

Like the setting, the underlying structure of the scene, and the complex of emotions with which it is charged are essentially the same in Boucicault's play and in Collins' painting. But where the painter seeks intensity in the greatest temporal concentration, and finds it at the point of highest anxiety, the playwright seeks intensity by giving the situation temporal extension, sustaining an alternating flow of anxiety and release before permitting a resolution. Both painter and playwright so invite the viewer's sustained contemplation and participation. And both take advantage (as the man from the *Times* said) "of the great effect which a bit of closely copied reality has upon a modern audience" to bring the drama of anxiety home.[18]

The excitement and expectations generated by the electric telegraph were never greater than in the years when the Pre-Raphaelite revolution (among others) was taking shape. A writer of 1847 notes that all the telegraphs of old—beacon fires and semaphores—"are associated either with scenes of blood and rebellion, or the secret policy of governments," but that the electric telegraph, this "expanding nervous system of our island," is rather "the servant of the *people*," and bids fair to unite in peaceful confederation all men and all nations. "Such is, then, the power which the Prosperos of science have called up for the service of man. A spirit more marvellous than fairyland can show. An Ariel or a Puck to traverse the fields of air faster than a beam of light—a gnome who trudges through the solid earth to do our bidding [a reference to the grounding of the wire to complete the circuit]—a spirit who realises more than the visions of the poet, and who, when you call him from the vasty deep, *will* come." [19]

In the course of explaining the effects on transmission induced by atmospheric disturbances, another writer, a notable chemist and natural scientist himself, indulges in a similar flight of fancy. George Wilson in 1849 finds "something exciting in the contemplation of these strange atmospheric influences."

> It must be not a little startling to the drowsy occupant of some solitary telegraph station, to be roused from his midnight slumber by the spectral clanging of his signal bell, bidding him quail at the wild quiverings of the magnets, now swayed plainly by no mortal hands. An imaginative man might then well recall the legends which tell of disembodied souls sent back to this earth, to divulge some great secret of the world of spirits, and seeking in vain for means of utterance which shall be intelligible to those in the body. A philosopher, too, might accept and interpret the legend. For it is sober truth, that the apparently aimless and meaningless movements of the magnetic-needles when vibrating at such times, are, after all, the expressive finger-signs of a dumb alphabet, in which nature is explaining to us certain of her mysteries; and already, too, we are learning something of their significance.[20]

The natural philosopher here evokes two versions of the imagination, one, the more profound, being "the sober truth" of the matter. It was this "real" form of the imagination that came closer to Collins' sense of his enterprise in creating his telegraph drama. Early in the life of Pre-Raphaelitism, Ruskin had found something truly scientific in its attentive, even microscopic detailing of every vein in the leaf. And indeed, one side of the original Pre-Raphaelite program of "a return to nature" had been to give ear to the phenomenal and find value and meaning in an observed reality. For Hunt this translated into an increasing tendency to localize spiritual values by clothing them in the material, and to read the material world symbolically, even typologically. Collins dramatized such thinking in *Convent Thoughts* (whose catalogue rubric was "I meditate on all Thy works; I muse on the work of Thy hands") and in the painting he completed shortly before he conceived *The Electric Telegraph*, titled *A Thought of Bethlehem*. In *The Electric Telegraph*, however, he turns the original Pre-Raphaelite program in another direction. In his modern-life painting, the phenomenal and the observed reality are not asked "to divulge some great secret of the world of spirits." They evoke no thought of Bethlehem. They represent no conflict between nature and culture, where nature alone speaks for the spirit. Instead the painting presents a continuity embracing modern dress, domestic anxiety, the forces of nature, human agency, invisible social organization, and "the little mahogany Instrument not two foot high"; the last, like gas lighting and railways, one of "the natural emanations from the modern mind" whose true significance is revealed, not through imaginative estrangement, but through an enhanced and empathic familiarity. Yet, informing this familiarity were the energies of the self, all the less manageable perhaps for eschewing conscious metaphor. It is possible that Collins' difficulties with *The Electric Telegraph* deepened as he sensed that the painting would, after all, speak more plainly than he wished of intimate mysteries, through "the expressive finger-signs of a dumb alphabet."

Liberty and Fraternity

Behind Collins' "Apology" in which, with painful objectivity, he attempts to distinguish his own creativity from that of the group, lie two family configurations. One is that of the PRB, whose puzzling initials on the unnerving canvases of Hunt, Millais, and Rossetti turned out to signify a brotherhood. The other is that of the Collinses. The latter of course had a great deal to do with Charles Allston Collins' personality and how he thought and felt about himself. But he lived and felt the crisis in his creativity, and more especially what has been so brilliantly and memorably named "the anxiety of influence," as a fraternal drama rather than as an oedipal history. In this I believe that Collins' experience was typical of many artists in what became the modern era, when rejection of the previous generation was simply a matter of course—not of itself a source of anxiety—and innovation was the normal point of departure. But such fraternal drama is probably also characteristic of many other working groups with an element of generational cohesion in the history of art and literature. Given a complex of emulation and fellowship, competition and mutual support, in a time of creative ferment, an artist is more likely to be nervously aware of what his contemporaries are up to than of the triumphant achievements of the past masters. Even the great runner runs his race against the immediacy of the pacesetter and the field, and only indirectly against the record. It may be that all anxiety has its roots in the oedipal and pre-oedipal rain forest (though I doubt it), but its preoccupations are with the threats and uncertainties in the indeterminate present.[21]

Anxiety is a wide field, and for an artist in what may be thought of as the first avant-garde, a distinction has to be made between anxiety over success (or the lack of it), and anxiety over influence. The two are not very well insulated from each other, but neither are they indistinguishable. In the beginnings of the modern era it was sometimes necessary to apologize to one's peers for success when weary of apologizing to one's elders for failure. In the rebellion of the present against the past, failure with the public was not a threat to integrity, but influence—when one was part of a fellowship that had declared its independence of authority, that valued autonomy, that insisted upon an unmediated relation between the artist and his material—influence could be felt as a profound threat to integrity and artistic identity.

Collins' case is instructive in that he grew up by his own account with no anxieties concerning his success in due course as a painter, in a world that encouraged him lavishly. It was a world, as it happens, where writing was important but always subordinate to painting. Collins' grandfather, William, who came from Wicklow and established the family in England, was a dealer in pictures and a writer whose best-known work was a life of his painter-friend, George Morland.[22] It was originally published together with a novel called *The Memoirs of a Picture*, full of the manners and customs of the art world of the day and its patrons.[23] The patriarch's son, also named William, took a wife from a family of painters, and through his considerable gifts became a Royal Academician of the inner circle. For his sons the whole pictorial establishment of the early nineteenth century was part of the familiar background. Both these sons were named after painters who were particular friends, David Wilkie and Washington Allston.

William Wilkie Collins, the elder by four years, was not expected to become a painter. In fact his father shifted him from apprenticing as a clerk destined for commerce to training in a profession, the law, only after he had demonstrated literary facility by publishing some small articles and producing a manuscript novel. Wilkie nevertheless had amphibious interests. He painted a landscape that was accepted and exhibited (though poorly) at the Royal Academy in 1849.[24] His first important publication, a year earlier, was the two-volume *Memoirs of the Life of William Collins, Esq., R.A.*, an act of piety towards his painter father who had died in February, 1847. His first published novel, *Antonina* (1850), set among fifth-century Goths and Romans, was conceived (according to the preface in the first edition) as a series of pictorial effects on the analogy of painting.[25]

Charles on the other hand impressed both his father and his father's friends with his gifts as a prospective painter and had their early encouragement. His father wrote in 1843, at the time of Allston's death, that Charles (then fifteen), "having been left entirely to his own choice as regards a profession, has determined to follow that of Painter; and is now carrying on his studies at the Royal Academy—I desire no better thing for him, than that he may follow the example of his namesake, both as a painter and as a man." [26] Writing many years after his intimacy with Charles, Holman Hunt reports a conversation in which he spoke enviously of his friend's "inconceivable luck" in knowing Wilkie, Turner, Constable, and other greats in his earliest days. Collins, he reports, replied: "I think you were more to be envied than I" in seeing obstacles, difficulties, and vast distances to be traversed; "I looked upon the diadem as a part of manhood that must come, and now I begin to doubt and fear the issue." [27]

The doubts came in the wake of more focused anxieties whose theme was originality and influence, the immediate product of Collins' association with a band of heterodox contemporaries. Pre-Raphaelitism was born in 1848, year of revolutions, and Collins, who had begun exhibiting in the Royal Academy in 1847, first shows his conversion to Pre-Raphaelite principles in an Academy painting of 1850. By that time, the beginning of his great intimacy with the leading members of the brotherhood, Rossetti was already about to cease exhibiting publicly, so that the standard bearers were Millais, at twenty-one a year younger than Collins, and Hunt, one year older. And the fraternal intimacy was very great, in a climate of mutual stimulus and mutual help. In the summer and autumn of 1850, Collins and Millais lived and painted together near Oxford, and drew mutual portraits (figures 5 and 6) that caught each other's youth and seriousness for posterity. But the peak moment for Collins was doubtless the long summer and fall of 1851, which Millais, Collins and Hunt spent together near Kingston and at Worcester Park Farm in Surrey, painting in the open air.

Fraternal intimacy, though grounded in a community of artistic aims and interests, expresses itself in life as well as art. Early on Collins reportedly fell desperately in love with Maria Rossetti, whose brothers, Dante Gabriel and William Michael, were founding members of the Brotherhood.[28] When Collins' mother, Harriet, wrote to Hunt in Jerusalem, she addressed him as "My dear Son N° 4," dear Son N° 3 being Millais, who stayed with the Collinses for extended periods, and otherwise visited constantly.[29] After the first summer near Oxford, Millais wrote to his Oxford patrons, "I see Charley every night, and we dine alternate Sundays at each other's houses. To-night he comes to cheer me in my solitude." [30] Four years later he could write, "I still half reside with Mrs. C., that strong-minded old lady." [31] And when Millais and Euphemia Gray, the former Mrs. Ruskin, returned from their honeymoon and settled in their house in Scotland, Charles Collins came to stay as their first house guest.

The characteristics that distinguish the Pre-Raphaelites as an early instance of the phenomenon of the avant-garde go beyond fraternal intimacy. The

Figure 5. Charles Allston Collins, *Portrait of John Everett Millais* (1850), pencil with grey wash, 16.5 × 12.5 cm., Oxford, Ashmolean Museum. By permission of the Visitors.

Figure 6. John Everett Millais, *Portrait of Charles Allston Collins* (1850), pencil, 16.5 × 12.5 cm., Oxford, Ashmolean Museum. By permission of the Visitors.

members of the group created a common platform to contain their diversity in a program with a rudimentary manifesto, a short-lived journal (*The Germ*), and a revolutionary attitude to the canons of their predecessors, notably Reynolds and his tribe.[32] They adopted the name "Pre-Raphaelite" as a challenge, to register scorn for the debilitated tradition that claimed to take its origin and ideal from Raphael, where, in the orthodox view, the struggling art of painting was supposed to have achieved full maturity. Their proclaimed standard, however, was Nature, immediate and unmediated, seen for oneself and meticulously rendered, rather than seen through the established practice of earlier schools. They appropriated nature for their argument, and they used it to assault conventions of color, the manipulation of light and shade for "effect," loose brushwork, limitations on subject matter, ideas of "beauty," and in sum the received idea of what was acceptable and what was canonical in art.

Such groups, often composed of strong personalities, tend to have a brief half-life. Though the core kept considerable cohesion into the mid 1850s, the original PRB as a formal organization was already partly unravelled by 1851, the time of Collins' sojourn at Worcester Park Farm. Interestingly, as the original group dissolved, its influence spread. Later it would spawn a second generation with different aims, built around an elder, Rossetti.

The record of the years of Collins' participation is rich with evidence of collaborative support, but also of competitive emulation. On the one side, for example, Millais campaigned strenuously to persuade his own patrons, the Combes, or their friends, to buy Collins' *Convent Thoughts* and Hunt's *Missionary*.[33] When Hunt, discouraged and impoverished, thought to give up painting in 1851, Millais arranged to pay Hunt's living expenses "for nearly two years" so he could continue to paint.[34] Looking back, Hunt registers his gratitude to Millais, speaking of him, however, as a generous rival who helped him until they were on a level as competitors.[35] As to the actual work of their hands, Millais designed the frame—"which, I expect, will be acknowledged to be the best frame in England"—for Collins' *Convent Thoughts*, incorporating its reiterated motif of lilies (see figure 1).[36] Collins in turn painted the firehose in Millais' *Rescue*, to help make the Royal Academy deadline. More significantly, the brothers shared technical methods and secrets, such as the difficult procedure of laying color on a wet white ground, whose striking results helped furnish the recognizable characteristics of a common style. They relentlessly publicized each other. And of course they inhabited each other's studios and abundantly discussed and made suggestions about each others' work in progress.

Away from their brothers in art, both their work and their spirits suffered. Even so stalwart and stoical a figure as Hunt complained to Collins from Jerusalem of the "want of sympathy" in his lonely labors.[37] Writing to William Rossetti, he wonders "whether there will ever be any thing like a repetition of our old fellowship in such disturbed times as seem to be coming upon us," and then, speaking of a painting sent to England some weeks before, he complains, "I cannot form any sort of notion of its merits. I had no one to show it to, and I should not like to be compelled to depend on my own opinion. In sending it away I did not consult my feelings but only my necessities." [38]

On the other side, the generous rivalry that Hunt later sees as the context for appreciating Millais' strenuous efforts on behalf of his friends evokes the uncertain line between mutuality and emulation. Certainly competitive feelings played their part in the centrifugal forces at work on the Brotherhood. Millais in particular was especially competitive, or perhaps seems so now because of his openness. Possibly for that reason he was especially concerned to avoid competition within the brotherhood, and to channel such combative energies outward. Accordingly, even after the core itself had scattered, he wrote to Hunt on the question of "an Exhibition of our own," that "One great reason why I think withdrawing ourselves from the body of artists a GREAT MISTAKE, is that they gain by *avoiding the comparison*, & we would lose by simply battling against each other. We should *court* comparison as much as possible & exhibit with the rest which is the only way we can expect to show superiority. I believe nothing in the world would please the general body of Painters better than our seperating ourselves, it would be called shagrine & cowardice [sic]." [39]

Early as well as late, Millais strove to direct his own competitive feelings and the fruits of fraternal emulation into a high-spirited and whole-hearted contest against painters following other notions. His success may be read in the unselfconscious modulations of a letter to Hunt, written during the period of greatest cohesion:

> . . . I was delighted to hear from Gabriel—his subject I think wonderful, I am afraid a smasher to all of us—We shall soon meet now in London—
>
> I quake at the idea of seeing your background as I know it must be splendid—
>
> I read Rossetti's Dante subject to Mr Combe; he is delighted and is likely to purchase it if it suits his taste (which is at my mercy). I think now we will spiffligate the sloshers. [40]

Here internal emulation elbows mutuality and support, and the conclusion is the common triumph of the whole group over the dominant school of facile painterly academicians, "the sloshers." Millais ends with Collins' desire for "brotherly affections," and signs himself "most brotherly." [41]

The fact is that whatever his anxieties about competition within the brotherhood, Millais throve on both mutuality and emulation, and seemed to be wholly impervious to anxieties about independence and influence. With his ebullience, his gregariousness, his technical gifts, his persistent good fortune, his partisan generosity, and perhaps his ultimate shallowness, he certainly had no doubts about his identity as a painter, or his originality, and in this he provides an extreme contrast to the neurotic and finally incapacitated Collins. Millais' confidence went hand in hand with what Hunt speaks of as "the 'Millais luck' (a phrase which became a proverb)." [42] And it expressed itself in an energetic activism in the lives and doings of his friends, and a vigorous impatience with scrupulous hesitations and delicate sensitivities of the sort Collins was prone to. It is noteworthy that none of Millais' contributions to *The Electric Telegraph*, as detailed in Collins' "Apology," approaches Collins' contribution in brushwork to *The Rescue*, a contribution that never troubled Millais. In the realm of ideas, Hunt significantly altered Millais' conception of *A Huguenot*, a crucial painting in Millais' oeuvre, from a generalized picture of two lovers by a garden wall to a particularized situation set in historical circumstances.[43] Yet Millais could write of the painting to his Oxford patrons, "I am in high spirits about the subject, *as it is entirely my own*, and I think contains the highest moral." [44] Only after Millais' marriage and separation from his artist brothers does the note of uncertainty about his art enter his correspondence, and does one encounter such a passage as the following: "I feel less and less command over the result of my work, and certainly much less belief in it whilst I am at it, than of old, when I used to paint ahead, and *never* doubt its goodness. Now what appears once a fortnight tolerable, the rest of the time appears really bad—I cannot help repeating this as it is a great feature in the change in me since you left us." Millais is writing to Hunt, now back in London, and he hastens to add, "I am really very happy here in other respects than Art, and I have every reason to be so." [45] A decade later, he would report, "I am working working alone knowing my own bitterness over the difficulty of painting." [46]

Being There

An argument—like that I have been advancing—which locates creative anxiety in the relations between contemporaries gives precedence, as a source of explanation, to the social dynamics of art over individual psychology. Certainly the social side is paramount in an argument that turns a particular instance of such anxiety into an illustration of the tensions between competitive emulation and fraternal reinforcement characteristic of an avant garde. But social explanation leaves a number of questions unanswered. Why did fraternal anxiety overwhelm the benefits of supportive mutuality in Collins' case, but not in Millais' or Hunt's? Why did it destroy only Collins' ability to turn his conceptions into paint? Why did the crisis come with this particular painting? It is worth putting such questions to the traces of what belongs, not to the group, but to Collins only: his intimate self.

Collins expressed his anxiety as a concern over his originality, not over the insufficient support, loyalty, and cohesion of the group (a common complaint in later avant-garde fraternities), nor even over his formal standing. His insecurity is not about belonging, but about autonomy, and it suggests a deeper anxiety over identity. A secure sense of self is what enables one to hold the balance between autonomy and community, liberty and fraternity; it doubtless takes form in the first sustained community we experience. This is generally familial, and it is reasonable to suppose that its comforts (provisional identity and relief from autonomy) and its anxieties (threatened identity and inhibition of autonomy) carry over into subsequent experience. What we know about the first community in Collins' life, however, is for the most part superficial, largely a matter of its public face. Some time after he left painting, Collins wrote an essay on the decline of the pious biography that must have given his brother Wilkie, author of the *Life of William Collins*, food for thought:

> Very often these books were written by relations of the deceased person, and how could he, or she, as the case might be, rip up the secret passages of the dead man's life, and dissect them for the benefit of society at large? Which among us would like this sort of revelation of his inner life to be made? And if it is not made, where is the use of the biography? To read of a life that is all virtue and integrity, and entirely free from weakness and folly, leads a man either to despair or to disbelieve. He either says to himself, "I am so utterly removed from this sort of thing that there is no hope of my ever doing anything;" or he ceases to believe a word he is reading, and sets the whole treatise down as a pack of lies.[47]

Thanks to the contemporary reticences and pieties, there is a limit to what can be conjectured on Collins' own inner life as formed in his family. Even so provocative a passage as that just quoted leads only to conjecture. Yet its profound ambivalence about revealing one's inner life may be traced even in the history of Collins' final painting. Who wants such a revelation, he asks, but without it, how are we to get on? Without it, what use is the work?

Given the limitations on direct evidence, one must turn, with a large reserve of skepticism and a dread of circularity, to indirect evidence. For example, it is perhaps significant testimony to the prevailing bias of Charles Allston Collins' first community that the nightmare threat to identity, to one's very name and nature, not just one's place in the world, is the obsessive central subject of his brother Wilkie's fiction. As with Wilkie, so with Charles: it is to the imaginative work that one must eventually turn for clues to the interior world. What emerges, however, are not revelations about the formative past, which remains obscure and conjectural, but rather further insights into the subjective present.

In the truncated pictorial gallery that Collins produced for the public eye, the anxiety over creative autonomy and originating power that he articulated in his "Apology" appears to have a sexual and existential counterpart. The connection lies in the partial embodiments of a recurrent narrative configuration incorporating anxiety over the absence of a potent and authoritative male. The absence strikes or is endured by a female protagonist, usually directly, sometimes empathically.

I would argue that this imagery, whose recurrence indicates its importance for Collins, should be read analogically and conservatively, as metaphor rather than as metonymy. That is, it should be read as a fictive substitution of one kind of anxiety for another, rather than as the substitution of cause (deficient or ambivalent sexuality) for effect (incipient creative impotence). It is of course possible that Collins' creative anxiety and disablement was the psyche's own metaphor for a sexual guilt or deficiency. But in that case, the psyche's metaphor would have been exposed and undone by the artist's, in his projection of the missing male. The true state of Collins' sexuality is in any case beyond establishing.[48]

The artist's narrative imagery points to a preoccupation with a more fundamental anxiety than that over sexual identity, though issues of sexual identity can be associated with it. The experiencing center of the paintings is always a woman; and it is rather to the point that in Wilkie Collins' novels the most notable instances of threatened and stolen identity concern women (as in *The Woman in White, No Name, The New Magdalen*). Contemporary literary and dramatic convention frequently make an innocent female the focus of pathos and peril, inviting empathy through an identification with our own vulnerable, open, and blameless selves. In Charles' paintings, however, his female protagonists are rarely directly imperiled. They regularly represent the self that feels and perceives, rather than the self that acts. It is that other self which is imperiled and absent.

The split is as telling as the absence. Though Collins' narrative configuration depicts anxiety for another, it is anxiety for one's self that is really at issue, an anxiety whose content is captured in the imagery of absence and division. The issue of identity is not simply a matter of ambivalence or uncertainty about who or what one is for Collins; it is a matter of wholeness, presence, and existence proper. It is an anxiety, in Collins' language, that "strikes you a blow and turns you sick" with the feeling of not being there.

Collins' known paintings are largely those he exhibited at the Royal Academy. Of these, three are portraits; seven, possibly eight, are subject pictures of single female figures—either children or young women—with a poetic or religious suggestion (*Convent Thoughts* is among these); one is an unusual and indeed highly original landscape (*May, in the Regent's Park*); and two are narrative paintings employing several figures. These two—*Berengaria's*

Figure 7. Charles Allston Collins, *Berengaria's Alarm for the Safety of Her Husband, Richard Cœur de Lion* (1850), oil on canvas, 96.5 × 125.7 cm., Manchester, City Art Gallery. By permission of the City of Manchester Art Galleries.

Alarm for the Safety of Her Husband, Richard Coeur de Lion (1850) and *A Thought of Bethlehem* (1854)—along with *Convent Thoughts*, a drawing that bears on one of the portraits, and the terminal *Electric Telegraph*, are the cluster that considered together provide the most intriguing signposts into Collins' interior world. All, in one way or another, are about the absence of a particular significant male. But even Collins' first two subject paintings, antedating his Pre-Raphaelitism, *The Temptation of Eve* and *Ophelia* (both 1848), tend in a similar direction.

Berengaria's Alarm for the Safety of Her Husband, Richard Cœur de Lion, Awakened by the Sight of His Girdle Offered for Sale at Rome, to give it its full title (figure 7), was the first of Collins' paintings to earn him recognition as one of the brash and offensive little band that included Millais and Hunt. In the year of Millais' *Christ in the Carpenter's Shop*, the *Athenaeum* called *Berengaria* "Another instance of perversion," while the *Times*, finding it "in the same grotesque style" as Hunt's *Converted British Family*, suggested it "might pass for an illuminated chessboard." [49]

Collins had found the incident in Agnes Strickland's *Lives of the Queens of England*, and the exhibition catalog quotes the significant passage: "The

Provençal traditions declare that here Berengaria first took the alarm that some disaster had happened to her lord, from seeing a belt of jewels offered for sale which she knew had been in his possession when she parted from him."[50] The peddler, who supplied the short title by which the painting was later known, is not mentioned in this source, but as inadvertent messenger, and a presence that underlines the absence, he has something of the function of the operator in *The Electric Telegraph*.

The absent person in *Berengaria*—a legendary distillation of male power and authority—is represented by the rich and colorful but sadly drooping girdle, and also by the embroidery that echoes its colors and displays the Ricardian emblem of a lion rampant. These lie just under the midline of the painting, between the Queen and the peddler. The absence of the figure these tokens represent is emphasized by the threefold division of the back wall, like a triptych, with two of its openings occupied or covered. The central third opening, arched, fully bounded, and flanked by the two principal figures, stands empty except for the garden backdrop. It appears almost like a vacant frame.

One of the double-framed rear openings is covered by a tapestry from the Joseph story, showing the scene where Joseph's brothers present the blood-stained coat of many colors to their stricken father. The analogy with the scene in the foreground is plain; it hinges on the recognition of a token, something worn on the person that speaks of disaster to the absent beloved. The analogy is reinforced by the scroll on the floor, which gives a version of Genesis 37:33, beginning, "And he knew it and sayde it is my sonne hys coate an evil beast hath devoured him." The scroll lies on the pages of an illuminated Bible opened to the beginning of the Gospel According to St. John. One whole leaf is the rendering of "In principio" into a labyrinthine pictorial design of whorls, letters, and figures. The other continues the rest of the Latin text of John's celebration of the Word. The illumination—which shows John producing the word, his Gospel, under inspiration—is in the most literal sense a translation of word into picture. As such, it is analogous to Collins' rendering of narrative as picture in this very painting. Richard's girdle and Joseph's coat tell a story: like them, Collins' painting is the many-colored visual emblem that speaks.[51]

Despite some undoubted insipidities of execution, there is enough conceptual intricacy in all this to suggest a degree of assurance in the artist at this stage of his development, and a confidence in his medium despite the priorities of St. John. Nevertheless, Berengaria's alarm and Jacob's despair—the beginning and end of anxiety—give the alert for what is to come. It is worth noting that the tapestry Jacob is no longer the potent actor of the past who could discharge anxiety by managing circumstances. Like Berengaria, he can now only suffer the experience of absence and loss, and he wrings his hands

Figure 8. Charles Allston Collins, *The Artist with Millais and Others* (1850), brown ink, 18 × 10 cm., Oxford, Ashmolean Museum. By permission of the Visitors.

in a closed gesture of grief. Moreover, it may be fortuitous, but it nevertheless hints at the incipient fault line of Collins' anxiety among the Pre-Raphaelites, that it was Joseph's brothers who brought about his disappearance, and it was Richard's nominal royal brother of the crusades who caused him to vanish from the face of the earth.

The summer following the exhibition of *Berengaria* was the first that Collins and Millais spent together near Oxford. In the fall they continued in the town, where Millais painted a portrait of his new patron, Thomas Combe, and Collins one of Mrs. Combe's elderly uncle, William Bennett. At the same time Collins also sketched the generous hospitality of the Combes in a drawing that retrospectively suggests Collins' initial vulnerability and the shape of the catastrophe to come. Identified as "The Artist with Millais and Others" (figure 8), the drawing shows a domestic group at its evening occupations. Millais is at the center of a semi-circle, seated on the floor, informal and at ease, between Combe and Mrs. Combe, but closer to the lady whose light he shares. At the left, in an imposing arm chair, sits Mr. Bennett, very much in the pose of his oil portrait, but with the angle reversed. The angle of view on Mr. Bennett in the portrait proper (which stops at the knees) would be that from the right side of the drawing, where indeed "the Artist," Collins, is placed. Oddly, Mr. Bennett's pose in the drawing, with hands together and ankles crossed, echoes or is echoed by Millais.

Mr. Combe, a vigorous man in middle age, sits working at the table to the right of Millais, with his back three-quarters to the spectator, for whom he is largely but not entirely in shadow. Collins is at the far right, almost at the picture plane, and little more than a silhouette. He is presumably sketching

Mr. Bennett, and his signature lies under him, but his presence, at the periphery, is almost as if through negation. Part of his figure is lost against the darkness of Combe, and more generally the ink and wash that normally assert themselves against the blankness of the paper here become deprivation of light and an approach to invisibility. The presence or absence of Collins would not be an issue if he had not included himself in the scene, if he had just assumed the customary invisibility of the artist who takes the point of view of the spectator. The ambiguous character of his presence suggests the nature of the issue for Collins: simply that of being there. And in the full light, exactly between the artist and his subject, and represented as if appropriating or inspiring the subject's pose, sits Millais.

Earlier in that companionable summer, Collins had worked on the background of *Convent Thoughts* (figure 1), and he finished the painting early in 1851, in time for the next Royal Academy exhibition. *Convent Thoughts* is a picture in which a young woman in religious dress is burdened with reconciling the claims of the spirit with those of nature and art. She turns from the illuminated book—which shows the Virgin and a Crucifixion—to meditate upon a withered passion flower, Nature's reminder of Christ's sacrifice and of the sacrificial meaning of a life of religious seclusion. Both the book and the flower speak of an absent male, both divine and imperiled, a figure of supreme power suffering extremity. But the walled garden, the nun's ambivalent stance, the vigor of nature, her novice's dress, also speak of an absent male who is secular and ordinary, the figure whose absence the choice of the cloister entails.[52]

After *Convent Thoughts*, the painting that most preoccupied Collins was the one that eventually became *A Thought of Bethlehem*. He began it soon after the exhibition of *Convent Thoughts* in similar circumstances of fraternal living and painting, but found it hard to complete. *The Electric Telegraph* was thus not the first of Collins' projects to cause him such difficulty, and because the record concerning this painting is confused and often misreported, it is worth trying to set it straight.

At Worcester Park Farm in the idyllic summer and fall of 1851, while Millais painted the backgrounds for *Ophelia* and *A Huguenot*, and Hunt the orchard for *The Hireling Shepherd* and the door for *The Light of the World*, Collins found and painted a broken-down shed amid sunlight and foliage, which he then thought to make the scene of a saint's legend.[53] Though Collins managed to send three canvases to the Royal Academy exhibition of 1852, the shed painting was not among them. Nor was it in the exhibition of 1853, in which Collins had one canvas. Millais issued occasional bulletins on Collins' progress to Hunt, including an account of trying to help Collins get models for the painting. (Among the requirements was a three-week old infant; "I pity him painting such a frightful thing.") In the spring of 1854, Millais reported, "Charley at last finishing the Saint subject."[54] Collins himself had already written in what he called "the first days of liberty [after] all the turbulent excitement of 'sending in'":

> I have seen no pictures but yours . . . and one, which I am sincerely glad that at this moment I do *not* see, one which has long occupied certain feet of what would otherwise have been air, in this room, and of which I have seen quite enough lately to last me some time; and which I need not allude to more specifically than to mention that its background was a representation of a shed in Surrey and to relieve your good natured anxiety for my welfare by telling you that, somehow or other it got finished in time for the R.A.[55]

The painting had metamorphosed into *A Thought of Bethlehem, Part of the Life of Madame de Chantal*, and it was respectfully but unenthusiastically received.[56] It formed part of the strong English showing at the Paris Exposition Universelle of 1855, however, where it attracted Gautier's attention. Collins by then was already at work on his next important painting, *The Electric Telegraph*, whose subject, he felt, would make it so much more immediately appealing than a pious scene of obscure and distant virtue concerned with spiritual meanings.

Most accounts of the Pre-Raphaelites convey the impression (reported as fact by J. G. Millais) that the shed painting was never finished. The view is made plausible by Hunt's account of Collins in death: "On his bed lay the canvas, taken off the strainer, with the admirably executed background painted at Worcester Park Farm." Hunt speaks further of Collins starting and abandoning subjects "until he had a dozen or more relinquished canvases on hand never to be completed."[57] What the more strictly contemporary evidence also shows, however, is Collins' extraordinary persistence with those paintings of whose worth he was convinced, and that the crisis that led him to abandon his art came to a head with one painting, *The Electric Telegraph*.

Whether the impediments Collins encountered in painting *A Thought of Bethlehem* had to do with the subject is not immediately apparent. The historical Madame de Chantal was a woman of ardent piety and powerful mind, a friend of Francis de Sales, who after fulfilling her duties in sixteenth- and seventeenth-century French society as daughter, wife, and mother, gave her life to charity, founded an order, and achieved sainthood. Collins' painting offered a typifying incident in her life as reported in Julia Kavanagh's *Women of Christianity*. He cites it in the Royal Academy catalog: "A poor strange woman * * * * was taken with the pains of labour in the course of her wanderings; she sought and found refuge in a stable, where she gave birth to her child. Madame de Chantal walked a considerable distance in order to visit her. * * * * All the time she was engaged in her pious office, Madame de Chantal confessed that she thought of the Infant Jesus in the stable of Bethlehem."[58]

The fullest description of the painting is in Gautier's exposition notice of 1855:

> Under the title of *A Thought of Bethlehem* [*Souvenir de Bethléem*], M. Collins has actualized a passage in the life of Madame de Chantal. The pious lady, visiting a poor woman in childbed, is reminded of the birth of Christ in a stable: M. Collins' scene evokes the thought quite naturally. Barely sheltered by a lean-to covered in thatch, the young mother, lying on an unravelling grass mat and covered with a thin rag of stuff, holds up her infant whom she looks at with a liquid and tender eye. Behind her, a little girl strips and scatters marigolds [*soucis*]—sad flower of the poor—as if to celebrate the happy arrival of the newly born. Several bits of dead wood, fire extinct, black embers clothed in a velvety white, are strewn on the ground, for there is no fireplace in this hut open to all the winds. Fortunately it is summer, and the sun plays among the transparent leaves. Otherwise, utter abandonment; no Saint Joseph, no ox nor ass breathing caresses on this little Jesus of wretchedness. But be easy; behold, Christian charity arriving in her nun's dress and, even as she walks, sewing a fustian vest, the first piece of the layette; this dear little angel will not die.[59]

Gautier goes on to acknowledge the surprising reality of the Pre-Raphaelite details and the sympathetic effect of the whole. He recognizes the affective importance of what is not there: the comforting presences in that other scene, in Bethlehem, and most significantly, the absent father. If God the Father is offstage in the sacred scene, even so honorary a father as Saint Joseph is missing from this secular echo.

Collins chose to show the entrance of Madame de Chantal, when she like the viewer is still a spectator responding to the central scene. He omits from the catalogue rubric a passage that tells how Madame de Chantal "knelt down by the poor creature, took the child, baptized it, and cared for its mother until she was able to leave the place and proceed on her journey." In both picture and text he avoids the kneeling configuration and its direct archetypal implications, and instead gives us the picture of "a thought." The fact is, in the incomplete domestic trinity of man, woman, and child, Madame de Chantal cannot supply the missing figure.

Charity enters to alleviate the "utter abandonment" (*abandon complet*) of the woman in travail, but has no permanent part in the picture. The relief she brings, like the shelter in the wood and the season, is only temporary. Nevertheless, for the moment at least, anxiety is thrust out of sight, and instead there is fulfillment in creation—expressed in the mother's loving look—and the assurance of friendly support. But anxiety is waiting in the wings, and it will emerge in *The Electric Telegraph*.

Sticking Fast

If Collins had completed *The Electric Telegraph*, anxiety would have achieved its fullest, most overt representation in his art to date, appearing as the true, affective subject within the narrative and visual idea. But as it happened, anxiety took charge of the painting in more senses than one. One result is that neither the painting nor the history of the painting can be known directly. Both have to be seen through the filter of Collins' own written account, and extrapolated from the evidence of the surviving drawings. But in the event, the painting and its history, like the "Apology" and the drawings, reinforce each other, by a species of cross reference. What follows is an attempt to take advantage of that circumstance, to read the "Apology" and the drawings in conjunction, and thereby chart the final movements and final imagery of the impasse.

When Collins first wrote to Hunt in February 1855 about his work in progress, he was still buoyant with excitement, conviction, and hope, though it was already becoming an anxious hope: "My dear Hunt do you know what it is to be full of intentions, full of thoughts of things one longs to paint and new thoughts of life one longs to write down—full of thick coming fancies and withal in dread lest one should go down to the grave before these things can be made available. No doubt you do, but you have made much of yours available already while I am not even (by a combination of circumstances) able to get the picture I have told you about ready for this years exhibition." [60] By April of the following year, when Collins wrote his "Apology," the buoyancy is long gone, and his dread has taken a concrete form. It is not now mortality and circumstance that could conspire to defeat Collins' longing to express the riches within. The very substance of what is to be expressed has now been undermined by doubt.

In his "Apology," Collins attempts to set down and evaluate the plain facts that bear upon the originality of his painting. He reasons to the conclusion that the painting is his, that his fears and anxieties are without material substance. But he knows, as others cannot, the weight and reality of their emotional substance. It is that reality he has to grapple with, and the "Apology" itself is a heroic attempt to do so.

The document takes the external form of a narrative with accompanying interpretation and conclusions. But this orderly progression gives way to a mingled stream wherein the conclusions are vitiated by afterthought and lingering "questions." The inner form of the document thus becomes the drama of an anxiety asserting itself and claiming its own. It is informative beyond Collins' intentions, all the more so because at various points it engages matters that appear in the external record.

The "Apology" attributes all the difficulties that have beset Collins and prevented him from completing the painting "to one cause—the fear of winning success by means of Millais' brains." Pertinent here is the fact that Collins had already spoken of the suffering and anxiety painting causes him, in his letter of February 7, 1855, where he announces the telegraph subject and celebrates its innovative modernity. But there modernity (contrasted with pseudo-Gothic imitation) seemed to be the very hallmark of originality, and therefore its implicit guarantee. The quest for a striking originality, the anxiety of influence, and Collins' turn to a modern-life subject, may so be seen as intimately linked.

In the "Apology," Collins sensibly excludes from consideration the general influence of Millais' opinions and conversation on art, and confines his audit to the particular. His first consideration is "the idea of the subject," which Collins shows to his own satisfaction was indeed his own. The leading importance for Collins of this aspect of a painting appears in his giving it pride of place in the audit and elsewhere, for example in his earlier letter to Hunt when he turns to his friend's own work in progress.[61] Concern for originality in "the idea of the subject" was necessarily more acute in the case of original narrative painting than where landscape or portraiture were concerned, especially where the narrative had a modern-life interest. Collins knew that were he to be anticipated in the use of the electric telegraph in a pictorial drama of domestic anxiety, his painting would lose more than half its effect. Even among the Pre-Raphaelites, an argument that accused Hunt's *Awakening Conscience* of stealing a march on Rossetti's unfinished *Found* did much to cool the relationship between those two Brothers and their partisans. The fierce arguments over priority in the use of "the railroad effect" between Boucicault, Daly, and others offer an analogy in the drama.

In his audit, Collins quickly concludes that not only was the idea of the use of the telegraph as a dramatic agent his own and not Millais', but so was the embodying dramatic situation, that of a wife asking after her husband's safety; so was the specification of the modern imperiling context, a railway accident; so was the actual configuration of the wife looking over the operator's shoulder as he records the message; so was the perception that the dramatic effect would be wonderfully enhanced if the writing were shown. Collins then scrupulously records a suggestion by Millais that the scale of the picture should be such as to make the writing easily legible, a suggestion that seems a self-evident corollary.

Collins' first sketch of the subject as he reports it in the "Apology" had the following elements: the lady and the clerk with the counter between them; the poster on Railway Accident Insurance; and the child reading it. Variations followed, including a sketch in which the lady was shown lifting her veil. Thereafter, using a model for the lady, Collins "tried the design in all sorts of ways," and decided he had to put the lady inside the counter with the operator in order to show her face properly.

What may be taken as the earliest of the four surviving drawings in the British Museum (figure 2) belongs to this phase of the experiment.[62] The drawing reflects the problem of organizing the space to show all that Collins wanted shown. As it stands, the lady's face is sufficiently evident, and she is—to judge by the position of the telegraph machines—inside the counter, but the operator's position is ambiguous. Moreover, the operator's relation to the machines and the lady's to the message seem independent of each other. It may be that, having found a view from the outside over the lady's back and shoulder unsatisfactory, Collins in this drawing began with a point of view from inside the counter with the operator, but with the lady still outside, beyond the bar, though facing the spectator. If so, then Collins altered the arrangement by extending the line of the counter through the operator's body. This put the operator and the lady on the same side of the counter, the inside, excluding only the viewer. Whatever its history, the drawing in its present form gives more direct evidence of experimentation and reworking than the others that survive, and it suggests an unresolved problem in spatial organization and point of view.

Apart from that problem, the design is less satisfactory than its successors for affective reasons. It is important that the lady rather than the operator, who is the foil for her engagement and anxiety, be closer to the viewer and on the same side of the counter. For the lady to be cut off from the viewer defeats what may be called the structure of empathy. Though shown from the left side in this drawing only, the figure of the operator, one heel hooked on the rungs of his stool, is fundamentally set. That of the lady is not. One of the lady's hands seems to be lifting her veil, but the other (though empty) seems to be in position to hold the veil up in the fixed attitude Collins attributes to a later suggestion by Millais. The poster Collins mentions is here present, but the child is not.

The remaining three drawings are much closer to each other, and share a point of view on the central configuration. In less essential matters, they vary in their indication of the child and in the shape of the machines. There is some logic in associating the two drawings showing the machines with rounded tops, particularly since they also happen to be without an indication of the child. The drawing (figure 4) that can be seen accordingly as bridging the one-and-three division differs from the remaining pair with which it shares point of view chiefly in the attitude and position of the lady. The lady here is distinctly forward of the operator, and her leaning figure impinges on his so that their heads are in closest proximity. Her eagerness to see and know is without restraint, without the ambivalence that fear creates as a dimension of anxiety. In this drawing the lady is all curves and the operator mostly angles; and her stance has the mannered grace and awkwardness associated with some of the backward-looking currents in early Pre-Raphaelitism. The drawing of the figure of the lady is particularly strong and assured, however, and represents an alternative possibility for the part of the design that Collins was to find most troublesome in trying to arrive at a secure conviction of his own originality.

Collins' attempts to work out the basic configuration of his painting occured, he tells us, while Millais was living with the Collinses and working on his Tennyson drawings for Moxon. This puts the time in the latter part of 1854, perhaps into January 1855, shortly before Collins sent his first letter mentioning the painting to Hunt. Collins reports that, besides working from the model during this period, he built something like a set in the studio, representing the telegraph office. What it was meant to look like can probably be seen in the one drawing that elaborately indicates the background (figure 9).

It is at this time also that Collins attempted to lay down rules on what Millais was permitted to say about the painting. He barred suggestions and allowed only opinions on alternatives of Collins' own providing. He credits Millais with recommending that the child be left out of the design as unnecessary and improbable, and Collins does not score this as "influence" against himself as he does less significant observations. Presumably Collins had already thought about it (and drawn it) both ways. The drawing with the fullest background has a vague indication of the child in two places (looking at the poster and filling a gap in the foreground). The drawing with the fullest indication of the child, however, is the one where Collins concentrates on the faces of the principle figures, and probably gives us the best sense of the affective qualities he sought in the central configuration (figure 10).

Collins reports that he returned often to a treatment in which the lady was lifting her veil, and that Millais had demonstrated a modified action of holding it up. In none of the three presumably later drawings is the lady so occupied, though in one the veil itself is indicated by shading. Rather, in all three drawings she clutches her shawl at her throat, an eloquent gesture for a scene of anxiety, and extends her other hand either before or behind her. Collins also notes that Millais, sitting as the clerk with the model for the lady, would tell her to press closer to seem more eager, and he worries that this could have influenced the compactness of his design. The three drawings suggest that once the basic configuration was arrived at, Collins kept the figures in close proximity, but that proximity and eagerness were only half the story. The version of the lady that best suggests the ambivalence of anxiety in the tension of her body is in the drawing where he concentrates on the face, and where only her upper torso is sketched. Her expression is eloquent, but so is her stance. The lady is shown craning her neck in a nervous thrust forward while holding herself back in fearful apprehension, touching the counter behind her for support. She is in effect peering over the shoulder of the operator while partly turned away (solving the problem of showing enough of her face and enough of the message). It is she who is here angular with anxiety in

Figure 9. Charles Allston Collins, Design for *The Electric Telegraph* (3), pen and ink, 26 × 20 cm., London, British Museum. By courtesy of the Trustees.

Figure 10. Charles Allston Collins, Design for *The Electric Telegraph* (4), pen and ink, 25.5 × 19.9 cm., London, British Museum. By courtesy of the Trustees.

contrast to the curve of the operator; and in defining the space between them, her dread is as potent as her eagerness. That Collins labels Millais' urging compactness as possible influence simply shows how well he is able to erode the elements of his own originality.

While registering this possible influence, Collins' account jumps to his stay with the newly married Millais "when down in Scotland I was painting his wife's head in the picture." Collins' language implies work directly on canvas, though how far he may have gone in paint, or what he may have let stand, is wholly unclear. However, the distinctive features of Euphemia Chalmers Gray appear in at least two, and probably three of the drawings (compare the wife's head in Millais' *Order of Release*, figure 11). Millais was eager for Collins to use his wife in the picture and had written to Collins' mother about it while still on his wedding journey:

First tell Charley to *work hard* at his "*Telegraph*," and get the background . . . finished, and he will find the head he wants I think in Effie. It is so difficult to speak for another that I could not of course promise that my lady will suit him, and yet I *should not hesitate* to paint her myself. Oh yes she will do PERFECTLY, and I will write and tell him when to come, I expect sometime towards the end of next month (*August*) as by that time we shall be settled in our house, and ways, and it will be more agreeable for him.—I promise him the *greatest quiet*, and as much time to work as he likes. I shall be working myself like a trooper.[63]

Collins' later concern was not that he had been influenced in the choice of a model whose distinctive features would associate his painting with the previous work and current notoriety of Millais. Rather it was that, when asked to take the attitude of the woman in the picture for a moment, Effie had done so so effectively that the image stayed with him indelibly. Collins reports drawing the figure again and again from the life on his return to London, only to find emerging just the qualities both he and Millais had noted in Effie's attitude. " 'So then' I said to myself 'the idea of this action is mine but the full beauty and energy and vigour of it are perhaps owed to Millais, and if anybody should praise those qualities how shall I feel?' " It is remarkable that Collins somehow manages to credit the full beauty and energy and vigor of the action to Millais the observer rather than to Effie the performer. His remedy, Collins tells us, was to flee to a wholly different treatment of the figure; where, however he discovered another association with Millais, stemming from a wholly different and quite trivial source. It is here that clarity and the air of objective reasonableness in Collins' scrupulous audit vanish.

From this history, Collins moves to his conclusions. The most important are that the idea and its narrative embodiment *are* his own, and that his sharing in a community of aesthetic ideas with Millais is irrelevant. However he also

Figure 11. John Everett Millais, *The Order of Release, 1746* (1853), oil on canvas, 102.9 × 93.7 cm., London, Tate Gallery.

feels that the idea and its narrative embodiment, the "subject," are so good that the painting will secure him an enviable (that is, secure) position in his profession, and that it will inevitably become the work by which he is known, the leading note in his artistic identity. And for Collins that would be unbearable if it meant being known by a work that despite his conclusions he still might not be able to feel is really his own. It appears that anxiety about influence varies directly for Collins with the prospective importance of the work and the chance of success, the very things that would offer him independence and an authority of his own.

Collins amplifies in a parenthetical note where he reflects on his suffering over *Convent Thoughts*, his best-known painting to date, because of Millais' part in suggesting the idea and its treatment. External evidence is here wholly against Collins in that it records Millais' vigorous dissent from Collins' conceptual shift from a Shelleyan subject based on "The Sensitive Plant" to one with high-church reverberations. Millais' only recorded contribution was the frame.[64]

At this point, in the midst of his conclusions, Collins introduces a new or previously suppressed question on the possible influence of Millais' *Order of Release* (figure 11) on *The Electric Telegraph*. Both, Collins observes, have as their subject a wife's care for her husband's well being. Collins then puts the thought aside on the somewhat contradictory grounds that, first, it is "to enquire too curiously," and second, if the influence is real it will be so obvious to the viewer that the matter should be of no real concern. Collins explains that it is only "clandestine assistance" he fears; that is, his own private knowledge, or feelings, or doubts. His anxiety reverberates between the express wish that everyone should know everything he owes to Millais, and the wish that he should owe Millais nothing. It is of course equality that provides the stabilizing force between liberty and fraternity in such a relationship and in such a band; the equality that subsisted between Hunt and Millais and permitted them to take support and inspiration from each other, and yet to develop as the logic of their individuality required. Such equality Collins could not achieve in his own imagination, and his failure expresses itself in the insatiable form of his anxiety.

After toying with the disastrous notion of reconsidering the whole design of the painting now that Millais was out of the way, Collins provides a coda to his "Apology." Actually the coda returns to matters Collins had already addressed, and erodes the principle he had established, that it had been legitimate to consult Millais on alternatives. Collins here approaches the perception that a residue of "certain vague feelings of mistrust" on what may or may not have come from Millais is independent of any matter of fact. He concludes with a statement, profoundly moving in its pathos, of the paralysis and despair that struck the brushes from his hand, of his near relief at finding himself missing the deadlines, and of his resolve to go on if he can be convinced of his right to do so.

If one reads *The Electric Telegraph* as reflecting something of Collins' own feelings about whatever distressed him, then it is plain that the dread of a clarifying resolution was as powerful as the longing for it. This appears, not only in the stance and expression of the wife in what I have called the fourth drawing, but in the formulation of the dramatic situation itself. The anxious inquirer dreads the discovery that what he or she imagines may turn out to be the case: that at the other end of the telegraph wire, there is no longer anybody there.

To fully enunciate the dread would be a way to confirm it, or dissipate it; and so the achievement of the painting itself, of this particular painting, became a doubly charged issue in Collins' inner economy. Successful completion of so momentous a project might prove his identity and autonomy, or it might confirm his worst fears. Successful completion could reveal, to Collins himself if not to the world, the image of his anxiety as in a mirror, divided between his emotion and its object. The feminine face of his emotion, revealed in expression and attitude, he had found difficult to project, but the masculine face of its object, realized as a blank, an absence, was a horror impossible to confront. To *see* that negative image of barren inauthenticity and vacuity would paralyze the beholder; while to avoid it, on such close approach, also entailed paralysis.

There is a progression in Collins' narratives, starting with *Berengaria*: from the medieval historical to the up-to-the-minute contemporary; and from alarm—the discovery of a cause for anxiety—to anxiety in full bloom. The latter is represented as at its most intense because it is set on the very brink of resolution. It seems to have been intense enough, and representative enough of Collins' own inner states, to have been in the end unmanageable. Consequently, despite his brave resolve to go on if he could—if he could believe, that is, that his anxiety was without foundation—Collins stuck fast. In giving concrete form to his general fears on identity and originality, by projecting Millais upon *The Electric Telegraph*, he found reason to delay and in the end to avoid seeing his project through. In an act that can be regarded as bravery or weakness, as self-assertion or self-surrender, as murder or suicide, he decided to cut the matter short. He gave up *The Electric Telegraph* and left painting.

Nessun Maggior Dolore

What Collins called Hunt's "encouraging review" of the documents apparently did nothing to convince Collins of his right or ability to go on with the picture. By 1858, if not before, he had turned his thoughts to a career as a writer. In that year Collins' first essay appeared in Dickens' *Household Words*, where Wilkie was on the staff and a regular contributor. Called "My First Patron," it was written in the persona of a mature painter looking back on his earlier frustrations and reporting the real state of impoverished unhappiness under the sometimes comfortable appearances. The worst of hazards was the genteel exploiter in Collins' title, who came from Collins' own early experience. The essay is written as if for the benefit of both would-be patrons and young aspirants, and as if by a successful artist who had weathered all the hazards of a career and had now reached a secure haven.[65]

Collins' abandoned vocation continued to appear in his writing in one guise or another. He soon began a series for *All the Year Round* in the character of "The Eye-Witness." Dickens urged, in a letter that had been quite hard on another Collins story, "Don't let the Eye Witness drop. It will certainly do you good; It's a capital name for you; if you went on with it, I think it would be the best name you could put upon the Title page of your book; it is your own idea, and one that you may stand by for years."[66] Never doubting in this case that it was his own idea, Collins did go on with it; and the book bore the title-page motto, "Seeing is Believing."[67]

The Eye-Witness essays make their way through church, theater, side-show, and various other public spectacles, to public art: "London Statues," "London Buildings," and the National Gallery. The Eye-Witness is severe and ironic on public art, and he roasts the acquisitions policy of the National Gallery, since 1853 especially, concerning "these purchases in such outrageous numbers . . . of works of the Pre-Raphael period."[68] The Eye-Witness points out his moderation in that "he does not affirm that the school of the Pre-Raphaelite painters should not be represented at all, but only that it should not altogether overwhelm us" (p. 299). He notes that recent visitors have laughed at the pictures in the gallery with some excuse, "the saints in some of the Pre-Raphaelite works being singularly calculated to stimulate a sense of the ridiculous in the spectator. One of these saints was shown gravely shaking hands with a lion" (pp. 303–4).

Collins is of course using the term "Pre-Raphaelite" literally and chronologically, in a brief for modern art. The argument in favor of the acquisition of modern art by public institutions is not startling (it had entered the debates over the creation of a national collection since the beginning of the century). But the reiterated use of the term Pre-Raphaelite, as if its meanings had not been altered by those who took the name only a decade earlier, is startling, especially remembering the ridicule reviewers had heaped on some of the awkward saints of the Brotherhood, including Collins' own. It was clear enough by 1860 that, despite the revivalist aspect of its avant-guardism evident in its chosen name and early practice, the most accomplished modern school of painters in Great Britain was undoubtedly that called Pre-Raphaelite. In his choice of language and illustration for framing an attack on an excessively reverential regard for the "painting of the past," Collins, one has to conclude, indulged a considerable ambivalence towards his former colleagues.

At about the same time, Collins published a fictionalized account of a visit to Hogarth's unprepossessing grave in Chiswick, "the only monument in England that bears his name," in which he counts over "the amount of anxiety and disappointment, ay, even of passionate distress, which the four walls of a painter's room witness." He notes that "sacrifices, great and cruel sacrifices, are exacted from the artist," including pleasures of the table, of society, of comfort,

> and one sacrifice more, the worst of all, the sacrifice of his work, of work completed, and beautiful in itself, and which must be scraped and cleaned from off the canvas on which it has been placed with such long effort and such arduous labour, because it is inconsistent with some part of the work in progress, and being so must go out of it. What do people know of the misery that reigns in an artist's whole household, when the members of it know that he is thus employed in undoing what it has cost so much to do? What do they know of an artist's career? Do they know that many who commence it break down under fatigues that few can undergo? Do they know that health has been destroyed, and that brains have softened, under the pressure of this work? . . . and that many of these canvases which they regard so carelessly have been touched with pencils dipped in tears? [69]

In his private writings, however, Collins' view of the time in which he too was a painter sometimes makes of it a lost paradise. In 1859, having looked over some old letters at Hunt's request, he writes: "This occupation has brought so forcibly before me the superiority of everything past to anything that is to be had now that I feel almost inclined to try and get back again by main force to the pleasures of ten years ago." [70] But news of his friends' present success could also evoke his ambivalence toward that era of innocence and unfulfillment. In the spring of 1860, when Hunt's *Finding of the Saviour in the Temple*, five or six years in the making, had a great critical and financial success,[71] Collins writes Hunt "half a dozen lines: which I implore you to consider. They are about yourself." He then warns Hunt about success—he has never known anyone who was not injured by it. He reminds Hunt:

> You were just the same man in worth and ability when we lived at the Farm House years ago. You will not let the opinion of society give you a different view of yourself I know.
> If I had succeeded since that time I think I should have been ruined. And even now I should be all the worse for a triumph or two. . . . The

success I am speaking thus about, I would have given anything to obtain, but now I should value it less.[72]

Hunt took the admonition in good part, and when Collins married Kate Dickens in the following month, he came down to Gadshill Place to act as best man. Five years later, Hunt turned to Collins for professional advice on the manuscript of an article on the symbolism of *The Light of the World*. (Collins worked assiduously as a writer; he published six books, including three novels, between 1859 and 1866, along with numerous shorter pieces.) Returning the essay, Collins makes a few useful suggestions, offers to do more when it is in proof, implies that Hunt is excessively civil to the public in taking pains to enlighten them ("but then as I have never succeeded yet in winning their interest as you have done perhaps I am no judge"). Then the tone changes:

> Apropos— Thank you a thousand times, my dear old friend, for your thought of linking honourably my name with yours and Millais' in that mention of our wondrous life in the Surrey Farm House.
> I have however, as you will see, put my pencil through each such allusion, feeling convinced that it is much better that my art career should not be spoken of while I am striving—and just now very hard —to succeed in another way. Such success once achieved—supposing such a consummation attainable—I should not feel as I do, but till that is done I cannot help thinking that all things connected with those old unhappy art-wrestlings is better left without mention [sic].[73]

The doubleness in Collins' thinking about the past suggests that the present had not resolved or concluded its tensions. "Our wondrous life in the Surrey Farm House" was redolent with "those old unhappy art-wrestlings." The "superiority of everything past" was infected by a craving "I would have given anything" to satisfy. The thought of the past, Collins having done violence to himself to escape its paralyzing weight, remained a present torment, both as the consciousness of loss and as the memory of pain. The paradox of an absence that is presence continued to haunt Collins in his unfortunate inversion of the generic myth of the modern artist. In Collins' "Artist's Progress," the bow of Philoctetes, the instrument of power, had turned into an open wound. The bow broken, the wound and only the wound remained to plague him.

A story Collins wrote for *Mugby Junction*, the 1866 extra Christmas number of *All the Year Round*, provides a final reflection on Collins' destruction as an artist through a neurotic anxiety over fraternal influence. The story is called "The Compensation House" after the house near the junction where the dying protagonist lives (already acquired by the railway "for compensation"). The tale is of a man who cannot tolerate a looking-glass. The curious narrator elicits the details of this obsession from the dying man's doctor-friend. The doctor speaks of meeting the protagonist while traveling, and finding him shortly after at an inn, frozen before a large, old-fashioned looking glass with a carved frame. The doctor then shook him into speech, whereupon the stricken man cried out in horror, "That face! . . . That face—which is not mine—and which—I SEE INSTEAD OF MINE—always!" Summoned to the bedside, the doctor and narrator now hear the dying man's explanation. He once had a wife, and after marriage they lived abroad, in Italy. "She liked the country, and I liked what she liked. She liked to draw, too, and I got her a master. He was an Italian. I will not give his name. We always called him 'the Master.' A treacherous insidious man this was, and, under cover of his profession, took advantage of his opportunities, and taught my wife to love him—to love him." Discovering his loss on a sketching expedition from a servant-maid whom the Master had deserted, the husband goes to his sup-planter's room, finds him engaged in writing to the wife, and shoots him. "But, before he died, he looked up once—not at me, but at my image before him in the glass, and his face—such a face—has been there—ever since, and mine—my face—is gone!" [74]

The story is about seeing; about the loss of what is most precious and intimate; about insidious displacement and self murder; about nemesis, or "compensation." The protagonist—once more an "eye-witness"—looks into the glass that happens to be framed like a painting and sees there, not himself, nor even a blank, but another. The other, a "master" artist, has robbed him of his muse and his potency, of what is most precious and intimate: of his very self. To destroy the power of the other is in effect to destroy oneself.

To free himself from the incubus of Millais—who looked out at him from his own canvases—Collins had to destroy himself as a painter. And the mirror story with its nightmare symbolism captures the complex equivalence between the unforgivable loss of self to another and a draconian self-mutilation; between the living obsession and its haunted aftermath. The story itself belongs, as far as Collins' life is concerned, to the aftermath, and it both confesses and enacts the ultimate failure of repression in a nightmare of recurrence. And indeed, in life as well as in art, recurrence seems to have been the order of the day. One further basis for associating the Master with (for starters) Millais, is that the story of the seduction comes uncomfortably close to the Ruskin-Effie-Millais triangle in Scotland. Moreover, eight years after its publication and a year after Collins' death, the story had a further echo in his widow's marriage to Carlo (that is, Charles) Edward Perugini, an artist and a Neapoli-tan by birth. In "The Compensation House," the dying man now at the last gasp looks in the glass one final time and gives a sign that the face that haunted him, the face of the other, is gone—a sign, as the narrator reads it, of a debt paid and of final forgiveness. Collins was not so lucky. [75]

Appendix

HH 1 in the Holman Hunt papers, Huntington Library, is a hand-written document in two sewn fascicles, each of five sheets folded, making a booklet of twenty pages. The fascicles are numbered, and the second is headed, "Summing up." On the back of the second fascicle, written vertically in another hand, is the docketing remark: "Charlie Collins / apology for his Art. / under a deep sense of / high minded responsibility." At the head of the first page are penciled "22 April 1856" and, in what appears to be the same hand that did the docketing, "Seddon?/ C. Collins?" Most of Collins' writing is on the recto pages, with the verso pages (with one exception) reserved for afterthoughts and rubrics, those in the first fascicle chiefly summarizing the possible influence of particular episodes involving Millais, and those in the second fascicle chiefly presenting numbered conclusions. The document is here reproduced by permission of The Huntington Library, San Marino, California.

1

What am I to do about the Telegraph—am I to give up the best subject I shall ever get, as I believe this to be. I have some notion of trying deliberately to examine the nature of the obstacles to my going on with it and how they may (if indeed they can at all) be conquered. One finds so many difficulties give way before a systematic and persevering attack that I am encouraged to take this trouble by the hope that it may get me out of mine. Now, in one word, the difficulties are attributable in this case to one cause —The fear of winning success by means of Millais' brains, or in any measure doing so. Let me then examine how much of this work is all my own or at any rate not the result of any advice of Millais on this particular subject, as to throwing off the influence of his conversation and opinions on art *generally* of course that is impossible. First then—The idea of the subject came into my head of its own accord and was not suggested by him, indeed I believe he was not in town when I thought of it as I shall presently show. / I may say at once that my reason for thinking Millais was away at this time was that I remember sending a Telegraph message (in one of my experiments) to his Father asking when he was expected./* I thought of the Electric Telegraph as a dramatic agent in a picture and determined that the subject should be a wife enquiring by means of it after her husbands safety. At first I thought it should be the wife of a traveller by sea who had heard of the wreck of the ship in which her

*Virgules indicate inserted afterthought.

husband was sailing. Then I thought it would be more completely a subject of our own day if it was a Railway accident which had caused her fears. My idea was that having heard that an accident had happened to this train in which her husband was travelling, she had hastened to the nearest station to enquire through the Telegraph after her husbands fate. As far as I can remember this was all my own. I found on going down to several stations (and sending messages myself that I might see what took place on such occasions) that the clerk writes down the answer to his message word by word as it comes on the instrument, and that the person interested in the intelligence might be looking over his shoulder as he does so. It subsequently became apparent to me that it would be a wonderful increase of the dramatic effect of the picture if this writing were shown, and Millais suggested that the figures ought to be done on such a scale that this writing might be easily legible.

Suggestion by Millais

I returned from these researches and set myself to develop the subject. I made a sketch with the counter of the railway station between the lady and the clerk. There was a third figure—her child reading one of the advertisements in large letters which the Railway Accident Insurance Company post about stations. I showed this sketch to Millais. I forget what he said except that he thought it a good subject[.] He may have said that he thought it might be treated yet better. I tried it several ways and made one sketch in which the Lady was lifting her veil the better to see what the man was writing. This idea Millais always liked—It was not suggested by him or any one else. Hitherto I had not drawn the figures from nature. About this time Millais came to stay with us and occupied himself in designing some illustrations to Tennyson. I got a model for the figure of the Lady and tried the design in all sorts of ways. I found that I could not if I had her outside the counter show such a view of her face as was necessary so I determined to have her inside it. But what of Millais all this time? He would say perhaps when the model was

standing in some attitude I was trying—
"That is good—how fine that is" speaking
of the model and the effect on her etc. Once
he said he saw, from a part of the room in
which he happened to be standing, a view
of the whole scene which he thought would
be the best (I had built up in my room a
kind of imitation of this office desk etc) I
came and looked and at this time thought
so too but rejected the idea because he had
suggested it, and over and over again
besought him *not* to suggest. I limited his
assistance to one thing—the helping me to
decide *which* of my own designs I should
adopt. He said he thought the child might
be left out of the design as it was not likely
that the mother would bring it with her
when so hurried and on such an occasion.

I returned oftenest to the treatment of
the subject in which the lady was lifting her
veil. I remember saying to Millais that I
doubted whether this was not too momentary an action for painting. He then put
himself into the attitude and assumed the
action of one *holding up* a veil while
following the words the man was writing
rather than of one hastily throwing it back
once for all. He would sometimes sit as the
clerk with the model and turning round
would tell her to press closer to him to seem
more eager. I remember once when down
in Scotland I was painting his wife's head in
the picture Millais was in the room. I asked
the lady to stand for a moment in the attitude of the woman in my picture. She did
so and both Millais and I were struck with
the grandeur of her action & Millais hastily
drew my attention to a few points in which
consisted the superiority of what we saw
over what I had previously drawn. I felt
this and months after at home when after
striving hard to make the figure what I
wished drawing it again and again from
nature when I was just getting it at last to
my mind, it appeared to me that it was
pleasing me just because precisely those
qualities which he had seen and pointed out
in the attitude were now becoming
developed. "So then" I said to myself "the
idea of this action is mine but the full
beauty and energy and vigour of it are

I doubt whether this incident may not have
influenced my drawing of the figure, a
drawing done long after.

This may have influenced my design making
it more compact possibly than it would
otherwise have been.

perhaps owed to Millais, and if anybody should praise those qualities how shall I feel?"

These thoughts sapped away my strength and I began to wish to abandon this treatment of the figure. I tried another which in many respects I liked better and was getting happy about it when it occurred to me that it reminded me of something. I set myself to think what and remembered that it was a figure in one of Millais slight pen & ink sketches of evening parties which he used to do in the evening at our house.

Such is a kind of brief view of the history of a very painful part of my life more painful than any one would believe.

This account is already almost a volume in itself and yet I find, I must say a little more and have recourse to a postscript or Supplement ———— — — In which I propose to "sum up" like a judge after a trial—

-2- "Summing up"

The original idea of the Telegraph used as a dramatic agent in a picture and of the subject in which it should be made to take a part — These are my own — and these in my opinion are enough to procure for me such a position in my profession as I should very much wish to have. Millais' influence on the education of my eye has doubtless been great, and must affect every thing I paint, whether I ever see him again or not. I cannot alter my opinion of what I believe to be the canon of right & wrong in art because his opinion has had a share in forming mine as to its laws.

Conclusion No. 1. That the subject should be painted

The idea, then, and the subject, must be made use of.

If made use of, it is probable that it is the picture I should be known by and that people would often say to me "Was not that picture yours of the Electric Telegraph"? It is therefore especially important that I should be able to feel that it is really my own, and that I should not be occupied half my life in trying to get known by some other work that I might not be tormented by feeling myself associated with what I should feel ashamed to claim.

Conclusion No. 2. That I should be especially careful to make it as far as possible all my own

Conclusion No. 3. That it is not necessary
to enquire how I came to think of the
subject at all

(I shall not soon forget what I have suffered
in having my name associated with the
picture of Convent Thoughts and in
receiving praise for it. The idea and
treatment of it having been suggested by
Millais.)

Conclusion No. 4. that the picture shall if it
is in my power be completed for the R.A.
Exhibition of 1857

Conclusion No. 5. The sooner the picture is
done the better

Question

Question

To enquire further whether my thinking
of the subject at all may have been in consequence of my having seen such a work of
Millais' as The Release and whether having
seen and admired it I may have said to myself "cannot I think of any such subject in
which a wife's care for her husband's well
being might be displayed." To go so deep
as this into the investigation of motive is
generally productive of little besides perplexity and I think that any one would
admit that it would be to enquire too
curiously and that I am justified in arriving
at Conclusion 3. and especially as, if the
subject was at all suggested by such an one
as the Release there is nothing to prevent
those who might be interested in the picture
from perceiving it—and it is a clandestine
assistance & not an obvious one that I
dread. For it is my wish that everyone
should know of everything that I owe to
Millais—

The picture should if I am spared be
completed for the Exhibition of 1857.

Would it not be well there being so
much time before that comes round to take
advantage of it and of Millais' absence to
reconsider the whole design seeking to make
it more & more my own.

I must not delay the consideration of this
subject because the time seems long.

Besides conclusions there must remain
certain questions which I must ask myself
and on which I should be glad of an
opinion.

Should I hesitate to make the wife
watching what the clerk is writing because
I have an indistinct recollection that when I
was undecided as to whether I would make
her do so or have her looking away I took
Millais' opinion on the question and he said
he thought she should be looking at the
writing. This is only an impression.

Should I hesitate to do the figures on a
tolerably large scale so that the words
which the clerk is writing should be legible,
because Millais was of opinion that they
ought to be so done that the spectator might
be able to read the writing.

Having stimulated my memory to the
utmost these are all the tangible objections

I can find to my proceeding with this work. There remain behind certain vague feelings of mistrust as to whether I may have received any other hints from Millais on this subject but I cannot (if there are any of any importance) bring them to mind.

Such then, is the condition of the case at present. Such has been the result of some two years of patient thought and laborious determination to do my best with this work cost what it might.

Such causes as those detailed above have operated to stifle the very breath of my professional existence. Such causes at last after months of struggling were too much for me. They seemed to strike the brushes out of my hand. And at last it was almost a relief to find that the year had advanced so far that the thing could not be done in time for the Exhibition.

Repulsed and foiled as I have been I am yet very far from having given up and if the conclusions arrived at above are justifiable and bear the test of examination If I can become convinced that I have proved my right to go on the picture shall be unlocked once more and once more I will open my siege against the canvass nor raise it unless compelled by ill health till the work is accomplished

2 Percy Street, Rathbone Place,
April 22, 1856

Notes

1 It was honored with a caricature in *Punch*, along with Millais' *Mariana*. On the whole it was treated more favorably than the other Pre-Raphaelite paintings in the exhibition.

2 Collins and his friends refer to the painting by that name, or abbreviated to "the Telegraph." The surviving drawings in the British Museum, however, are identified as for *The Railway Accident*, probably because of the words on the poster in three of the drawings. Titles are especially important in narrative paintings; and *The Railway Accident* might have worked even better than *The Electric Telegraph* to clarify and interpret the depicted situation for the beholder. But Collins is consistent in using the name of the instrument that he expected to make the center of interest.

3 A.L.S., 10 May 1856, Huntington Library, HH 70. All manuscripts designated HH in subsequent citations are in The Huntington Library, San Marino, California, and are quoted by permission. Letters to Collins from Hunt or Millais concerning his crisis (e.g., Hunt's written commentary on Collins' "Apology") are unlikely to have survived, judging by a letter from Collins' widow, Kate Perugini, to Alice Stuart Watley (née Millais) in the Morgan Library ("Bowerswell Papers," n.d., Folder A I): "My dearest Carrie. I have

gone right through your fathers letters to Charles Collins and his mother. I was obliged to destroy at least ten of these, as they spoke of private matters connected with C C. alone, and were better destroyed."

4   Augustus Egg, then A.R.A., one of the first of the older generation of painters to befriend the Pre-Raphaelites.

5   A.L.S., 7–14 February 1855, HH 68.

6   "And the Lord spake unto Moses, saying, / See, I have called by name Bezaleel the son of Uri, the son of Hur, of the tribe of Judah: / And I have filled him with the spirit of God, in wisdom, and in understanding, and in knowledge, and in all manner of workmanship, / To devise cunning works, to work in gold, and in silver, and in brass, / And in cutting of stones, to set them, and in carving of timber, to work in all manner of workmanship. / And I, behold, I have given with him Aholiab, the son of Ahisamach, of the tribe of Dan: and in the hearts of all that are wise-hearted I have put wisdom, that they may make all that I have commanded thee; / The tabernacle of the congregation, and the ark of the testimony, and the mercy seat that is thereupon, and all the furniture of the tabernacle."

7   "Charlie Collins apology for his Art under a deep sense of high minded responsibility," autograph MS, subscribed 22 April 1856, HH 1.

8   For this vocabulary and its application, see Martin Meisel, *Realizations: Narrative, Pictorial, and Theatrical Arts of the Nineteenth Century* (Princeton: Princeton University Press, 1983), chapter 5.

9   George Wilson, commenting in 1849 on the rapid spread of the telegraph system "like some swift-growing tropical plant," notes that "it would have done so, however, twenty years ago, had the mechanical conditions for its extension existed:—and we must thank the railroads for its early maturity. Till they provided a secure pathway for its progress it could only exist in embryo." *Edinburgh Review* 90 (October 1849), p. 472.

10 "Suspected Murder at Salt-Hill," London *Times* (3 January 1845); a report of the coroner's inquest at Slough.

11 *Annual Register, 1845*, p. 367, from a full account of the trial (pp. 365–78) and the execution (pp. 42–44).

12 G. M. R. Garratt, "Telegraphy," in *A History of Technology*, ed. Charles Singer, E. J. Holmyard, A. R. Hall, and Trevor I. Williams, vol. 4, *The Industrial Revolution c. 1750 to c. 1850* (Oxford: Clarendon, 1958), p. 659.

13 *Ibid.*, pp. 645–47. When the *Liverpool Telegraph and Shipping Gazette* took its name (1826), it did so from the semaphore device as especially appropriate for shipping news. When the resoundingly successful London *Daily Telegraph* took its name (1855), it had the rapidity, modernity, and potential for drama of the electric telegraph in mind. But the visuality in the term persists in the latter paper's announced intention to "sacrifice all decorum to the desire to make the journal a remunerative spectacle." The "acoustic telegraph" was first introduced in England in 1854, and came into use on the lines of at least one of the numerous telegraph companies, the British and Magnetic. The visual system remained in general use, however, until after the state purchase of the system and its transfer to the Post Office in 1870. Trollope's story, "The Telegraph Girl," first published in 1877 and contemporary in setting, touches on the shift to acoustic reception and its traumas for the operators.

14 See chapter 17. Clifford also refers to "these rapping spirits" as "the messengers of the spiritual world." The Spiritualist movement in America, which took wing between 1848 and 1851, invested itself in metaphors of electric or magnetic telegraphy. The rapping method of telegraphy between worlds was then discovered (and attributed to Benjamin Franklin), manifesting the alliance between the scientific up-to-date and the spiritual or immaterial so characteristic of American culture. For an account of the "intimate

connection between the magnetic telegraph of Samuel F. B. Morse and the spiritual or celestial telegraph," see Werner Sollors' lively paper, "Dr. Benjamin Franklin's Celestial Telegraph, or Indian Blessings to Gas-Lit American Drawing Rooms," *American Quarterly* 35 (Winter 1983), pp. 459–80.

15 John Forster, *Life of Charles Dickens* (London, 1872–74), III, p. 252, (dated by a similar passage in a letter to Forster of 25 August 1862). The notion was never used.

16 Cf. Dion Boucicault, *The Long Strike: A Drama in Four Acts*, French's Standard Drama, no. 360 (New York: Samuel French, n.d.), act 4, scene 1. The scene direction in this American edition, which nevertheless seems to represent the common script of the first productions, reads as follows:

> *Telegraph office in 3; box scene; circular counter; real apparatus; tormenter doors used only; painted window C. of F.; curtain painted on window to appear rolled up; letters on window to read backward—"Telegraph Office—Messages sent to all parts of the United Kingdoms." Chair at R. end of counter; gas-lights with shade's [sic] over operatives desk, (lighted); high stools behind counter for operatives; writing materials on counter and different desks; two small desks on counter with blank despatches [sic] and writing materials; two kerosene lamps by desks and desk and counter telegraph operatives working as curtain rises.* SLACK [telegrapher], TWO OPERATIVES *and* ONE MESSAGE BOY *discovered.* GENTLEMAN *passing on and off.*

17 *Athenaeum* (22 September 1866), p. 376.

18 The only telegraph scene to rival Boucicault's in nineteenth-century drama was in William Gillette's *Secret Service* (1896), where the situation and its emotional appeal are fundamentally different, and only the technical fascination is the same. In Gillette's scene, the sustained effect comes from the virtuoso efforts of the hero, a sympathetic Yankee spy, to send out a message from Confederate headquarters amid interruptions, suspicions, and the unannounced nearby presence of his counter-spy nemesis and his patriotic Southern sweetheart.

19 Andrew Delap, "The Electro-Magnetic Telegraph," *The People's Journal* 2 (1847), p. 210.

20 George Wilson, *Edinburgh Review* 90 (October 1849), pp. 471–72; reprinted in America in *Littell's Living Age* 23 (8 December 1849), pp. 449–50.

21 Harold Bloom, who articulated "the anxiety of influence" and gave it currency in literary studies, argues that relations between contemporaries (e.g., Tennyson and Rossetti) have to be "read" through relations to the predecessor (e.g., Keats). Influence for him is a matter of filiation, sonship. Bloom admits one kind of influence with elements of mutuality, influence "through a generosity of spirit, even a shared generosity." But "where generosity is involved, the poets influenced are minor or weaker; the more generosity, and the more mutual it is, the poorer the poets involved." *The Anxiety of Influence: A Theory of Poetry* (New York: Oxford University Press, 1973), pp. 11–12, 26, 30. I do not think this view accounts for the interactions in schools, especially fraternal avant-garde groupings, nor for the kind of support and emulation to be found in pairs like Wordsworth and Coleridge, Shelley and Byron. Strength of course is relative, though Bloom tends to treat it as an absolute attribute. As we shall see, among the Pre-Raphaelite painters the relatively strong makers were confident enough in themselves to be able to nurture *and* use each other; the relatively weak maker, Collins, was disabled by his anxiety from reaping the benefits of such mutuality.

22 *Memoirs of that Celebrated, Original and Eccentric Genius; the Late George Morland, an Eminent Painter* (London, 1806).

23 "William Collins," *DNB, s.v.*; and W. Wilkie Collins, *Memoirs of the Life of William Collins, Esq., R.A.* (London, 1848), 1:5.

24 *The Smuggler's Refuge*, noticed in the *Illustrated London News* (26 May 1849) as "By the son of the late Royal Academician, whose sea-shore scenes will long preserve his

name. There is something of the father in the treatment and execution of this subject. The very title is somewhat similar."

25 For his earlier life, see "Wilkie Collins," *DNB*, *s.v.*; Kenneth Robinson, *Wilkie Collins: A Biography* (New York, 1951); and Nuell Pharr Davis, *The Life of Wilkie Collins* (Urbana: University of Illinois Press, 1956).

26 W. Wilkie Collins, *Memoirs of the Life of William Collins*, 2:242; from a letter to Richard Henry Dana, Allston's brother-in-law, dated 26 April 1843. Given its ironic fulfillment, Collins' wish for Charles could serve as a folk lesson against wishing. Allston had also suffered a crisis over a painting which effectively ended his active career. The painting in his case was a *Belshazzar's Feast* that he labored over for twenty-five years and left incomplete at his death.

27 W. Holman Hunt, *Pre-Raphaelitism and the Pre-Raphaelite Brotherhood* (London, 1905), 1:298. On a portrait of Charles in death that he gave to Wilkie Collins, Hunt inscribed a passage from Charles's first published volume, *A New Sentimental Journey* (1859), including the following: "For surely of all the ingredients in the horror which death inspires, there is not one that has a larger share to make it terrible than the bitter thought that we are forgotten" (*Pre-Raphaelitism*, 2:313). Wilkie, in thanking him, offered to hold the drawing at Hunt's disposal and to leave it to Hunt's son, " — for you too were his brother, if love makes brotherhood." A.L.S., 11 May 1873, HH 93.

28 Davis, *Wilkie Collins*, pp. 99–101; and S. M. Ellis, "Charles Allston Collins," in *Wilkie Collins, Le Fanu and Others* (London, 1951; original ed., 1931), pp. 59–60.

29 In an appendix to Collins' letter to Hunt of 7–14 February 1855, HH 68. Harriet Collins there mentions that Millais (now off to Scotland and Effie) had been with them recently for nearly two months, "and he kept us alive with a vengeance. Never was such spirits." Millais treated Mrs. Collins with affectionate irreverence and the language of extravagant flirtation.

30 Millais to Mrs. Combe, 10 February 1851, in John Guille Millais, *The Life and Letters of Sir John Everett Millais* (London, 1899), 1:99.

31 Millais to Combe, 30 January 1855, in *Life and Letters*, 1:245.

32 The best brief summary of the enabling effect of fraternal union on the members of the group, and of how cohesion enhanced their impact on press, public, and patronage, is in Ford Madox Hueffer's little book, *The Pre-Raphaelite Brotherhood* (London and New York, [1907]), pp. 61–77. Hueffer's account of the dynamics of the group and "what made Pre-Raphaelism a powerful engine" (p. 69) draws on his experience of other successful avant-garde movements.

33 Millais to Combe, 10 May 1851 and 28 [May] 1851, in *Life and Letters*, 1:102–3; and Hunt, *Pre-Raphaelitism*, 1:232–36. See also Mary Lutyens, "Selling the Missionary," *Apollo* 50 (November 1967), pp. 380–87.

34 A.L.S., 16 March 1882, HH 12973, in *The Forty-Fourth Volume of the Walpole Society*, (Glasgow, 1974), p. 76. See also Hunt, *Pre-Raphaelitism*, 1:262.

35 Hunt writes, "What an act of practical generosity . . . my brotherly rival thus performed! I was at the time helpless and without the prospect of carrying on the emulative competition we had entered into . . . but he, regarding my welfare as dear to him as his own, again secured to me the opportunity of carrying on the contest with him, which, it will be seen, he continued to do until I had found my fair chance of making my effort by his side" (*Pre-Raphaelitism*, 1:236).

36 Millais to Combe, 1 April 1851, in *Life and Letters*, 1:100.

37 Repeated by Collins in A.L.S., 7–14 February 1855, HH 68.

38 A.L.S., 12 August 1855, HH 197.

39 A.L.S., 16 May 1858, HH 402.

40 Millais to Hunt, 8 November 1850, in "Selling the Missionary," p. 386.

41 The story exists in the literature on Collins that Millais was instrumental in preventing his formal election to the Brotherhood on the resignation of Collinson, and in fact covertly subverted Collins' artistic opportunities even as late as Collins' attempt to illustrate *The Murder of Edwin Drood* (1870). The historical record is all to the contrary. William Michael Rossetti makes it clear in *The P.R.B. Journal*, ed. William E. Fredeman (Oxford: Oxford University Press, 1975), that Millais was Collins' chief advocate, supported by Hunt, F. G. Stephens, and Dante Gabriel Rossetti, while Woolner, supported by W. M. Rossetti, was "savagely" opposed (5 November 1850, p. 78). After Collins' *Convent Thoughts* of the following year, however, even W. M. Rossetti was prepared to support Collins' "strong claim to P.R.B.-hood" (May 1851, p. 91). Hunt, in *Pre-Raphaelitism*, 1:266–67, reconstructs a conversation where he explains the undercurrents in the rejection to Millais, and attributes it to the "supernumeraries" and "sleeping members." On the *Edwin Drood* episode, Dickens wrote to Chapman, his publisher (28 November 1869), "Charles Collins finds that the sitting down to draw, brings back all the worst symptoms of the old illness that occasioned him to leave his old pursuit of painting; and here we are suddenly without an Illustrator! We will use his cover of course, but he gives in altogether as to further subjects" (*The Letters of Charles Dickens*, ed. Walter Dexter [London, 1938], 3:753).

42 Hunt, *Pre-Raphaelitism*, 1:263.

43 Millais, *Life and Letters*, 1:136–38; and Hunt, *Pre-Raphaelitism*, 1:283–85, 289–90.

44 Millais' emphasis, in a letter to Mrs. Combe, 22 November 1851, in Millais, *Life and Letters*, 1:135.

45 A.L.S., [January-May 1856], HH 384 (first page missing).

46 A.L.S., Millais to Hunt, 6 January 1867, HH 410.

47 "Biography at a Discount," *Macmillan's Magazine* 10 (June 1864), p. 159.

48 In *Charles Dickens and His Original Illustrators* (Columbus, Ohio, 1980), Jane R. Cohen reports a family legend that Collins was either a homosexual or impotent or both, and that his marriage might never have been consummated (pp. 211 and 270). Since other family legends (e.g., that Charles posed for Millais' Black Brunswicker, as Kate truly did for the lady) are only appropriate fictions, this one cannot be allowed much authority.

49 *Athenaeum* (1 June 1850), p. 591; London *Times* (9 May 1850), p. 5.

50 *Exhibition of the Royal Academy of Arts* (London, 1850), no. 535. The catalog chastely substitutes "in his possession" for Miss Strickland's "on his person" (*Lives of the Queens of England* [London, 1873], 1:211). It further identifies Berengaria's companions in the scene as her sister-in-law, Queen Joanna, and Richard's quasi-captive, the Princess of Cyprus.

51 The illuminated page—identified by Julian Treuherz in "The Pre-Raphaelites and Mediaeval Manuscripts" (*The Pre-Raphaelite Papers*, ed. Leslie Parris [London, 1984], pp. 156–57)—derives from the Arnstein Bible (MS Harleian 2799), probably by way of Henry Noel Humphreys' and Owen Jones' facsimile in *The Illuminated Books of the Middle Ages* (London, 1849), plate 9. In the illumination, John's seat rests on the shortened right riser of the huge N belonging to the IN that occupies the left two-thirds of the image (a vertical PRINCIPIO, with a separate column for the three I's, occupies the remaining third). John is writing with a quill on a manuscript held in a lily-like stand, under a Christ holding a book. The visible words in the writing are: "In p . . . / cipio . . . / verbum / et verbū." As part of the interplay between word and image, more extensive than I have indicated, the artist closes a remarkable endless loop where creation is incorporated in the created.

52 On the imagery of the nun in Victorian painting, and the argument between the cloister and the hearth as it bears on *Convent Thoughts*, see Susan P. Casteras, "Virgin Vows:

The Early Victorian Artist's Portrayal of Nuns and Novices," *Victorian Studies* 24 (Winter 1981), esp. pp. 170–73.

53   Millais, *Life and Letters*, 1:133.

54   A.L.S., November 1852, HH 355, and 10 April 1854, HH 380.

55   A.L.S., 6–7 April 1854, HH 63.

56   The *Illustrated London News* noted the Academy's hanging committee "has deservedly assigned places to honour [several paintings including] Charles Collins's pre-Raphaelite, 'Thought of Bethlehem' " (29 April 1854, p. 390). The *Athenaeum* (6 May 1854, p. 560) found the subject uninteresting, but "redeemed by the religious feeling that vivifies it. . . . The child arranging the flowers, the grateful mendicant and the Dorcas herself, all interest though they do not attract. The chestnut trees in the background are wonderful; and the accessories, though somewhat hard, are good in detail."

57   Hunt, *Pre-Raphaelitism*, 2:313–14. In *The Pre-Raphaelite Landscape* (Oxford, 1973), p. 83, Allen Staley speculates that Collins may have subsequently reworked or partly effaced the painting.

58   *Exhibition of the Royal Academy of Arts* (London, 1854), no. 607. The first ellipsis describes the woman as "perchance a sinner too, but one assuredly whom the merciful Jesus would not have rejected." See Julia Kavanagh, *Women of Christianity, Exemplary for Acts of Piety and Charity* (London, 1852), p. 178.

59   Théophile Gautier, *Les Beaux-Arts en Europe, 1855* (Paris, 1855), 1:79–80.

60   A.L.S., 7–14 February 1855, HH 68.

61   "I was especially struck with the noble idea of the scapegoat. It is a glorious subject full of wild terror . . . it becomes a theme of the utmost and most touching interest and importance. I envy you the subject, only glad that it has got into better hands than mine" (A.L.S., 7–14 February 1855, HH 68).

62   The four drawings may be arranged in a developmental order where first the point of view and general configuration are worked out, and finally the concrete representation of the principal figures in vibrant relationship is achieved. This is an ideal order, however, rather than an actual one. As the written evidence makes clear, Collins' progress with his subject was not linear; rather he circled back continually, starting fresh, reviving earlier ideas, undoing and redoing previous work. Moreover, in the absence of a painting as the result of the drawings, there is no convenient final state of the image to work back from. The most sensible procedure might be to ignore sequence entirely, and assume that each drawing addresses a different compositional problem: point of view (figure 2); placement of the heads and bodily attitude (figure 4); placement in a background (figure 9); inclusion of the child (figure 10). However, the ideal order is useful in eliciting some of the possibilities in the painting and arguable because the contents of the drawings correspond to events and concerns in Collins' history of the enterprise, so that a developmental order is compatible in broadest terms with a chronology.

63   A.L.S., [29 July 1855], Bowerswell Papers, Morgan Library. The marriage had taken place on 3 July. Millais also wrote to Collins on 29 July, on the joys of marriage and the foolishness of his prior fears (Morgan Library). Collins seems to have stayed with the Millais for several weeks. A thoroughly garbled version of the visit appears in J. G. Millais' *Life and Letters*, 1:288: "Among their first visitors was Charles Collins. He, however, was not bent on amusing himself; he wanted to paint, and at his request my mother sat for him every day for a fortnight. Then, seeing that the picture made very slow progress, and that she was presented as looking out of the window of a railway carriage—a setting that would have vulgarized Venus herself—she refused to sit any longer, and the picture was never finished."

64   Collins' earlier conception may be seen in a sketch in the British Museum, reproduced in

Hueffer's *Pre-Raphaelites*, p. 147. Millais reportedly blamed the shift on Collins getting "hipped about a fancied love affair, and becoming a High Churchman" (Hunt, *Pre-Raphaelitism*, 1:294). Allen Staley, who argues that as a painter Collins "did little more than caricature Millais," points to a similarity between the composition of *Convent Thoughts* and that of Millais' *Ferdinand Lured by Ariel*. There are indeed similarities (e.g., the arched top and the placement of the horizon). But Collins' distress over owing Millais "the idea and the treatment of it" was not a matter of composition; it involved the subject and its conceptual embodiment.

65 *Household Words* (13 February 1858), pp. 201–5.
66 *The Letters of Charles Dickens*, ed. Walter Dexter (London, 1938), 3:138 (19 November 1859).
67 *The Eye-Witness, His Evidence about Many Wonderful Things* (London, 1860).
68 *The Eye-Witness*, p. 288. The original version in *All the Year Round* (16 June 1860), p. 225, has "pre-Raphaelite period."
69 "An English Painter's Tomb," *Macmillan's Magazine* 1 (April 1860), p. 491.
70 A.L.S., 16 July 1859, University Research Library, University of California in Los Angeles.
71 The painting was exhibited on its own after Gambart, the great art dealer, bought it to be engraved for the then staggering sum of 5,500 guineas. (Through the good offices of Wilkie Collins, Hunt was able to tap Dickens for sound commercial advice on negotiating the price.) At about the same time, Gambart was reported to have acquired Millais' *Black Brunswicker* for similar purposes even before its exhibition at the Royal Academy. See the *Athenaeum* (21 April 1860), pp. 549–50, 588.
72 A.L.S., 20 June 1860, HH 74. Another hand, probably that of Hunt, pencilled a head-note on this letter: "A real friend!!"
73 A.L.S., 12 June 18[65], HH 71. Collins misdates this letter as "June 12, 1856." He mentions taking his wife (married 1860) to see her father "after his late narrow escape," i.e., the Staplehurst railway accident, 9 June 1865.
74 *All the Year Round*, extra Christmas number (10 December 1866), pp. 28–35.
75 Gladys Storey in *Dickens and Daughter* (London, 1939), p. 157, says that the Collinses first met Perugini in Leighton's studio; she doesn't say when. As Mrs. C. E. Perugini, Kate, who had taken to art herself, began exhibiting at the Royal Academy (thirty-four paintings between 1877 and 1904), often taking her subjects from Dickens. That Millais had much earlier dubbed Charles "Saint Carlo" is an especially heavy-handed touch in life's narrative.

Willing Frame-Ups, After Henry James
Mary Ann Caws

She had framed it all. James, "In the Cage" (ET, 245) [1]

Our will to framing and reading frames, to seeking out figures of some interest in our own carpets, are forms of involvement we may have learned from Henry James.[2] We have seen, in his passionate work-on-us, what an intense concern with the conditions for seeing and surrounding some posited center of focus, present or absent, leads to: this is frame-involvement to the literary spiritual extreme.

Framing is taken here in the sense of what encloses the object we want to make sense of, isolating it from the context that surrounds it, cutting it out, as it were, from the wall behind it to enable its own figures to take on more importance and its gestures, greater depth.[3] Verbal framing can be often seen in a patterning effect: the repetition of words and phrases, or their reversal in a chiasmus, or the deliberate interruption of a series, draw attention to the border of an especially meaningful scene or one that we read as such. The border here would be a detectible *different* against a more ordinary ground of the *same*, like the ornamented edges of a picture we are meant to focus on. Within the framing edges, the picture is held in what seems a static freeze, which effectively halts the full flow of narrative, so that we may read and reread what we think significant in it. The halt can be perceived spatially, so that heavy framing architecture surrounds the principal figure, or temporally, so that a *delay* holds the scene before our eyes, or (and more usually) both. In short, the framing impulse in narrative is a circumscriptive preparation which writes around and works toward a sense of at least temporary closure and enclosure. Thus, a framing moment would combine temporal and spatial modes to arrest the telling action by a deliberate suggestion of special meaning, held down to be more closely observed; it could be described as an extraordinary picture, held in a perceptual and conceptual delay against the ordinary flux of what is to be read and told.

Within a given frame, there is often what I call a *developing object* which points to the center of the scene or to the principal figure, and which seems to concentrate within itself the story told, enabling all the gestures associated with it to appear larger than life. In the particular instance of a high-raised frame such as those Henry James is master of, the whole scene and its transfixed moment are set on a special rise and in an almost unbearable tension by the intensity of the holding action.

James the Master carpet-maker is also James the master framer in his late works, particularly that superb paradigm of framing called "In the Cage," which questions the whole idea of message and of transmission by making a mock picture, taking us in, and delivering us to the side of blindness. This quite remarkable frame-up of an empty or at least undiscoverable message shows all the characteristics of the framing tale, of a reading and writing frame-up, a send-up of hermeneutics and a mockery of message, with a terrible clarity. The cage itself, the high borders of a telegraph desk, mocks the idea of James' own standard architectural surround (Nanda appearing naive in the doorway of *The Awkward Age*, the mother in the door confronting Ned's mistress/model in *The Tragic Muse*, Kate or Milly in *The Wings of the Dove*, and Charlotte or Maggie in *The Golden Bowl* in their respective doorways and windowframes) and works to surround the very idea of the undiscoverable, undeliverable message in a paradigm of framing. The telegram itself, that developing object within the cage, is, despite the transmitting girl's constant interpretations, held in a drastic delay, until each of the interpretative moments is seen, like a parody of Reception Theory, to be suspended in utter triviality, as the multiple and central misreadings work out their full uselessness.

The reading of that cage and of the Jamesian figure, present or absent in the author's and reader's carpets—probably not of the same pattern—those emblematic objects doubly his and our obsession, lie underfoot in our attempts to get back to what preceded them, and on to what follows. This essay will briefly explore, in that light, a few paradigms of the framing impulse, in writing and in our reading. Without making any pretense as to the inclusive nature of these examples, my choice nevertheless is intended to represent different perspectives that our reading of James might lead us to view, and to view from, differently.

First, the architectural and conceptual framework of Hawthorne as James saw it and which no doubt influenced him greatly, with its ominously imprisoning devices, and then those of Poe, whose stories present, in their rhythm and reversals, a claustrophobic and obsessive inframing of reader as of included and narrated figures. Third, Flaubert's play of mobile against static framing in a doubly determined ship/land background/foreground passage setting off the central figure in a pre-Jamesian Portrait of a Lady. Borges and Cortázar will represent the willing confusion of in and out: more particularly the analysis of the interference of camera work in its problematized enlargement or "blow-up," which can be made to suggest the power of impersonal lens over personal subjective vision, of "modern" techniques and their relation to focus and frame. The reader is taken into their duplicity of absence and presence.

The essay in its own marked end-framing will end with what questions it all and our question with it, one French labyrinth as seen by Robbe-Grillet. In a brilliantly mocking parody of the stifling inclusionary mode, the *frame-up mode* itself, in a labyrinth both verbal and visual, the painting he describes is its own rhetorical frame and the story its own over-full and finally empty setup, like a myth worked out and at last deserted.

My own view of framing is, of course, determined by the objects I have chosen to see, and they by it, as well as by my relatively Western and win-dowed outlook on the frame and how it takes in and sets out. This outlook, Jamesian as I am presenting it here, with specific allusions to the cage, as a reading conundrum ("In the Cage"), and to the fount, as a parody of the sacred source of inspiration (*The Sacred Fount*) corresponds to a relatively static opposition between interior and exterior, inside and out, and the intrinsic/extrinsic stances.

From another and more current viewpoint, all the tales alluded to here could be retold within a currency of exchange poetics, where dialogue might lend to the flexibilization of inside and out, to the complexification of the framing categories. That will have to be for a future frame.

Hawthorne's Baroque Borders

Here I sit in my old accustomed chamber . . . and now I begin to understand why I was imprisoned so many years in this lonely chamber, and why I would never break through the viewless bolts and bars. Hawthorne, *Notebooks*

For the present-day reader, Hawthorne's melodrama is hard to take. Its heavy structures exude their own gloom, without apparent interior motivation. James, fascinated from an early period with Hawthorne, and the author of a book on him, was himself to learn a great deal from these constructions, even while he criticized their unnatural air. Even Hawthorne's sense of sin, said James, had to be "imported into his mind, existing only for a literary pur-pose" (HJ, p. 58). There is something stiff, he continues, about "The Birth-mark," "as if the kernel had not assimilated its envelope" (HJ, p. 64).

As in Poe, the surround is of paramount interest because it is architectural, psychological, verbal, and metaphysical all at once. And as in James, any ex-plicit reading is foredoomed, in favor of a multiple reception of meanings. Hawthorne's letter, scarlet or black, like the Birthmark, will be difficult to construe and unsure in its construal. Hawthorne's "Intelligence Office" bears a close parallel to James's remarkable story of a misreading, "In the Cage," where the text within the text remains obscure, even to the author. (" 'What in fact was the message?' " James was asked about this tale. "How should I know," he responded.) The reader is constantly shut out from the record-ing sessions and deprived of all clues, except to the misreadings committed by the character involved. "What further secrets were then spoken remains a mystery. . . ."

James' own "figure in the carpet," unfindable and uninterpretable, perhaps existing only in the mind of the reader as projected by the author, is intimately related to the tapestry in Hawthorne's *Marble Faun*, whose mystery is not to be undone: "The gentle reader . . . is too wise to insist upon looking closely at the wrong side of the tapestry, after the right one has been sufficiently displayed to him" (*MF*, p. 275). Hawthorne's framing impulses work, finally, to exclude the observer and the reader; if those of James seem finally to permit more readerly play, it may be only because we are, by his genius for the subtle slant of the construction, so very well taken in.

Hawthorne's whole concern in *The Blithedale Romance*, as he says in the preface, "is merely to establish a theatre, a little removed from the highway of ordinary travel" (*BR*, p. 21). The scene is to be odd, the viewpoint, sideways: Miles Coverdale, the narrator, is constantly presented as on the edges of the view, outside the general framework of the story and the sympathy of its personages. He does not see straight on, but rather through a deformation of coldness, camouflage, and distance. His peculiar and chilly slant is constantly visible as he spies upon the others in all self-righteousness: "For, was mine a mere vulgar curiosity?" (*BR*, p. 19). Speaking of himself as the tragic Greek chorus, he seems a "pasteboard copy" of a man. Duplications of this kind further the chill of events and the catastrophe. Each thing has its copy: some material or conceptual, some mimetic or metaphoric, some artistic and innocent or purposely duplicitous. When an entire scene is copied, rather than existing twice, it places existence at a distance by reframing it; so "the snowy landscape, which looked like a lifeless copy of the world in marble" prefigures Zenobia's own "cold and bright" eventual transfiguration from her early passionate and idealizing or communitarian self. This worldly change is reflected in glass as cool as stone: "Pictures, marbles, vases,—in brief, more shapes of luxury than there could be any object in enumerating . . . and the whole repeated and doubled by the reflection of a great mirror which showed me Zenobia's proud figure, likewise, and my own" (*BR*, p. 198).

Yet her reflection is already a warning of her end: "But I caught the reflection of her face in the mirror, and saw that it was very pale—as pale, in her rich attire, as if a shroud were round her" (*BR*, p. 202). Even as it is turned aside, this pale shrouding is at once a copy of Priscilla's inserted tale of the Veiled Woman, and a prefiguration, seen twice as it is reflected, of her final end by drowning, by her own choice. Typically, this latter and terrible incident is perceived by Coverdale as only an *imitation* "of drowned persons in lithe and graceful attitudes" (*BR*, p. 276). His warped framework permits even this remarkably cold-hearted perception to be preceded by a veiled statement of his own self-deception, doubling in the guise of honesty: "A reflection occurs to me that will show ludicrously, I doubt not, on my page" (*BR*, p. 276). And so it does, within the readerly framework.

This is, quite openly, a vulgar tale of spying and of curiosity: as an ideal natural eavesdropping hideout, a leafy cave between the boughs of a sheltering tree provides a concentrated viewing place for the always covered Coverdale. This natural peeping-place will be recovered in the architectural, social, or cultural peeping-place of the room given to Coverdale and his curiosity in the boardinghouse, where he looks out upon the rear window of the final dwelling of the erstwhile community, which has come to culture from nature. The observed picture is framed by what borders the viewing place as well as the surroundings of the seen.

The aggressively curious look that is Coverdale's and the passive and submissive look that is Priscilla's are set in a dialectical relation, as are the look directed in from out and that directed out from in. The frame is made to include both, in its arrest of the double look — so the images are open to reading against and upon each other in their highly curious overlay: the multiple spying and reflecting scenes have many possible readings. Like copies of the real landscapes in marble, in glass, the images can be read forwards, backwards, into, and through.

In the following scene, the narrow passageway of the space both protected and set off gives a double glimpse into the inside (as it opens upon the outside) and the outside (as it invades the space within). "The sense of vast, undefined space, pressing from the outside against the black panes of our uncurtained windows, was fearful to the poor girl, heretofore accustomed to the narrowness of human limits, with the lamps of neighboring tenements glimmering across the night" (BR, p. 59).

Windows, which are in their most usual sense the apertures through which we look out upon the outside world, become here the doorways for that outside world to push in threateningly upon the little world within: "The evening wore on, and the outer solitude looked in upon us through the windows, gloomy, wild and vague, like another state of existence, close beside the little sphere of warmth and light in which we were the prattlers and bustlers of a moment" (BR, p. 61). Even the personal metaphors work in much the same way, as passageways between two spaces: "My fit of illness," says Coverdale, "had been an avenue between two existences; the low-arched and darksome doorway, through which I crept out of a life of old conventionalisms, on my hands and knees, as it were, and gained admittance into the freer region that lay beyond. In this respect, it was like death" (BR, p. 87). Whatever the view opens upon, it is not at its most intricately worked moments a one-way passage.

The view is complicated still more in the case of an included observer, unreliable and observed by yet another pair of eyes, so that the spectacle makes a double frame:

Zenobia was in the doorway, not far from Hollingsworth. She gazed at
Priscilla in a very singular way. Indeed, it was a sight worth gazing at,

and a beautiful sight, too, as the fair girl sat at the feet of that dark, powerful figure. Her air, while perfectly modest, delicate and virgin-like, denoted her as swayed by Hollingsworth, attracted to him, and unconsciously seeking to rest upon his strength. I could not turn away my own eyes, but hoped that nobody, save Zenobia and myself, were witnessing that picture. It is before me now, with the evening twilight a little deepened by the dusk of memory. (BR, p. 105)

The infatuated narrator, as observer, suffers an attraction to Priscilla so strong as to infuse the entire portrait, which no one is privileged to see but himself and Zenobia: it is the picture of a passion developing, far from some neutral pastel portrait. That is, of course, the case in the tale as a whole, strongly colored by the look, not so much of curiosity as of an obsession, in which the position of the frame is askew.

In the most extraordinary double-framed scene of all, Coverdale, in exile from Utopia—as they all are—stares out from his boarding house window on to the backs of the windows across from that house, and, as at a theater illuminated for his sole benefit, glimpses, in that "backside of the universe," a sort of reality from the rear. The picture is such as would appeal to his speculative interest, and is more revealing of his nature than of the persons spied upon, in its frost, its general unpleasantness matched to the surrounding weather, "lowering, with occasional gusts of rain, and an ugly-tempered east wind, which seemed to come right off the chill and melancholy sea" (BR, p. 179).

The parallel with his own nature is made clear ten pages later: "That cold tendency, between instinct and intellect, which made me pry with a speculative interest into people's passions and impulses, appeared to have gone far towards unhumanizing my heart" (BR, p. 188). In keeping with this, the sight of the familiar figures "arraying themselves before me, and presenting their old problem in a shape that made it more insoluble than ever," makes the hope of some catastrophe the only one (BR, p. 190). The inhuman has plainly gained dominance in this onlooker, more "voyeur" than simple observer.

In a further reversal, like that of the night beyond the window panes staring back in, the observed persons look back at the observer, and Zenobia lets the curtain fall, shutting off the sight, having signaled that she recognizes and dismisses Coverdale's efforts to be at once the onlooker and involved: "The next moment, she administered one of those pitiless rebukes which a woman always has at hand, ready for an offender (and which she seldom spares, on due occasion), by letting down a white linen curtain between the festoons of the damask ones" (BR, p. 193). But it falls like a "drop-curtain," separating the acts one from another.

For the window of this picture, this real but rear picture window is a privileged one: the "golden wine" of the sunbeams inmingled with water

casts a glow up to the very spire, before the twilight falls, making an illuminated place for the spirit to rest. As in the preceding scenes, the opposites are
clearly pictured, just as for the tableau captured in the preceding window as
an interior oasis against a barbarian outside, or the reversal, with the outside
dark peering in. As Coverdale peers, is discovered, is shut out, intrudes, and
is shut out again while the final events take their course—it is only he who
unmasks his terrible apartness:

> As for me, I would look on, as it seemed my part to do, understand-
> ingly, if my intellect could fathom the meaning and the moral, and, at
> all events, reverently and sadly. The curtain fallen, I would pass onward
> with my poor individual life, which was now attenuated of much of its
> proper substance. (*BR*, p. 192)

In this story of utopian spirits and a place set apart, of secrecy and spying,
of the veil and the peeping place, the original duplication of metaphors adds
to the final picture: veil and cover, patch and falsity, as opposed to the genuine
Hollingsworth, who is the final rescuer of the Veiled Lady, the making present of what was only seen as covered. After that strong scene of rescue, there
is a delay marked in the text, a description of the way wending back from
civilization and its rear windows to the rural calm of the rediscovered Blithedale, captured in the narrator's memory, forever: "The pathway of that walk
still runs along, with sunny freshness, through my memory. I know not why
it should be so" (*BR*, p. 242).

And now, in an underplayed but none the less significant transferral, the
earlier reversal inside/outside, light/dark, permits Coverdale to usurp the
place of dark nature, peering into the simple interior and its tranquil scene:
"Had it been evening, I would have stolen softly to some lighted window of
the old farm-house, and peeped darkling in, to see all their well-known faces
round the supper-board" (BR, p. 244). Longing for a quiet entrance, a re-
absorption into the familiar scene, this revisitant precedes the tale of Zenobia's
drowning by his contemplation of the black pool of the river, and on the
other hand repeats his own spying in a reframed or *self-imitative* pose.

And the reader, caught in the same reformulations of framing and reframing, spying from the edges like Coverdale, is finally imprisoned like Coverdale,
in a self-imitation of what it is to read, while what seems most real drowns
in a reflecting pool. Zenobia has had the last word: "Is it you, Miles Coverdale? . . . Ah, I perceive what you are about! You are turning this whole affair
into a ballad" (*BR*, p. 261). Poets, she continues, give us either "glittering
icicles or lines of fire." This poetic tale includes both icicles and fire, both
presence and distance, spying and hiding, but not so that the reader should,
like Coverdale, turn it into a ballad for the mind. Structure and its perception
may mask feeling; the perfection of some picture glimpsed in a window or

from the peep-holes of a tree may glaze it into an accepted frame, to the detriment of what is really to be observed within it.

Hawthorne, who may indeed never have felt himself able to break through those "viewless bolts and bars" of his early imprisoning chamber, also refuses final entrance to the viewer of his architectural schemes. His perversion is the ground for our obsession with his enframing exclusions of his readers, all the more engaged in their reading for the perversity of the paradox.

Poe's Constructions and Circumscriptions

If ever mortal painted an idea . . . Poe, "The Fall of the House of Usher"

In Poe's picture, the techniques of metatextual reference are intensified and exaggerated to the extreme, the over-determined structural effect framing mansions, chateaux, houses, as well as the page. An airless inclusion permeates the text and composes surrounds of baroque swerves and windings, of swaying draperies, windows reddening, velvet curtains closing across the view. Rare is the presentation simple or straight, for the elements are either doubles (two ladies, two black cats, two William Wilsons, two beating hearts), or else oddly angled with niches, projections, and protusions, with rooms opening through each other, gates turning upon their hinges, and doors collapsing.

The frequent, even typical, final consummation gives a particularly intense claustrophobic cast to the stories where the metatextual element at the center causes the turn and the ruin: in Poe the text absorbs itself into its own narrated decor, never retreating into simple "novel," but rather walling itself up, flooring itself over, or dissolving entirely. Some "frivolous device" in the margin or in the typography, some "quaint shadow falling aslant on the tapestry or upon the door" may serve as the *incitamentum* or First Cause of the reflection, as the focus for the ensuing meditation; so the teeth of Berenice, for example, frame a tale from inside and to enameled perfection, within an absolute and horrible concentration:

> Not a speck on their surface—not a shade on their enamel—not an indenture in their edges—but what that period of her smile had sufficed to brand in upon my memory. . . . The teeth!—the teeth!—they were here, and there, and everywhere, and, visibly and palpably before me; long, narrow, and excessively white, with the pale lips writhing about them. . . . They alone were present to my mental eye, and they, in their sole individuality, became the essence of my mental life. I held them in every light. I turned them in every attitude. I surveyed their characteristics. I dwelt upon their peculiarities. I pondered upon their conformation. I mused upon the alteration in their nature. I shuddered as I assigned to them in imagination a sensitive and sentient power, and even when unassisted by the lips, a capability of moral expression. (SW, pp. 180–81)

The insistence of the verbs, in their feverish activity and their exaggerated repetition of pattern, imposes itself with a terrible regularity upon the contemplation of those regular and repeated fixtures of the mouth, a sort of high camp metonymy for the speaking voice and a recall of the "furniture for the mouth" of the Precious School. Everything is in its right place and patterned in the sentence exactly as in the mouth: "I held/I turned/I surveyed/I dwelt/I pondered/I mused/I shuddered."

The object or observation that is to be set apart, no matter how singular, must hold the attention, and just as the poem must be short, the place of action must be tightly enclosed: "It has always appeared to me that a close *circumscription of space* is absolutely necessary to the effect of insulated incident: —it has the force of a frame to a picture" (*SW*, p. 488). The sense of enclosure is haunting, and often referred to a picture whose two dimensions are still more imprisoning, whose textual cross-reference pervades everything.

"The Fall of the House of Usher," for example, is at once a scene, a landscape, and a painting, easily modifiable merely by the "different arrangement of the particulars of the scene, the details of the picture" (*SW*, p. 139). An intense visual consciousness here is responsible for the almost abstract design of the downward lines in formal parallel to the thick atmospheric touches of the gloom descending, the evening hanging densely, the torches smothering, and the Lady Madeline succumbing.

In the inserted ballad, an abandoned palace is crowded with pale forms and time entombed: this *inset* shadows forth in its depth the fate of the falling house, but here too the grey stones, the fog, and the decaying trees make an arrangement then duplicated and repeated in the waters of the tarn, like a still life, more impressively with all the linguistic force of a *nature morte*, already dead in its expression, however natural that expression.

A coffin enframes yet another *nature morte*, in the sense of a life stilled as well as a still life: "the mockery of a faint blush upon the bosom and the face, and that suspiciously lingering smile upon the lip which is so terrible in death" (*SW*, p. 151). The lid is screwed down, but the sight serves as the border for future ones, as the outer or framing narrative suddenly converges with the narrative enframed, for instance, in Ethelred's gaunt hand tearing down the door during the reading of the story itself.

At the core of the correspondences like these reside the paintings Usher meditates upon and whose images he communicates to the narrator, who would in vain erase their accumulation, showing the text as faulted, in its lack as in its excess. Usher paints his idea, casting shadows and lights on his canvas in an abstraction even more vivid than Fuseli's "too concrete reveries"; here the painter's occupations "shadowed forth . . . in words" include a small picture of the interior of a tunnel flooded by a radiation which the narrator finds inappropriately splendid, for there is neither outlet nor inlet for light. The tunnel shape includes and encloses, like an optical illusion turning inside and out, writing in and writhing out, tunneling and traveling faster and faster, to guarantee "the success" of the design, as the narrator says. His design encompasses the fragments of the remainder of the construction, from the initial fissure to the closing waters, over the inner and outer walls as they merge.

The most celebrated purloined letter, folded back upon itself so as not to be noticed, offers another image for doublings and reversals classic in form. Poe's reversals, thus stressed, tend to make similar points, that on the *other side* (as of the plaster behind which there is a murdered woman, or of the floorboards in *The Tell-Tale Heart*) some secret is to be found. The text is always on the side where it is not expected to be.

Like the sourceless light in the tunnel, the removal of an eye suppresses, in the text, the I opposed to the narrating eye: the eye-like windows of the house of Usher and the thousand menacing eyes in the pit have not the same personal horror as the eye in *The Tell-Tale Heart*, removed as the head is cut from the corpse, or eye of *The Black Cat* cut out in a criminal act whose possible reappearance haunts the text in its own reversed likeness on the other side of the wall. The act is seen, and subsequently cut off, or out.

The projection already made upon the wall behind which the dead wife is inserted—surely the most macabre insetting in any of these tales—serves the reader as a mark of the obsessive imagination, further manifested by the character irrepressibly moved to speak of the "excellent construction," as before of the "success of my design." To the extent to which Poe's own *design* is successful, the text enframes the reader in that design and in that construction. Always here the narrator informs upon himself, so that the plot carries its own reversal, so that his "solid" construction may be seen, in reverse, as "decayed." Such revelations undo the excellent construction, reversing the effect for the observer's and the reader's reconstruction of the crime through the informing voice, itself sounded within the text, as if to try it out for the observer or listener.

Vision is here obstructed for its effect, for the senses see much and much too clearly, unless they are veiled over, like the soul; the excessive and hypernervous concentration on one spot or one feature forces a vision so close that it blurs, serving the same obstructive function. Staring at the teeth of Berenice or at the color of Ligeia's eyes may cancel the vision on the outside, whereas an intense insetting may, on the contrary, open the way to a meditation or a reflection within. The text veiled over, walled up, and mirroring in its self-construction and self-annihilation, the construction in imaginative collapse, repeatedly instructs us in its own reading. That reading serves to illustrate the positive-through-negative reading impulse; hooked on a detail or a set of clues, as in James, the reader is made to lose the whole outer picture for an inner and obsessing one. The picture, shifted in its scope and terms, holds us framed in a tighter grip than the initial telling of the story had promised, or threatened.

Flaubert: Subjective Outlining

It was like an apparition . . . *Sentimental Education*

The initial portrait of Madame Arnoux as she appears to Frédéric in Gustave Flaubert's *Sentimental Education* shows a typical and high-tone outlining of one figure: the scene has the memorable quality we associate with the dramatic pictorial presentations of James, but has also the solemn overtones of religious imagery, like a Madonna in a stained-glass window, with thick lead borders enhancing its iconic significance and paradigmatic value.

The first announcement of the portrait sets it formally into the text, like a visual analogue of one of Molière's portrait scenes, such as that which Célimène furnishes in the famous salon passage of *The Misanthrope*. This is in fact a set piece, situated in a dazzle of central radiance with strong backlighting; the central figure is presented as almost a mythic being, standing out in drastic relief against the flatness and dullness of everything around her. She is, literally, a figure to be read against a ground; the slow-moving pace of the view, as it closes in, throws the portrait in a temporal relief to match the spatial one. The iconic picture is in contradistinction to the meaninglessness or "insignificance," to use the words of the text, of all the other travelers: of course this scene is given its interest, which is its skewing of reality or its deformation, through the eyes of the love-struck Frédéric, so that it is an example of subjective outlining.

Three stages mark the gradual intensification of the gaze. (1) First, the smallness and slowness of the scene and the vessel's motion, halted as if by boredom at the unimportance of it all: "Some little white clouds were halted in the sky—and a vague sense of ennui seemed to slow down the motion of the boat and make the travelers seem still more insignificant" (*SE*, p. 36). (2) Next, the announcement of the apparition is unnamed as befits that of a mythic figure, preceding the centralization of the queen, enthroned in her dazzling isolation and her instant assertion of authority over the passive worshipper, who has eyes for no one else in her all-encompassing presence. She has only to raise her head slightly in order for him to bend his shoulders and retreat, in order to free the space for her miraculous being and the deserved obeisance:

> She was seated, in the center of the bench, quite alone; or at least he saw no one, in the radiance with which her eyes dazzled him. As he went by, she raised her head; without meaning to, he bent his shoulders; and when he had taken up a position further along, on the same side, he looked at her. (*SE*, p. 36)

(3) In the last stage, the details have come clear. She is so centralized and so beautiful to the eyes of love that the amorous pressure of her hair around her face and the extension and expansion of her skirt convey the sheer erotic delight to the text, generating a pleated profusion of detail:

> She had a large straw hat, with rose-colored ribbons which trembled in the air behind her. Her black hair came down low around the tip of her large brows and seemed to press lovingly against the oval of her face. Her dress of light muslin, with polka-dots, spread out in numerous pleats. She was embroidering something; and her straight nose, her chin, her whole person was outlined against the backdrop of the blue air. (*SE*, pp. 36–7)

For the apparition to take on such passionate force of description, or rather, vision, the very clouds are halted to make a delay, so that the radiance from her eyes which have taken on the dazzle of the sun is shown as the only vigorous element in the entire scene. Opposed to this outspreading and in-pressing of love, the insignificance of everything else around is as striking as it is illogical in an objective sense: the impersonal ennui of the landscape and the personal boringness of the other travelers remain as unspecified as the "something" she is embroidering, a textual marker of vagueness. She embroiders something material, and probably no more than "something," whereas he embroiders everything in the scene, which is his alone. He will not read her text as she will be given to read his. The two frames on which they embroider are completely different; nothing, finally, has any importance in the eyes of love but the loved object as it is so framed.

The apparition of the figure occurs before it is named, so that the text is presented to the ignorant eye as it is to Frédéric's own. His sight is the model for ours.

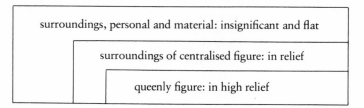

The two paragraphs setting off this vision from that of the flat border begin by evocations of the central figure, by means of the simplest verbs: "she was . . . ," "she had . . ." The outline of her body against the blue air of the background is sharp; she sits motionless as if posing for this portrait, and suddenly on the border of the picture there appears a nurse with her child, who is then handed to her. This Mother-with-Child motif then adds to the inset piece of the beloved woman the motif of the Madonna with Child to be revered. The proof of this within the text comes on the next page, as Frédéric gives a large coin to the beggar, moved by a benevolent feeling associated with her, at once a blessing and an impulse "almost religious."

Abruptly, the spectator's eyes switch to a shawl, about to fall into the water, a metonymy of the figure herself: to rescue it and her Frédéric leaps forward, so that their eyes meet. The play of looks works toward a center of intensity:

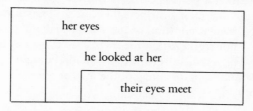

Then the scene is cut off as the figure is identified from the outside, by a figure unvalorized aesthetically—no dazzling background, no outlining, just a reductive language: "Wife, are you ready?" (*SE*, pp. 36–37). Now the vision that was dazzling in sunlight darkens, and the outside edges of it are portrayed as landscapes, apparently moving as seen from the ship, whereas of course in reality the ship moves and they do not. (Proust adopts this technique in *Remembrance of Things Past*, in the passage where the bell towers of Martinville are seen by the young Marcel looking from the back of Dr. Percepied's carriage, shifting their outlines with the carriage in movement. From our present perspective, the ship and carriage scenes seem to shift their outlines and merge, as we see them from our vehicular vantage point in the textual passage now being carried out.)

Like the "traveling" of a film camera, the camera of the eye moves along, giving its own notion to what is observed. The impersonalizing of the expression contrasts each time with the personal rhythm of vision, in which Frédéric lingers, until the scene goes blank: "Then everything disappeared . . ." (*SE*, p. 39). The scene is radiantly and obviously set, and the techniques of visual découpage are perfectly illustrated.

Borges and Cortázar: Self-Inclusion and Implication

I swallow my soup. Then in the midst of what I am reading, I think: "The soup is in me. . . ." Then the soul is born: "No, I am not that." Now that (let's be honest for once) yes, I am that. With a very pretty means of escape for the use of the finicky: "I am also that." Or just a step up: "I am in that." Cortázar, *Hopscotch*

The wit of South American fiction has dealt a joyful death blow to previous assumptions about linearity and logic, circling about the topics of self-inclusion, limits and transgressions thereof, nestings and insettings. No one perhaps has pointed out as convincingly as Borges the implications of readers in their reading, going one step beyond the protagonists of Don Quixote who were already reading the first part of their own novel or Hamlet's staging of the Hamlet tragedy.[4] One of Borges' best illustrations of the *mise-en-abîme* is taken from Josiah Royce, *The World and the Individual* (1899); my quoting Royce from Borges, in an article translated from the Spanish, figures the complexity of this border around the map in the mind:

> Let us imagine that a portion of the soil of England has been levelled off perfectly and that on it a cartographer traces a map of England. The map is perfect; there is no detail of the soil of England, no matter how minute, that is not registered on the map; everything has there its correspondence. This map, in such a case, should contain a map of the map, which should contain a map of the map of the map, and so on to infinity. (*L*, p. 196)

Borges explains that the "disturbing" element of these nested inclusions consists in the way they suggest the possible fictitiousness of readers.

"The world is my representation. The man who confesses this truth clearly understands that he does not know a sun nor an earth, but only some eyes which see a sun and a hand which feels an earth" (quoted in *F*, p. 47). Borges' fascination with Schopenhauer seems based on the same problematization of knowledge. We know only within the limits of our processing of knowledge, and cannot exceed them into the "real." All the tools for reflection and naming and accumulation — mirrors, dictionaries, lists — serve as so many graspings after some all-inclusive process of assurance, which would guarantee us and what is beyond us, reaffirming our knowing and what we know.

But our assurance is that of an "unnerving mirror" and a "misleading encyclopedia" in "Tlön, Uqbar, Orbis Tertius." Misinformed, we see the final deformation of what framing devices could do in their ideal state. The encyclopedia would provide a taxonomy of framing devices and their analysis; the mirror would provide a reflection upon each, and also on the reflecting mind considering what corridors and junctures and paths, forking, duplicating, or self-annihilating, are relevant.

"There is no intellectual exercise which is not ultimately useless" (*L*, p. 53): and even *The Secret Mirror* — a story, as Borges says, close to James — includes the frustration of "The Circular Ruins" (*L*, p. 78). Yet the overlapping of frames, the undermining of reference or of probable use, in no way precludes the Mallarmean hope of a "total book." Like Rilke's unicorn, who is fed only with the possibility that it may be, and so becomes, "it is enough that a book be possible for it to exist" (*L*, p. 85). The ideal book of pictures, the picture book as it could be, in its most absolute interference, interior and exterior, would be Borges at his most willingly "disturbing."

Cortázar's "Blow-Up," no less disturbing, is an intricate study of *interference*. On the outer border, uncertainty poses its questions: what person the story should be told in, how to separate the clouds from the figures, how to manage to have the machine type the story without personal input? The presentation is reminiscent of Magritte's *The False Mirror*, with the clouds and the sight interchangeable, the outside superposed upon the seeing itself, blocking or *clouding* the sight and again, looking back at the eye. The *intrusions* made upon the frame of vision by a pigeon, two or three sparrows, and a murder, are finally equalled out: what registers is the detail, what counts is the camera's record of the sight rather than a judgment of events.

The tale can be read as a tale of frame-up, where, as in James, the story is uncertain but the recording of and wonder at it are sufficiently complex to compose a patterned border to surround it, as if the center were clear. The fact that it is not ceases to matter: value resides in the attention paid directly to attentiveness, like the Surrealists' valuing of the state of expectation itself. The camera as arm against neutrality (the "level-zero of passive acceptance") works to frame events, bringing them to life as they are brought to sight: ". . . in all ways when one is walking about with a camera, one has almost a duty to be attentive, to not lose that abrupt and happy rebound of sun's rays off an old stone, or the pigtails-flying run of a small girl going home with a loaf of bread or a bottle of milk" (*EG*, p. 116). Distraction is, on the other hand, a camera-less stroll, an easy interpretation of the world just as seen, without arrangement, "knowing that he had only to go out without the Contax to recover the keynote of distraction, the sight without a frame around it, light without the diaphragm aperture or 1/250 sec" (*EG*, p. 118). But his tale is now told through the frame of the viewfinder itself, with a tree included to "break up too much grey space." The aesthetic takes precedence over substance, over thought: "I got it all into the viewfinder (with the tree, the railing, the seven o'clock sun) and took the shot" (*EG*, p. 124). To "get it all in" is to possess it. Later, the enlargement of the photograph in repeated stages works like the enlargement of a surrealist rose in a poem by Desnos, for example: as the rose is compared to more and more elements, each is added on to it and the image finally outstrips the poem, growing steadily larger and larger, with the formal details visible as, always, through the eye of the lens. This focus replaces the "normal" human focus of vision, until the detail becomes the whole, and the eye becomes the lens, "something fixed, rigid, incapable of intervention . . . my impotent eye" (*EG*, p. 130).

The *move* into the picture by the lens is accompanied and framed by the rhythmical sway of the branches of the tree—placed, we remember, to break up the grey space—and the focus lights upon an irregularity, as the perceptual psychologist would say, the place where the railing is tarnished: "The woman's face turned toward me as though surprised, was enlarging, and I turned a bit, I mean that the camera turned a little, and without losing sight of the woman, I began to close in on the man who was looking at me with the black holes he had in place of eyes," closer and closer, increasingly rapid until "the game was played out." The picture is *cropped*: some is cut off, until only the black tongue of the man occupies the center, and the horrified spectator, who is the narrator, breaks into tears. Clouds return across the eyes and their own sky, rain falls over the picture in the final shot:

> like a spell of weeping reversed, and little by little, the frame becomes clear, perhaps the sun comes out, and again the clouds begin to come, two at a time, three at a time. And the pigeons once in a while, and a sparrow or two. (*EG*, p. 131)

In this clearing of the sight, the border of the few birds is repeated, at the moment when the emotion of the spectator is transferred to the picture and the focus shifts from inside reaction to outside climate. (This picture might be superimposed as a transparency over the extraordinary scene in James' *The Wings of the Dove*, when at the turn of the weather in Venice and the turn in the story, all the emotional weight of tragedy and tears is transferred to the rain and its effect upon the veil, effectively veiling the wet eyes of the dying girl's companion.) Here the clouding and clearing, of the sky, the eyes, and the camera lens, make the final frame for the enlargement, or blow-up, of the picture and of our perception.

Blown up, the picture may reveal what we could not have seen, even in a deliberate choice of content, border, form. As the camera replaces human gesture in its motion, human sight is superseded by what exceeds it without reassuring it. But just so, the slippage from our "natural" frame to the "cultural" frame, superimposed and victorious, casts retrospective doubt on how we—as "intellectuals"—frame our own most serious endeavors.

An ironic example of this reframing is served up by an oddly self-questioning editorial epilogue, the exchange of letters between the two translators Anthony Kerrigan and Alastair Reid, which closes Borges' so-called *Personal Anthology*. Reid wonders, as he says (following the famous meditation by Borges called "Borges and I," about the split between the person Borges and the author celebrated as Borges, which closes by wondering which one wrote this particular text), if, having made Borges "exist in English," these two translators might just have made him up, if they "may have made him exist altogether—if he has any existence at all. . . . You may be Borges, whoever he is." And, he continues, of himself, "I am translated." (*PA*, 205–6).

Framing our work, as we work it through, putting our final *touch* on it, may involve in itself, and us in it, what we would neither have chosen nor perceived.

Robbe-Grillet: Enframing of a Labyrinth

This labyrinth permits access only through an image of a grotto or then of a lying-in room, for the sake of creation as well as for that of covering: "I am here alone now, under cover" (*IL*, p. 29). Just outside the room, the repetitions which mark the linguistic border of the scene thus enframed or nested play with oppositions, paradoxes, and stress: "Outside it is raining, outside you walk through the rain . . . outside it is cold, the wind blows between the bare black branches; the wind blows through the leaves . . . outside the sun is shining" (IL, p. 29).

Then the reader and text are returned to the womb, or the room sufficient unto itself, where traces are made directly in the dust: inscriptions within the text already circumscribed. What is written here is written from the inside:

> The sun does not get in here, nor the wind, nor the rain, nor the dust. The fine dust which dulls the gloss of the horizontal surfaces, the varnished wood of the table, the waved floor, the marble shelf over the fireplace, the marble top of the chest, the cracked marble on top of the chest, the only dust comes from the room itself: from the cracks in the floor maybe, or else from the bed, or from the curtains or from the ashes in the fireplace. (IL, p. 29)

The captured or privileged look (for nothing else "gets in here") is greatly intensified by this sheltered presentation, a massing of elements which attract the eye in rapid succession. Each circle, each square, each rectangle left in the dust by the displacement of small objects forms an indication of the past to which responds, in visual echo, the projection of the lampshade in its own circle of light, cutting into the background shadow, itself cut into by the line of the vertical wall, hidden from top to bottom by thick red curtains. The circle of the lampshade answers the circle traced by an ashtray, these circles fitting into smaller and smaller ones. Directly after this concentration, set off by the interior and mental representation of labyrinth and picture, the reader's look is forced once more towards the outside of the picture and the room, where diverse mobile forms create a dizzying pattern in the snow. No sound penetrates this room, heavily cropped at the sides and so severely limited by the white landscape or snowscape. The excess of concentration, isolation, and claustrophobia exacerbate our sensitivity to the smallest details we are given to picture:

> The street is too long, the curtains too thick, the house too high. No noise, even muffled, ever penetrates the walls of the room, no vibration, no breath of air, and in the silence tiny particles descend slowly, scarcely visible in the lamplight, gently, always at the same speed, and the fine gray dust lies in a uniform layer on the floor, on the bedspread, on the furniture. (IL, p. 30)

The slightest traces leave their mark; in the dense expectancy of some meaningful inscription, we read into what bears no reading. The traces of slippers shuffling across the floor in the dust form their own meaningless and mute witness to the past. But in contrast to the domestic comfort suggested by the cliché of felt slippers, a dagger-flower now is seen to point to the clear trace of an ashtray, the opposite of the inscription in the floor's dust, and yet no more significant. Papers have been shuffled about, but we have no indication of what they might have been said to say; only the blur of their outline in the dust remains, as the proof and mockery of past action or thoughts. In the airless scene, the traces in time are to be read against the background always of the white page, matching the snow, untouched by sense. Neither brushed by the wing of time nor penned by any other implement, bearing no mark at all.

The table inside, with its dusty surface and the white snow outside both serve to collect traces, records of movements and actions, being passive receptors of largely useless signs. The claustral path here, for reading the text, leads only from the actual and unreadable bed to the frame of an equally unreadable picture, framed in varnished wood and occupying the center of the story as labyrinth. It is within this central picture that the story unfolds.

But in fact, the bed, unreadable as it is, can all the same be imagined to lie at the very source of the picture being dreamed, as it is enveloped within the presentational borders in this "chambre double," like Baudelaire's room in and out of time. This sitting room with its curtains, dust, and traces of eternity, is reminiscent of Igitur's own room, where a clock marks, as here, the arrested hour, taken in its flight as the mirror fixes the image, as a frozen lake fixes a swan outside in the snow, and inside, as the frame fixes the picture.

After all the inscriptions in the dust are read, as if they were so many paths leading to the center of the picture, the frame sends the observing look back to the outside, and the end makes a résumé of the whole, undoing itself, fading out in a pattern exactly reversed from the beginning. Now the lines of the text are turned towards the exit, as they begin repeating:

> Outside it is raining. Outside you walk through the rain. . . . The rain does not get in here, nor the snow, nor the wind; and the only dust . . . the only dust comes from the room itself, perhaps from the cracks in the floor, or else from the bed, or from the ashes in the fireplace, or from the velvet curtains whose vertical folds rise from the floor to the ceiling. . . . But the image grows blurred by trying to distinguish the outlines, and, beyond the door, the dark vestibule where the umbrella is leaning against the coat rack, then, once past the entrance door, the series of long hallways, the spiral staircase, the door to the building with its stone stoop, and the whole city behind me. (*IL*, pp. 159–60)

The path from inside to out leads past the umbrella, which functions like the "real" protruding object in a "trompe-l'oeil" canvas, showing up the fake and the fictive by contrast. The attentive glance leads out and in, down to the corridors of passage and the stairs and the door, all of this traceable in both directions until a confrontation of self and town is reached: "and the whole city behind me." The narrator, absent in person from the rest of the text, reappears to set the final frame as he set the initial one, so that it is thus entirely inscribed with his inspiraling view.

The book has disappeared, having absorbed the entire experience within its corridors, its labyrinth, and its covering frame, to make its breathless picture, or parody of one.

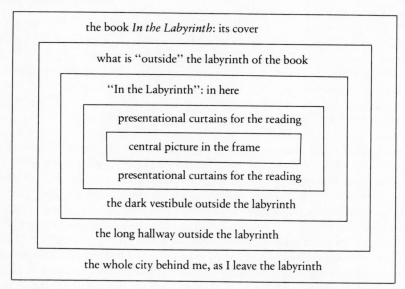

the book *In the Labyrinth*: its cover

what is "outside" the labyrinth of the book

"In the Labyrinth": in here

presentational curtains for the reading

central picture in the frame

presentational curtains for the reading

the dark vestibule outside the labyrinth

the long hallway outside the labyrinth

the whole city behind me, as I leave the labyrinth

This is, finally, the extreme of the cage rethought in contemporary terms: Robbe-Grillet's labyrinth is, in its utter *self-enclosure*, a pseudo-labyrinth, a verbal and psychological picture about our reading a picture of a labyrinth.

The central picture towards which the lines of the text seem to tend already dominates our thought, so that while we believe ourselves to be outside, reading a maze to see how it works, we are looking at just what the labyrinth in fact is, and all it is. A pseudo-trap set for the reader, by the reader, self-propelled into *amazement*. As we want to think we are drawn in, we are just drawn into thinking we want to be drawn in. It works because we want our outer references not to work, our criticism taking to them as little as it does. We want the labyrinth to take us in, longing for some textual entrapment of the suspenseful kind, just as if we were longing for a real world. Ready to play with Minotaurs and maidens, we end up playing with wanting to play, entrapped in a combination as obvious as one of M. C. Escher's involving patterns, or one of Saul Steinberg's figures drawing itself into its drawing: except that we, wanting to be drawn in too, are not.

This is what James leads to, not some croquet game with slow gestures and subtle conversation on one of those Jamesian lawns on some summer afternoon, not even a good read about it, but a reflection on words alone, on his favorite words "summer afternoon." The referent disappearing even in the text as the subject disappears even in the picture, as the parodistic *Sacred Fount* is finally about our wishing the *Sacred Fount* had some enigma at its center. We have lost, and it is apparent, not only the sacred, but also the possibility or fount of a myth of origins.

The question that is begged here begs its own conclusion: to what extent is this convincingly a labyrinthean procedure, and to what extent a send-up of how we read, after Theseus, any labyrinth at all? No Ariadne figure is likely to be leading us, since we have forsaken myths along with exterior reference.

All we have is our own will-to-amazement, and these few pictures, emblems of our fascination with what ropes us in. "In the Cage" of reading, at the "Sacred Fount" of our consecrated lack of source and sacred, all the lines intersect and the lack of enframed message is final. James is the greatest teacher, after all, about ambivalent figuring and how it cannot all add up to anything. What we long for: being told a good story, being really taken in; being the able interpreters of figures static and in motion, silent and carpeted, or rhythmic and rhetorically inclusive, that we must ourselves select and arrange. Our frames finally have to be of our own construction, using whatever received knowledge and reception theoretical self-inclusion we most gladly deal with. But it may all, as we suspected all along, add up to exactly nothing.

Let me suggest that the problem may lie in our models of additions and accumulation (thus, adding up to . . .), as well as in our expectations about progression, focus, and selection. Having tried to "get it all in," into whatever frame we think of ourselves as using, we expect to have surrounded at least something in our effort and our obsession with surrounds. We should perhaps treat our very obsession with getting it in as what we are getting— that is, in fact, James' most ironic lesson, which we have still to learn.

Notes

1   The books referred to in this essay are listed herewith. Page numbers given in the text are to these editions. Jorge Luis Borges, *Ficciones* (New York: Grove Press, 1962), *Labyrinths* (New York: New Directions, 1962); Julio Cortázar, *End of the Game and Other Stories* (New York: Harper, 1967), *Hopscotch* (New York: Avon, 1966); Gustave Flaubert, *A Sentimental Education* (Harmondsworth: Penguin, 1964); Nathaniel Hawthorne, *The Blithedale Romance* (New York: Dell, 1960); Henry James, *Eight Tales*, ed. Morton Dauben Zabel (New York: Norton, 1969); *Hawthorne* (Ithaca, N.Y.: Cornell University Press, 1966); Edgar Allen Poe, *Selected Writings* (Harmondsworth: Penguin, 1967); Alain Robbe-Grillet, *In the Labyrinth* (New York: Grove Press, 1960).

2   On James' figure in the carpet, one of the most intelligent studies is that of J. Hillis Miller in the "Narrative Endings" special issue of *Nineteenth Century Studies* (June 1978), pp. 3–7.

3 The subject is part of a collective fascination. Framing is involved in some of the most notable current critical work: Derrida, Felman, Hamon, Johnson, Kermode, Lotman, Miller, Said, Smith, Todorov, and others in literary studies; Gombrich and Schapiro in art; Dennett and Hofstadter in psychology; Bateson and Goffman in sociology; Minski in computer science.

4 See the "Partial Magi in the Quixote," in Borges' *Labyrinths*.

The Philological Fictions of Fernando Ortiz
Gustavo Pérez Firmat

It is hardly an overstatement to say that, since the Romantic period at least, one of the overriding preoccupations of Spanish-American literature has been its own relation to its Spanish or European analogues and precedents. From Bolívar and Bello to Martí and Rodó, from Vasconcelos and Varona to Retamar and Paz, Spanish-American thinkers have returned time and again to the question of the New World's cultural and literary autonomy. In general, this preoccupation has passed through two stages: in the first stage, America's originality, its radical newness is affirmed. This view, whose seeds were sown in the chronicles of discovery and conquest, flowered in the nineteenth century during the Wars of Independence and reached full development in the work of the *criollistas*, with its attention to native landscapes, regional dialects, rustic characters, and autochthonous themes. The second stage arises from a recognition of the difficulties inherent in this first view. It is always naive to assert, without a great deal of qualification and nuance, the originality of Spanish-American literature or culture; even the novels of the *criollistas*, for all of their "local color," essentially followed the (non-autochthonous) canons of the nineteenth-century realist fiction. As Juan Marinello once pointed out, no amount of indigenous overlay can cover up the transatlantic roots of much of Spanish-American literature.[1]

For this reason, recent criticism has drawn attention to the connections between Old World and New World culture, connections that do not imply, however, intellectual subservience. Although the concern is still with autonomy, with cultural and literary independence, it is recognized that this will be achieved not through some radical beginning, but through the distinctive — and often polemical — assimilation of the New World's unavoidable cultural inheritance. Using notions adapted for the most part from contemporary Continental criticism, advocates of this view have sought the indicia of Spanish-American literature in its manipulation of peninsular or European models. Thus, for Alfred A. MacAdam, to cite a representative opinion, modern Latin-American fiction constitutes "a carnival literature, a world-upside-down literature, combining the Western literary tradition with the cultural contradictions of Latin America."[2]

MacAdam's reference here to the "Western literary tradition" helps to clarify some of the issues involved. Tradition implies continuity, linear descent, the orderly transmission of a code of devices, motifs, or attitudes. Many of the best—and best-known—works of Spanish-American literature are not traditional in this sense, for they deviate from, and at times violently break with, European genres and conventions. MacAdam is surely right, thus, to speak of Spanish-American literature's "carnivalization" of the Western literary tradition. But it is sometimes forgotten that there is another (semantic) tradition in "tradition," since the word's etymological doublet is "treason." In Spanish, the similarity between the two words—*tradición* and *traición*—makes the filiation evident. To traduce tradition is to affirm it: nothing is more traditional, according to this second acceptation, than the break or discontinuity of an act of treason. In this sense of the term, the literature of Spanish-America is nothing if not "traditional." One can say, indeed, that the task of the Spanish-American writer is to come to terms with the doubleness, the treacherousness of tradition. The ambivalence of the word may then serve as an appropriate emblem for the dialectic of dependence and autonomy, loyalty and betrayal, that defines Spanish-American literature.

In the present essay I would like to study the working of this dialectic in a few texts by Fernando Ortiz (1881–1969), and particularly in one of his better-known works, *Un catauro de cubanismos*, a compendium of Cuban words and idioms that may be seen as a treacherous, disloyal version of one of the ornaments of Spanish literary culture, the *Dictionary of the Spanish Royal Academy*.[3] What is a *catauro*? The entry in another dictionary of *cubanismos* gives: "A kind of portable, rustic box or basket, made from palm bark, and used to keep or carry fruits, eggs, etc., and even to get water from wells."[4] A *catauro*, then, is an all-purpose box, an American portmanteau. As we will see, an examination of the contents of this box will allow us to study in detail some of the ways in which the New World assimilates and carnivalizes, reproduces and traduces its cultural heritage.

Fernando Ortiz may seem, at first glance, an odd choice for this project, since he is neither a poet or novelist, nor do his essays often deal with matters literary. Sometimes called Cuba's third "discoverer" (after Columbus and Humboldt), Ortiz is esteemed for his seminal contributions to the study of the "transculturation" (a term Ortiz himself coined) of African customs in Cuba.[5] What has been overlooked, I think, is that Ortiz's texts are themselves, quite often, excellent examples of transculturation. That is to say, his essays also have foreign roots; they too are creole or Cuban adaptations of exogenous models and forms. Before proceeding to my principal text, let me illustrate what I mean by briefly mentioning a couple of other examples. One of Ortiz's early works is *El caballero encantado y la moza esquiva* [*The Enchanted Gentleman and the Disdainful Maiden*], a curious piece that its author labels a "free and American version" of Pérez Galdós' novel, *El caballero encantado* [*The Enchanted Gentleman*], which Ortiz says he has only "translated."[6] Ortiz's translation, however, is actually a plot summary with comment. And both summary and commentary are transparently tendentious, for Ortiz is interested only in drawing attention to the "American" dimension in Galdós' allegorical novel, a dimension embodied in Cynthia, the character in the novel that symbolizes Spain's former colonies. Thus, to the title of the original, *El caballero encantado*, Ortiz has added a reference to Cynthia, the emblem of America: "the disdainful maiden." He has, in effect, "transculturated" the novel by giving the symbol of America equal billing with the character that symbolizes Spain (Tarsis, "the enchanted gentleman"). The political animus behind such rewriting is succinctly illustrated in the translation's subtitle, for when Ortiz calls his text a "free" version ("una versión libre"), he is obviously punning on the dual meaning—political and literary —of the adjective.[7]

Though in less obvious ways, other texts by Ortiz embody the same problematic. His well-known *Contrapunteo cubano del tabaco y el azúcar* [*Cuban Counterpoint of Tobacco and Sugar*], for example, places itself in the genre of the medieval debates. Ortiz begins by invoking the dispute between Carnival and Lent in the *Libro de buen amor* [*Book of Good Love*], which he labels his "literary precedent."[8] What then follows is a transculturated, creole version of the dispute, with sugar and tobacco taking the places of Carnival and Lent. Thus, there is a double dialogue, a compound counterpoint in Ortiz's text, for the dialectic of foreignness and autochthony that Ortiz finds in the interplay between sugar and tobacco is reproduced, on a textual plane, in his transculturation of the medieval genre of the allegorical debate. Even the short essay where the word *transculturación* is introduced may serve as an example, since Ortiz here changes a foreign term, acculturation ("la voz anglo-americana"[9] ["the anglo-american word"]), so as to make it more reflective of native realities. What is at issue in this essay, as in all of Ortiz's work, is the finding of a vernacular "voice" (*voz*: word/voice).

This brings me to *Un catauro de cubanismos*, for in this work the issue of finding a native "voice" is reduced to its simplest, most fundamental level, that of words, *voces*, singly considered. Leaving aside Ortiz's lexicographical contributions, which will not concern me here, the principal issue raised by the *Catauro* has to do with Cuba's cultural autonomy. Since language sediments human culture, a nation's most radical autonomy and its most degrading dependence are linguistic. A recognition of the determining influence of language leads to an awareness that, in the New World, Spanish (like English, like Portuguese, like French) is a "foreign" tongue, one imported from Europe and thus not always responsive or sensitive to New World specificities. Juan Marinello, in a fundamental essay to which I have already alluded, put the problem this way:

> El escritor americano es un preso. Primero el idioma. Los grillos sabios de Europa, después. La lengua es en lo literario mucho más de lo que

imaginan los gordianos. Si fuese sólo medio expresivo, elemento tra-
ductor, no sería cárcel. Sería sierva, no dueña. Pero el idioma es cosa
viva, de vida incoercible, inmortal. Como en lugar alguno se advierte en
nuestras tierras indohispánicas. La lengua es en nosotros la más fuerte
españolidad, el más grueso aislador de lo vernáculo porque nacemos a la
lengua como a la vida, sin oportunidad de elección: cuando pensamos,
cuando existimos, el lenguaje de Castilla es ya nuestro único lenguaje.
Somos a través de un idioma que es nuestro siendo extranjero. A lo
largo de nuestra existencia el idioma vivirá ya vida propia. Sudaremos
de echar criollismos sobre la lengua matriz y cuando queramos innovar
seriamente el habla derivaremos formas que tuvieron hace siglos vida
lozana en Andalucía o Extremadura. O que pudieron tenerla. Es que la
sangre claustral que es toda lengua recuerda fatalmente a sus padres y
enniña sin quererlo nietos que se le parecen.[10]

[The American writer is a prisoner. First, because of his language. And
then, because of Europe's learned fetters. In the literary realm language
is a great deal more than what the Gordians imagine. If it were only an
expressive medium, a vehicle for translation, it would not be a prison.
It would be a servant, not a master. But a language has a life of its own,
and it cannot be coerced—as is evident in different parts of our Indo-
Hispanic lands. Language is the truest mark of our Spanishness, the
most powerful obstacle to a vernacular idiom, for we are born into a
language, as into the world, without the opportunity for election: as
soon as we begin to think, as soon as we begin to live, Castilian is
already our only language. We exist through a language that is our own
while being foreign. Language has a life of its own. We strain to in-
seminate our mother tongue with native expressions, only to find that
our innovations were already alive centuries ago in Andalusia or Extremadura. Or that they could have been. The cloistral blood of language binds parents and children, and unwittingly engenders grandchil-
dren that resemble them.]

Marinello's melancholy meditations underscore that what is at stake in this
war of words is nothing less than the New World's intellectual integrity. If
Marinello's dictum is true—"We exist through a language that is our own
while being foreign"—Spain's old colonies suffer from a peculiar schizo-
phrenia for which there is no treatment. As Roberto González Echevarría has
pointed out, Marinello's statement is a version of the Rimbaldian declaration
of otherness, *je est un autre*,[11] for to be constituted as/through another's language amounts to experiencing one's self as one's other—and vice versa: not
only *je est un autre* but also, *l'autre, c'est moi*. Grammatically what is rendered problematic is the first person and the singular number: one is at least
two; behind the first person there is always a second. Culturally what is de-

nied is the possibility of a native tongue or an autochthonous literature, that
is to say, the possibility of finding a distinctive *voz*, in both senses of the
word.

To be sure, Marinello is probably right. Language can be alienating, and
not just for those born in "Spanish" America. The idea of a purely American
sociolect or culture, a notion that achieved some currency in the early decades
of this century, seems sheer delusion. To the present-day reader a tract like
José Vasconcelos' *La raza cósmica* [*The Cosmic Race*], with its millenary
promise of a radical beginning, reads less like social science than like science
fiction.[12] The point is that one cannot escape what Marinello, in the same
passage I have quoted, labeled "Europe's learned fetters."

Ortiz's *Catauro*, while not making any of the extravagant claims of a work
like Vasconcelos', still represents an attempt to escape the Old World's gravi-
tational pull by securing a partial autonomy for the Spanish spoken in Cuba.
In this respect the *Catauro* is less a work of "objective" scholarship than a
committed, polemical demonstration of Cuba's cultural autonomy, a demonstration built on this culture's linguistic foundations. Ortiz's recursive title,
which creolizes the *vocabulario* or *diccionario* of similar collections, already
anticipates the book's encompassing aim. It is no exaggeration to say that
the *Catauro* is a profoundly political treatise, a declaration of cultural independence addressed, as we shall see, to those peninsular arbiters of linguistic
propriety whose task is to "establish, purify, and polish" the mother tongue.
The *Catauro* does just the opposite: it deranges, defiles, and pollutes the
mother tongue by seeding it with barbarisms, with "cubicherías lexicográ-
ficas" ["Cuban slang"] (p. 15). In this sense, the book voices one of those
typically American (North *and* South) barbaric yawps with which the New
World responds to Old World polish.

In order to understand better Ortiz's polemical stance, it is useful to look
first at another compilation of American expressions, Miguel de Toro y Gisbert's "Reivindicación de americanismos," published in the *Boletín de la Real
Academia*—where else?—a couple of years before the appearance of the
Catauro.[13] Toro's title is every bit as revealing as Ortiz's; how does one "re-
vindicate" Americanisms? Simple: one shows that they descend from fine
Castilian stock. The article consists of a long list of items that, according to
its author, have been wrongly entered as Americanisms in various reference
works—words like *calimba, manjúa, guagua, jabado, bullarengue, mamalón*
and many more. Interestingly enough, one of the revindicated words is none
other than *choteo*, a term that has often been employed to designate the specificity of the Cuban temperament.[14] A look at this entry will show us how
the revindication is accomplished. The entry begins:

> *Chotear*: Lo encontramos en la Academia como cubano. "Poner en
> ridículo, mofarse de una persona." Ha sido adición de la última edición
> del *Diccionario*.

También es mejicano, según Ramos.

La palabra es española. En Besses encontramos, como voz de caló, *Chotiar*, en sentido de escupir. En Pío Baroja (*Busca*, 102) leemos un derivado: "Menudo choteo que tuvimos con las marquesas." [15]

[*Chotear*: According to the Academy, a Cuban word. "To ridicule, to make fun of someone." It has been an addition of the last edition of the *Dictionary*.

It is also Mexican, according to Ramos.

The word is Spanish. In Besses we find, as a *caló* word, *Chotiar*, in the sense of to spit. In Pío Baroja (*Busca*, 102), we find a derived word: "That was some *choteo* that we had with the ladies."]

Toro goes on to relate *choteo* to *chota* and gives *choto*, small calf, as the root. He thus employs two complementary techniques of revindication. One is to trace an *americanismo* to its Spanish root-words. In the world of lexicography, etymological determinism takes the place of genealogical determinism; the lexical antidote to transculturation is excavating the Spanish roots of American words. Toro's other ploy is to cite peninsular precedents for each of his entries. He seems to assume that the use of a word by Baroja or Pardo Bazán or Pereda (all three favorite sources) furnishes sufficient proof of its Spanish origins, even though, of course, by the nineteenth century Castilian Spanish had incorporated a good number of American borrowings. Interestingly, Ortiz will evince an antithetical blindness, for he assumes that no date of entry is too *early* to preclude contamination. His *Catauro* regularly cites Spanish authorities from the sixteenth century with the claim that the currency of the word in Spain is due to the residence of black slaves in Andalusia.

More important than the accuracy of Toro's rerootings is the purpose they serve. This purpose is made clear in the introduction to the catalog, where Toro charges American lexicographers with ignorance of Castilian Spanish:

No causa poca sorpresa al lector español que hojea algunos Diccionarios de provincialismos americanos la increíble cantidad de voces netamente españolas que figuran en dichos libros, atribuyéndoles cada autor su respectiva nacionalidad.

Se queda uno admirado a la vez de la pobreza increíble de nuestros Diccionarios y de la ignorancia en que algunos escritores americanos están respecto del idioma castellano.[16]

[The Spanish reader who leafs through some dictionaries of Spanish-American provincialisms is more than a little surprised by the incredible number of purely Spanish words that appear in these books, words that each author attributes to his own country.

One is astonished by the incredible shabbiness of our dictionaries as well as by the ignorance of some Spanish-American writers with respect to the Castilian language.]

This ignorance is dangerous because it creates the impression that a wide gap exists between Castilian and American Spanish, and this impression may make American readers, who are "less informed," give up the struggle to speak with Castilian correctness, *castizamente*. The political undercurrent of the diatribe comes to the surface a few sentences later: "Some Spanish-American writers, misguided by a faulty sense of national pride, and having no knowledge of our modern literature, figure that their political emancipation has endowed them with such linguistic vitality that they have been able to create a new language. I have already spoken several times in my books against such an absurd theory." From Toro's perspective, the collection of Americanisms obeys illegitimate political ends. Toro is warning his American colleagues, in effect: do not think that political independence entitles you to linguistic autonomy. Etymology is destiny. Even though Spanish America may no longer be a complex of colonies, culturally it remains under the Spanish flag. A bit later, in an aside on the pains and pleasures of lexicography, he adds:

> Este trabajo de identificación es sumamente largo y penoso; pero ¡qué placer el nuestro cuando tropezamos con la filiación de tal o cual palabra, expresiva, elegante, castiza, olvidada hoy entre el polvo de los escritores antiguos o desdeñada por lugareña en tal o cual rincón de provincias, mientras vive lozana y honrada en alguna comarca americana! ¡Y cómo nos alegramos al ver cómo se estrecha más cada día el lazo indisoluble del idioma que, a través de los siglos, nos reúne con nuestros hermanos de allende el océano! [17]

> [This tracking down of sources is long and tedious. But what a pleasure it is to stumble across the filiation of one or another word, expressive, elegant, Castilian, words which in Spain today are gathering dust in libraries or are disdained for their provincialism, while they lead youthful and vigorous lives in some Spanish-American territory! And how it cheers me up to see how, day by day, the indissoluble bond of language tightens more and more, reuniting us with our brothers from across the ocean!]

I find something unsettling in that gradual tightening of the "lazo indisoluble del idioma," perhaps because it reminds me of Marinello's somewhat different metaphor for the same idea, that of "Europe's learned fetters." One man's lasso is another man's noose. In any case, Toro's elation has a definite imperial quality. His implied comparison of the American nations to the Spanish provinces suggests that the New World is to the Old as the provinces are to the metropolis; moreover, the fledgling republics are identified only as *comarcas*, territories, and not as autonomous political entities. For Toro the American continent remains on the margins, geographically as well as culturally. And the fraternal kinship mentioned at the end is somewhat jeopardized by the filial image he had earlier employed ("what a pleasure it is to stumble across the filiation of one or another word"). Toro's is the delight of the colonizer who realizes that, political dispossession notwithstanding, in a deeper sense than the political these lands remain under his sway. He is an embattled Prospero, a magus of philological savvy who makes up for his deficit in political power by what he regards as a surplus of knowledge.[18] Note his superior attitude vis-à-vis his transatlantic brothers. A "lector español" like himself immediately perceives the flaws of Spanish-American lexicography; but the "lector americano," being less knowledgeable or alert ("poco advertido"), is easily duped. The whole catalog is nothing more than an exercise in linguistic recolonization, the repossession for Spain of what, in Toro's bull's-eye view, rightfully belongs to her. Hence the title.

"Reivindicación de americanismos" reveals strikingly the ideological substratum of seemingly impartial scholarship. Toro y Gisbert's erudition, which is considerable, is nourished by a centrist bias in favor of Spanish cultural hegemony. In the *Catauro* a similarly impressive scholarly apparatus will be put to the service of a decentralizing impetus or centrifugal force. Although Ortiz uses much the same ploys as Toro, particularly etymologies, they are used to sever, not cement, Cuba's peninsular connections.

One can identify three different stratagems or devices that work toward this end. The first consists in deracinating a word from peninsular soil by proposing a non-Spanish (usually Amerindian or African) etymology. Again *choteo* can serve to illustrate. Even though Ortiz concedes that *chotear* may well be related to its homonyms in *caló*, he argues that the derivation from *choto* is "arbitrary" and advocates instead a different derivation from the word *achote*, a red substance used by some Indians for body decoration. Since *choteo* embarrasses, makes its victims blush, it could be a metaphorical extension of the Indian word for the red dye. *Chotear* would then evolve from *achote* through the hypothetical middle step, *achotear*: "And this being the case, we would thus have another verisimilar etymology for *choteo*, through a common apheresis of the initial *a*" (p. 211).

In the *Glosario de afronegrismos* he goes a step further, suggesting, in addition to the Indian one, several African etyma for *choteo*. Again he discards the Academy's etymology: "The Academy supposes that the word comes from *choto* or "baby goat." This etymology is entirely unverisimilar. If the most learned Spanish corporation did not deserve our highest respects, we would say that this etymology was a *choteo*."[19] Ortiz's quip itself, of course, is an act of *choteo*. By incorporating the term under discussion into the rhetoric of the debate he is not so much begging the question as mocking the answer; he is making a *choteo* out of the convention of scholarly disputation. He will perform this gesture many times. The same joke had already been used in the *Catauro*; after mentioning that *chotiar* in *caló* means "to spit," Ortiz asks: "Isn't *chotear* to spit morally on someone, a suggestion I make without *choteíto*, or with only the indispensable amount of it?" (p. 36). So that, in effect, Ortiz himself is spitting on lexicography, turning an erudite disquisition on *choteo* into a *choteo*.

The disparagement of the Academy's etymology is followed, in the *Glosario*, by a new theory. *Choteo* did not evolve from *choto*, nor even from *achote*, but from a *lucumí* or *yoruba* word meaning "to speak."

> No obstante lo antecedente, es más verosímil la tesis africanista, fundada en el vocablo lucumí o yoruba *soh* o *chot*, que significa "hablar," "decir" y, además, "tirar," "arrancar," "arrojar," lo cual armoniza con el sentido despectivo del choteo criollo. De esa raíz *cho* o *soh* se derivan *sohroh* "conversar," *sohrohjehjeh* "murmurar," *sohrohlehin* "hablar de uno en su ausencia," *sohwerewere* "hablar sin ton ni son."
>
> Asimismo, en pongué, *chota* es "acción de espiar," "acechar," y en lucumí *cho* es, también, "vigilar" o "espiar," lo cual evita la etimología gitana de *chota*, como asimismo la de *choteo*.

> [In spite of the foregoing, the Africanist thesis is more verisimilar, founded as it is on the *lucumí* or *yoruba* term *soh* or *chot*, which means "to speak," "to say," and, besides, "to throw," "to tear," "to cast out," all of which harmonizes with the despective sense of our *choteo*. From that root *cho* or *soh* are derived *sohroh* "to converse," *sohrohjehjeh* "to murmur," *sohrohlehin* "to speak of someone behind his back," *sohwerewere* "to speak without rhyme or reason."
>
> Likewise, in *pongué chota* is "act of spying," "to pry," and in *lucumí cho* is, also, "to keep watch," "to spy," which avoids the gypsy etymology of *chota*, as well as that of *choteo*.]

Taken together, the entries in the *Catauro* and the *Glosario* propose no less than three different etyma for *choteo*: one *caló*, another Indian, and another African. The "Africanist thesis" itself has two variants, for Ortiz suggests roots not only in *yoruba* or *lucumí* but also in *pongué*—all with a view to avoiding, as he says at the end, the "gypsy etymology." But the upshot of these multiple derivations is that *choteo* itself becomes a gypsy word, a lexical exile, wandering from continent to continent in search of its authentic "roots."

Typically, Ortiz's defense of the non-Spanishness of the word is multifaceted. Not satisfied with one alternative etymon, he goes in for philological overkill. And all of this, it must be mentioned, from someone who had no firsthand knowledge of the African languages he so insistently exploited. Ortiz's procedure was to ransack dictionaries and grammars of African tongues (most of these works written in English or French; hence the peculiar-looking —to Spanish eyes—transcriptions of the African roots) in search of homonyms or paronyms of words used in Cuba. Having found them, he then tried to confect a semantic link between the African word and the Spanish one. Once this connection was established, the rerooting (and rerouting) was complete. Needless to say, etymologies thus elaborated are far from reliable, especially in view of Ortiz's fanciful interpretive leaps (*choteo* as a form of "throwing," for instance), and the excesses of his method are apparent even to the nonspecialist.[20]

But for my argument Ortiz's eccentricity is beside the point. Or rather, it is precisely the point, since I regard the *Catauro* as a work of philological fabulation, a "logofiction" that obeys a logic and incarnates a consistency different from those of scientific inquiry. I approach the *Catauro* as one would approach a novel—and perhaps as one should approach works of criticism as well: with an eye for the motif rather than for the syllogism, for texture rather than for truth. The accuracy of Ortiz's etymologies interests me less than the role they play in the book's plot, and I use the term "plot" advisedly, for in its mixture of the political and the literary the word traces precisely the contours of the book.[21] The *Catauro* is a philological fiction with a political theme. One important motif in this theme is the excision of Cuban Spanish from its peninsular matrix, what Ortiz terms the "avoidance" of peninsular etymologies. And the questions that need to be asked of the book are: why should one feel compelled to avoid such etymologies? What is to be avoided by such avoidance? What danger or harm in a gypsy etymon? The answer to these questions will not come from the field of philology; it will come from a discipline sensitive to the play and display of forces even in "dry" works of scholarship, works seemingly barren of the layering and emplotment that enable interpretation.

The irony of Ortiz's avoidances, of course, is that Cuban Spanish is not Castilian only to the extent that it is African or Amerindian. Ortiz can only replant roots, not remove them altogether. One can imagine, nonetheless, that the discovery or invention of his African etyma must have caused him a pleasure similar to that felt by Toro. For both men the pleasure arises from recognition, from finding the familiar in unfamiliar surroundings. But whereas for the Spaniard the familiarity of the American lexicon reassures him about the filial or fraternal ties between Spain and her former colonies, for the Cuban the pleasure of recognition attaches to the cause of cultural autonomy. Toro imaginarily travels to the colonies in order to retrieve the mother tongue; Ortiz imaginarily travels to Africa or to pre-Columbian America to show that our mother tongue is forked, since it has multiple origins.

The *Catauro*'s second device cuts deeper than the first, for Ortiz will now bring his erudition to bear on words that, besides being used in Cuba, are also current in Spain. As a corollary to the same ploy, he will recommend acceptance by the Royal Academy of a number of words that, for one reason or another, have no good equivalent in peninsular Spanish. One example of a *cubanismo* used on both sides of the Atlantic is *garapiña* (*Catauro*, pp. 34–35); another is *mojiganga*, which he discusses at length in the *Glosario*, arguing that the word derives from the Congo language and its diffusion in

Spain stems from the participation of Congo slaves in Spanish carnival festivities.[22] Examples of words whose acceptance he urges are: *pucha, financiar, enseriarse, vuelto, turismo, control, entresemana,* and *culear,* all of them entered in the *Catauro.* The effect, if not the purpose, of this dual device is to reverse the cultural flow between the peninsula and the continent. Ortiz inverts the center-periphery relation with the result that America becomes the cultural center that exports its verbal riches to Spain. The colonies threaten to colonize their colonizers. Since these entries demonstrate not the presence of Spain in America but of America in Spain, they constitute the exact opposite of those in "Reivindicación de americanismos." One might venture that what motivates them is a kind of peninsular envy, a vindictive wish to play the part of the usurper. By pointing out the Afro-Cuban provenance of a word like *mojiganga* or the need for other words like *pucha* and *culear,* Ortiz shows that the American nations have not limited themselves to absorbing Spanish culture; rather, their absorbent capacity has been complemented by procreative power.

Thus, if the first device implements a desire for *autonomy,* the second one implements a desire for *influence.* The *Catauro*'s third device, in turn, will implement a desire for *legitimacy.* Strictly speaking, this last desire may not be consistent with the other two, for now we observe Ortiz arguing for the Spanishness, the *casticidad,* of a number of Cuban words. He will say that *cubanismos* like *calimba, fajatiña, moringa,* and *sabina* are in fact of peninsular ascendancy, even though by so doing he is actually rehearsing Toro's argument, trying to outbully the Spanish bull. All this, strictly speaking. But if one insisted on strict speaking, one would never venture beyond the pages of the *Royal Academy Dictionary.* A text like the *Catauro,* from its title onward, is the work of a loose tongue, one that aims, precisely, to unloosen, to relax the strictures of strict speaking.

Two things need to be said loosely in explanation of the third device. The first is simply that Ortiz's wish to legitimate the Cuban sociolect manifests the characteristic ambivalence that the colonized feel toward their colonizers. The American predicament inheres not only in the New World's fateful obligation to emulate Europe; part of the problem is that the New World persists in *selecting* Europe as the model to emulate. Those "learned fetters" that Marinello talks about are, to some extent, self-imposed. In his classic study of the North-American ethos, *The American Adam,* R. W. B. Lewis organizes the nineteenth-century debate about the United States' separation from Europe by placing the participants in one of three camps: the party of Hope, the party of Memory, and the party of Irony.[23] The party of Hope was made up of those, like Whitman or Thoreau, who advocated a clean break from Europe. Ortiz's first two devices, and particularly the Africanist thesis, are stratagems of the hopeful. The party of Memory comprised those who, like the long line of Calvinist preachers, insisted on shouldering the burden of the past. The *Catauro*'s third device can be situated in this camp. The third party, made up of Ironists like Melville, mediated between Hope and Memory by showing their intrication. This party argued that one could escape the past no more than one could avert the future. In its blending of hopeful and mnemonic motifs, the *Catauro* may be labeled an ironic text. Its contradictions, its janus-character—backward and forward looking, loyal and treacherous—faithfully reflect the American cultural predicament.

The second thing that should be said about Ortiz's third device is that, on occasion, the memory exercise can be turned into a weapon. Consider the entry for *torcaza*, [dove]. After pointing out that the Academy accepts *torcaz*, the adjective, but not *torcaza*, the noun, Ortiz adds: "But we have to agree, against what Pichardo thought, that *torcaza* is not a corrupt word, but a healthy and pure one, one which—like several others—was kept alive in Cuba even after falling into disuse and being *corrupted* in Castile" (p. 181; italics in the original). Thereupon follow two verses from the *Libro de buen amor* in which the word appears:

Vino el cabrón montes con corcas y torcaças . . .
A las torcaças matan las sabogas valyentes. (*Catauro*, p. 181)

[The mountain goat came with deer and doves . . .
The brave shads are killing the doves.]

Since "archaisms" like this one are for Ortiz vital signs of health and purity, Cuban Spanish maintains a less corrupt, more pristine state of the language than its Castilian counterpart. This device thus involves metaleptic reversal, for what is being claimed is that certain items in the Cuban lexicon are actually "older" than their supposed ancestors. *Torcaza* is presumably a corruption of *torcaz*; and yet one finds it already in the Arcipreste. In this sense Cuban Spanish antecedes that being spoken at the same time in the peninsula. The fatherland is temporally posterior to its offspring and perhaps less hospitable to the mother tongue.

The devices I have now mentioned circumscribe the three principal motifs in the plot of the book: autonomy, influence, and legitimacy. Something remains to be said, however, about the book's form and style. I have so far discussed the *Catauro* as if it constituted a response of sorts to Toro y Gisbert's "Reivindicación de americanismos." Conceptually this is true enough; but historically Ortiz's compendium needs to be situated with respect to two other works. One is the fourteenth edition of the *Royal Academy Dictionary*, to which Ortiz constantly refers. The other is Constantino Suárez's *Vocabulario de voces cubanas*, which spurred Ortiz to publish his *papeletas*. This is how Ortiz describes his text's relation to the other two: "If Suarez's *Vocabulario cubano* is an appendix to the fourteenth edition of the *Diccionario de la Lengua Castellana por la Real Academia Española*, this small notebook that follows will be, in turn, a kind of appendix to Suarez's *Vocabulario* and also, by extension, to the well-known academic catalogue" (p. 17). The *Catauro* is an appendix to an appendix, a supplementarity evident already in the title, since *catauro* is one *cubanismo* one will *not* find in *Un catauro de cubanismos*. If one is not familiar with the word, one has to resort to Suárez's vocabulary for a definition. For the non-Cuban reader, that is, for the reader who would perhaps find such a compendium most useful, the intelligibility of the title presupposes acquaintance with Suárez's work. And on a more abstract level, of course, this intelligibility rests on the reader's memory of the titular labels that Ortiz has displaced and replaced.

The *Catauro*'s supplementarity manifests itself in another way. Since its materials are actually a by-product of Ortiz's research into Afro-Cuban folklore, this collection derives from some of Ortiz's other works. "This year we hope to finish the *Glosario de afronegrismos*, which I have been working on; and the entries that make up the *Catauro* are like the shavings left behind as I chisel away to uncover the ebony heart that is the object of my unceasing labor" (p. viii). The *Catauro* is a chip off the old block, a box constructed from shavings left over from the author's work on things Afro-Cuban. These "Cuban odds and ends," then, consist only of "the jottings gathered as a result of other projects on Cuban lore, like poor shavings produced by the chisel or the plane during our long-standing work on the culture of the Afro-Cuban underworld" (p. 255). It is somehow appropriate that a work so concerned with etymologies should so clearly uncover its duplex origins. Like some of the words Ortiz studies, his dictionary has both Spanish and African roots. Its derivativeness or secondariness with respect to these two sources seems a fitting emblem for the Cuban vernacular generally.

The residual, supplemental composition of the *Catauro* helps to explain its stylistic and structural quirks. As my reader will surely have noticed, Ortiz's tone is unlike what one would expect in a work of this nature. One can describe it as festive, or carnivalesque. His entries are full of puns, of outrageous suggestions (*marconigrama* for telegram; *autorista* for chauffeur), of amusing asides, of jibes at the Royal Academy.

> *Guayabo*—El árbol que produce la *guayaba*, dice el Diccionario de la Academia. ¿Pero por qué aÑade: "En francés: *goyavier*"? ¿Quiere decir con esto que es un galicismo? ¿Sí? ¿Pues qué, acaso en cada otra papeleta del Diccionario se trae a colación la traducción francesa de cada vocablo? ¡Fuera, pues, el *goyavier*! Esa etimología, si se propone como tal, *no vale una guayaba*, para decirlo en criollo. Recuérdese en cambio alguna de las 22 acepciones y derivados de *guayaba*, traídas por Suárez, que, como *guayabal*, *guayabera*, *guayabito*, harían mejor papel en el diccionario castellano que esa inexplicable etimología gabacha. ¿Que no nos venga la Academia con *guayabas*!, y consignemos así, de paso, otro cubanismo.
> (p. 43)

[*Guayabo*—The tree that produces the *guayaba*, according to the Dictionary of the Academy. Why does it add: "In French: *goyavier*"? Does it mean to suggest that it is a gallicism? Really? Well, does the Dictionary by any chance provide the French translation of every word? No? Then out with the *goyavier*! The etymology, if that is what is being proposed, is not worth a *guayaba*, as we say. Let's recall, instead, some of the 22 acceptations and derivatives of *guayaba*, cited by Suárez, that, like *guayabal, guayabera, guayabito*, would look better in the Castilian dictionary than that inexplicable Frenchified etymology. This *guayaba* is just too hard to swallow!, and let us thus note, in passing, still another Cuban idiom.]

On occasion, Ortiz even parodies the style of academic dictionaries:

Cuajo—La Academia da en su 4a acepción el sentido siguiente: *Cuajar*, 1er. artículo. Este dice: Unir y trabar las partes de un líquido, convirtiéndose en sólido. Nos parece poco atinada esta definición en lo que debiera ser de química, como en lo de lógica; pero no ocupándonos de ella, digamos que en Cuba, *cuajo* tiene otro sentido, que académicamente pudiera ser expresado así: *Cuajar*, 3er. artículo. Y leyendo entonces la referencia tendríamos: Lograrse, tener efecto una cosa. (Pp. 39–40; see also *meter*, p. 42)

[*Cuajo*—The Academy gives in its 4th acceptation the following meaning: *Cuajar*, 1st entry, which says: To unite and thicken the parts of a liquid, turning it into a solid. This definition seems to us off the mark, as regards both chemistry and logic; but leaving this matter aside, let me say that in Cuba *cuajo* has another sense, which could be expressed academically in the following way: *Cuajar*, 3rd entry. And reading the reference we would have: To accomplish, to have an effect.]

These passages embed a reflexive dimension that sets the *Catauro* apart from the academic dictionaries it supplements. Entries like these not only complete or correct the information in the *Royal Academy Dictionary* but also expose, indeed toy with and undermine, the conventions of the dictionary form. Nowhere is this more evident than in the disconcerting fact that the *Catauro* is a dictionary whose entries are not arranged in alphabetical order—nor in any other kind of order.[24] Since the work also lacks an index, the reader who wants to locate a particular *cubanismo* has to skim the whole compendium. He has, in effect, to *read* the *Catauro*, to treat it as one would an essay or a novel and not as one normally uses a dictionary, by "looking up" the item in question. One cannot look anything up in Ortiz's wordbook, for one would not know where to look—a situation complicated further by Ortiz's habit of discussing some words in more than one place (without cross-referencing) and of proposing a different theory each time.

The curious thing, however, is that occasionally one detects in the *Cataure* traces of alphabetical order. That is to say, one encounters clusters of entries that begin with the same letter or with consecutive letters; for example, *Pilotaje—Pintorretear—Pintorreteo—Revirarse—Revirado—Ribeteado—Saltaperico—Sanjuanero* (p. 56). This sequence is ordered to the extent that *p* is followed by *r* and *s* and that words that begin with the same letter are grouped. The semblance of order is momentary, nonetheless, since the words that immediately precede this sequence are *manguera, lucernario,* and *control*; and those that follow it are *novenario, tumbadero,* and *bocabajo.* But the *Cataure* contains many such discrete interludes, which cumulatively create the impression that at some stage in the book's prehistory the entries were indeed arranged alphabetically. Whatever the stages in the book's actual elaboration, the finished product gives the impression, not of randomness, not of haphazard disarray, but of deliberate deconstruction. It is as if, at some hypothetical time before publication, Ortiz's *papeletas* were indeed alphabetized; something then intervened —the "devil of *choteo*" [25] perhaps—and disheveled the list. Or perhaps the box fell. The obvious analogy is with a deck of cards that, after shuffling, retains scattered vestiges of its former numerical ordering. Ortiz seems to have submitted his index cards to a similar shuffling.

Consider also the book's heterogenous contents. Its author acknowledges that he has filled his box with "lexicographical notes, a sampling of words overlooked by earlier studies of the vernacular language, casual comments on uncertain etymologies, clarifications of the meaning of words, and evocations of forgotten Cuban folklore" (p. 256). This aggregation of diverse ingredients only increases the book's untidiness; one is reminded of the multiple uses of a *cataure:* "to keep or carry fruits, eggs, etc., and even to get water from wells." And then there is the *Cataure*'s external form: it begins with a preface, "Al lector," followed by Ortiz's review of Suárez's *Vocabulario de voces cubanas,* followed by another preface, and then by the list itself. The list is in turn succeeded by a brief section of Cuban idioms, "Locuciones cubanas" (p. 248), and a conclusion, "Cerrando el *Cataure*" (pp. 248–53). The box does not stay shut for long, however, since "Una ambuesta de cubanismos," an addendum to the main list, comes after the conclusion. In its contents and external appearance, the book is as much a hodgepodge, as much an *ajiaco criollo,* as the list itself.[26]

Because of its festive tone, disheveled structure, and miscellaneous materials, the *Cataure* is a barbaric dictionary of barbarisms, a carnivalization or *choteo* of the dictionary form, a "contradictionary." Its generative nucleus is either the carnival principle of motley or the equally carnivalesque notion of excremental disarray (as is suggested by Ortiz's statement that his box contains overripe and even rotten fruit, p. 255). Robert Adams has pointed out that some of the greatest literary works of this century have an unequivocal tumular or dungheap quality, since they have been confected from scraps, bits and pieces, literary and cultural debris.[27] If this is so, Ortiz's dictionary is one of our most typical and modern texts, a philological fiction comparable in its way to *Ulysses* or *The Waste Land*, of which it is almost the exact contemporary. *Un catauro de cubanismos* is *The Waste Land* of modern dictionaries.

I want to leave the *Catauro*, however, not in the wide spaces of modernist culture but in the bounded textual universe of Spanish-American literature. In its self-consciousness, its heterogeneity, its apparent disarray, its parodic or subversive intent, Ortiz's contradictionary exhibits features that we have come to associate with a great deal of twentieth-century Spanish-American literature, and particularly with its fiction. This should not be surprising: since the central concern of Ortiz's work is the relationship between Cuban culture and its Western and non-Western antecedents, his texts, as I mentioned at the outset, often revive and revise, portray and betray, traditional genres and forms. That is to say, Ortiz's books frequently get caught up in the problematic that constitutes their subject matter. Thus, the same sort of analysis that I have performed on the *Catauro* could be done many times over in the rest of Ortiz's vast and varied output. More than a philologist, more than an ethnologist, Fernando Ortiz is, above all, a fine and nuanced writer, one whose works address many of the same issues that define the best and most representative (that is to say, the most traditional), moments of modern Spanish-American literature.

Notes

Unless otherwise indicated, translations are my own.

1 Juan Marinello, "Americanismo y cubanismo literarios," in *Ensayos* (La Habana: Editorial Arte y Literatura, 1977), p. 49. This essay was originally published in 1932.

2 Alfred A. MacAdam, *Modern Latin American Narratives: The Dreams of Reason* (Chicago: University of Chicago Press, 1977), p. 9. A programmatic statement of this position may be found in Emir Rodríguez Monegal, "Carnaval/Antropofagia/Parodia," *RI* 45 (1979), pp. 401–12.

3 Ortiz's work was originally published in several parts in the *Revista Bimestre Cubana* during 1921 and 1922. A revised edition appeared posthumously under the title *Nuevo catauro de cubanismos* (La Habana: Editorial de Ciencias Sociales, 1975). I will be quoting from the first edition (La Habana: n.p., 1923). For reasons that will become apparent later on, page numbers are needed in order to locate the entries in the *Catauro*.

4 Constantino Suárez, *Vocabulario de voces cubanas* (La Habana: Librería Cervantes, 1921).

5 For a general overview of Ortiz's life and work, see Salvador Bueno's two essays, "Don Fernando Ortiz: al servicio de la Ciencia y de Cuba," in *Temas y personajes de la literatura cubana* (Habana: Ediciones Unión, 1964), pp. 209–18; and "Aproximaciones a la vida y obra de Fernando Ortiz," *Casa A* 113 (March–April 1979), pp. 119–28.

6 *El caballero encantado y la moza esquiva (Versión libre y americana de una novela española de D. Benito Pérez Galdós)* (La Habana: Imprenta "La Universal," 1910), p. 30. Ortiz's

"translation" of Galdós originally appeared, in several parts, in volume 5 of the *Revista Bimestre Cubana*; the book version is actually a reprint from the journal.

7 Although it would take me too far off the track to discuss the political dimension of Ortiz's rendering of Galdós, let me just say that Ortiz's regarded *El caballero encantado*, which was inspired, in part, by the "panhispanic" movement of the early decades of this century, as covertly neo-imperialistic; for Ortiz, in fact, the whole panhispanic movement, which stressed the spiritual affinity between Spain and her former colonies, was only a thinly veiled attempt at cultural recolonization. Ortiz's writings on this subject are collected in *La reconquista de América* (Paris: Sociedad de Ediciones Artísticas y Literarias, [1910]). *El caballero encantado y la moza esquiva* is again reproduced in this collection.

8 Fernando Ortiz, *Contrapunteo cubano del tabaco y el azúcar* (Barcelona: Ariel, 1973), p. 17. The *Contrapunteo* was originally published in 1940.

9 Ortiz, "Del fenómeno social de la 'transculturación' y de su importancia en Cuba," in *Contrapunteo cubano del tabaco y el azúcar*, p. 135.

10 Marinello, "Americanismo y cubanismo literarios," pp. 48–49.

11 Roberto González Echevarría, *Alejo Carpentier: The Pilgrim at Home* (Ithaca: Cornell University Press, 1977), p. 29. González Echevarría adds: "Marinello subverts the notion that the Latin American identity can be found on an ideal level, where the stock answers will supply satisfactory solutions, and makes the language in which they are cast part of the problem itself."

12 In a lucid discussion of New World Utopianism, Peter G. Earle rightly labels Vasconcelos' essay an "aesthetic fantasy." "Utopía, Universópolis, Macondo," *HR*, 50 (1982), p. 148.

13 Toro's article appeared in several installments: vol. 7 (1920), pp. 290–317, 443–71, 603–27; vol. 8 (1921), pp. 409–41, 481–514.

14 The best and best-known discussion of *choteo* is Jorge Mañach's *Indagación del choteo* (La Habana, 1928). Other discussions may be found in: Mario Guiral Moreno, "Aspectos censurables del carácter cubano," *Cuba Contemporánea*, 4 (1914), pp. 121–22; Calixto Masó, *El carácter cubano* (La Habana, 1941; written in 1922); Fernando Ortiz, *Entre cubanos* (Paris, 1914); and José Antonio Ramos, *Manual del perfecto fulanista* (La Habana, 1916).

15 Miguel de Toro y Gisbert, "Reivindicación de americanismos," *BRAE* 7 (1920), p. 459.

16 *Ibid.*, p. 290. The quotations that follow are taken from the same page.

17 *Ibid.*, p. 298.

18 The "American" reading of *The Tempest* to which I allude here has been developed by Roberto Fernández Retamar in *Calibán: Apuntes sobre la cultura en nuestra América* (México: Editorial Diógenes, 1972).

19 Ortiz, *Glosario de afronegrismos* (La Habana: El Siglo XX, 1924).

20 Ortiz's Africanist view of *choteo* apparently has not found favor with professional philologists. It is not mentioned by J. Corominas in his *Diccionario crítico etimológico de la lengua castellana* (Madrid: Gredos, 1954).

21 I should underscore that my discussion makes no claims about what Ortiz "intended" to accomplish in the *Catauro*. Though I do not doubt that some of the notions I impute to his text were also harbored by its author, my argument addresses only what exists in the text, not in the author's psyche. If I sometimes say "Ortiz" where, strictly speaking, I should say "*Catauro*," it is only because of stylistic convenience.

22 Corominas, who thinks that the word derives from *vejiga*, does not accept the African etymology. He states in the *Diccionario crítico etimológico*: "Don Fernando Ortiz writes me that he is not convinced by my etymology and continues to believe in the one he has proposed. I record here, with due deference, the opinion of the master of Afro-Cuban research, while I wait for the proofs that he promises, but I must say now that the origins

of the documentation indicate a Spanish etymology, rather than an African or Caribbean one, and that the fact that blacks took over the word later is not evidence of its black origin; as regards the *bantú* etymology suggested by Ortiz in his glossary, it is too far-fetched to appear probable."

23 R. B. Lewis, *The American Adam* (Chicago: University of Chicago Press, 1955), p. 7. There exist enlightening parallelisms between the cultural situation in the United States at the beginning of the nineteenth century and that in Cuba a hundred years later. It is enough to leaf through the pages of reviews like *Cuba Contemporánea* or *Revista Bimestre Cubana* to ascertain the resemblances between the "dialogue" (Lewis' term) that took place in Cuba during the early years of the Republic and that which unfolded in this country a century before. The most obvious difference, however, is that in the "Cuban myth" the Adamic figure has been replaced by its antitype, the *pícaro* (as in Carlos Loveira's *Juan Criollo*, for instance).

24 In the second, posthumous edition, the entries have been put in alphabetical order.

25 Mañach's phrase, in *Indagación del choteo*, 2d ed. (1940; reprint, Miami, Fla.: Mnemosyne Publishing Co., 1969), p. 64.

26 It is worth remarking that Ortiz has proposed the *ajiaco* as the culinary emblem of Cuban society. See "Los factores humanos de la cubanidad," in *Orbita de Fernando Ortiz*, ed. Julio Le Riverend (La Habana: U.N.E.A.C., 1973), pp. 149–57.

27 Robert M. Adams, *Bad Mouth* (Berkeley and Los Angeles: University of California Press, 1977), pp. 122ff.

"Pernicious," "Pessimistic," and "Foreign": The Controversy over Literary Modernism in The People's Republic of China / Robert Kiely

"We can discern in works of a few young writers traces of egoism, social-Darwinism, religious idealism and Western bourgeois modernism. Critics should provide effective guidance for these writers." Liang Dalin, *Hongqi*, 1983.

"The true Marxist does not reject outright any cultural legacy whether ancient or modern, Chinese or foreign, but should study its historical significance and assimilate whatever is useful." Zhu Hong at the James Joyce Centenary, Beijing, 1982.

During an eight-month period from August 1982 through March 1983, I was a visiting professor of English and American literature at Sichuan University in Chengdu, the People's Republic of China. I gave a seminar on contemporary American writers to a group of professors from nine provinces; courses in nineteenth-century American literature to graduate students and seniors; and a number of public lectures in my own university and as a guest in Beijing, Wuhan, Nanjing, and Shanghai.

My students—despite understandable gaps in reading—had, for the most part, an astonishingly good command of English and a profound sensitivity to literature. Because of the censorship of Western literature since the 1950s and the virtual black-out during the Cultural Revolution (1966–76), the greatest curiosity I encountered was about literary trends and movements in the twentieth century.

I soon learned that terminology, including literary jargon, has a distinctive flavor and political coloration in China. Terms like "stream of consciousness" or "romantic irony"—loosely bandied about in American classrooms—had an effect comparable to "abortion-on-demand" or "school prayer" in certain parts of the United States. At first, I thought it best to avoid using controversial language altogether. If "humanism," "symbolism," "impressionism," etc. had alarmingly negative associations to my listeners, they were, for me, only crude indicators of complex phenomena. In discussing individual authors and texts, I could easily live without them.

But one term would not go away. That was "modernism." (The word as used in China tends to include most twentieth-century literary and artistic innovations, including those now commonly referred to by Western critics as "post-modern.") My students and colleagues were irrepressibly curious about it; Chinese newspapers and literary journals regularly featured debates about it; national conferences were held to discuss what "it" was and whether it should be tolerated; and wherever I went to lecture, including the Institute of Foreign Literature of the Academy of Social Sciences and the College of Foreign Affairs in Beijing, I was asked to comment about it.

Though some Westerners and Chinese dismiss the controversy over modernism as a purely political fracas created by bureaucrats with little or no knowledge of literature, the longer I listened to and tried to follow the intricacies of the discussions, the more I realized that the problem was not so clear-cut. Tangled within the arbitrary and often poorly informed judgments of the censors were questions and difficulties of a genuinely ideological and cultural nature raised by intellectuals and writers as well as by party officials. Rather than dismiss the controversy as one of narrow public policy, I wanted to understand it in the context of contemporary Chinese culture as China once again opens itself to the West, but this time, on its own terms.

From a Western point of view, it seems that no people on earth should have a better or more natural understanding of certain aspects of modernist aesthetics than the Chinese. The compound ideographs of Chinese calligraphy, the enduring abstractions from the earliest dynastic periods, the rich symbolism and austere economy of much Chinese painting and poetry look, to many Western eyes, surprisingly "contemporary." It appears paradoxical, if not perverse, that the post-revolutionary leadership continues to be worried about the "polluting effects" of modernism when so many of its attributes are intrinsic to what is best in the great tradition of Chinese art and literature.

It is frequently and a little too easily argued that since the feudalistic and autocratic systems out of which the cultural tradition grew have been abandoned, so too must the characteristics of its art. But, whatever has been claimed, the Chinese Revolution did not put the entire past away. Much of Mao's genius as a revolutionary leader was derived from his ability to make Marxism Chinese, to blend Lenin and Confucius, to search out ways to change China and, at the same time, preserve it. Aside from undoubted feats of courage, endurance, and determination, the Revolution succeeded because politically and socially it brought the Chinese character, with its inherited strengths and weaknesses, into dynamic contact with new ideas of international origin and significance. Since the Revolution, it is precisely this kind of interaction that has not been allowed to occur without interference in literature and the arts.

One of the most striking attributes of revolutionary realism (the Chinese version of socialist realism) as one encounters its manifestations throughout the People's Republic is how poorly assimilated most of it is with the rest of the culture. Statues and posters of huge, muscular Slavic-style heroes and heroines look like gigantic images of Brobdingnagian aliens, the originals of which can be seen nowhere in the crowded lanes and open fields of China. Similarly, the stilted dialogues and moralistic formulas of much post-revolutionary fiction bear little resemblance to the way most Chinese speak and behave and none whatever to the elegant stylizations of classical Chinese fiction and drama. Whatever else modernism may mean in the West, it virtually always involves a coming to terms of past and present. Not a slavish imitation of the past and rarely a harmonious bridge to it, the work of modern literature or art nonetheless recognizes and in some way incorporates its ancestry. The recognition may involve struggle, even repudiation, but it remains recognition. Western modernism is not built on amnesia.

"The arts are inseparable from the customs, feelings and even the language of the people, from the history of the nation." Mao Zedong, "A Talk to Music Workers," August 24, 1956

One of the attractions of Chinese culture for Western writers from the earliest years of the modern period was its way of reflecting the past. As is always the case in the transfer of signs from one culture to another, Westerners read Chinese art and literature in terms of their own situation and in accord with their own perceived needs. To contemplate the extraordinary length of China's history, often a burden to the Chinese themselves, was, for the American and even the European, to see his own shorter history in perspective. Not only did Chinese history seem infinite but, for the Westerner who knew few of its details, it represented an almost miraculous pattern of survival despite every conceivable variety of catastrophe.

Ignorance of Chinese history was a prerequisite for the American and European writers who looked to Chinese art for serenity and stability during the period of the two world wars. To those Chinese intellectuals who had time to think about it, this phenomenon must have seemed more than ironic since the first half of the twentieth century in their own country could hardly have been more chaotic. Furthermore, few if any Chinese writers had the luxury of contemplating a foreign culture without feeling the blunt and immediate effects of its economic, political, and military designs on their own territory. For Lu Xun (unlike Ernest Hemingway) there were no safaris in Africa. For Ding Ling (unlike Gertrude Stein) there was no Parisian salon. Whatever their own politics may have been, the modernist writers in the West were sons and daughters of powerful and imperialistic nations for whom, despite war, the word "foreign" was an invitation, not a menace.

China, its art and the *idea* of a long past unspoiled by facts, could be a symbol of eternal tranquility to Western writers precisely because it posed no political or military threat. While for the Chinese, foreign cultures imposed themselves in the unaesthetic forms of merchant fleets, militia, and missionaries, for the Westerner, the very name "China" was synonymous with "far away." In the Western imagination China was, quite literally, an artifact. Ezra Pound's China was imbedded in the ideograph; T. S. Eliot's in the "stillness" of "a Chinese jar";[1] Yeats' in a piece of lapis lazuli carved into the semblance of a mountain scene by a Chinese sculptor. It is as though the Chinese might have known us first and for a long time almost exclusively through Praxiteles, Donatello, and Emily Dickinson.

This difference in perspective is so crucial to understanding the contemporary discussions of Western modernism in China that it is worth illustrating and analysing. Yeats' "Lapis Lazuli" is not only characteristic of the Western tendency to conceive of China in aesthetic terms but it is also one of the classic expressions of modernism. The poem begins with a reflection on the increasing criticism (in the 1930s as war again approached) of art and artists for being irrelevant and impotent in the face of disaster. The poem refers to great achievements in Western civilization, to the works of Shakespeare and sculptures of Callimachus, and acknowledges that these too are subject to ruin. The reader is led toward a resolution that is neither pessimistic nor sentimentally hopeful, but rather resigned, stoical, and mysteriously resistant to the ravages of war or the detraction of critics.

> All things fall and are built again,
> And those that build them are gay.
>
> Two Chinamen, behind them a third,
> Are carved in lapis lazuli,
> Over them flies a long-legged bird,
> A symbol of longevity;
> The third, doubtless a servingman,
> Carries a musical instrument.
>
> Every discoloration of the stone,
> Every accidental crack or dent,
> Seems a watercourse or an avalanche,
> Or lofty slope where it still snows
> Though doubtless plum or cherry branch
> Sweetens the little halfway house
> Those Chinamen climb towards, and I
> Delight to imagine them seated there;
> There, on the mountain and the sky,
> On all the tragic scene they stare.
> One asks for mournful melodies;
> Accomplished fingers begin to play.
> Their eyes mid many wrinkles, their eyes,
> Their ancient, glittering eyes, are gay.[2]

Like the Chinese carving it describes, the poem is concentrated into a small space. With a few lines, it suggests much more than it actually shows. The poet must speculate and imagine beyond what he sees, for example, that there are flowering blossoms in the halfway house and that the little group does eventually reach this place. Perhaps the most important of the poet's suppositions is that the old men's eyes are glittering and gay, since, in the kind of carving he describes, such a detail would be impossible to detect. Thus, the poet, otherwise an impersonal, anonymous voice, is himself one who responds to, "reads" another's work of art and is led by it to create images and possibilities of his own.

The poem, like the carved piece of stone, is a flight from reality, a celebration of art for its own sake, and, simultaneously, an article of faith in the creative potential of the human mind and the power of the work of art to set it in motion. That "all things fall" does not necessarily negate the builder's work if one thinks of the spoilers and the builders not in individual but generic terms. History, that is, Yeats' "reading" of time experienced through a Chinese filter, is a compression of past and future into an eternal present. The poet does not deny historical time and its tragic events nor does he gloss over ruin since he knows that is impossible. Yet he does not presume to suggest in social or political terms the parts and dimensions of a new "building." His chosen role, in a time of crisis, is to bear witness to the builder's art rather than to provide a blueprint.

The questions of egotism and alienation in modern literature are of great interest to Chinese critics and are of considerable importance in this poem. The poet's own personality does not intrude; there is nothing autobiographical in the verse. And since the three Chinese figures are generalized almost to the point of abstraction, the poem gives the impression of universality and objectivity. Still, as any Marxist will notice, the view of civilizations and their rise and fall in time is so detached as to overlook the particular ways in which institutions and groups of people are organized. Such a view of things, it can be argued, is itself the privilege of certain classes. The two old men do have a servant with them. And Yeats wrote the poem because he was in possession of a precious stone that someone had given him. The artist's view may not be, after all, a universal one available to all men. There are multitudes who cannot rise out of the "tragic scene" to contemplate it from afar. Despite its impersonal tone, the poem does finally seem to be the expression of a privileged, individualistic view of history and its relation to art. Those who climb mountains and write poems in time of trouble are those who can *afford* to do so.

For most Western modernists, a certain distance from what Yeats refers to as "the tragic scene" is an inevitable aspect of the artistic act insofar as it requires observation and reflection as its central disciplines. According to this view, whatever the artist advocates morally or politically and whatever his economic situation, he is to some degree alienated from the institutional norms according to which the majority of men and women conduct their daily lives. This form of separation from society is the poor cousin of the aloof detachment of the aristocratic scholar-poet. Far from being a privilege, it is more commonly perceived as a burden, yet a necessary one for the artist who is determined to be true to himself. This determination, though fraught with the dangers of arrogance, egotism, subjectivity, may be the only way in which the artist can give something of value back to the society from which he is removed. Alienation is not equated with inaction or despair in Yeats' poem. The old men gazing at the turmoil below are identified with "those that build" and are "gay" while waiting their turn.

Perhaps nothing is more characteristically modern, in the Western sense, in "Lapis Lazuli" than the way it invites variant, even contradictory readings. All literature is open to different interpretations, but many of the most esteemed modernist works appear to flaunt their openness to multiple explanation. "Lapis Lazuli" may be read as a charming but rather shallow reflection on a minor piece of exotic decorative art, or as a profound meditation on the enduring spirit of human nature despite the fluctuations of history. It can be read as a cynical and pessimistic view of a world which turns in a never-ending cycle of destruction, or as sign of hope in the indestructable power of the "builders." It can be assumed to be advocating art as a form of escape from reality or to be pointing the way toward the artist's fundamental role in the preservation and rebuilding of a harmonious civilization. For the Western admirer of modern literature (and the Chinese ideograph), such openness is a desirable appeal to the reader's freedom. The poet does not impose an idea through his verse, but rather constructs a configuration of images of sufficiently uncertain significance as to demand the reader's active participation as a creative partner. The danger, as Chinese critics of Western modernism have repeatedly pointed out, is that most readers will simply find the whole process too bewildering, that the "obscurity" will be a deterrent to the majority and a possible danger to the minority of readers who may use their freedom to draw "decadent" and "anti-social" conclusions.

"Our aim is to make literature and art serve the people and social progress." Zhou Yang, Vice-Chairman of the China Federation of Literary and Art Circles, January 1980

While Western modernists like Yeats and T. S. Eliot expressed anxiety over the loss of a central tradition that once gave coherence and moral purpose to literature, they nonetheless guarded their individual authority as poets. It appears to be one of the givens of modern literature, as it is of capitalist democracy in the West, that conditions of nearly anarchical autonomy are theoretically preferable to yielding control to an arbitrary authority. Well before the Marxist revolution, indeed for centuries before, this was not characteristic of the Chinese culture. Perhaps the vastness of the terrain and population and the harshness of the natural environment made the realities of anarchy too familiar in China to represent a liberating and, at the same time, safe pseudo-alternative. Furthermore, Western modernists, especially those from English-speaking countries, took for granted certain institutional stabilities and legal guarantees, even while reviling the societies that produced them, while to their Chinese contemporaries—Lu Xun, Lao She, Ding Ling, Shen Congwen [3]—so comfortable an option was inconceivable. In short, it is neither new nor surprising that there are those in China who wish to define the purpose and control the limits of artistic and literary creativity.

As in any system, it is easier to proclaim general aims, such as "service to the people" and "social progress," than it is to determine precisely how to realize them. Moreover, though stability and consistency may be desired, political leadership and the powers behind various government bureaus are, in their nature, subject to repeated, and often sudden, change. Thus, as is so often seen in the tragic pattern in China since Liberation, even the most loyal and patriotic of writers and artists are likely to find themselves in and out of favor with predictable unpredictability. They must try not only to please themselves and their readers, but must also satisfy the demands of various arbiters, often unknown to them, who may be of uncertain education and motivation. To the Western reader, literary criticism in China often does not seem to involve analysis as much as peremptory political judgment. When words like "clique," "revisionism," or "pernicious" appear, the writer is in trouble.

Soon after the downfall of the Gang of Four and the end of the ten-year Cultural Revolution in 1976, there was a period of relaxation during which Chinese writers produced works of fiction and poetry of a more vigorous and experimental kind than had been tolerated for over a decade. One of these, *Figure-carved Pipe*,[4] by Feng Jicai, a young writer from Tianjin, won a prize in a national short-story competition in 1979. Though any similarity between Feng's story and Yeats' poem is almost certainly coincidental, there is much to be learned about the modernist dilemma by comparing the two. Feng's story is also a meditation on the function of art in times of crisis; it is a highly compressed narrative with strong symbolic overtones; its central image is a small and intricate carving; and the artist's alter-ego is a mysteriously wise old man.

The story begins with the visit of a once-famous painter to a greenhouse. The time is during the Cultural Revolution and the artist is not allowed to paint. "Barbed wires were stretched all over the literary scene and the art academy was filled with mines" (p. 496). At the very outset the reader sees that the artist has not lost his imagination or his taste for beauty. When he sees a large pot of chrysanthemums, his mind is filled with images—"a fountain," "a shimmering peacock's tail," a "waterfall," a "young woman's hair, free from restraint." The old flower-grower recognizes the artist, praises his past work, and admires his carved pipe. At first, the artist is suspicious of the old man; he thinks he wants something or that he is just too ignorant to know what he is saying when he keeps muttering about the pipe, "beautiful —very beautiful." Despite himself, however, the artist is encouraged by the old man's attitude, and decides to continue carving pipes, a pastime he had turned to when his painting was forbidden.

The description of the creative process involved in the carving is central to the story:

> Somehow his eyes were caught by the deep red, smoothly polished bowl of the pipe. He noticed the grain of the pipe, thinking that it suggested the flying angels painted on the walls of the Dunhuang Grottoes. The thought propelled him to get hold of a carving knife with which he traced his imagined picture. . . . The effect was a surprise to him. . . . All of a sudden he discovered a new world in his artistic prison. (p. 497)

Like the lines on the lapis lazuli which make use of "every discoloration of the stone/every accidental crack or dent," the carving on the pipe follows "the grain." But even while the artist makes use of the natural coloration and contours of his medium, he engraves them with concentrated images suggested by other artists distant in time and place. As Yeats had built on Shakespeare, Callimachus, and the unknown Chinese sculptor, so the artist in this modern story draws inspiration from the Dunhuang painters. Indeed, as the artist continues to carve, his work becomes, in a time of ignorance and desolation, a recapitulation in miniature of the history of world art, incorporating as it does, images suggested by "the six steeds of the Han Dynasty, l'Arc de Triomphe, the stone reliefs of Wuliang Temple, . . . the Sphinx of Egypt, and even Walt Disney's cartoon characters" (p. 499).

To try to picture too literally what these pipes might look like is to miss the poignancy and near desperation reflected in the effort of the artist to keep alive the community of artists as it cuts across borders and historical periods, as well as to preserve, in whatever form possible, some remnant of what has been achieved. While Feng's artist copies and preserves, he does not merely imitate the past. He "tapped the wealth of both the world of civilization and all . . . the visions reachable by the human imagination. . . . His designs were bold and original. . . . Often he abandoned the familiar contours of recognizable things to convey their spirit . . . (and) what he felt inside of him" (p. 499).

In the course of the story, the artist is rehabilitated and finds himself once again admired by reporters, critics, and officials. Throughout everything, the old flower grower maintains his faith in the painter-sculptor. He delivers chrysanthemums to him, says little more than "beautiful . . . very beautiful" or "you must paint," and remains happy even when ignored by the painter and his friends. "Sometimes the wrinkles on his face deepened as though what he heard puzzled him," but usually "he sat quietly in the corner, a picture of perfect contentment" (p. 504).

At last the artist gives the old man one of his least prized pipes. And then, when the winds of fortune have shifted once again and he finds himself alone and out of favor, there is a knock at his door. A large pot of chrysanthemums appears, but the messenger is the old man's son. He relates how his father had died several months earlier, and how until the end, the carved pipe had been his most prized possession. The artist, ashamed of his mistrust and condescension, no longer sees the wrinkled old man as an ignorant oddity. "Instead the image (was) transformed into a beautiful soul."

To a Western reader accustomed to the fictions of Faulkner, Joyce, and Borges, Feng Jicai's story looks, on first reading, like a conventional and somewhat transparent piece of revolutionary realism. The situation is grounded in a recognizable time and place, the characters are representative types, the narrative line and vocabulary are clear, and the moral appears to be an uplifting one about the artist's need to trust the instincts of the common man. Such a reading is comparable to that a Chinese reader educated in the doctrines of Mao and Marx might bring to Yeats' "Lapis Lazuli." He would doubtless condemn it as an example of bourgeois self-indulgence and escapism centered on the image of just the kind of decorative art prized by the leisured class. The poem appears to project a timeless, placeless mood, to describe that which has never happened, a non-event. The "setting" is a work of art, a semi-precious stone, an import, carved many years ago by an unknown artist in a place unreachable to most Westerners except through the imagination. Its narrative line is a series of fragmentary speculations, and its moral, shrouded in ambiguity, seems to be that the way to true happiness is to climb a mountain and "fiddle while Rome (Peking, Paris, or London) burns."

But neither the Irish poem nor the Chinese story is reducible to the conventional markings of its frame. Both invite the reader into a "new world" of surprising dimensions despite the narrowness of the confines within which it is discovered. Yeats' carved stone does not yield to expectations of quaint and cameo-like perfection. On the contrary, it reveals visions of "a watercourse or an avalanche," a "lofty slope," of mixed seasons of snow and plum blossom, and of a flying crane, the symbol of longevity. The stone, like the short poem, becomes a means for projections that lead beyond its own limits. Whether sublime landscape or ancient symbol, the tiny markings, requiring concentration and focus from the viewer, reward him with a reversal of their own initial triviality. Seeming to acknowledge the irrelevance of art by choosing a bourgeois collector's item for his emblem, Yeats instead makes the boldest of claims for the virtually infinite scope and durability of what the builders see and perennially recreate.

Within Feng Jicai's modest and conventionally realistic framework, there are also significant signs of contradiction. The time scheme, though superficially related to recent Chinese history, is vague and dreamlike. When the story begins, the artist is out of favor; then suddenly he is back in favor and crowds appear at his door; then just as suddenly he is out of favor again. The cause of these changes is as unclear as the timing of them: "His painting had been labeled poisonous art—and the labeling was done by none other than the chief of the art division who had once requested a carved pipe from him. . . . He (had) had to accommodate himself to some crazy theory about art from the higher-ups, and his own desire to mount another rung on the political ladder triumphed" (p. 509). The only thing that seems certain is that these fluctuations are part of a constant rhythm over which the artist has no control. On close inspection, the time scheme of Feng's story bears more than a little resemblance to the timelessness of Yeats' "All things fall and are built again."

The artist's visit to a greenhouse to relax and have a smoke also seems ordinary enough until one reflects on the author's choice of this closed environment where beauty is cultivated even during times when beauty is suspect. The greenhouse is a place of "culture"—where life and harmony are sustained. While official and public behavior is destructive and ugly, and language is debased to the point that an anti-cultural movement is called a "Cultural Revolution," the silent greenhouse assumes the attributes of a shrine. What the artist (and therefore the reader) first notices there is a huge pot of chrysanthemums, which becomes the dominant image in the story. One of the loveliest of Chinese flowers and a favorite of poets and painters, the chrysanthemum stirs in the artist myriad subjective impressions. What remains unstated but obvious to a Chinese reader is the traditional association of the flower with a retreat from the pressures of society to the simplicity of nature and its symbolic identification with that which is "defiant of frost and triumphant in autumn."[5] Thus, in a modern Chinese setting, Feng combines the free creative urge of the artist with a culturally inherited emblem.

Aside from the artist, the most important figure in the story is the flower-grower, the old man who cultivates the chrysanthemums and delivers prime specimens to the artist's apartment as gifts. It is as easy to see him as a representative of the proletariat as it is to see Yeats' old men with their servant as members of the scholar-poet class. His clothes are simple and poor, his hands rough with work, his few words unsophisticated. It is he who cultivates beauty in good times and bad, who encourages the artist and remains loyal to him, and, like Yeats' old men with eyes "glittering and gay," who maintains a mysterious contentment in times of adversity.

But even as one identifies the class and type of the old man, the questions persist, as they do after one reads Yeats' poem, "Who are these old men? What is their role? And why are they so important in the visions of these twentieth century writers?" Though the old man of Feng's story is not aloof from his society by virtue of privilege, he, like the old men in "Lapis Lazuli," is detached from it. He is "overlooked" by the Cultural Revolution because he and his work are insignificant. When the old man discovers crowds of admiring officials in the rehabilitated artist's apartment, he is not particularly surprised or hurt when they ignore him. Though these officials are always speaking of "serving the people" or "the people benefiting" from this or that, when one of the people enters in their midst, they do not seem to notice. Thus, Feng makes a simple point relevant both inside and outside of China, that those who presume to speak for the people do not necessarily do so.

If, therefore, the old man of the story is "a man of the people," he is not so in the sense referred to by the usual political jargon. He is not a statistic or a theory or a cliché of forgotten origins nor is he the passive recipient of politically authorized intentions. He is a cultivator of beauty, a grower, a giver of gifts, a mysteriously potent partner to the artist, totally confident in his knowledge of beauty, oddly untouched by the crazy fluctuations in "popular" taste and the officially permissible. If he is "alienated," it is not by his own choice, but rather the consequence of those in the leadership who have *separated themselves from him.* For the artist, however, there is, in spite of himself, no possibility of separation from the old man in whom he recognizes so much of himself. He recognizes in him the poverty and strength of the human flesh, aging, wrinkled, yet surprisingly rugged and durable. He recognizes in him the product of an ancient culture imprinted to the bone which, like "a black ceramic pot dug up from a 2,000-year-old burial site," can be covered over by historical change but never lost. Finally, after the old man has died, he recognizes in him "a beautiful soul" that survives misjudgment and the destruction of time.

Compared with Yeats' carved figures, there is no question that Feng's old man is a more authentic representation of Chinese wisdom. Yet the parallels remain striking. The insistence on the serene endurance and power of the creative spirit; the blending of individual talent and the inherited tradition; the inevitability of detachment, whether by choice or necessity; and the miraculous habit of finding a space for beauty in conditions of extreme limitation (in the crack of a stone, a greenhouse, or on the bowl of a pipe) suggest that artists under attack in this violent century have responded with fascinating similarity within frameworks determined by their own cultures.

" 'Thirty stormy years' refers to the great changes in our country, the setbacks suffered. The vicissitudes in the life of one individual may seem incredible. This change in content requires a change in form." Wang Meng, *My Exploration*, January 1981

As Feng Jicai's story illustrates and Wang Meng's comment makes explicit, the realities of Chinese life in recent decades have placed a strain on conventional literary and artistic forms, whether derived from classical norms or the orthodoxies of socialist realism. Though there are countless ways in which the Chinese situation—its ancient culture and contemporary political upheavals—is unique, it is important not to overlook the ways in which it resembles that of other nations. The disruptions of war, the displacement of large numbers of people, the rapid growth of cities, the changing patterns of family life, the swelling of bureaucracies, the incursions of technology—all are occurring within a peculiarly Chinese context and yet all, in one way or another, are an increasing part of worldwide experience of life in the twentieth century. It is little wonder that a growing number of Chinese writers, like writers around the world, sense that these subjects cannot be adequately or faithfully treated within conventional formats. Experiments with time sequence, theme, characterization, and the use of symbols can be found not only in the fiction of Feng Jicai and Wang Meng, but also in that of Lu Hsinhua, Shen Rong, Jiang Zilong, and many others.[6]

The fears expressed in China about the "modern" elements in the works of these writers reflect a mixture of political, sociological, and literary concerns, unfamiliar to many Western readers. But they are fears that must be taken seriously and, if possible, understood in the Chinese context. With Yeats' poem and Feng's story in mind, it will be useful to summarize them in a manner that is comprehensible to both Chinese and American readers. To put the case most graphically, I would like to imagine how a Chinese scholar, knowledgeable about the West and loyal to his own culture, might explain it to an American. His argument might well include the following points:

1. Modernist techniques such as compressed symbolism and distorted time sequence make literature too difficult for the common reader and appeal only to an elite. Though, as Feng Jicai's story makes clear, political leaders are not necessarily the best judges of what is comprehensible to the "people," this is a serious problem, especially in a vast country trying to forge a sense of national coherence, and one that has not been satisfactorily solved in the West. Though technically there is freedom of expression in the United States and there is no governmental constraint on what can be published, most forms of popular culture are controlled by a relatively small group of people whose concerns are not political but commercial. It is taken for granted that television and film-making are "industries," and the growing number of pulp novels and romances in supermarkets suggests that the same is true in large segments of the world of publishing. Though the bulk products of these industries—moronic, crass, sentimental, violent, unedifying—are commonly defended as the price one pays in a democracy for the absence of controls, these industries and their products are, in fact, tightly controlled and monitored in the interest of financial gain. The American counterpart of the Chinese cadre who knows what is best for the "people," is the producer or publisher who "knows" what "pleases" (sells best to) the American public.

American writers and artists, obviously free not to join these industries, are nonetheless affected, and to some degree circumscribed, by them. The channels available to them are limited and their audiences relatively small not always because their work is "difficult," but because the opportunities to reach and educate large numbers of people are costly and therefore rare. Often, out of despair or indifference, Western writers and artists seem to be addressing only one another and a small coterie of highly educated people. Occasionally, a gifted writer crosses over from one realm to the other, manages, like Robert Frost or Seamus Heaney, Saul Bellow or Alice Walker, to remain faithful to his or her imaginative experience and, at the same time, to reach out in a rich but comprehensible language to a large human community. In the works of these writers, the uses of symbolism, the distortions of time, the exploration of character are not fashionable ornaments, but profound reflections of life in the twentieth century. They can be understood by those, like Feng Jicai's flower-grower, who do not have a Ph.D.

2. Modernist tendencies are pessimistic and do not encourage or inspire readers. Western modernism "does not feel satisfied with the status quo; it does not have faith; it has not yet found its ideal, but it is continuously fumbling for it." [7] When Chinese critics review the characteristics of much modern literature in the West, they never fail to notice the prevalence of anti-heroes, failed dreams, broken promises, and fruitless relationships. It is difficult not to see these as the signs of decadence, the last gasps at the dead-end of capitalist democracy. Of course, some American writers and readers would agree with that interpretation, but most see the self-criticism and sobriety of such literature as a healthy and familiar aspect of a democratic culture in which the prophetic and satiric have always played an important and corrective role. Americans may be alternately charmed and appalled by Jay Gatsby as a fantasy life idol, but if Chinese critics wish to understand the "other side" of the literature of modern American decadence, we should not ignore Nick Carraway, the midwesterner, the faithful friend, a hard worker on vacation, who lives to tell the story.

Much modern fiction has a Nick Carraway in it, a solid, prudent, rational person without the glamorous ambitions of the more exaggerated characters but also without their self-destructive faults. But the majority of American readers do not require such a figure, nor do they necessarily miss it when it is absent, since they typically approach even the most pessimistic of modern works from a position of strength. It often seems to Chinese readers that Americans can afford to dwell on their weaknesses precisely because they are so prosperous. And though this may put the case too simply, there is much truth to it. In their position of material wealth and relative social stability, Americans do not need, or do not think they need, to depend on literature to help buttress their sense of security and well-being.

Nothing could be further from the Chinese situation in which readers and writers alike have all suffered what Wang Meng euphemistically refers to as "vicissitudes" and therefore would quite naturally look anywhere, including to literature, for strength, support, and encouragement. "She grew accustomed to walking long distances barefoot; she learned not to expect trains, or roads, or even mules to ride in the rough terrain over which she travelled; she held it no discomfort not to wash face or teeth for days on end, and dressed in simple army clothes, with a cap on the back of her head." [8] This is a description of the way Ding Ling, one of modern China's most distinguished novelists, lived in 1937, the year before Yeats published "Lapis Lazuli." It could apply to any one of millions of Chinese. To these Chinese, and not only to their political chiefs, the pessimism and despair of some modern Western literature looks like a bourgeois luxury.

3. Modernism accentuates the importance of the individual at the expense of society. It is frequently argued by Chinese critics that Western modernism is subjectivity run rampant. Chinese writers and readers are fascinated by the techniques of "interior monologue" and "stream of consciousness," yet they are regularly warned that these are signs of an unhealthy, anti-social, unproductive preoccupation with self. It is nearly impossible for a Chinese reader (as it may be for some Americans) to read the poetry of Anne Sexton or the fiction of Philip Roth and deny the charge. At the same time, there is a tradition in the West, at least as old as Socrates, that holds that self-knowledge is the beginning of wisdom. A later development of this idea, with particular potency in the history of democracy in America, is that the understanding and cultivation of the self is fundamental to a dynamic and progressive society. Though modern literature may give its own expression to this view, the concept is not peculiar to the twentieth century. Similarly, it must be said that the Chinese misgivings about it did not originate with Mao and the Revolution. The teachings of Confucius and Mencius and their followers stressed obedience to familial and imperial hierarchies and the attainment of wisdom and virtue through conformity to elaborate and well-established forms of thought and behavior. Whatever emphasis was placed on individual perfection by Lao Tse or the followers of Buddhism tended to point away from social involvement to a life of solitude or retirement. The Maoist-Marxist insistence on placing the state above the self was an idea of the Revolution, but not, for China, a revolutionary idea.

Complicating these disparate views of the individual's relation to society in the twentieth century is the rapid development in the West of the science of the unconscious. It is a commonplace of cultural analysis in the West to say that Marx and Freud are the two single greatest influences on twentieth-century thought. Yet the works of Freud are still virtually unknown in contemporary China. (One of the exotic charms for the Western traveler in the People's Republic is that it remains a pre-Freudian culture!) There are a number of practical reasons for which the Chinese leadership might well wish to discourage the wide dissemination of Freudian ideas in China. The Freudian emphasis on the persistent power of the irrational and unconscious poses an enormous threat to a system dedicated to warding off anarchical impulses. The prolonged exploration of inner chaos does not appear a constructive activity to a leadership anxious about the effects of flood and famine, to say nothing of the potential of massive political disturbances and foreign invasion. Though Freudians might argue that the facing of internal devils strengthens people for the battle against external ones, the logic of that argument is not obvious to the Chinese.

Explicit analysis and descriptions of sexual behavior and fantasies are also antithetical to the Chinese aesthetic. Multiple concubines and trysts notwithstanding, classical Chinese literature is rarely, in the Western sense, openly erotic. Though in pre-Liberation days there was a sub-class of pornography, there has never been a Chinese Rabelais or Chaucer, and there is no evidence in the twentieth century of a Chinese D. H. Lawrence. Similarly, in painting and sculpture there is no tradition of the nude, except for the round, asexual, scantily draped Buddhas. The contemporary Western preoccupation with sexuality seems just as puzzling to many Chinese as the absence of it in China seems to many Westerners. And it is interesting that even educated Westerners, though they deplore the old-fashioned cultural imperialism of the missionaries and traders, find it difficult to repress the idea that somehow "it would be good for the Chinese" to join the sexual "revolution." Once again, the logic of this is likely to be lost on a Chinese leadership faced with a devastating problem of overpopulation and determined to divert the minds and energies of youth to less provocative enterprises.

4. The aims of modernism are unclear; they may not coincide with those of the state; they may do harm to the public good. A common charge against modernist literature is that its authors and characters are exceptions to general rules, that they are peripheral figures, even outcasts, who see their society as bystanders rather than participants. In short, modern literature is a literature of alienation. Like "egoism," "humanism," and "individualism," "alienation" is a charged word in the post-Liberation Chinese vocabulary. It bears connotations and heavily judgmental overtones virtually unknown in the West.

For Westerners, alienation is a condition experienced by most people some of the time. It is an increasing and seemingly inevitable aspect of life in this century. Urbanization, technology, bureaucracy, it is thought, are bound to produce feelings of estrangement in people culturally and perhaps genetically predisposed to an existence of a simpler and more directly comprehensible kind. Furthermore, there are people, whether by virtue of education or innate sensibility, who are more keenly conscious of the odd and ironic ways in which the parts relate to the whole (or fail to relate to the whole) than those who flow uncuriously with the mainstream. This "alienated" condition, though understood in its exaggerated form as a malaise is also seen in the West as playing a necessary and constructive role in the process through which the social organism sees, analyses, and ultimately shapes and controls itself. The communal attitude is never a simple one, but frequently if belatedly, the detached artist or intellectual, is embraced by the society he had criticized.

The Chinese were not alone in celebrating the Joyce centennial. Ireland also honored the memory of her self-exiled son.

For the Chinese, "alienation" is understood in the Marxist sense as a sign of socio-economic maladjustment. Because workers and peasants once had no control over their own destinies, no economic power, no political voice, no active part in their own culture, they were physically and spiritually excluded from the society which they fed and supported with their labor. They were alienated through no fault of their own. The Marxist Revolution in China was intended to bring about the dictatorship of the proletariat, the communal division of land, universal literacy, shared responsibilities in factories, fields, and offices, a fair assignment of tasks, and a just distribution of profits. In such a society, the causes of alienation are theoretically eliminated. Evidence of alienation in literature is interpreted as a sign of a counter-revolutionary or reactionary spirit or, even worse, of some fundamental imperfection in the new society.

The question in modern China is not really whether such disaffected spirits and imperfections exist. There are regular official acknowledgement that they do. The issue is whether fiction, poetry, and drama are the proper contexts in which to expose them. The problem for the writer is how to remain faithful both to a political and social ideal and to the truth. The problem for governmental leaders is how to maintain the discipline and motivation necessary to further the achievements of certain ideals and to prevent people from becoming discouraged or confused along the way.

A typical and perhaps self-satisfied Western reaction to these problems is to dismiss them as unnecessary. Americans especially like to argue that a just society and its government cannot flourish unless continually exposed to public scrutiny. Nothing is more important and characteristically American about the Watergate scandal than the way in which it was made part of the public imagination, without government control, through newspapers, television, books, and films. This prolonged unofficial reveling in the details of a tawdry and seemingly minor political indiscretion appeared to many Chinese one more sign of American inscrutability. For most Americans, unlike the Chinese experience during the trial of the Gang of Four, Watergate was not an occasion for confusion, fear, or shame, but rather one for self-congratulations and pride in a system that worked, laws that prevailed, an organism that healed itself. Few Americans fully realized how rare the balance of institutions allowing such a prolonged public display of political self-criticism without the risk of ruinous consequences was. Americans did not expect blood in the streets, troops in the White House, or empty shelves in the markets. They were raucous in rhetoric, but prudent in action—a familiar pattern in domestic, as in literary, affairs in twentieth-century America, and one that appears an unfathomable mystery to the Chinese observer.

5. Modernism is a foreign phenomenon uncongenial to the Chinese cul-

ture. In a typical outburst, Yao Wenyuan, one of the Gang of Four, once attacked a new Chinese novel as "pernicious" because it advocated "revisionism" and dealt with "a clique of scientists and their relationships with foreign countries."[9] Throughout Chinese history the ultimate in derogatory or laudatory labels in reference to ideas, fashions, or things has been that they are "foreign." There rarely seems to have been a middle way. The United States in her early decades showed a similar ambivalence toward Europe, especially England. Often feeling a moral and spiritual superiority, Americans continued for a long time to feel culturally and materially inferior to the Old World. The American solution to this problem was absorption. What had been foreign—people, languages, customs, ideas, even food—was imported, mixed and stirred, and eventually "Americanized." China, for all her vast size and ancient civilization, has often perceived herself as, and sometimes been, susceptible to absorption by other cultures. It is ironical that what to the Western eye looks like China's most deeply rooted and indestructable resource—the culture imbedded in her language, literature, philosophy, and art—seems to many Chinese fragile and vulnerable.

Whether an actual Chinese scholar would put the case in quite the same way that I have is less important than the value of the exercise for the Western observer of contemporary China. The West still has a good deal to live down with regard to its past record in Asia. It is easy but dangerously naive for politicians and journalists to speak of capitalism and the "American way-of-life" as just around the corner in Beijing. There is every reason to believe that the Chinese want progress, but on their own terms and in their own way. The modernist "threat," even in its literary guise, symbolizes to China a necessary but risky encounter with the world of the future.

Perhaps one of the most valuable lessons that Chinese writers can learn from Western authors like Joyce, Eliot, Yeats, Faulkner, Woolf, and Lowell (and contemporaries like Bellow and Walker) is not this or that technique, but the need to face a new age with a sense of the legacy—positive and negative—of their own past. Writers and artists are rarely among those who are responsible for the destruction of a culture. However radical, experimental, or "alienated," the serious writer, through the inheritance of language, engages in a dialogue between past and present, familiar and strange, here and there. Writers and artists are, as Feng's story and Yeats's poem imply, the growers and builders.

"We have to give up the useless and irrelevant elements of traditional literature and ethics, because we want to create those needed for the progress of the new era and new society." *New Youth, 1919*

The inroads of modern life—the new city, the new technology, new forms of industry, transportation, communication—will inevitably have their effect on the Chinese people, including their artists and writers. If these effects bring about new forms in Chinese art and literature, it will not be because they are foreign, but because they are new. Of course, one of the consequences of modern life is the increasing contact among nations. It is certain that one of the major political as well as cultural problems of the twentieth century is how to establish mutually beneficial relations among nations without domination of one by another. It would seem that culturally at least the key for each nation in approaching the foreign is to do so with a clear knowledge of its own identity and values. Foreign ideas are unlikely to overwhelm Chinese writers who are firm in their knowledge of China and her culture. On the contrary, as in all the most fruitful of foreign exchanges, they can only clarify and enhance what is most precious in the Chinese experience.

No Westerner—Irish, English, or American—reading Yeats' "Lapis Lazuli" could possibly mistake it for a Chinese poem. The voice, the tone, the rhythm, the diction, the sentiment belong incontrovertibly to a Western tradition. The literary use of a Chinese artifact neither absorbs the poem's cultural identity nor wrenches it from its own time and place. It provides a means for contemplating that tradition from a fresh perspective. It is a link with readers and "builders" of other times and places, but the poet keeps faith with his own language and temper, with his native inheritance. Similarly, Feng Jicai's story, its stylistic innovations and mention of Walt Disney notwithstanding, is unmistakably Chinese. The retrieval of the chrysanthemum —a seemingly too familiar and static image in certain contexts—through a startling juxtaposition with the discordant realities of contemporary history, is an achievement of a uniquely Chinese kind. Only a Chinese writer, keenly aware of what is ancient and new, could bring into modern relief the contours of this old symbol, "defiant of frost and triumphant in autumn," and make it live again.

For the Westerner, writer or critic, complacent about his freedom, including the illusory freedom from politics, the Chinese literary situation has its relevance. The Chinese cannot forget that human discourse is never entirely detached from the structures of power and that literature influences as well as reflects human behavior. Detachment is a relative, not an absolute condition. If the Chinese writer may need to be reacquainted with himself, with his own venerable tradition, and with the ways of the foreigners' world, the Western writer needs to recall that he or she is part of a social organism, that what he or she writes or refuses to write has political implications, and that despite the dictates of the producers and publishers, there is a wide audience waiting.

Notes

1 T. S. Eliot, "Burnt Norton," *Four Quartets*, in *The Complete Poems and Plays, 1909–1950* (New York: Harcourt, Brace and Company, 1958), p. 121.
> "Only by the form, the pattern,
> Can words or music reach

The stillness, as a Chinese jar still
Moves perpetually in its stillness."

2   William Butler Yeats, "Lapis Lazuli," *The Collected Poems of W. B. Yeats* (New York: Macmillan Company, 1959), pp. 291–93.

3   For an extended discussion of the careers of these writers and a number of their contemporaries, see Jonathan D. Spence, *The Gate of Heavenly Peace: The Chinese and Their Revolution, 1895–1980* (New York: Viking Press, 1981).

4   This story first appeared in Chinese in *Contemporary Literature*, no. 2 (1979). The text quoted in this essay is from a translation by Kai-yu in *Prize-Winning Stories from China, 1978–1979* (Beijing, Foreign Languages Press, 1981). Page references in parentheses follow quotations.

5   The fourth-century scholar-poet Tao Yuan-ming in "Home Again" is responsible for one of the earliest and best known references to the chrysanthemum. Also see Mai-mai Sze, *The Way of Chinese Painting, Its Ideas and Technique, With Selections from the Seventeenth Century Mustard Seed Garden Manual of Painting* (New York: Random House, 1959), p. 49.

6   Among the examples of innovative fiction by these writers are Wang Meng's *Butterfly* (1981), in which "stream-of-consciousness" narration is used; Lu Hsinhua's "The Wound" (1979), one of the first stories to dwell on the suffering caused by the Cultural Revolution; Shen Rong's *Middle Age* (1980), a powerful depiction of the stresses endured by professional middle-aged women in contemporary China; and Jiang Zilong's *All the Colors of the Rainbow* (1982), in which impressionistic imagery is employed in the presentation of character and setting.

7   These remarks are translation of part of a commentary by Xu Chi that originally appeared in an essay entitled "Modernization and Modernism" and were elaborated upon in the November 1982 issue of *Wenyi Bao*.

8   Spence, *The Gate of Heavenly Peace*, p. 309.

9   This is quoted in Gu Zhicheng, " 'The Second Handshake,' A New Bestseller," *Chinese Literature* (January 1980), p. 10, in reference to a remark made by Yao Wenyuan in 1974 about the popular novel by Zhang Yang.

Notes on Industrialism and Culture in Nineteenth-century Britain / *Charles Dellheim*

And this notion we all have—ancient England steeped in her traditional ways? Forget it.
—John Le Carré, *The Little Drummer Girl* (1983)

"In this work I have to examine the capitalist mode of production, and the condition of production and exchange corresponding to that mode. Up to the present time, their classic ground is England." [1] Thus Karl Marx in a famous passage of *Capital* (1867) written when Britain's industrial and technological supremacy still seemed secure. [2] Those days are, of course, long gone. The economic decline of Britain belies Marx's reading of nineteenth-century British society, to say nothing of his predictions for its future prospects. From Marx to W. W. Rostow, Britain occupied a privileged place in social theory as the paradigm case of industrial capitalist society. Since the mid-1970s, Britain has occupied a far less honorable position. It has served unwillingly as an exemplar of economic stagnation and industrial strife. What ails Britain and how to set it right is a question that continues to provoke controversy on both sides of the Atlantic and all shades of the political spectrum. The condition of Britain and its causes has become a testing ground for debate on the virtues and vices of capitalism and socialism. This debate has produced an increasingly corpulent scholarly and journalistic literature on the set of ills popularly known as the "British disease." [3] The "British disease" is itself an epiphenomenon of broader social transformations. They can be viewed optimistically as the coming of a post-industrial Britain, a humane society rich in leisure and services; or pessimistically as the advent of a de-industrialized Britain, a moribund society hampered by the persistence of archaic attitudes and institutions. [4] For all the differences in these perspectives, they share one common feature. Both minimize the role of industrialism in Britain's past and present.

The preoccupation with economic decline frames contemporary approaches to the British past. Whereas the Whig historians of the nineteenth century explored the national past to celebrate the sources of Victorian political stability and economic supremacy, contemporary historians are concerned with isolating the historical origins of Britain's decline. What I want to do in this essay is to examine and evaluate recent generalizations in nineteenth-century British history. I am concerned, in particular, with the following thesis: Britain never became a complete industrial society despite or perhaps because of the fact that it was the first industrial nation. The cultural values associated with industrialism were contained by the triumph of a pre-industrial aristocratic-gentry culture that idealized the countryside and the past. The gentrification of the middle class led to the waning of the industrial spirit and thus to the economic decline of Britain. Although several scholars argue this case, no one has done so more skillfully than Martin J. Wiener in his important study, *English Culture and the Decline of the Industrial Spirit, 1850–1980* (1981).[5] This thesis repays close analysis for its intrinsic significance and growing influence, but especially because it provides an opportunity to reconsider the complex relationship between industrialism and culture in nineteenth-century Britain.

Recent generalizations in modern British history begin with the idea that Britain, far from being the model of industrial society, never modernized fully. Daniel Bell argues this case in "The future that never was," an acute analysis of the British predicament. He begins his historical analysis with a critique of the "mortmain of Marx." Marx mystified British capitalism by drawing "a picture of the bourgeoisie that has informed (i.e., misinformed) every sociological cliché regarding the transformation of *Gemeinschaft* into *Gesellschaft*."[6] Never was England the atomistic, egotistic civil society imagined by Hegel and anatomized by Marx. Bourgeois capitalism did not sweep away, as promised, all "ancient venerable prejudices" any more than the middle class drove the landed aristocracy from the seats of power. Far from it! Indeed, Bell turns Marx on his head. His thesis is that "while England was the *first* country to industrialize, it never became a *full* industrial nation."[7] Hence, the "future that never was" is England's future conceived by Marx and duly ignored by the English, a people disinclined to accept the counsel of foreigners or the imperatives of history. The central "imago" of English society remained the gentleman because the middle class accepted and emulated the style of life and values of the aristocracy and gentry. Cast by Marx to play "a most revolutionary part" in that much-rehearsed historical drama "The Fall of the Ancien Régime," the English bourgeoisie changed its role in the middle of the action. They fell in love with the world of their intended victims. It was more pleasant to live in country houses—or look forward to weekend invitations—than to burn them down. And so it came to pass that "in its social and political institutions, England has been a *traditional* society, managing an arrested industrial economy, and, if it can be compared with anything at all, resembling Venice. . . . England has not been the great industrial-capitalist power whose integument would burst asunder for the socialist society to step forth."[8]

Other scholars put forth this thesis from different perspectives. Waiting in the wings for the oft-predicted death of capitalism, the Scottish neo-Marxist thinker Tom Nairn provides a revisionist interpretation of the British state. His provocative account emphasizes the "logic of priority." Britain was the "pioneer modern liberal constitutional state." The English Civil War proclaimed the supremacy of Parliament and the rule of law. Yet the British state "never itself became modern." Political power remained in the hands of a patrician elite dedicated to rule from above. The political culture of Britain retained its organic, hierarchical, and deferential character even as it became a parliamentary democracy.[9] Although Martin J. Wiener is more concerned with the character of English cultural values than the nature of its political system, he also stressed the limits of modernization. He observed that

> the transition to modernity was relatively smooth and involved no political upheaval. . . . If society was transformed, with a minimum of violence, the extent of the transformation was more limited than it first appeared to be. New economic forces did not tear the social fabric. Old values and patterns of behavior lived on within the new, whose character was thus profoundly modified. The end result of the nineteenth-century transformation of Britain was indeed a peaceful accommodation, but one that entrenched premodern sentiments within the new society, and gave legitimacy to antimodern sentiments.[10]

The peaceful compromise between the middle class and the aristocracy that the Whigs hailed as a source of England's much-envied stability is now seen as a cause of its stagnation.

The thesis that Britain is an incomplete industrial society is in many respects brilliant, elegant, and persuasive. There is much in contemporary Britain that cannot be explained with reference to the recent past alone. The persistence of the old order manifests itself in the continuing vitality and power of the monarchy, the House of Lords, the Church of England, the ancient universities of Oxford and Cambridge, and the Inns of Court. It is also true that the triumph of the middle class heralded, for quite different reasons, by Karl Marx and Thomas Babington Macaulay was never completely realized. As Richard Cobden explained in 1863: "We have," he observed, "the spirit of feudalism rife and rampant in the midst of the antagonistic development of the age of Watt, Arkwright and Stephenson. Nay, feudalism is every day more and more in the ascendant in political and social life. So great is its power and prestige that it draws to it the support and homage of even those who are the natural leaders of the newer and better civilisation."[11] Recent research in social history, in particular the work of W. D. Rubinstein, suggests that the impact of industrialism on the social and economic structure of nineteenth-century Britain has been much exaggerated. He underlines the close ties which bound the Tory, Anglican middle class which was so prominent in commerce, finance, and the old professions—medicine, law, army, and Church—to the aristocracy and gentry. The wealthiest men in nineteenth-century Britain, landowners notwithstanding, were engaged in commerce and finance rather than industry. What emerges from his studies is a conservative, traditionalist England certain to delight the Tory and enrage the Radical.[12]

Yet there are major problems with the argument that Britain is not a full industrial society. Literally speaking, it is simply wrong. Britain is, of course, one of the most heavily industrialized, urbanized societies in the world today. Moreover, if we define modern societies as differentiated, dynamic, specialized, urbanized, and literate, then by this conventional sociological standard, Britain is indubitably modern and indeed was so prior to industrialization.[13] The idea of an incomplete industrial society is itself as relentlessly teleological as the Whig or Marxist interpretations of modern British history that it purports to replace. And the notion that Britain is not fully modern imposes a value-laden, normative model of modernization on the British experience and then finds it guilty of failure to conform to the alleged laws of historical development. Furthermore, the normative model is founded on the erroneous assumption that all industrialized societies will eventually converge. This premise ignores the impact of different national histories on the shape modernity assumes in different societies. So too does it overestimate the totalizing effect of an industrial economy on culture, government, and social structure.[14]

Perhaps the main conceptual problem with the current debate on the character of British society is that it suffers from inadequate, one-dimensional conceptions of tradition and modernity and the relationship between them. This is largely the legacy of classical sociological theory. The classical sociologists used different terms and concepts to explain the transition from traditional to modern societies. Henry Maine distinguished between status and contract; Ferdinand Toennies between "Gemeinschaft" and "Gesellschaft"; Emile Durkheim between mechanical and organic divisions of labor; and Max Weber between traditional, charismatic, and rational-legal forms of authority.[15] So intent were they on explaining the vast social transformations they witnessed that they overstated the gulf dividing traditional and modern societies by presenting them as mutually exclusive systems. Historians and social scientists demonstrated that the antithesis between tradition and modernity is unsatisfactory in several respects. First, the modernization of some societies took place under the aegis of traditional elites and traditional symbols, not in opposition to them. Second, old elites were often able to reestablish their power and status in new, modern settings. They did not simply fade from the scene to make way for the ever-rising bourgeoisie. Finally, modern societies are not traditionless. The prescriptive power of tradition fades, but at the same time it is reconstructed to suit new masters and altered circumstances. Seen from this perspective, traditions are not mere "vestiges" or "survivals" of the past. Instead they are vital, if not necessarily beneficent, forces in social and cultural life.[16]

Nowhere, perhaps, is this more true than in Britain. Modernization took place there under the banner of the aristocracy and gentry. Thus there was only a limited rearguard assault on modernizing forces.[17] The relative absence of reactionary traditionalism is one reason why tradition retained much of its appeal as a reservoir of symbols and values in British society. (Whether the appeal of preindustrial ideals in the late nineteenth century conflicted with continuing economic growth is a question that I will address later.) Although I do not deny the persistence of certain traditional ideals and institutions in modern Britain, it does not follow that Britain is therefore an incomplete industrial society any more than the same could be fairly said of Japan. And for that matter, the persistence of traditional forms and values is itself deceptive. As Walter Bagehot observed in *The English Constitution* (1867):

> When a great entity like the British Constitution has continued in connected outward sameness, but hidden inner change, for many ages, every generation inherits a series of inapt words—of maxims once true, but of which the truth is ceasing or has ceased. As a man's family go on muttering in his maturity incorrect phrases derived from a just observation of his early youth, so, in the full activity of an historical constitution, its subjects repeat phrases true in the time of their fathers, and inculcated by those fathers, but now true no longer. Or, if I may say so, an ancient and ever-altering constitution is like an old man who still wears with attached fondness clothes in the fashion of his youth: what you see of him is the same; what you do not see is wholly altered.[18]

Britain's ancient political institutions survived, but the apparent continuity of forms disguised the substantially different meanings and uses they had. It is not unimportant that the British state is still suffused with the symbols of a monarchical and aristocratic society. But hierarchical as Britain is, it is also nonetheless a parliamentary democracy.[19] Tradition—one of those big words which Stephen Daedalus believed make us so unhappy—was a weapon which cut in different directions. The British invoked the symbols of the past as much to justify reform as to squelch it.

Misleading as it is to present Britain as an incomplete industrial society, it is true that the rise of industry did not transform Britain as completely as other societies. In the nineteenth century, two social systems competed for dominance. The first was a preindustrial hierarchy based on land in which status followed birth and everyone knew who owed him deference and to whom he had to defer. The highest ideal of the old society was the landed gentleman. He was distinguished not simply by gentle birth, but also by personal elegance, grace, and bearing. The second social system was a class society that developed during the industrial revolution. In the new society, status depended on income and its sources and men were bound together by voluntary contract and cash payment. The entrepreneur was the hero of the industrial world.[20] Neither side was able to displace its opponent or rule unaided. As Asa Briggs put it: "No single group has been able to establish unqualified dominance; no code from one group has won total acceptance; no political party has a built-in, permanent majority." [21]

Related to the idea that Britain is an incomplete industrial society is the argument that the cultural values of industrialism were contained by the pre-industrial culture of the aristocracy and gentry. Martin J. Wiener argues that "the cultural revolution of industrialism" reached its high-water mark during the Great Exhibition of 1851. Thereafter, the enthusiasm of the educated classes for industrial capitalism and technological innovation faded. The great Victorian social critics, Thomas Carlyle, Matthew Arnold, John Ruskin, and William Morris led a counterrevolution of values. From different perspectives and with different aims, they denounced the world created by the provincial, industrial middle class and derided the materialism and philistinism of an increasingly commercial society. Their vision might not have been so influential were it not for the complicity of the English middle class. Those who had been prosperous for two or three generations tended to discard their fathers' emphasis on self-help, enterprise, and practicality. Instead of subverting the old order, many businessmen proved anxious to assimilate into landed society through the purchase of a country estate and perhaps the acquisition of a coat of arms or a title. Failing that, they had to content themselves with obsequious imitation of the life-style and ethos of their betters. It was, above all, the reformed public schools that became the crucibles for turning the sons of businessmen into faultless gentlemen, or in any event gentlemen with gentlemen's faults. The classical curriculum of the public schools promoted hostility, or at best indifference, to the work-a-day world of industry and technology. The masters of Eton, Harrow, Rugby, and Winchester dedicated themselves to shaping the character of the educated amateur; for the trained technical specialist they had little interest and less tolerance. They directed their boys away from capitalist values and toward prestigious careers in the established professions or the civil service. Better, far better, for a gentleman to lead the natives in New Delhi than to seek brass amid the muck of Manchester. As the meeting-ground, and of course the playing-ground, of the sons of the middle and upper classes, the public schools were instrumental in consolidating a national elite loyal to gentry values and dedicated to the proposition that men are created unequal and so shall they stay.

In the late nineteenth and early twentieth centuries, writers and artists adopted a "conception of Englishness what eventually excluded industrialism." [22] The "English way of life" was identified with the values of the "agricultural" South of England: tranquility, stability, idealism, and spirituality.[23]

Thus the dynamism, enterprise, materialism, and pragmatism associated with the industrial North of England were relegated to the periphery. The true England was to be found in the beauties of the countryside and the virtues of the past. Its characteristic symbols were the village, the parish church, the country house, and the cathedral town. The ugliness of the industrial city and the vulgarity of the contemporary world were aberrations.[24]

Martin J. Wiener's account of English anti-industrialism is unsurpassed in its appreciation of the ambiguity of modern English history and in its analysis of the values of the English elite. He demonstrates the strength of anti-industrial sentiment and thought through a subtle analysis of literature, architecture, politics, and historical thought. Yet his interpretation of the relationship between industrialism and culture requires qualification on three counts. First, it overestimates the unity of English culture. Second, it underplays the continuing strength of the culture of provincial, industrial England. And, finally, it oversimplifies the meanings and functions of the allegedly anti-modern idealization of the past and the countryside.

Both the defenders and the critics of English culture often remark on its unity. And there is good reason to do so. The English upper class was, and is, unusually homogenous and disproportionately influential. The ideal of the gentleman was a powerful social archetype with wide appeal. Yet the consensus is easily exaggerated. Neither the notorious gulf between "U" and "non-U" nor the distance separating insiders and outsiders is imaginary. Granted that the "Southern" vision of England as "an old country" and a "green and pleasant land" became increasingly dominant in the late nineteenth and early twentieth centuries. But the "containment of industrialism" was itself partial. This is especially striking when we approach British culture from a regional vantage point. It is true that at the turn of the century, the lure of London reasserted itself and did so at the expense of provincial cities such as Manchester, Leeds, and Birmingham. Even after the nationalization of provincial cultures, however, regional differences between the North and South of England persisted.[25] The economic and cultural strength of the provincial, industrial, dissenting middle class waned as mills were deserted and fortunes exhausted. Yet it survived throughout the early twentieth century as did the universities and the musical and literary institutions they founded and nurtured. This was the world of the cultured Northern middle class J. B. Priestley evoked in *Bright Day* (1946). No simple capitulation to the culture of the aristocracy and gentry took place, at any rate not until the 1950s.[26] "Achievement is what matters in Manchester," A. J. P. Taylor wrote in his wonderful evocation of the city, "not a historic name or a cultivated accent. It is an added advantage, of course, that Manchester is in Lancashire and can have its own way of speaking without anyone worrying about it."[27] Nor did Manchester men take their lead from the South. "Manchester looked at southern England in Cobden's spirit. It cared little for what was going on 'down there.' London was not expected to provide either ideas or material direction."[28] In *English Journey* (1934), J. B. Priestley noted the eagerness of some Northern businessmen to leave the city for the country and the chapel for the church at the first opportunity. They did so at their peril in his native Bradford. "If having made some big lucky gamble in wool, you made a fortune there and determined to set up as an English gentleman, you never stayed in Bradford, where everybody was liable to be very sardonic at your expense; but bought an estate a long way off, preferably in the South."[29] The question is not whether there were deserters from the provincial middle class—obviously there were—but how numerous they were and what effect they had. Here, systematic study of twentieth-century local and national elites is necessary.

As for the attachment to the past and the countryside, there is no doubt, as Wiener's excellent account demonstrates, that both were profoundly ingrained in English culture. He suggests that "a shift from the use of the past to make innovation palatable to a preoccupation with the past for its own sake began to become visible in the eighteen-seventies and eighties."[30] The chronology put forth for changing attitudes to the past is untenable. There was indeed widespread public enthusiasm for local and national history during the later nineteenth century. But this predated the so-called Great Depression and was neither a consequence nor a cause of it. The booming interest in local history began in the midcentury when local archaeological and historical societies proliferated throughout England.[31] Moreover, there was no clear shift from using the past to justify innovation to exploring the past for its own sake. Both attitudes informed late nineteenth-century approaches to the past. It is true that old and new towns alike made much of their distant past, even to the point of inventing historic pedigrees where none existed. Yet they did so more from civic pride or provincial consciousness than from dissatisfaction with the industrial world.[32] Wiener rightly insists that the past provided a source of alternative values for those alarmed by commercialism and ugliness. Yet the middle-class acceptance of the Gothic style, exemplified by the Manchester Town Hall and the Bradford Wool Exchange, did not signify "the cresting of the new culture of the industrial revolution, and the beginning of a yielding by its new men to the cultural hegemony of the old aristocracy."[33] Both these buildings are testimonials to the values and archives of the history of liberal, middle class, industrial England. Their iconography celebrates the romance of trade and industry and their medieval style recalls the liberty-loving medieval burghers who threw off aristocratic tyranny. In their choice of the Gothic style for their municipal buildings, the City Fathers of Manchester did imitate a favorite aristocratic idiom. Doing so, however, was more a gesture of defiance than a sign of submission. Anxious to create buildings that would establish their city as a place of good taste, they consulted leading architectural experts. The approval they sought was that of professionals rather than that of the aristocracy.[34]

Did the concern with the past, then, conflict with the values of an industrial society or contribute to an outlook inimical to economic growth? Yes and no. The concern with the past had different meanings and uses because various individuals and groups interpreted the meaning of tradition and the demands of modernity in very different ways indeed. Thus, the concern with the past expressed both progressive and conservative values. It was part and parcel of the culture of industrial England, but it was also used to criticize its values and aspirations. There were, of course, conflicts between the appeal of the past and the demands of the present. Yet myths of historic continuity mitigated the tension between them as did the "invention of tradition," notably the rituals surrounding the Crown that were devised in the late nineteenth century.[35] The potential power of historic forms and symbols to undermine the values of the industrial world was largely defused by institutionalizing the lure of the past in cultural activities such as local archaeology and tourism, historic restoration and preservation, and architectural historicism.

Much the same ambiguity is evident in the idealization of the countryside. The image of England as a garden did conflict, on one level, with the image of England as a workshop. Garden suburbs, however, proved that the clash was not irreconcilable. The great Quaker cocoa and chocolate manufacturing firm, Cadbury Brothers, called its Bournville works "the factory in a garden." George Cadbury, a true lover of nature, ensured that the homes he built for working-class families in the garden city of Bournville—their style, incidentally, was medieval or tudor—had lovely gardens so that they might enjoy the pleasures of country life in close proximity to the city. His hope was to keep them at home, out of mischief and away from drink: the fact that no pub was permitted in Bournville certainly aided the cause. In no sense did George Cadbury's appreciation of the countryside and his dissatisfaction with the squalor and sins of the city interfere with his concern with maximizing industrial efficiency.[36] The love of nature, as Wiener aptly points out, was shared by many city-dwellers. What he underplays is the fact that this passion could, and did, coexist with the affairs of the industrial world. As J. B. Priestley wrote of industrial Bradford:

> Thus Bradford is a city entirely without charm, though not altogether ugly, and its industry is a black business; but it has the good fortune to be on the edge of some of the most enchanting country in England. A sharp walk of less than an hour from more than one tram terminus will bring you to the moors, wild virgin highland, and every mill and warehouse will be out of sight and the whole city forgotten. . . . However small and dark your office or warehouse was, somewhere inside your head the high moors were glowing, the curlews were crying, and there blew a wind as salt as if it came straight from the middle of the Atlantic. That is why we did not care very much if our city had no charm, for it

was simply a place to go and work in, until it was time to set out for Wharfedale or Wensleydale again. We were all, at heart, Wordsworthians to a man.[37]

From this perspective, the city and the countryside complemented each other. The fact that the delights of the garden and the countryside could be relished on the weekend made the inadequacies of the factory and the city more tolerable than they might have been otherwise. There is no reason to believe that weekend Wordsworthians were inefficient managers or workers.

The conservative, anti-industrial bias of English culture had destructive, practical effects on business performance. "In business, too," Martin J. Wiener argues, "industrial and anti-industrial values were joined. . . . Businessmen increasingly shunned the role of entrepreneur for the more socially rewarding role of gentleman (landed, if possible). The upshot was a dampening of industrial energies." [38] The gentrification of the middle class led to the waning of the industrial spirit which, in turn, contributed to the economic decline of Britain, in particular of industry. This manifested itself in several ways. First, the growth of anti-industrial bias discouraged the growth of technological education or branded it inferior when and where it did develop. Second, the idealization of the landed gentlemen spurred the sons of successful businessmen, if not their fathers, to become rentier capitalists rather than enthusiastic entrepreneurs. Third, the graduates of public schools were either drawn away from business careers or brought to them gentlemanly values inimical to innovation, productivity, and growth. Finally, the social hierarchy of the business world came to embody aristocratic-gentry values insofar as it found the "clean" careers of finance and commerce in London preferable to the "dirty" jobs of industry and engineering in the provinces.[39]

Here again the argument is an impressive *tour de force* that explains much of what happened, and failed to happen, to the British economy. Here again, however, like Voltaire's Zadig, I am compelled to say "But."

Certainly there is powerful evidence supporting the thesis that the gentrification of the middle class contributed to the economic decline of Britain. Many late nineteenth- and early twentieth-century commentators decried the woeful consequences of the decline of the work ethic. In *Imperial Germany and the Industrial Revolution* (1915), Thorstein Veblen offered a devastating critique of English gentility and its economic costs. For Veblen, the essence of the gentlemen is conspicuous wastefulness. Sports played a major role in the world of the leisure class.

Sport, on the scale, and with the circumstance attending its cultivation in the United Kingdom, can not be incorporated in the workday scheme of life except at the cost of long and persistent training of the popular taste. It is not to be done by a brusque move. It is quite beyond the reach of imagination that any adult male citizen would of his own motion go in for the elaborate futilities of British shooting or horse-racing, e.g., or for such a *tour de force* of inanity as polo, or mountain climbing, or expeditions after big game.[40]

The style of life of the "conventionally accredited wasters" had destructive consequences, direct and indirect, on economic performance. No longer the world leader in industry, "the English today lead the Christian world both in the volume of their gentility and in its cost per unit."[41] The numerous residences of the English gentleman required a host of servants who were thus removed from potentially useful labor. Far more worrying was the fact that the inanities of the genteel provided a dubious model for the lower classes. "This preoccupation with the emulative and invidious interests of sportsmanship unavoidably has an industrially untoward effect on the temper of the population, bends them with an habitual bias in the direction of trivial emulative exploits and away from that ready discrimination in matters of fact that constitutes the spiritual ground of modern technological efficiency."[42] Thus, the useless life of the upper class undermined both the moral integrity and the industrial efficiency of the middle and lower classes alike.

The "pursuit of Ease" did to some extent undermine the middle-class ethic of self-help and hard work. It could hardly have been otherwise for those who found the pursuit of foxes preferable to the hunt for profits. (Who could blame them? The hours were amusing, the company agreeable, and the fox, for all his speed, better quarry than the bounders pushing at their heels.) Certain business dynasties did indeed disintegrate as later generations found the pleasures of country life more enticing that the rigors of the business world. The Marshalls of Leeds are a famous example of those who used the wealth they earned in industry to win social status and acceptance. As they blended into landed society, they gradually severed their ties to the family firm, which decayed and ultimately died as a new county family fashioned a future colonel.[43] Testifying before a Parliamentary commission in 1903, the economist Alfred Marshall explained that England's early industrial and technological lead encouraged many businessmen to believe, quite wrongly, "that an Englishman could expect to obtain a much larger real income and to live more luxuriously than anybody else, at all events in an old country; and that if he chose to shorten his hours of work and take things easily, he could afford to do so."[44] Thus, many of the sons of successful businessmen were, he continued, "content to follow mechanically the lead given by their fathers. They worked shorter hours, and they exerted themselves less to obtain new practical ideas than their fathers had done; and thus a part of England's leadership was destroyed rapidly."[45] No such retreat took place in the great financial and commercial dynasties such as the Rothschilds and the Barings. This was true partly because finance carried social prestige not to be found in industry. But there too a gentlemanly style was de rigueur.

D. C. Coleman raised the issue of precisely how a public school education affected business performance. What does it matter if a man has been to Eton?[46] On the one hand, the public schools may have contributed to the later business success of their old boys by fostering "leadership qualities" and forging social connections. On the other hand, the leisurely style and anti-technological bias of the public schools were hardly likely to encourage aggressive entrepreneurship or spark hard work. It was more likely to prove disadvantageous in, say, heavy industry than in merchant banking. "Callisthenes," the anonymous house writer of Selfridge and Co., the leading London department store built by H. Gordon Selfridge, an American tycoon from Chicago, took up the question of "The Public Schools in Business" in a series of articles published in the press in the early 1930s. Although Selfridge's had done much to recruit public school graduates, their attitudes presented certain problems for both the managers and staff of the Store. He pointed out that public school boys labor under the illusion that they are *entitled* to a good position and a good salary. Not so, responded "Callisthenes," who claimed that "business pays a man for what he does, not for what he is, . . . not for having capabilities, but for exercising them."[47] A shocking idea for some, but there it is. Public schools taught their boys the importance of "playing the game" and of course playing it as an amateur. There is much room for fine ideals in business, but none, alas, for amateurism. At least not at Selfridge's, where professionalism was encouraged. There a man has "got to apply himself constantly and unashamedly and proudly to make himself more efficient in order to gain a stronger place in the economic world."[48] As for the much-vaunted habit of command deliciously cultivated at the public schools, "Callisthenes" notes: "It is, however, a very different thing to arrive in business with no other equipment except a facility for giving orders. Business in London is not manned from the backward races. It is manned by people who in the essentials are very much the same as the Public School Boys themselves."[49] Not until they gain business knowledge and practical experience through hard work and steady application will their power of command be useful and justified.

"Callisthenes'" strictures confirm the assumption that gentility and business are not natural allies. But several additional points need to be made about the "gentlemanly economy" of Britain. First, it is easy to overestimate the impact of genteel values on the actual conduct of business. The aggressive, performance-oriented business philosophy of Selfridge's, "Americanized" as it admittedly was, had little place for class snobbery or the higher laziness. As "Callisthenes" put it: "There are few joys like the joy of working at high pressure. Men love it. They will look back on a day of such work with more a thrill of satisfaction than on any day of idleness."[50] Management propa-

ganda perhaps, but no less telling as an index of business attitudes for being
so. Second, it is equally easy to be deceived by taking the gentlemanly style
at face value, especially in view of the gentleman's penchant for mild self-
mockery and irony. It is not surprising that a "gentrified industrialist" like
Samuel Courtauld would downplay the importance of material gain as a primary motive in business.[51] It is "not the done thing" for a gentleman to
indulge in greedy chatter about the delights of money-making or behave as if
he had labored to win his fortune. Far better to act as if one's wealth was a
fortunate, though well-deserved, accident or as if it had been in the family
for years like one's good looks or Grandfather's old tweed coat and hunting
rifle. But the fact that gentlemen affect indifference to money reveals as much
if not more about their public style than their private ambitions. The desire
not to appear a bounder or vulgarian should not be construed as a sign of
profound idealism or abiding spirituality. There are many things that one
could say about the City of London: lack of interest in wealth and profit is
not among them. Were that so, it would be difficult indeed to explain the
continuing financial success of the City, not to mention the propensity of
some City men to be taken in by outsiders who sometimes prove themselves
to be scoundrels.[52] The self-professed amateur status of the gentlemanly businessman is also somewhat misleading. Amateurism requires casualness and
effortlessness at all times, but it does not necessarily mean not knowing one's
business. Finally, the gentlemanly style sometimes coexisted with technical
efficiency and business competitiveness. Such was the case at Brunner, Mond
and Co., an innovative, aggressive chemical firm that was one of the fore-
runners of Imperial Chemical Industries. Its historian, W. J. Reader, points
out that the corporate life of Brunner, Mond centered on the Winnington
Hall Club, whose atmosphere was like an Oxbridge college and whose structure was founded on class distinction. "That might," he observes, "under
other circumstances, have fostered the kind of amateurishness which British
management has often been accused of, but at Winnington, on the contrary,
if Brunner, Mond's pre-1914 results are anything to go by, it sharpened the
edge of professionalism."[53] In fact, the existence of the Club was an incentive
for the university-trained scientists that the firm wanted to recruit.[54]

The extent of the gentrification of the middle class is also questionable. So
much has been said recently about the primacy of the gentlemanly ethos in
England that we now tend to ignore the persistence of the industrial spirit.
The fascination with technology, the pride in industry, and the gospel of work
survived, especially in the North of England. In *The Romance of Modern
Industry* (1889), James Burnley took up a long-standing theme:

> Industry and Romance have long been regarded in the popular mind as
> "thing apart", or at all events, as having their kinship only in a remote
> past, when the spirit of personal adventure entered more largely into

trade enterprise than is the case in our own time. It needs but a moment's reflection, however, to dispense this notion; for, although in the magnitude of modern industrial operations the element of picturesqueness which appertained to the days of home handicrafts has disappeared, we have still present—and in stronger force than ever—those conflicts of human motives and human passion which the struggle for wealth and power always engender.[55]

While some businessmen retreated from the industrial world, others celebrated its unique "poetry."

Katharine Chorley's memoir, *Manchester Made Them* (1950), furnishes interesting evidence on the social values of the provincial middle class at the turn of the century. She described her home as "pretty nearly a microcosm of north-country English bourgeois and professional life in those golden Edwardian days which were the culmination of a century of middle class endeavor."[56] In search of "cleaner air and country surroundings" the Campbell family moved from Manchester to Alderley Edge in Cheshire, "the residence of the merchant princes of Manchester."[57] Their move to the countryside did not mean withdrawing from the business world, rejecting the industrial spirit, or blending into county society and adopting county ways. Her mother's family were Ulster Irish with a "long-secured and easy family position, industrial now, but with memories which went back to the ownership of land and . . . a feudal and personal sense of responsibility."[58] Her father, Edward Campbell, came from a rising Manchester Nonconformist family, "proud of its achievements; proud of its education."[59] He was a "vital unresting man radiating energy," who "lived in the world of affairs and practical problems."[60] He and his brothers were Oxbridge scholars; this was more the exception than the rule among Manchester men in the 1870s and 1880s. "Charged up with ambition," Edward Campbell, a Cambridge Mathematics Wrangler, went into "applied electricity."[61] After coming down from Cambridge he returned to Manchester, joining the firm of Mather and Platt. Unlike conservative entrepreneurs who preferred the practical man who had been through the works, Sir William Mather "believed in the application of science in industry."[62] Mather and Platt was innovative in other ways. Sir William conceived business as a "joint moral Partnership," much as the Quaker chocolate manufacturers, the Cadburys and the Rowntrees, did.[63] Mather and Platt was also the first British engineering firm to change over to the forty-eight-hour week in 1893. Sir William purchased the right to manufacture Thomas Edison's dynamo in Britain. Edward and John Campbell modified the dynamo and used it to design the first electric locomotive engine for the London underground. When the firm became a limited company in 1898, Edward Campbell became managing director. This case demonstrates the persistence of the industrial spirit and of aggressive entrepreneurship at the turn of the century.

Whether it is representative is an open question, but the same question applies to well-known examples of gentrification.

The connection posited between gentrification and economic decline is based partly on the premise that there was a "failure of entrepreneurship" in the late nineteenth century.[64] Whatever the validity of this thesis for heavy industry with a strong technological component, it does not apply to light industry and retailing, both of which were vigorous and innovative at the turn of the century. The exhaustion of established firms and families needs to be seen alongside of the rise of new men and new methods.

Take the case of Jesse Boot, founder of Boots the Chemists, still the largest pharmaceutical chain in Britain. "The day of romance in business is not yet past," commented one writer in 1926 of Jesse Boot, "when just about forty years ago a little boy who helped his widowed mother keep a small shop in Goose Gate, Nottingham, is now the head of a concern with 5,000,000 capital, 40,000 shareholders, and a staff of 13,000 including 1,000 fully qualified chemists, huge factories and distributing warehouses, and 700 of the finest retail shops in every part of the country."[65] The rise of Jesse Boot would have made a good chapter in Samuel Smiles' *Self-Help* or *Industrial Biography*. He was raised in a pious Nonconformist working-class family in Nottingham. Until his health failed him, Jesse Boot worked sixteen hours every weekday as he built his business. He broke the monopoly of established private chemists by relying on low profit margins and high turnovers, and by manufacturing many of his own lines of pharmaceutical articles.[66] He captured public attention by extensive advertising campaigns and by building shops as attractive in appearance as they were convenient in layout. Even his love of building served his commercial flair. In response to the pleas of the local antiquarian society in the cathedral town of St. Albans, Boot commissioned the restoration of a picturesque Jacobean shop that he had purchased for the value of its site. Public approval and patronage proved that "good taste" was also good business. He capitalized on the public enthusiasm for local history and historic architecture by building new shops in historic towns such as Winchester, York, and Exeter, in medieval and Tudor styles and graced them with statues, stained-glass windows, and heraldry that celebrated major figures and events from the local past.[67] Throughout his life, he remained a loyal Liberal and religious Nonconformist. Never really secure in his wealth, he did not identify with the upper class or move easily in their company even when he became Sir Jesse Boot, and shortly before his death, Lord Trent. The same could not be said for his son, John Campbell Boot, second Lord Trent, whose career illustrates the ambiguities of gentrification. His posh style of life was antithetical to that of his ascetic father. He was a hunting, shooting, fishing lord who loved farming his 45,000-acre estate. He fancied himself a Scottish laird and indulged his fancy by reading Scottish history and hiring his own piper. On the face of it, we might assume the second Lord Trent to be one of the dim who inherit the earth and squander it at their leisure, a fine candidate for a Monty Python farce. In fact, he was an extremely successful businessman. Much like his father, he was a dictatorial chairman of Boots Ltd. who thoroughly knew the retail trade and Boots' ever-growing branches.[68]

There were other late nineteenth-century entrepreneurs who were as dynamic, inventive, and successful as Jesse Boot. Outstanding among them was Boot's friend, William H. Lever, later Lord Leverhulme. Born in a lower-middle-class family in Bolton, Lancashire, he was brought up to appreciate the virtues of respectability, piety, business integrity, and hard work. Not for nothing did Charles Wilson, the historian of Unilever, call him "Mr. Smiles's Disciple."[69] "I know that people," he wrote, "are inclined to scoff at Smiles and his gospel of Self Help, but my advice to the young man of the present generation is to act on the principles taught in Smiles's philosophy. He will go further than his competitor who does not."[70] Those principles had served Lever well as he used his family grocery store as a base for becoming the largest wholesale grocer in Lancashire, and then in building the giant soap-manufacturing firm, Lever Brothers. Like Jesse Boot, a Liberal and a Nonconformist, Lever was also a forceful, autocratic entrepreneur who brilliantly exploited advertising to popularize "Sunlight" Soap and related products through prize schemes, slogans, and verse. Like Sir Thomas Lipton, he adopted the advanced methods of retailing and marketing that impressed him in his travels in America. A forward-looking, enlightened capitalist, he named his company magazine *Progress* and labored to fulfill the ideal it promised in his model factory and community, Port Sunlight. Its architecture was largely in the "Old English" style with Dutch and Flemish buildings added on later. At Port Sunlight, as in Bournville, historic architecture and rural prospects provided the setting for industrial experiments.[71]

The connection between the waning of the industrial spirit and the economic decline of Britain is ambiguous. Granted that the gentrification of businessmen contributed to Britain's loss of industrial supremacy at the end of the nineteenth century. But it is not a sufficient explanation. Other factors must be taken into account. First, Britain's industrial priority proved disadvantageous. Heavy investment in textiles, coal, iron, and railroads discouraged serious commitment and quick adaptation to technological innovations. For all Thorstein Veblen's caustic comments on English gentility, he did not believe that they had "sinned against the canons of technology." They were only paying the "penalty for having been thrown into the lead and so having shown the way."[72] The result was ultimately systematic "depreciation by obsolesence."

An industrial system which, like the English, has been long engaged in a course of improvement, extension, innovation and specialisation, will in the past have committed itself, more than once and in more than one connection, to what was at the time an adequate scale of appliances and schedule of processes and time adjustments. Partly by its own growth, and by force of technological innovations designed to enlarge the scale or increase the tempo of production or service, the accepted correlations in industry and business, as well as the established equipment, are thrown out of date. And yet it is by no means an easy matter to find a remedy; more particularly is it difficult to find a remedy that will approve itself as a sound business proposition to a community of conservative business men who have a pecuniary interest in the continued working of the received system, and who will (commonly) not be endowed with much insight into technological matters anyway.[73]

As long as businessmen could make a profit, albeit a diminishing profit, using existing technologies, there was little incentive to make huge capital investments in new processes. The failure to do so, however, meant that Britain's infrastructure and technologies became obsolete. The current situation of the United States is a telling parallel, and a disheartening one. Second, the alienation of capital and labor undermined productivity by encouraging little more than the worker's grudging obedience to the boss. Loyalty and commitment cannot be quantified, but recent management theory underlines the impact of what Seebohm Rowntree called "the human factor in business," and what we call corporate cultures on business performance.[74] Third, the conservative attitudes of managers and workers contributed to the technological shortcomings of British industry. The capitalist who preferred "the lad who had been through the works" to the university-trained scientist or engineer resisted the adoption of new scientifically based industrial processes, as did the workers who feared displacement. Henry Phelps-Brown suggests that this led to a lag in development that "impaired international competitiveness and impaired competitiveness in turn inhibited development."[75] The cult of the practical man, no less than the code of the gentlemanly amateur, proved destructive. Finally, Alfred D. Chandler contends that late nineteenth- and early twentieth-century British business' shortcomings are better explained as managerial failure rather than entrepreneurial failure. The ongoing dominance of family firms blocked the development of large-scale managerial enterprise. Thus, Britain was deprived of the cost-advantages and market power of American firms. The failure to quickly adopt new methods of mass production and distribution allowed American and German firms to make substantial inroads in British markets. The relative lack of engineers and managers in Britain proved particularly harmful in the chemical, machinery, and electrical equipment industries. And it was precisely in those sectors of the "second industrial revolution" that Britain lost ground most rapidly.[76]

Recent generalizations in modern British history represent a genuine intellectual advance, but they require considerable qualification on conceptual and empirical grounds. We are now far more aware of the paradoxes of British culture and society: the ambivalence to industrialism in the first industrial nation; the idealization of the countryside in an increasingly urban world; and the development of parliamentary democracy in an hierarchical state. Revisionist historians have contributed substantially to understanding the origins of Britain's economic and political decline. The danger is, however, that the preoccupation with what went wrong in the twentieth century will dominate and distort perceptions of the nineteenth century. This is not to deny the importance of anti-industrial thought and feeling, archaic attitudes and institutions, but only to insist they be seen as one face of an extremely complicated historical reality. It would be a mistake to interpret the ambiguities of British history as symptoms of incomplete modernization; the fault lies as much in our conception of modernity as in our view of Britain. As we approach the post-industrial world we are in a far better position than the classical sociologists were to discern the links between tradition and modernity as well as the chasm separating them. Now that it is clear that modernity is not the end of the historical road, it is possible to place it in proper historical and sociological perspective. The British experience underlines the problems of using industrialization as an all-purpose explanatory tool and industrial society as an all-embracing theoretical category. It is as erroneous to do as to invoke the omnipresent bourgeoisie to explain the origins of the Renaissance, the Protestant Reformation, the Spirit of Capitalism, the Scientific Revolution, the Enlightenment, the French Revolution, and the Industrial Revolution. There is much in the modern world that simply cannot be explained by industrialism alone. The notion that industrialism completely transformed modern culture mistakes a revolution for the apocalypse. It is based on the questionable premise that culture is an epiphenomenon of social and economic forces rather than a shaping power in its own right.

The relationship between cultural values and economic behavior in modern Britain has thus far been studied largely from a macrocosmic perspective. Well-informed as we now are about responses to industrialism, more remains to be said about how attitudes to finance, commerce, and industry differed and how capitalists and workers were depicted in visual and literary media. So too is further study of the attitudes of different class and regional subcultures necessary. But the only way to really advance our understanding of the impact of values on business performance is through microcosmic analysis of the business world. Business needs to be examined from the inside by exploring the self-perceptions and world views of businessmen and the architectural symbols of business. What requires intensive analysis, above all, is the cultures of different firms: their folklore, rituals, symbols, philosophies, and ethics must be studied in the context of their structure, strategy, and performance. I insist on the plural "cultures" because it is misleading to view capitalism monolithically or to assume that the values of all capitalists were identical. In so doing, it may prove possible to better understand the "successes" and "failures" of British society and to provide models for the future that will help reconcile the claims of social justice and industrial efficiency.

Notes

1   Karl Marx, *Capital* (New York: International Publishing Co., 1967), 1:8.

2   By the Paris Exhibition of 1867, some observers, notably Lyon Playfair, were well aware that England was already falling behind technologically in certain areas. See Michael Fores, "Britain's Economic Growth and the 1870 Watershed," *Lloyds Bank Review* 99 (January 1971), pp. 27–41.

3   On the "British disease," see "What is the British Disease?" London *Times* (29 April 1971); Peter Jenkins, "A Nation on the Skids," *Manchester Guardian Weekly* (8 October 1978); Isaac Kramnick, ed., *Is Britain Dying? Perspectives on the Current Crisis* (Ithaca: Cornell University Press, 1979); Bernard D. Nossiter, *Britain: A Future That Works* (Boston: Houghton Mifflin, 1978); R. Emmett Tyrell, ed., *The Future That Doesn't Work: Social Democracy's Failure in Britain* (Garden City, N.Y.: Doubleday, 1977); Tom Nairn, *The Break-Up of Britain* (London: Verso, 1981); Ralf Dahrendorf, *On Britain* (Chicago: University of Chicago Press, 1982); Robert Bacon and Walter Eltis, *Britain's Economic Problems: Too Few Producers* (New York: St. Martin's Press, 1976); James Alt, *The Politics of Economic Decline* (Cambridge: Cambridge University Press, 1979); Patrick Hutber, ed., *What's Wrong with Britain* (London: Sphere Books, 1978); William B. Gwyn and Richard Rose, eds., *Britain: Progress and Decline* (London: Macmillan, 1980); Samuel Beer, *Britain Against Itself: The Political Contradictions of Collectivism* (New York: Norton, 1982); Charles Hampden-Turner, *Gentlemen and Tradesmen: The Values of Economic Catastrophe* (London: Routledge and Kegan Paul, 1983); Nevil Johnson, *In Search of the Constitution: Reflections on State and Society in Britain* (Oxford: Pergamon Press, 1977); Anthony Lewis, "Notes on the New York Skyline . . ." *Atlantic* (June 1971), pp. 58–62; and *The United Kingdom in 1980: The Hudson Report* (New York: Halsted Press, 1974).

4   On Britain as a post-industrial society, see Nossiter, *Britain: A Future That Works*, and the thoughts of John Kenneth Galbraith reported in Krishan Kuman, "A Future in the Past?" *New Society* 42 (24 November 1977), pp. 418–19. On deindustrialized Britain, see Frank Blackaby, ed., *De-industrialization* (London: Heinemann, 1979).

5   Martin J. Wiener, *English Culture and the Decline of the Industrial Spirit, 1850–1980* (Cambridge: Cambridge University Press, 1981); Daniel Bell, "The Future That Never Was," *The Public Interest* 51 (Spring 1978), pp. 35–73; and Tom Nairn, "The Twilight of the British State," *The Break-Up of Britain*, pp. 11–91. This thesis was anticipated by Perry Anderson, "Origins of the Present Crisis," *New Left Review* 33 (January–February 1964), pp. 26–53. See the excellent critique by E. P. Thompson, "The Peculiarities of the English," *The Poverty of Theory* (New York: Monthly Review Press, 1978), pp. 245–301.

6   Bell, "The Future That Never Was," p. 54.

7   *Ibid.*, p. 55.

8   *Ibid.*, p. 60.

9   Nairn, "The Twilight of the British State," pp. 14–19.

10 Wiener, *English Culture*, p. 7.

11 Quoted in *ibid.*, p. 14.

12 W. D. Rubinstein, *Men of Property: The Very Wealthy in Britain Since the Industrial Revolution* (London: Croom Helm, 1981).

13 S. N. Eisenstadt, *Tradition, Change, and Modernity* (New York: John Wiley and Sons, 1973), pp. 3–29.

14 On the "convergence theory" of modernization, see C. Kerr, F. H. Harbison, and C. A. Meyers, *Industrialism and Industrial Man* (Cambridge: Harvard University Press, 1960).

15 Eisenstadt, *Tradition*, pp. 3–10.

16 *Ibid.*, pp. 98–115; Joseph R. Gusfield, "Tradition and Modernity: Misplaced Polarities in the Study of Social Change," *American Journal of Sociology* 72 (January 1967), pp. 351–62; and Reinhold Bendix, "Tradition and Modernity Reconsidered," *Comparative Studies in Society and History* 9 (April 1967), pp. 292–346.

17 Barrington Moore, *Social Origins of Dictatorship and Democracy: Lord and Peasant in the Making of the Modern World* (Boston: Beacon Press, 1966), pp. 3–39.

18 Walter Bagehot, *The English Constitution* (Ithaca: Cornell University Press, 1963), p. 59.

19 Edward Shils, *The Torment of Secrecy* (London: Heinemann, 1956), p. 49.

20 Asa Briggs, "Modern Britain," in Norman F. Cantor, *Perspectives on the European Past: Conversations with Historians* (New York: Macmillan, 1971), 2:185–87; R. H. Tawney, *Equality* (New York: Barnes and Noble, 1965); and Harold Perkin, *The Origins of Modern English Society, 1780–1880* (Toronto: University of Toronto Press, 1969).

21 Briggs, "Modern Britain," p. 187.

22 Wiener, *English Culture*, p. 5.

23 *Ibid.*, pp. 41–42.

24 *Ibid.*, pp. 41–80.

25 On North and South, see Charles Dellheim, "Imagining England: Victorian Views of North and South" (paper presented at North American Conference on British Studies Conference, 25 March 1984).

26 Edward Shils, "British Intellectuals in the Mid-Twentieth Century," *The Intellectuals and the Powers and Other Essays* (Chicago: University of Chicago Press, 1972), pp. 135–53.

27 A. J. P. Taylor, "Manchester," *Essays in English History* (Harmondsworth, Middlesex: Penguin, 1976), p. 311.

28 *Ibid.*, p. 317.

29 J. B. Priestley, *English Journey* (Harmondsworth, Middlesex: Penguin, 1977), p. 154.

30 Wiener, *English Culture*, p. 43.

31 Charles Dellheim, *The Face of the Past: The Preservation of the Medieval Inheritance in Victorian England* (Cambridge: Cambridge University Press, 1982), pp. 45–57.

32 *Ibid.*, pp. 58–69.

33 Wiener, *English Culture*, p. 64.

34 Dellheim, *Face of the Past*, pp. 153–75.

35 David Cannadine, "The Context, Performance and Meaning of Ritual: The British Monarchy and the 'Invention of Tradition,' c. 1820–1977," in *The Invention of Tradition*, ed. Eric Hobsbawm and Terence Ranger (Cambridge: Cambridge University Press, 1983), pp. 101–64.

36 On Bournville, see George Cadbury, *Town Planning, with Special Reference to the Birmingham Scheme* (London: Longmans, 1915).

37 Priestley, *English Journey*, pp. 166–67.

38 Wiener, *English Culture*, p. 97.

39 *Ibid.*, pp. 127–54; and Alastair Mant, *The Rise and Fall of the British Manager* (London: Macmillan, 1977), p. 7.

40 Thorstein Veblen, *Imperial Germany and the Industrial Revolution* (New York: Viking, 1954), p. 142.

41 *Ibid.*, p. 141.

42 *Ibid.*, pp. 148–49.
43 W. G. Rimmer, *Marshall of Leeds* (Cambridge, England: Cambridge University Press, 1960).
44 "Memorandum on the Fiscal Policy of International Trade," *Official Papers by Alfred Marshall* (London: Macmillan, 1926), p. 405.
45 *Ibid.*, p. 406.
46 D. C. Coleman, "Gentlemen and Players," *Economic History Review*, 2d ser., 26 (February 1973), pp. 92–116.
47 *Callisthenes* (London: Selfridge and Co., 1933), p. 330.
48 *Ibid.*, p. 331.
49 *Ibid.*, p. 333.
50 *Ibid.*, p. 87.
51 Wiener, *English Culture*, p. 149.
52 On the City of London, see Paul Ferris, *The City* (New York: Random House, 1961), and Anthony Sampson, *The Changing Anatomy of Britain* (London: Hodder and Stoughton, 1982), pp. 263–85.
53 W. J. Reader, *Imperial Chemical Industries: A History* (London: Oxford University Press, 1970), 1:219.
54 *Ibid.*, pp. 218–19.
55 James Burnley, *The Romance of Modern Industry* (London: W. M. Allen, 1889), p. v.
56 Katharine Chorley, *Manchester Made Them* (London: Faber and Faber, 1950), p. 12.
57 *Ibid.*, p. 13.
58 *Ibid.*, pp. 47–48, 76, 81.
59 *Ibid.*, p. 47.
60 *Ibid.*, pp. 16, 21.
61 *Ibid.*, p. 54.
62 *Ibid.*, pp. 103–5.
63 *Ibid.*, p. 99.
64 For the debate on late-Victorian entrepreneurship, see especially Derek H. Aldcroft, "The Entrepreneur and the British Economy, 1870–1914," *Economic History Review*, 2d ser., 17 (August 1964), pp. 113–34; Charles Wilson, "Economy and Society in late-Victorian Britain," *Economic History Review*, 2d ser., 18 (August 1965), pp. 183–98; David Landes, *The Unbound Prometheus: Technological Change and Industrial Development in Western Europe from 1750 to the Present* (Cambridge: Cambridge University Press, 1969); S. G. Checkland, "The Entrepreneur and the Social Order," *Business History* 17 (July 1975), pp. 176–88; A. L. Levine, *Industrial Retardation in Britain, 1888–1914* (New York: Basic Books, 1967); Donald McCloskey, "Did Victorian Britain Fail?" *Economic History Review*, 2d ser., 23 (December 1970), pp. 446–59; N. F. R. Crofts, "Victorian Britain Did Fail," *Economic History Review*, 2d ser., 32 (November 1979), pp. 533–37; D. H. Aldcroft, ed., *The Development of British Industry and Foreign Competition, 1875–1914* (Toronto: University of Toronto Press, 1968); Eric Hobsbawm, *Industry and Empire* (Harmondsworth, Middlesex: Penguin, 1970).
65 William Henry Beable, *Romance of Great Businesses* (London: Heath Cranston, 1926), p. 245.
66 My account of Boot is based on S. D. Chapman, *Jesse Boot of Boots the Chemists* (London: Hodder and Stoughton, 1974), chap. 3.
67 *Ibid.*, p. 87.
68 *Ibid.*, pp. 191–94.
69 Charles Wilson, *The History of Unilever: A Study in Economic Growth and Social Change* (London: Cassell, 1954), 1:21–44.
70 Quoted in *ibid.*, 1:24.

71 *Ibid.*, 1:144–58; and W. L. George, *Labour and Housing at Port Sunlight* (London: Alston Rivers, 1900).

72 Veblen, *Imperial Germany*, p. 132.

73 *Ibid.*, pp. 129–30.

74 See Seebohm Rowntree, *The Human Factor in Business* (London: Longmans, Green, 1921); and Terence Deal and Allen A. Kennedy, *Corporate Cultures: The Rites and Rituals of Corporate Life* (Reading, Massachusetts: Addison-Wesley, 1982).

75 Sir Henry Phelps-Brown, "Then and Now, the British Problem of Sustaining Development, 1900s and 1960s," *Essays in Honour of Lord Robbins*, ed. Maurice Peston and Bernard Corry (London: Weidenfeld and Nicholson, 1972), p. 195.

76 Alfred D. Chandler, "The Growth of the Transnational Firm in the United States and the United Kingdom: A Comparative Analysis," *Economic History Review*, 2d ser., 33 (August 1980), pp. 396–410.

Contributors

Mary Ann Caws is Distinguished Professor of French and Comparative Literature at the Graduate School of the City University of New York, and at Hunter College, and is the Executive Officer of the French Ph.D. program. Among her recent publications are *A Metapoetics of the Passage: Architextures in Surrealism and After*; *The Eye in the Text: Essays on Perception, Mannerist to Modern*; and *Reading Frames in Modern Fiction*. She is editor of *Le Siècle éclaté* in Paris, the co-editor of *Dada/Surrealism* and of the French Modernist Series for Nebraska (the first publication will be her translation of Breton's *L'Amour fou*), and the editor of a book series, Reading Plus, for Peter Lang.

Charles Dellheim received his Ph.D. in History from Yale University, where he specialized in modern European cultural history and modern British history. He is the author of *The Face of the Past: The Preservation of the Medieval Inheritance in Victorian England*. His current research focuses on comparative business cultures. Recently, he was awarded a Fellowship for Independent Study and Research from the National Endowment for the Humanities to study "Cultures of British Business, 1880–1914."

Robert Kiely is Loker Professor of English and American Literature at Harvard, where he teaches courses on the Victorian, Modern, and Contemporary Novel, and the English Bible. Among his publications are *The Romantic Novel in England* and *Beyond Egotism: The Fiction of James Joyce, Virginia Woolf, and D. H. Lawrence*. He is currently at work on a book on self-consciousness in the nineteenth-century novel.

Jürgen Klein is Professor of English Literature at the University of Siegen in West Germany. His most recent literary criticism includes *Virginia Woolf: Genie, Tragik, Emanzipation* and *Studenten Lesen Joyce, Interpretationen zum Frühwerk*. He is editor for the Peter Lang book series entitled Aspects of English Intellectual and Cultural History.

Martin Meisel is Professor of English and Comparative Literature at Columbia University. His most recent book is *Realizations: Narrative, Pictorial, and Theatrical Arts of the Nineteenth Century*. He is currently writing a broad study of the imagination and representation of chaos.

Jeffrey Mehlman is Associate Professor of French at Boston University. He is the author of *A Structural Study of Autobiography; Revolution and Repetition; Cataract: A Study in Diderot*; and *Legacies: Of Anti-Semitism in France*.

William Moebius is Associate Professor of Comparative Literature at the University of Massachusetts at Amherst. Author of a book of poems, translator of Sophocles and Philodemus, he is currently writing a series of essays on children's and folk literature, of which this is one. He is also co-translating two contemporary children's books (from Austria and Belgium) and developing a poetics of the picturebook.

Gustavo Pérez Firmat is Associate Professor of Spanish at Duke University. He is the author of *Idle Fictions: The Hispanic Vanguard Novel (1926–1934)* and *Literature and Liminality: Festive Readings in the Hispanic Tradition*, as well as of a collection of poetry, *Carolina Cuban*. He is now working on a book on the Cuban literature of the 1920s and 1930s.

Julia Przyboś, Associate Professor of French at Hunter College, has just completed a book on the nineteenth-century French melodrama. She is the author of articles on popular theater, Balzac, Gobineau, Huysmans, and Villiers de l'Isle-Adam. She is currently working on a book on decadent literature.

Hillel Schwartz is a poet, playwright, choreographer, and historian. His previous publications include *Knaves, Fools, Madmen and That Subtile Effluvium*; *The French Prophets: The History of a Millenarian Group in Eighteenth-Century England*; and *Phantom Children*. This essay was presented in an earlier version as a President's Scholar paper at the University of Florida. His present research concerns the history of dieting in America, which will be published by The Free Press/Macmillan.